The Drumbeat of Jimmy Sands

Murray Davies was born in South Wales. After doing an MA in First World War poetry, he became a journalist and spent more than twenty years on Fleet Street as a news reporter and a feature writer on three national newspapers. *The Drumbeat of Jimmy Sands* is his first novel.

MURRAY DAVIES

THE DRUMBEAT OF JIMMY SANDS

HarperCollins*Publishers*

HarperCollins*Publishers*
77–85 Fulham Palace Road
Hammersmith, London W6 8JB

A Paperback Original 1999
1 3 5 7 9 8 6 4 2

A catalogue record for this book
is available from the British Library

ISBN 0 00 651155 4

Typeset in Meridien by Palimpsest Book Production Limited,
Polmont, Stirlingshire

Printed and bound in Great Britain by
Caledonian International Book Manufacturing Ltd, Glasgow

For Glen

AUTHOR'S NOTE

Fact. Members of D Squadron SAS destroyed Argentine Pucara aircraft on Pebble Island in the Falklands war. Some of the same squadron were at the Loughgall ambush when they killed eight IRA terrorists and innocent victim Oliver Hughes.

Fact. The IRA operation to destroy Loughgall police station was betrayed by a woman who was then abducted by an IRA revenge squad and rescued by the RUC when she pressed her panic button.

Fact. A British soldier deserted to become an IRA commander and used his inside knowledge to blow up the members of his ex-regiment.

Fact. A mystery sniper has killed at least five soldiers in Ulster over the past four years with a single shot at long range. He has never been captured.

The Special Forces techniques mentioned are those taught in the Regiment. The slang and the abbreviations are those of Stirling Lines.

While the veil has been partly lifted from the SAS in recent years, the Regiment remains extremely skilful at manipulating what information is released. Most of its work is still top secret.

This account was written in collaboration with noted former SAS soldier Peter McAleese, whose autobiography *No Mean Soldier* was published in 1995. McAleese was the prime adviser on a recent Carlton TV series on the SAS.

Interlude

'What's this? An army funeral? Full military honours.'

'It's that wee laddie shot in Northern Ireland last week.'

'Och, poor bairn, and I thought there was supposed to be a ceasefire.'

The two old biddies scurried towards the grave and stopped a regretful, respectful, all-seeing distance away.

'They say his death was a mistake.'

'That's a great comfort for his ma. There she is now. Oh bless her . . .'

A small, grey-haired woman in a well-worn, black-braided coat holding her headscarf against the cold wind sweeping across Dalbeth cemetery from the slow Clyde, a rivet's throw away.

'Who's that taking her arm?'

'Must be the brother.' Slight, fair hair and piercing blue eyes, holding his ma, biting her lip against the tears.

'Not his real brother. The family took the laddie in after his own ma died when he was two.'

'Still, you feel it's your own blood.'

The swish of polished boots as the carrying party glided over the loose chippings.

'Inside, outside; inside, outside.' The sergeant's whispered commands. Don't swing the coffin.

'Don't those laddies look bonny in their tartan trews and Glengarries. Fusiliers, from his regiment.'

The priest, intoning from his prayer book, led the drab procession of mourners in ill-knotted ties and blue chain-store anoraks. A helicopter circled in the distance.

'Surely they wouldn't do anything here. Not against Catholics.'

1

'He was a Catholic and they shot him.'

'Look, there's his da walking by himsel'.'

'Done that all his life. Fierce one, he was.'

Old and shuffling now. White bristles under an ear where he had failed to shave. A shirt collar too large for his creased neck.

'All the wee laddie ever wanted was to be like his brother. Even after that terrible accident, he was set on being a soldier.'

'Look where it got him.'

A short prayer blown away on the wind and the coffin lowered into the waiting earth.

The tremulous cadences of the Last Post.

'Och. That sends shivers down my spine. They say he'd only been in Northern Ireland a week when he was killed.'

'Ay, and what did that do but break an old woman's heart?'

Fusiliers formed two lines at the head of the grave, brought their SA80 rifles to their shoulders and pointed at the sky over the looming Victorian mass of Belvedere Hospital.

'Load, ready, fire. Ready, fire. Ready, fire.' Three volleys.

The lone piper took one pace forward. 'The Flowers of the Forest' swirled around the open grave. Women and old men dabbed their eyes with white handkerchiefs.

The mother and father who brought him up each dropped a morsel of the thick grey earth to rattle on to the coffin.

The brother shook his head in a brief gesture of finality and picked up a handful of the damp, tenacious clay with his left hand.

His lips moved as he fed the gaping grave. In his right hand he grasped a small silver object.

'The wee laddie worshipped him. He must feel responsible.'

'Doesn't he look grim? Purposeful, somehow.'

'What a waste. Ay, well, that's the end of it . . .'

But the story began twelve years before and eight thousand miles away and it had not finished yet.

Part One

Chapter One

I hate this waiting. Duggie Fife ran his fingertips over the silken coverings of the plastic explosive packages inside the haversack. He felt the sweat on his palms and stealthily wiped them on his para smock. Excitement and fear churned inside him and he wished he'd had a piss back at the bergen dump. He told God he wasn't afraid and asked for his help not to fuck up. His left hand stole up to the medallion of Saint Michael, God's warrior doing overtime as the patron saint of paratroops, and his right thumb traced the safety catch on his M16. He glanced at his watch on the inside of his wrist and told himself to stop fidgeting. Over the pounding of his heart a generator chugged away in the darkness. The smell of the kerosene mingled with the damp freshness of the grass. Fife caught himself trying to hold his breath and released it gradually. In his mind he checked and rechecked and then checked once more. The PE4, the detonators, cortex, det cord, timers, fuses. Shit, the minute hand hadn't moved. Fucking mental. He looked at his watch again.

Well, Paddy boy. This is it. The big one. Come a long way, all the way from the Falls Road to the Falkland Islands. Via Brum, Aldershot and Hereford and a few other places. Paddy O'Keefe. Acting troop sergeant. He hummed 'Kevin Barry' silently and turned to take in the deep shapes of his seven men. We'll have a right piss-up when this is over. He ran over Actions On, decided it was too late to worry and continued with the second verse. *A lad of eighteen summers* ... facing execution by the occupying English forces. But the lad of eighteen summers had slotted two fourteen-year-old drummer boys, Duggie said. He deserved topping. Trust bloody Jimmy Sands to know that. They had solemnly shaken hands when they cached their bergens. 'I'll never forget you, Jimmy Sands,' they'd pledged each other as they wished each other luck. At least he knew he could trust Fife. He had doubts about his rupert. He had reservations about all officers, but he distrusted this new one in particular. He'd come from the Guards, why hadn't he joined G squadron? Wish he bloody well had. Just hope he'll look after his half of the troop. O'Keefe switched to the last verse. *Lads like Barry are no cowards, From the foe they will not fly.*

What am I doing here? I never foresaw anything like this. I never thought the British army would actually go to war, groaned Simon Baines-Hickey to himself. Life in the army was a succession of frights – not fights. Bit different from ceremonial duties in a bearskin outside Buck House. It'll look good on my cv – if I get out alive. No reason why I shouldn't. It's a good plan and after all the Argies aren't exactly your crack opposition. But I'm not going to hang about. There's not much time allowed to exfil to the war rendezvous. The men know their business. They know it better than I do – leave it to them. Politics, that's the future. The City and politics.

The crescent moon freed itself from the ragged cloud, throwing a silver light over the mown stubble of the runway. On the edge of the airfield the row of propeller aircraft cast raven dark shadows over the longer grass. Soft amber light glimmered out of the temporary hangars on the far side of the strip. The Argentine troops were being sloppy about the blackout. Who'd expect a raid up here? On a small island on the edge of the Falklands?

Fife pulled his black woollen hat down firmly over his head so it wouldn't work loose when he moved and watched the sentry's cigarette end glow as he ambled past. He was going to get slotted if he was still mincing around in two minutes. Fife turned his head into the breeze, his mouth slightly open so the sound of his own breathing didn't impair his hearing. His night vision was perfect now – better than the sentry's with that fag going.

The rest of 16 Troop were scattered in cover behind him. To his left on the rising ground the blokes from 17 Troop were ready to give covering fire and distract the Argentine troops from the Pucara aircraft Fife and his oppo Molecatcher, the thinnest, sexiest man in the Regiment, were about to destroy. Paddy O'Keefe was crouched behind Molecatcher ready to give him the off. Paddy had squeezed the tube of black camouflage cream over his fingers and then dragged them down his face so that he looked like a tiger with the whites of his eyes glistening. Fife caught his eye and O'Keefe grinned, exposing large gleaming teeth. He tapped his watch and gave the thumbs up. Fife jerked two fingers in reply. If Paddy wanted his Rolex that much he'd have to take it off his corpse.

The 4.5-inch shell smashed into the end of runway 27 with a blue-white flash, the ground erupting in a fountain of earth and stones. Fife felt the hill shudder under his body, his stomach heaved with the explosion and sweat prickled his armpits. The sentry was legging it towards shelter, fag still in his mouth. A machine gun opened up in short bursts. The sentry tumbled in a forward roll, poised for a second like a high board diver, arms outstretched ahead of him, then threw himself into a trench.

Fife rose, feeling the heavy canvas bags sway against his body, and then he was off, ducking in a crouching run towards the drainage ditch. Through the thicket of undercarriages he saw Argentine soldiers piling out of their tents, shouting and screaming. Hell was breaking loose.

In the middle of the line of ten aircraft, Molecatcher turned to the right and Fife to the left. The stench of oil and kerosene filled his nostrils as he cuddled up to the fuselage of the first Pucara. Reaching up to the high wing, Fife placed a two-pound standard charge into the port engine's air intake. From the other bag he drew out an SAS initiation set consisting of a time pencil and a length of green cortex running into a detonator. Alongside he had taped a shorter length of safety fuse, which joined the cortex just before the detonator, and a safety fuse ignition percussion. He slid the detonator into the PE4 and squeezed.

His action released acid inside the pencil which slowly ate through a lead strip holding back a spring. The released spring would ignite a .22 cap of gunpowder setting off the cortex which, burning at 400 feet per second, would fire the detonator to ignite the explosive charge, causing a rapid expansion of gases to a temperature of 4,000 degrees Centigrade.

The bang should take place in 20 minutes.

P for Plenty. He repeated the operation with the starboard engine. A fiery stream of tracer hissed and burned along the runway, keeping the Argentines away from the Pucaras. Fife heard the cackle of M16s with their 5.56mm rounds against the heavier thump of the Argentines' FNs. The rattle of a GPMG played somewhere in the background. A 66mm rocket hit the smaller hangar and an oil drum exploded in dull red flames, flinging a trail of red pinpricks in a sparkling arc which glowed for an instant and then vanished. Thick pungent smoke drifted across the aircraft.

It was all happening in slow motion. Except Fife knew it wasn't. It only appeared to do so because his mind was racing. Racing faster than it had ever raced in his life.

He crawled to the second aircraft, placing the charges in identical positions to prevent the Argentines cannibalizing the damaged Pucaras. The desperate cry of a wild animal in pain chilled his blood. The man screamed over and over again. Shut up, for fuck's sake.

A 4.5-inch shell overshot and crumped a hundred yards away near the ground he had just left. He grinned, imagining Paddy's language on the radio net to the forward gunnery observer. A blue on blue was the last thing they needed. The moon disappeared and it began to drizzle. Fine and piercing; the sort you don't notice until you're wet to your soul.

Twack. Twack. Twack. Holes appeared across the starboard nacelle. Holy shit! The engine coughed, spluttered and with a roar the propeller kicked into life. Fife threw himself out of the way of the whistling blades as the plane jerked forward. The Pucara slewed to the right, the other engine started up in a cloud of blue smoke and the aircraft taxied down the strip until it lurched to the right again. Fife glimpsed Molecatcher flinging himself clear as the Pucara's starboard propeller chewed into the wing of a stationary aircraft and came to a halt.

Shit and double shit. That was one way of attracting attention. Argentinian soldiers were running towards him across the runway and behind him his troop opened fire. Getting warm out here. Fife was pleased he was so detached. A professional getting on with his job. Only one more aircraft to do.

A Schermully flare exploded, its brilliant white light washing out all shades and colour and turning the blackness into a monochrome grey. Fife could clearly hear the hiss of the flare 1,500 feet above him. He looked up and saw the parachute swaying on the breeze, its 17,000 candlepower turning the rain into silver slivers. The descending flare pushed out long deep shadows so that every gesture was miscast and magnified. There was a crack and whistle of a bullet; behind Fife a deformed giant twitched and fell.

O'Keefe gave an aimed three-round burst at the scurrying figures on the airstrip. The last two rounds were tracer, telling him his magazine was about to run out. He clipped on another banana mag with thirty rounds, threw the empty one into his para smock and took stock: 17 Troop were giving the airfield a right beasting, but the Argies were starting to regroup. That bloody plane had scared the shit out of everyone and compromised the guys placing the charges.

Through his night vision goggles he saw Molecatcher turn away from the extreme right-hand aircraft and begin to make his way back.

That's my half done. Time to pull out.

'One seven. This is one six bravo. Preparing to move to Thunderbolt. Over.'

'One six bravo. This is one seven. Roger.'

'One seven. This is one six alpha. Also preparing to move to Thunderbolt. Over.'

His rupert wasn't wasting any time.

'One six alpha. This is one seven. Roger. Out.'

O'Keefe was the first at the shallow declivity on the reverse slope where the troop had cached their bergens. Seven looming figures, all breathing hard, moved swiftly past him. He hit each one on the shoulder and counted quietly.

'Last man,' muttered the seventh.

The guys were in motormouth mode, each desperate to tell their own stories. The adrenalin was pumping and they were safe.

'When that fucking plane went off by itself . . .'

'Did you see the way I slotted that bastard . . .'

'A stoppage! A fucking stoppage!'

'Fucking shut it. All round defence.'

Nearby in the blackness, a man made two clicking noises with his tongue. A pond full of frogs replied as every man in the half troop answered. It should have been O'Keefe's job. High spirits were breaking out.

More dark shapes glided to the row of bergens, then fanned out waiting for the order to move. Another flare lit up the treeless landscape in its harsh glare and O'Keefe saw one bergen still waiting to be claimed.

It had a small piece of white material knotted around a buckle to show it contained vital equipment.

Like a demolitions man would have tied to show he was carrying explosives.

Like Fife's.

Shit.

'Sir, sir, you've got a man missing.'

Baines-Hickey lay on the ground, struggling into his bergen. O'Keefe knelt down beside him and put his hand on the officer's shoulder.

'Sir, you've a man missing,' he repeated in a fierce whisper which emphasized his Belfast accent.

The flare died as the men peered into the shadows trying to make out who had not returned. Baines-Hickey said nothing.

'Harry.' O'Keefe addressed the corporal in charge of four men under Baines-Hickey. 'Have ye got your stick together?'

'Yeh, Paddy, all here.'

'He's one of yours, sir. Did you see a man go down?'

The officer hesitated. 'I think it was Fife.'

Baines-Hickey's cut-glass voice told him apart in the darkness.

'What the fuck do ye mean, you *think* it was Fife? Did ye see him go down or didn't ye?'

'I believe he was hit placing the charges.'

'Christ.' O'Keefe spat his anger. 'Jimmy Sands, are ye here?'

Silence.

'Who was the last to see him?' No one replied. 'It must have been you, sir. Where did you see him?'

'I told you. He was placing the charges.'

'Let me get this right,' rasped O'Keefe in disbelief. He grabbed the shoulder of the officer's camouflage smock. 'Ye saw him go down and ye did nothing?'

'He went down just as we were withdrawing. He was killed outright.'

'How the fuck do you know that? You should have fucking checked.' O'Keefe's lips were drawn back into thin bloodless lines of fury.

'I believe he's dead.'

'We've got to go back.' O'Keefe thrust his face up into

13

the well-bred features of the captain who, caught in the slanting light of another flare, bore an uncanny resemblance to a racehorse with his thin face and high forehead.

'There isn't time, corporal.'

'We've got to know if he's dead. We cannot leave him. Sir.' His hard, corncrake voice rang with contempt and scorn.

'I'm not going to jeopardize the troop for one man.'

'Fife could be lying injured under those aircraft and those charges are going to go off.' O'Keefe made his decision. 'Fuck it. I'm going back.'

Fife was his closest friend. But it wasn't just that. The Regiment never left a wounded man behind. In the SAS you depended on each other. You trusted your mates with your life and they trusted you with theirs.

'Join the troop, corporal.' Baines-Hickey spoke hesitantly, unable to withstand the searing heat of O'Keefe's hostility. He was aware the men were listening keenly and he knew which side they were on. Sod them, he was the officer. 'We're running late already.'

At that moment O'Keefe wanted to beat the shit out of Baines-Hickey. With an enormous effort, he made his training overcome his rage. Ignoring the officer, he turned to another shape.

'Molecatcher, take my stick. I'm going back. Exfil to the war RV. If Jimmy Sands has beaten the clock I'll catch you up.'

He tugged at the bow of the quick release on the top of the medic's bergen and pulled out the troop medical pack.

'One seven. This is one six bravo. Over.'

'One six bravo. One seven. Over.'

'One seven. We have a man down believed to be in vicinity of the aircraft. One man returning to assist. Can you provide covering fire? Over.'

'One six bravo. This is one seven. Stand by.'

14

They must wonder what the bloody hell we're playing at, thought O'Keefe.

'One six bravo. This is one seven. Affirmative. We are receiving heavy fire from left flank. We are preparing to exfil in figures five. Can provide you with assistance until then. Over.'

'One seven. This is one six bravo. Moving out to Foxtrot. One man returning. Over.'

'One six bravo, one seven. Roger. Out.'

O'Keefe dropped into the drainage ditch, brushed the fine rain out of his eyes and peered at ground level among the undercarriages. No unusual shape on the grass, no bundle to indicate the body of a fallen man. If Fife had been killed he'd be here. If he'd been wounded, he'd crawl somewhere – somewhere not too far. O'Keefe knew he didn't have much time.

That PE is going off soon and I don't want to be near those Pucaras when they do.

Twenty metres along the ditch he made out a huddled form. Fife looked asleep, his head resting alongside the haversack, his right hand clenched around his M16. As O'Keefe knelt beside him, he opened his eyes and a pale recognition seeped into them.

'Didn't think I would forget ye, did ye, Jimmy Sands?'

Fife tried to smile. It emerged as a grimace of pain. 'Left thigh.'

O'Keefe hacked away at the blood-sodden fabric of Fife's trousers, switched on his pencil torch and winced at the butcher's slab mess of pulped red meat and sinew. The bullet had ripped through muscle, exposing white bone and gristle; blood was steadily oozing from the gaping wound. The injury alone would not kill, but Fife was in shock and that could – would – kill.

'Right, Jimmy Sands, let's have you.'

He pulled a shell dressing out of its waterproof pack and pressed it on the open wound. At first they had been taught to tie the ends of the dressing around the thigh, but then they found that if the leg swelled, the bandage acted as a tourniquet cutting off circulation. Now they held the dressing in place with a crepe bandage.

'That'll staunch the bleeding until we're away from here, then I'll get you stabilized.'

Fife lost interest. His eyes closed.

Fuck it.

'Jimmy! Jimmy! Fucking wake up. You're not going to beat the clock, so open your fucking eyes and stop pissing about.'

Fife's face creased in concentration as he tried to obey.

'I told you. You're not getting your name on the clock tower in Hereford yet. Right, up you come.' With difficulty, O'Keefe hauled him across his shoulder in a fireman's lift. 'Let go your fucking weapon, you wee Jock bastard. I'm not carrying that as well.'

'Bollocks.'

This is insanity. He's half dead, no use to anyone and he's still got his weapon and belt kit on. Still thinks he's the Lean Mean Killing Machine. O'Keefe grinned to himself. He picked up his own M16 and scrambled out of the trench. Someone in 17 Troop must have been sweeping the area with passive night goggles as a torrent of automatic fire descended. Good boys. He guessed they must be about to pull out and were putting on one last show for his benefit.

A bullet sang over his head and O'Keefe instinctively ducked. He stood stock still, but no further rounds came in their direction and he began stumbling over the rough ground.

Two hundred steps on, Fife retched.

'Don't ruin my para smock, you dirty sod.'

Fife retched again and O'Keefe knew he was going to have to stop, even though they were too close to the airfield for comfort.

The first charge exploded with an echoing thud. Gunfire erupted. It sounded as though the Argies had declared war

16

on themselves. Good time to halt. O'Keefe gently lowered Fife on to the wet turf on the far side of a large flat rock overgrown with lichen. Fife's sunken face had taken on a ghostly tinge as beads of cold sweat ran into the congealed camouflage cream. His lips were purple. Shock was setting in.

O'Keefe pulled out the shock pack from his medical pouch. Remember your training. ABCDE.

A is for airways.

'Give me some morphine, you bastard,' gasped Fife.

At least his airways are clear.

B is for bleeding. O'Keefe took another gauze dressing out of his pouch and put it on top of the saturated one on Fife's thigh.

C is for circulation, chest wounds and comfort. Not much comfort in this boggy hole.

D is for drugs, drips and documentation. O'Keefe reached into the pack and produced a small toothpaste tube with a needle at one end – a syrette of morphine. There were two around Fife's neck and another two around his own. Use the medical pack's first. He jammed his knife into a fissure in the rock above Fife's head, unrolled a plastic bag containing the saline drip and hung it from the knife. Then he rolled up Fife's left sleeve and tapped heavily with the back of his hand on the exposed inside forearm to bring up the vein.

This was the dodgy bit. Miss the vein and it would collapse. He held the torch between his teeth and concentrated. Fife twitched as O'Keefe inserted the needle into the soft flesh with a satisfying spurt of blood. He placed the tube from the drip into the catheter and jabbed the needle of the syrette into the bung of the giving set. He squeezed the other half into the drip itself. He was going to run the drip quickly. Twenty minutes, that was all. He wrote a big M and the time on Fife's forehead in indelible pencil.

E is for evacuation. Which is what we've got to do when you've stabilized, sunshine.

Fife smiled dreamily, a sense of euphoria creeping over him as the morphine began to course through his veins.

'I knew you wouldn't forget me, Jimmy Sands.'

O'Keefe wet Fife's lips from his water bottle and took a swig himself. As he waited for the morphine to run, he calculated. Eighty-five per cent of the island was peat bog and they had almost three miles to cover to the emergency RV where the chopper would sweep at first and last light carrying out lost drills for stragglers. Three miles across treacherous, broken country with gorse, heather and tussocks of grass, each one an invitation to turn an ankle.

'Come on, Jimmy Sands, I'll carry you.' O'Keefe pulled Fife to his feet and, with a heave of his broad chest, hoisted the slight Scot over his shoulders. 'Leave your fucking weapon.'

'Bollocks.'

'Are you all right there?'

'Fucking grand, Paddy.'

The morphine was sending Fife into his own rose-tinted world. He saw his wee mother in her kitchen in the council house in Glasgow. She was pouring a cup of tea. He was stepping out with Elsie and it was a summer's day. They walked over the slag heaps covered with grass and they lay down in the evening sun. It was warm and drowsy. A blackbird fussed and Elsie smelled good and soft and womanlike. She had a miniskirt and long legs. They dozed off in each other's arms. He smiled at the memory.

The drizzle became heavier and O'Keefe turned his face sidewards to catch the refreshing drops.

'If you were the real Jimmy Sands you'd be lighter than this,' he panted to Fife, now humming tunelessly to himself.

'If I was the real Jimmy Sands I'd be dead.' Fife continued humming.

In spite of his exhaustion, O'Keefe grinned. Jimmy Sands had become their own private joke. It was a reference to Bobby Sands, an IRA man who starved himself to death in

18

the Maze prison. The Republicans pledged in six-foot-high letters on gable walls: *We'll never forget you Bobby Sands*. Within days the Proddies were joking: We'll never forget you, Jimmy Sands. It appealed to their sense of humour. O'Keefe and Fife began to call each other Jimmy Sands.

The wind carried only silence and the steady plod and creak of O'Keefe's soaking wet boots and the taint of vomit from Fife's mouth. The six-inch-high tufts of grass were the worse, O'Keefe didn't know whether to step on them or over them. Step on them and he risked turning his ankle, but having to raise his legs those extra inches was wearing him down. Already his thighs felt as though someone had lit a fire inside them and a red hot pain seared through his right calf. The rain stopped and a few faint stars pricked through the jackdaw-black sky. There was a growing pain across his chest and he knew he would never make the ERV.

The pewter dawn caught O'Keefe staggering onwards towards the ghostly hills, his burden over his shoulders and his knees literally shaking with the mammoth effort of putting one foot in front of the other. Banks of heather and waves of long grass faded away up the slope until they receded into the darkness. His shirt was stuck to his back with sweat; flaming knots of cord were tying up his calves and his breath rasped in his chest. He was taking baby steps now, tottering as though he was on high heels. At each step, his kneecap locked into position. The small of his back felt crushed in a vice and every fifty paces he stopped, bent over double to rest. He pulled in huge chunks of air, grabbing every piece of oxygen as though trying to suck up the sky. Fife was asleep or unconscious, still clutching his bloody M16. Weaving from side to side like a punch-drunk fighter, O'Keefe focused his hatred on that fucking rupert.

How could Baines-Hickey leave one of his men behind? The injustice seared through him as much as the molten metal rods piercing his legs. His Irish Catholic dislike of the

English gentry coalesced with his professional soldier's contempt for Baines-Hickey's behaviour. Officers were largely irrelevant to the running of the troop. They served only three years at a time with the Regiment. The senior NCOs really ran the squadrons. All officers are useless until they become majors and then you begin to get some work out of them.

O'Keefe was on his chin strap now; only his anger kept him going step after mind-numbing step. When the eastern sky turned to slate he laid Fife gently into a shallow depression protected on three sides by outcrops of rock. Fife's pale blue eyes glazed out of the white rings of his sunken sockets. His black pupils were dilated and the happily vacant half-smile had been replaced by a sagging mouth reeking of stale puke.

Shit! Shit! Shit!

O'Keefe's hands were shaking so much that he had difficulty setting up the drip. Fife's circulation was closing down and it took for ever to find the vein in his forearm. O'Keefe squeezed a second syrette directly into the bung of the giving set. The two shell dressings were sodden with blood. More blood had congealed in black blotches on Fife's tattered trousers. His bare leg looked obscenely white and his skin was cold and clammy as his body fought to retain its core temperature.

A brew-up. O'Keefe crumbled two hexamine blocks and watched as the blue flame licked the bottom of his mug. He sweetened the tea with condensed milk and put the mug to Fife's lips while cramming slabs of chocolate into his own mouth. When they had drunk, O'Keefe carefully pulled Fife's woollen hat down over the Scot's straight sandy hair. Then he wrapped his space blanket around them, its inner silver side reflecting their heat back to their bodies while the green outer skin merged with the dark moss. He wrapped his arms around his mate and hugged him so he shared the Irishman's body warmth.

I'm buggered if I'm going to lose him with hypothermia.

20

Then O'Keefe too began to shiver and cramp gripped his calves. He tried to curl his toes and became aware that the soles of his socks had compressed into cardboard inside his boots.

The two SAS men huddled stiff and shivering as the cheerless day grew. In the cold, raw light the purple and dun countryside showed itself as desolate and wild with stretches of brown bracken, rough-edged grasses and the occasional withered gorse bush bent by the winds. Between two hills, O'Keefe could make out the steely sea. A skein of white geese flew overhead honking loudly. The only other living beings.

O'Keefe glanced fondly at his best mate. They say opposites attract. Fife was like a bright sixth-former: intolerant, naive, opinionated, anxious to please and difficult to impress. A hothead, always in trouble with his temper. At the same time so serious and intense. And all that reading. He's a terrier. Give him a task and he's remorseless, implacable. One day he'll make regimental sergeant major – if he's not returned to the paras for fighting first.

And me? Every day's party day for Paddy O'Keefe. I never pick a fight – ended a few though.

'Where are we?' Fife's voice was little more than a croak.

'On the way to the ERV.'

Fife drifted off into another morphine-induced dream. This time he was a wee bairn. He'd been put in a class of girls for making trouble at school and he was learning to knit. The repetition of purl one, plain one pleased him. Pretty Aggie McCleod was helping him and letting him hold her hand. He'd got a belting from his da, but even at that young age he was ceasing to feel the hard blows which rained down so frequently.

The wind rose, gusting and buffeting the tufts above their shallow hole. The average wind speed in the Falklands, O'Keefe knew, was seventeen knots – equal to a drop of seventeen degrees Fahrenheit. And Fife needed all the warmth he could get.

All morning they huddled together as Fife drifted in and out of consciousness. O'Keefe permitted himself a few minutes' sleep at a time. Once, he was woken by hoarse cries on the wind and saw an extended line of Argentine troops performing a perfunctory sweep on the high ground well away to their left. Vapour lifted off their damp clothes: by afternoon, baked by their body heat, they would be dry and hard.

Fife became delirious and started to mumble to himself.

'I'll be all right, hen. Dinnae fret.'

His pulse was turning over slow and ponderous, his eyes were open, yet what he saw was far away in another time. O'Keefe became alarmed.

'Yer wee Jock shit. Come back. I didn't carry you all this way here for you to go out on me. Look at me. Talk to me. Fucking well talk to me.'

With effort Fife focused on O'Keefe. 'How far?'

'Over half way. I'd have done better if I'd had the real Jimmy Sands on my back.' He could see Fife drifting away again.

He clasped Fife's wrists in his big red shovels of hands. 'What constituency was he elected to?'

Fife did not answer.

'Come on, you tosser. You reckon you know more about Irish history than meself and me only born and brought up there. Which constituency?'

Fife opened his eyes. It took a great effort. 'Who?'

'Jimmy Sands.'

'Never was.'

'All right, smart arse. Bobby Sands.'

'Fermanagh and South Tyrone.'

'When did he die?'

'Last year.'

'When?'

'May the something.'

'How long did his hunger strike last?'

22

'Sixty-five days.' Fife stirred. 'You Irish like your martyrs. If he hadn't died, no one would have heard of him.'

'There's nothing wrong with Ireland.'

'You left.'

'Would you want to live off the Falls Road in Belfast?'

'I lived in Glasgow.'

'Ay, all right. Point taken.'

O'Keefe rubbed his large hand over the dark stubble of his chin, flaking off the congealed cam cream, and wondered if the Argentines had found their bergens. Maybe that's what this morning's sweep had been about. Fife would not survive another night unless he received proper medical care. The wound trauma was proving too much for him and he needed to be stabilized.

They were going to have to go for the RV and stuff the risks.

When O'Keefe judged there was an hour of daylight left, he ripped off a syrette of morphine from Fife's neck, loosened his trousers and jabbed the drugs directly into the upper outer quadrant of his buttocks. For good measure, he gave him a jab of penicillin as well.

'Okay, see if you can stand on your own feet.'

'Get ye away. You don't have to carry me. I'll manage, don't you worry.'

O'Keefe grinned as Fife struggled to rise, leaning heavily on the rock. That's Jocks for you. Press the pride button and they're good for another ten miles. He swooped down and picked up Fife, still clutching his M16.

Within twenty metres, O'Keefe stumbled and fell. Fife stifled a grunt of pain and sat swaying as he fought against the red waves of agony which threatened to suck him down into the swelling sea of unconsciousness. His face turned ashen and all the morphine in the world wasn't helping. O'Keefe watched anxiously as the right side of Fife's face seemed to collapse inwards.

'Ye okay, Jimmy Sands?'

'Aye, aye, I'll do,' he replied in a tortured whisper.

As he manoeuvred Fife back over his shoulder, Fife's arm knocked off O'Keefe's woollen hat exposing his shock of black curly hair. It was too much effort to pick it up. Bent almost double, O'Keefe set off again to climb the rise towards the sea and the setting sun. Soon he became aware of Fife's body becoming heavier. He had been trying to hold on to O'Keefe's belt, now his hand hung limp. He was slipping back into unconsciousness and felt like a dead weight.

'Wake up, you bastard.' The words came out in a hoarse whisper. 'Jimmy. Hey, Jimmy. Remember that time you got crabs?'

No reply.

'Jimmy Sands! Fucking wake up. Jimmy!'

'What?' Fife's speech was slurred. Every word an effort.

'That time you got crabs. From the Yellow Submarine. Do you know who gave them her?'

'No.'

O'Keefe tripped over a root and lurched forward. 'Me.'

'You bastard. I didn't know you'd been there . . .'

'You give them to that Sunday school teacher and she dumped you.'

Fife croaked as he tried to chuckle at the memory. 'Aye, she went fucking mental.'

'She smashed you over the head with that pop bottle, remember?'

Fife did not answer.

'Jimmy Sands. Jimmy Sands, talk to me.'

'She gave a good blow job.' His words seemed to come from the distance.

'Not as good as the Hereford Hoover. She spent so much time in the troop basha that her name was down on the detail for room jobs. What was her name?'

But Fife had gone again.

Talk to me, pleaded O'Keefe in his head. Talk to me. Say something, any fucking thing, but talk to me. Don't go out on me now.

O'Keefe heard the faint sound of the helicopter on the

westerly wind. Shit. It's early. The chopper was flying a pattern along the coast – more than a mile away – to conceal the actual ERV. They weren't going to make it in time.

A second later there was the sound of a shot. He didn't know if it was a negligent discharge or whether someone had taken a pot shot at a rabbit – if there were rabbits in the Falklands. But it meant that someone with a gun wasn't far behind them. And that someone would have company. Enemy troops. In one last desperate effort, O'Keefe broke into a staggering trot, legs wide apart for balance, and with lungs bursting and neck muscles bulging cleared the ridge.

The sound of the chopper faded away on the wind.

Now or never. He considered putting Fife down, but knew that if he did he'd never be able to pick him up again. His reserves were spent. Better to keep the weight distributed around his shoulders. O'Keefe transferred his rifle to his right hand already hooked over Fife's legs and reached for the TACBE on his belt. The TACBE could act as a distress beacon to alert overflying aircraft and also as a short-range radio set.

O'Keefe pulled the tab on the TACBE and the antennae sprung out. Within seconds he heard a clipped and precise voice.

'Hello, unknown station. This is Cyclone. Do you read?'

Thank Christ!

'Cyclone. This is Delta one six bravo. Over.'

'Delta one six bravo. Cyclone. Reading you fours. Over.'

'Cyclone. Delta one six. I am approximately one and half miles north-east of spot code red. Two pax. One wounded. Can you assist? Over.'

'Delta one six. Direct me to your location. Over.'

A Sea King helicopter rose from behind the low hills to the south of O'Keefe.

Shit. His navigation was faulty. The chopper was heading off to the right. It would miss them literally by a mile. And the pilot wasn't hanging around.

'Cyclone. I have you visual. Correction. Come left. Come left.'

The Sea King, skimming the heather just feet above the hillside, stood on its nose. Engine protesting, it banked so the tips of the whirling blades seemed to touch the grass, pivoted and swung violently to the left.

'Cyclone. Come left . . . come left . . .' The chopper was hugging the contours, travelling nose-down at a furious lick. 'Come left . . . level out . . . I'm one hundred yards to your left . . . left . . . under you . . . NOW.'

The chopper overshot.

'Delta one six bravo. Cyclone. We have a hot extraction.' The pilot was ice. 'You have hostiles four hundred yards to your north and closing. Give me smoke. Over.'

'Giving you smoke.'

O'Keefe pulled the smoke canister off his webbing, yanked the tab and tossed the canister down wind. Clouds of purple smoke billowed out. The Sea King was already heading back. He could hear automatic fire as the Argentines let fly at the chopper.

'Delta one six bravo. This is Cyclone. Confirm smoke. What colour smoke?'

'Giving you purple smoke.'

'Delta one six bravo. Cyclone. Confirm purple smoke. We have you visual. Enemy closing rapidly. I can give you one pass. Repeat one pass. Stand by.'

The downdraught flattened the surrounding grass and knifed through O'Keefe's sweat-sodden clothes. Instinctively he ducked as the chopper came to a quivering ground hover just feet away. He lurched towards the swishing blades and heard the crack of a bullet pass near his head. Two crewmen wearing harnesses and microphones reached out. O'Keefe bent forward and they pulled Fife off his back like a sack of coal and laid him on the floor.

The Sea King soared off in an evasive climbing bank with O'Keefe's legs still dangling over the edge of the open door. He scrabbled frantically for something to hold on to before a crewman hauled him in and the last things he saw as they dropped over the far side of the hill were the muzzle-flashes of the rifles trying to kill them.

Chapter Two

'Careful. Drop that and you're dead.'

O'Keefe blinked at the object in his hand with nervous fascination.

'You drop that and my mam'll murder you. She brought it back from her honeymoon in Blackpool.'

O'Keefe placed the small china dog carefully back on the mantelpiece. 'Why does it say "Present from Morecambe", then?'

A small, busy woman in a blue pinnie bustled back into the kitchen, assumed her rightful place at the stove and continued stirring and turning the ingredients in a vast, blackened frying pan.

'How many eggs will ye have, Paddy, two or three?'

'Oh, just one please, Mrs Fife. I'm putting on too much weight.'

'Get away with ye, ye'll have two, same as any other man. Duggie, gi' that fire a poke. It's going into the next room.'

Duggie stirred in his chair by the fire, leaned forward and rattled the coals around the grate.

'I don't know why you want a fire on a nice day in summer.'

'Makes the room friendlier. Honestly, ye'd watch it go out before ye'd shift.'

'I've a poorly leg, mam.'

'Ay, well that comes and goes. Ye can get down the pub fast enough when it suits you.' Then Kate Fife's voice softened. 'He's looking better, isn't he?'

'He's looking better than the last time I saw him,' laughed O'Keefe.

'Ay, of course, you've not been back, have ye? Well, it

was a grand thing ye did for our Duggie. Come to the table. A good fry-up will set you right after your long journey.'

She began ladling out food, chattering and scolding like a brown, dusty wren.

'You've done me proud, Mrs Fife,' said O'Keefe, regarding the plate laden with three rashers of bacon, two sausages, a thick slice of black pudding, tomatoes, tatty scones and two eggs. 'Truly you have.'

He splashed brown sauce over the mound and began eating, steadily and strongly, and for the first time since he arrived twenty minutes ago, looked around the council house kitchen.

It wasn't much different from the ones he remembered in Belfast ten or so years ago. Blue and yellow plastic flowers in a polystyrene tub on the window sill, the smoking coal fire even in summer, the crucifix and the religious calendar, the unevenly painted cupboards and the thin metal draining board held up by wooden struts with the rubbish bin underneath. No fitted kitchens here in Shettlestown, Glasgow. Nor in the Falls Road, either. Late afternoon sunlight fell on the table covered with brown oilcloth and the fug of hot grease lay heavy in the air. Through the window he saw the small wilderness of a garden with the charred remains of a bonfire and an upturned metal bath without a bottom. Beyond a narrow path of cinders and black earth was another garden and another identical council house.

A black and white photograph of a determined-looking young woman and a man upright and proud caught his eye. The man wore a sharp double-breasted suit with shoulder pads and she had a ridiculous little hat.

Noticing O'Keefe looking at the photo, Kate said, 'That's me and Duggie's father on our wedding day. That was taken outside St Peter's church, just down the road.'

Fife let out a bellow of laughter. 'If you look closely you can see me. I'm that slight bulge in the skirt.'

'Whist ye.' Kate spun round on him and looked about to

peck him to death in her bird-like fury. 'So did you drive straight from Hereford?'

She already knew the answer, but felt she had to say something to hide her embarrassment.

'No, I called in at Birmingham to see my father and sister. Most of my family left Belfast looking for work and ended up there.' He balanced a triangle of egg white on a sliver of bacon and thrust them into his mouth.

'But you joined the army?'

O'Keefe managed to swallow before answering. 'Ay, well. I came across when I was sixteen, but it didn't work out so I joined up. Didn't seem much else to do.' He didn't mention his father's endless infidelities or the fights or the vain pursuit of a worthwhile job that didn't involve sweeping floors or filling shelves.

'Same as me,' said Fife.

'Where's your ma?'

'Mam.' Fife made a warning noise.

'She died five years ago when I was nineteen.' O'Keefe speared a lump of black pudding.

'Oh. I'm sorry.'

Fife raised his eyes to heaven while his mother gave him one of her well-I-didn't-know-did-I looks.

Kate approved of O'Keefe's nice table manners, cutting his food into small pieces rather than shovelling it all into his mouth. He was eating to a pattern. Bacon then egg then sausage, then tatty scones followed by black pudding and tomatoes. Then he started over again. He was built, if not like an ox, then like a young bullock with broad chest and a thick neck.

It was around that neck that he had carried her son to safety and it was that chest and lungs that had given him the strength to do it. He could eat in her house every day until eternity and he still would not have supped enough. But she didn't say that. Wee fierce Glaswegian women weren't given to articulating their gratitude. They merely demonstrated it in practical ways. He had nice eyes, she thought. Laughing eyes. And a lovely ready smile which showed his white teeth.

'You all right there, Jimmy Sands?' Fife felt he should try to cover his mother's gaffe. 'Would you like a beer to wash it down?'

'You finished the booze last night. I'll send Billy to the offie. He doesn't know you're here, otherwise he'd be here like a shot. Army barmy, that boy.' Kate rolled up her sleeves and sunk her arms deep in the sink full of soapy water. 'And anyway, who's Jimmy Sands when he's at home?'

'He's the man the Irish will never forget, mam,' replied Fife quickly.

'That was Bobby Sands and it's no laughing matter. The poor boy starved himsel' to death for something he believed in.'

'It was his choice, mam. More of a choice than the IRA give their victims,' said Fife.

'Ye sound like that Thatcher woman and ye know I'll not have that kind of talk in this house.'

'Ma. Ma . . .' A tousle-haired boy in a green army tee-shirt many sizes too large came running into the kitchen in a flurry of thin arms and legs and stopped dead at the sight of the ruddy-faced man with black curls eating at the kitchen table.

'Are you Paddy O'Keefe?'

'That I am. Are you Billy?'

'Ay.' Then the boy ran out of words and just stared at his hero. This was the superman who carried our Duggie all that way in the Falklands and saved his life. This was the man who had given Billy and his gang their latest game. One boy was the wounded Fife while another played the hero who carried him to safety across the overgrown slag heaps at the edge of the large estate. The others were Argies, lying in ambush. The hero always won through.

O'Keefe worked his way to the last bite of sausage, dipped it in a pool of sauce and wondered what to say.

'Leave Mr O'Keefe alone when he's eating,' ordered the mother.

'Paddy or Mick will do. I don't mind which.' He smiled confidingly at the boy. 'So you want to join the army?'

'Ay. I want to be a troop sergeant like you.' The words came out in a rush and Fife exploded in laughter.

'I was only acting troop staff sergeant. I've only got two stripes really. Do you know what two stripes mean?'

'That you're a complete arsehole,' interjected Fife swiftly.

'Shut it. I will not have that language in this house.' Wee Kate wagged an angry finger at her son. 'Especially in front of our Billy.'

'A corporal, that's easy.'

O'Keefe wiped the last smear of egg yolk off his plate, put down his knife and fork, sat back and blew out contentedly.

'I don't think I can move. That was grand. Thank you.'

'Our Billy's military schooling is well past that, isn't it, Billy? Tell Paddy what different tasks the troop sergeant and the troop officer perform.'

Billy put his hands behind his back, took a deep breath and stared at a point three feet above the mantelpiece.

'It is the responsibility of the troop sergeant to administer the battle and the responsibility of the troop officer to run the battle.' He stumbled over the long word as though he was repeating a poem in a foreign language. 'It is the sergeant's duty to gather the men at the point of departure and ensure they are properly equipped. The officer should never be directly involved in the early stages of the battle. He is the decision maker. He should stand one tactical bound away from the battle so he will have clarity of thought and not be distracted.'

Fife grinned with pleasure. 'Good boy, Billy. What's your six battle drills?'

Again the blond-haired lad took a deep breath. 'Preparation for battle; reaction to effective enemy fire; location

32

of the enemy; winning the firefight; the assault; and the reorganization,' he repeated parrot fashion.

'Och, there's only one thing he wants to do, isn't there, Billy lad?' said his mother.

'I'm going to join 2 Para and then the SAS – just like our Duggie.'

'How old are you, Billy?'

'Seven and a half.'

O'Keefe knelt beside his bag, still by the door where he had dumped it when he came in. After fumbling inside, he pulled out a glittering bayonet.

'Here you are, Billy. An Argie bayonet all the way from the Falklands.' Billy's face lit up in delight. As an afterthought, O'Keefe suddenly asked, 'Is that all right, Mrs Fife? He can put it on the wall in his bedroom.'

'Och, ay. Bairns round here have knives in the cribs instead of rattles. What do you say, Billy?'

'Thanks,' he whispered. 'Ay, thanks.' He turned the bayonet, like a sword in his small hands, feeling the cool steel and running his finger down the central runnel.

'That's called the blood channel,' instructed Fife. 'If you didn't have that, the suction makes it hard to pull it out of a man's body.'

'Ye're not to take it out of this house, did ye hear?' said Kate. 'If you want to show it to the gang, they'll have to come here. It's not going over this doorstep. Now go and get the men some cans from the offie.'

'It's all right, mam. Me and Paddy'll go for a drink. I need to get out and have some exercise. Is that all right with you, Paddy?'

'Let the poor man's food get down,' protested Kate.

'Billy, fetch me my coat.' Billy was still staring spellstruck at the bayonet.

'Did this kill anyone?'

'Dozens,' replied Fife. 'Now get my coat.'

Fife limped past a knot of bored young teenagers standing

around a ruined bus shelter; a younger group played football in the middle of the street, ignoring a van with no
wheels on the halfway line. Billy had finally torn himself
away from his new prize and walked just behind them. Fife
became aware of his presence and grew angry.

'Billy. Sod off. You're like a shadow to me.'

'Let him be. He's no harm. Just let him walk to the pub
with us.'

At that moment Billy's admiration for O'Keefe knew no
bounds.

'So the leg's getting better, then?'

'Ay. It's healing well now. Took some time, that bloody
secondary infection didn't help, but I'm glad to be out of
the Queen Elizabeth Hospital. Should be back with the
Regiment in a month or two. How're things with you?'

'Fine. Fine.'

It was the first time they had been alone to talk openly
and both felt an awkwardness; their only communication
since Fife had been choppered to the *Canberra* had been
the odd ill-written letter and a hurried phone call.

Fife insisted on buying the first round. They sat at a
bolted-down table on ripped plastic seats against the wall
of the modern cavernous box already looking shabby and
worse for wear. Thick glass bricks took the place of windows
– too easily smashed when the fights started. The few men
who lined the long bar drank alone, each with his tumbler
of whisky and a bottle of lemonade. No one spoke.

Fife felt he had to get the embarrassing bit over first.

'Paddy, I just want to say . . .' He began pompously
then stuttered to a halt, rubbing his chin with his left
hand and pulling a face. 'I just want to thank you for
saving my life. I wouldn't be here but for you. Thank
you.'

He wanted to make his speech of gratitude as formal and
correct as his soldiering. He lifted his drink and toasted
O'Keefe.

'Away with ye.' O'Keefe felt the colour rise in his cheeks

and hid behind his pint. 'You'd do the same for any idiot daft enough to catch a bullet. Duck next time.'

Fife was not willing to leave it alone. 'Someone should slot that rupert. I've spoken to a couple of blokes in the troop. They reckon you were a gnat's fart from a court martial.'

'You know me. Always in the shit, it's only the depth that varies.' O'Keefe shook his head regretfully. 'Too many faces had seen us fall out and the squadron sergeant major had to get involved, which didn't do anyone any favours. By the time Boss Doughty heard my side of it, Baines-Hickey was up for his MC. The boss wasn't too chuffed, but it was too late. The troop kicked up holy fuck and every word got back. There was enough shit flying to sink the *Ark Royal*. They had to be seen to back the rupert so I was put in with 18 Troop. I had a good time with the Marines on Mount Kent and I got a write-up, so that helped smooth things over.'

O'Keefe took a deep pull on his pint and wiped the froth off his lips with the back of his hand in an agricultural gesture.

'Yeh, I heard you got a mention in dispatches. I also heard you'd have got the MM if it hadn't been for the shit over me.'

O'Keefe shrugged. 'No big deal.'

'What happened to Baines-Hickey?'

'The new troop sergeant had a run-in with him and the blokes wouldn't talk to him. They totally ignored him, so it all went lumpy. In the end Boss Doughty transferred him to Group out of the way. Hope the bastard rots there. I've been sweating my cobs off in Belize.'

He saw Fife pose the question and held up his hand to fend him off. 'It was their way of keeping me away from home as long as possible. They're thinking about posting me to the TA.'

'You're going to teach the bounty hunters!'

'No, I am fucking not.' Paddy became animated. 'I only

joined the Regiment because 2 Para tried to get me into the depot. I'm a soldier. I'm from a long line of warriors . . .'

Fife pulled a face. 'It's too early in the evening. You've only had one drink.'

'. . . I'm not going to Invergowrie with a bunch of chouchters. They can stick it.' O'Keefe's dark brows bristled.

'There was talk about setting up a permanent Irish troop over the water – that would get you away.'

'Can you see me in Ireland and me a good Catholic boy from the Falls?'

'You've done it before,' Fife reminded him. 'Anyway, forty per cent of Paras are Catholic boys from working-class areas and they're the hardest bastards on the streets. They hate the Ulster Catholics for what they've become.'

'But I'm all for Irish Liberation. I've got Republicanism in my blood.'

'No, Paddy. You've got Guinness in your blood; you've got Republicanism in your imagination.'

'Bollocks. Did you know my ancestors fought at the Battle of the Boyne?'

'On which side?'

O'Keefe burst out laughing, his humour restored. 'Well, most of them were with James but the family had a row the night before the battle and some crossed over and fought with King Billy. The family's tried to keep it quiet ever since.'

'That's all right, they were on the same side as the Pope,' grinned Fife.

'What?'

'At the Battle of the Boyne, the Pope supported the Protestant side because he and the French were in the middle of a quarrel and France was backing Catholic James. Did you know the Penal Laws which followed the battle forbade any Catholic to own a horse worth more than five pounds?'

'You and your history. Irish history is not about facts, it's about feelings. You remember with your heart, not your head. My forefathers were at Vinegar Hill and inside the Post Office in Dublin.'

'And I bet they drank with Wolfe Tone as well.'

'That they did.'

'Bullshit.'

'Anyway, that's why I don't fancy doing Ireland full time. By the way, there's a wee souvenir in my bag for you. A nice little 9mm Browning with full mag and untraceable. It was like Hamleys out there.'

Fife waved his hand over his head and indicated two more pints.

'I'll get them,' said O'Keefe.

'No, you stay there. They'll bring them over. I'm the local hero.'

'Too right. Isn't that your Billy at the door? He's a good kid.'

Billy spotted them and began to make his way over.

'Ay, he's not bad,' said Fife grudgingly. 'But he's got his heart set on being a daft squaddie.'

'What else is there to do? My school had no higher expectations of me than to become a carpenter.'

'My school expected me to be expelled. And I was . . . Stand to attention, Billy, when you're addressing a soldier with a pint in his hand.'

Billy solemnly squared his narrow shoulders, brought his heels together and placed his thumbs along the seams of his football shorts.

'Please. Our mam says she forgot to remind you about seeing the fizzy lady. Mum's arranged for Kevin Twistygob to give you a lift and Dad's on his way down to keep Paddy company. Our mam'll be down later.'

'God help ye, then,' exclaimed Fife.

'What's a fizzy lady?'

'He means the physiotherapist. I'd a lot of muscle wastage. This girl who looks after Celtic offered to do it free after work. I won't be more than an hour if you can put up with my old man. Talk of the devil.'

A squat, bulky man rolled towards them. The gait suggested a sailor, but as he got closer the small blue scars on the forehead and the ingrained grime around the eyes told of a miner. The immense cauliflower left ear and the pug nose told of a miner who had fought all his life.

O'Keefe was taken unawares by Shug Fife's handshake. It was a straightforward confrontation. His hand, though not as big as O'Keefe's shovels, felt like something between untreated leather and coarse sandpaper. The grip was convulsively strong. O'Keefe found himself having to quickly apply pressure to prevent his hand being crushed. Shug Fife looked directly into O'Keefe's eyes and nodded in recognition. There was nothing malicious in the handshake. Just the same test he gave everyone.

Fife stood up with difficulty and pulled an inch-thick wad of ten pound notes from his back pocket. He slowly peeled off the top one. 'Get yersel' a drink, da, and get us one too.'

'Ay, ay. Thanks. Same again is it?' Shug tore his eyes away from the money and rolled towards the bar.

'What the hell are you doing with all that money?'

Fife gave a mischievous grin and holding the wad close between them, he pulled back the top two notes to reveal pages of a book cut neatly to size.

'This way the old beggar'll be on his best behaviour all night hoping for a bung. He can carry on hoping, as well,' he added with unexpected bitterness.

His father returned with a tray holding two pints of Guinness for Fife and O'Keefe and a lager and whisky for himself.

'Where've you been, da?'

'Buying shoes in the town.'

It seemed there was not a great deal of love between father and son. Not even mutual respect. Just an abrading mistrust of each other.

'Not bad, are they?' He sat down and held out his feet for inspection. 'Special leather. From the Bata Islands in the Far East.'

'It's okay, da, keep the change,' said Fife with heavy sarcasm.

'Ay.' There was no shame. Pocketing the change was just something he had done. Confront him with it, if you liked. He didn't care. If his son had insisted, he would have handed over the money, but it would have been Fife who would have seemed the smaller.

'Duggie said you were a miner,' said O'Keefe to Shug. 'Not something I'd ever do myself. Too dangerous.'

Shug inclined his head in the semblance of a gracious gesture. 'Ay, there were many who couldn't take to it. It doesn't matter if they do or don't now. There's no work for them. No pits left. It's no way to finish your life – on the buroo.'

'The dole,' explained Fife, adding, 'There's no way I'd have gone down the pits. I'd rather catch a bullet.'

'You did,' laughed O'Keefe.

'Ye should have used incidenary bombs,' said Shug, turning to O'Keefe. 'Better than creeping round in the dark. Incidenary bombs. From mortars. Those planes were full of petrol. They'd have gone up like Roman candles.'

'Do you mean incendiary devices?' asked Fife with a malicious note in his voice.

'Incidenary I said. Incidenary I mean.' O'Keefe saw that the years in the mines and the fights had taken a toll. His pale blue eyes were almost translucent and very tired.

'Car's here, our Duggie.'

'Shouldn't be long. You'll be okay here, Jimmy. Make the bleeder buy his round.'

'Och, away. I'm content here,' Fife's father answered for O'Keefe. 'Your mate's fine. There'll be people coming in who'll be wanting to see him. We're having a bit of a gathering, ye ken. You'll enjoy it.'

By the time Fife returned the bar had become loud, crowded and smoky. The solitary drinker had left with his bottle for his solitary night in front of the telly. Paddy's naturally red face was beginning to glow and Fife reckoned he had missed an hour of ferocious drinking. Paddy was holding court to a large circle. Billy sat rapt at his elbow, hoping he was invisible. Fife recognized the story immediately.

'. . . So anyway, we came back off three days' patrol in the desert and we were gagging. Gagging. We got into this mess tent and started to get it down our necks as if it would run out. Just after dusk the crap-hats started coming in when . . . wheee . . . crump. Mortars landed on the edge of the camp. The crap-hats were out of there so fast they left scorch marks on the matting. The guys behind the bar legged it too, so we had the place to ourselves. Duggie turns barman and we're getting stuck in. Our 105s are firing back and there's a fine old din going on. Then the mortars began landing closer. Duggie says: "I'll bet you a bottle of whisky they don't get one within a hundred yards." No sooner did he open his mouth, than . . . wallop. One lands dead outside the tent. We're out of that flap, but it's dark and we didn't know the camp and we'd had a few . . .'

The men nodded understandingly. They knew what it was like to have a few.

'. . . I careered off, tripped over a bloody rope and pitched headfirst into a slit trench, cutting open me head and knocking meself out. When I opened my eyes, there's a couple of medics from the Irish Guards, with polished tin hats and neatly ironed shirts, and they're trying to put me on a stretcher. The more I shouted the more this sergeant kept telling me I was concussed. I tried to tell him I'd been on the piss, but the next thing I knew I was in an operating theatre and there was a surgeon with a mask and a scalpel in his hand. He took one look at me, put his face next to mine, sniffed and shouted: "This man's not injured, he's drunk. Get him off my table."'

Everyone laughed and slapped O'Keefe on his broad back. He was obviously going down a treat.

'Your da's good company,' he said to Fife, slipping alongside him.

'Ay,' said Fife in a clipped way that made O'Keefe look at him keenly.

'He's proud of you, you know.'

'Only cos he can cadge money offa me and cos when I came home the wounded hero, he can drink for free.'

'You're being hard.'

'Paddy. Do you know the only reason I wanted to grow up?' Fife looked directly in his friend's eyes. 'So I could be big enough to batter my da the way he battered me all those years. That's the only fucking reason. An' I'll tell you what . . . I can still see the look in his eyes when I dropped him for the first time. Defeat and humiliation. I saw it and I fucking loved it.'

'My da battered me, too, but only cos he reckoned he had to do it to show he cared a bit.'

'My da didn't care a shite. He just battered me.'

'Well at least he didn't go chasing everything in a skirt and making an arse of hisself and his family.'

'Only cos he knew no woman would ever fancy him.'

'God, you're a hard, merciless people, you Scots. Live and let live. You're dead a long time. Still, there's lots of Irish who can't keep it in their trousers for long. We'd have had Home Rule if Charlie Parnell hadn't kept getting a hard on at the wrong time.'

'You know he was a Proddie, don't you?' demanded Fife.

'He was a randy old goat who put cunt before country. We almost had our freedom but he had to go and poke wee Katie whatsername.'

'O'Shea. Yeh, but it wasn't as close as the third Home Rule Bill in 1912. It was rejected twice by the House of Lords. Even the King got stuck in on the Proddie side. Did you know fifty-seven ruperts in the Cavalry Brigade at the Curragh threatened to resign rather than force Ulster to join a united Catholic Ireland. And when a boatload of illegal arms for the Ulster Volunteer Force landed at Larne, the police just stood by and helped direct traffic. But it was

41

different when the Catholics tried to land guns, the police started a battle and three were killed. Then Edward Carson threatened civil war . . .'

O'Keefe, who knew Fife would recite the dry dusty facts of Irish history for hours, sparked into life.

'I know, I'll give you Roger Casement's speech from the dock.' He swayed to his feet, flushed and glowing.

'He was a shirt-lifter. They examined his arse after they hung him,' said Fife, but it was too late. Paddy O'Keefe was back in the dock of Number One Court at the Old Bailey in 1916.

Two tables away, a small, pretty girl with light brown hair, a square jaw and stubborn eyes nudged her friend.

'Who's that doing the show time?'

'Don't know, Mary. He seems to be a mate of that headbanger Fife, so he must be a squaddie. Fancy him, then, do you?'

'Might do, Martha. Though not so much at the minute. Seems to be making a fool of himself.'

'Och, he's enjoying himself and no one around here minds that.'

Paddy, encouraged by the cheers which greeted his rendition of Casement's speech, launched into a maudlin version of 'Kevin Barry', his voice quavering in an uncertain baritone, tears seeping from his closed eyes as he felt the song in his heart.

'In Mountjoy Jail one Monday morning, High upon the gallows tree . . .'

The sinews in his neck stood out like whipcord. A mass of dark curls had fallen over his eyes and his face was tomato red with beads of sweat. He sang with clenched fists and he only just held on the last high note. He sat down, pleased with himself.

'That's a grand song, Paddy.'

'Sing us one about Robert Curtis,' called Fife.

'Who's he?' O'Keefe had changed to lager and sank half a pint in one huge swallow.

'The first British soldier to be killed in Ulster in the modern troubles,' explained Fife. 'Killed by a mob in Belfast in 1971. He'd only been married for a year and never saw his baby daughter. Sing about that.'

O'Keefe dismissed Fife's suggestion with an airy wave of his hand. 'I don't write the bloody things. I just sing them.'

'Fuck the facts as long as it rhymes, eh?' said the small pretty girl quietly, passing behind O'Keefe's chair.

'What!'

'Every time the Irish have a piss they make up a song about it.'

'Paddy O'Keefe is here and I couldn't give a shite for no man,' he bellowed.

'Nor woman either,' she murmured.

O'Keefe opened his mouth to reply but she moved away to rejoin her friends, picking her way over the floor tacky with spilled beer.

Bollocks.

'We're off to Dublin in the green, in the green, Where the helmets glisten in the sun . . .'

'Is he always like this?' asked Kate, who had just joined them.

'Only when he's enjoying himself, mam.'

'I'm worried he might burst a blood vessel. Will ye look at the colour of him now. I reckon he might explode.'

'I've always hated slavery since the day that I was born, So I'm off to join the IRA and I'm off tomorrow morn . . .'

'He's not really for the IRA, is he?' asked Kate. 'I'm surprised you're allowed to be in the army.'

'Don't be daft, mam,' replied Fife. 'He's been on operations against them. He's actually shot them.'

Next morning Kate, getting up early to clear the ashes and lay the fire, was surprised to see O'Keefe in an old tracksuit sitting at the table looking bleary-eyed and finishing a cup of milk. Billy sat across from him, fingering his bayonet and plotting how to get it out of the house to show his gang.

"Morning. We're just going for a run. Billy's going to show me where to go and then we'll run back together. See you later, Mrs Fife.'

Kate watched from the doorstep as O'Keefe, with Billy at his elbow, jogged off towards the overgrown coal tips and the fields beyond. The men she knew would be in bed until midday; piggy-eyed, unshaven, foul-smelling, slurping Irn-Bru and complaining about a headache while refusing to blame last night's drink.

At the bottom of the first grass-covered slag heap, O'Keefe put Billy on his shoulders and jogged up. It was the finest ride of Billy's life. At the top he pointed out the fields and O'Keefe promised to return in half an hour.

'Why can't I come with you?'

'You're a wee bit young to run this far. Maybe next year, yeh?'

Billy nodded hopefully.

'I just need a bit of a blow to clear the system. Need to run off yesterday's food to make room for today's.'

'And make room for the Guinness . . .' chirped Billy as a parting shot.

O'Keefe was still grinning to himself as he ran from the coal waste into the fields. This was the only way he could keep his weight down. Everything in excess, Paddy boyo. Drink until you drop and train until you stop. The Regiment's obsession with fitness and stamina suited him. It also allowed him to grow his hair. In the Paras he'd believed what was under his beret was his and what was outside was the army's. Sergeant majors were always amazed just how much he could stuff under his beret. Now it didn't matter.

He felt at home with Fife and his family. A working-class Catholic family in Glasgow wasn't much different from one in the Falls or Andytown. Nice to have a proper family. O'Keefe wished he did. What with his dad always moving in with or just leaving a different woman every month and his sister doing her own thing and showing quite clearly she didn't want to know, you couldn't really call it a family.

The only cloud on the horizon was the threat of being sidelined to 23 SAS. No way. He wanted to fight. That's why the Falklands were the finest days of his life. He was a corporal at twenty-five and doing well. Good money, especially with the Special Forces allowances. Sergeant wasn't too far away. If it hadn't been for that bloody rupert.

So he ran on, sweating out last night's alcohol, vaguely wondering whether he had disgraced himself and only worrying that he might have done something to embarrass wee Kate Fife. It was a perfect summer morning and he ran longer and further than he intended, lost in his thoughts. He was puffing well when he returned to Billy.

'There ye are, Billy boy. Sick, shit, shave, shower, shampoo. Same every morning. Now the world can throw what it likes at Paddy O'Keefe. I'm ready.'

''Morning, Jimmy Sands. What time do you call this to get up?'

Fife was sitting at the table, his walking stick by his side. There was no sign of Shug. The transistor radio was turned on and his mother looked severe.

'Och, those poor wee boys. Those poor horses. Bastards should be shot.'

O'Keefe cocked a questioning eye at Fife.

'Two IRA bombs in London. Blown up a band and a mounted troop. One device under the bandstand and another by the roadside. At least six dead. Early days yet.'

Kate scurried around, finding small tasks around the kitchen on which to spend her pent-up anger. 'Och, they should let the women sort out the problems of Ireland. They'd bang a few heads together. The whole of Ireland isn't worth the life of a single soldier. Sorry, Paddy, but there it is.'

She looked so set and sad in her blue pinny that O'Keefe

45

could only nod and go off to the bathroom to wash and dress.

When he returned Kate had wound herself up into a passion. The TV carried pictures of the scenes of carnage. There were at least eleven dead and fifty injured now. A lovely summer's day in a London park had been turned into a bloodbath.

'And what harm were they doing? Playing music for the pleasure of others. And those soldiers on the horses. Looking pretty for the tourists.' She compressed her lips in her fury. 'I'd like to get my hands on the murdering bastards – just for five minutes. They'd never plant another bomb. Don't put them on trial so some clever lawyer can get them off – hand them over to the mothers, they'd know how to deal with them.'

She put down two laden plates on the table with a thump which made the egg yolks quiver.

'I don't understand why the army doesn't just do away with all the trouble-makers.'

'It's not as simple as that, ma,' replied Fife. He quoted from his training manuals. 'It's a fundamental rule of counter-terrorism that to combat terrorism effectively, the forces of the government must adhere to the rule of law.'

'Tsk. I don't want your lectures. They know who the terrorists are, just kill them.'

'Then you become another terrorist.' Fife remembered the discussion they'd had with the CRW lecturer when they had raised exactly the same points. 'Of course, they know who the players are – but it's another matter proving it in a court of law. The Government must keep the moral high ground. The IRA are hoping we'll fight as they do. That's what they want. It'll mean they are winning.'

'It's all very fine talking about the rule of law and moral high ground,' sniffed Kate. 'Tell it to the mothers of those poor boys lying dead down in London.'

Her maternal feelings swamped any romantic notions she had possessed the previous night of the glamour and righteousness of the Republican cause. That could have been her boy lying there by the roadside, torn, mangled and bleeding.

'Bastards.'

In the afternoon Fife took O'Keefe to see the sights of Glasgow, which involved pub crawling the larger hotels until they ended up at Stevenson and Taylors. Everywhere TV sets in the corners carried the morning's attack and drinkers shook their heads in sorrow and resignation at the slaughter.

'It's only the Scottish regiments that can understand Ulster,' asserted Fife. 'We understand it because it's the same here. We have different tribes in Glasgow. Catholic and Protestant, Celtic and Rangers. Regiments like the Welch or Royal Anglians don't have a clue. They've never experienced it at home.'

'And how's the voice today?'

They turned to see the fair-haired girl who had been in the pub last night. O'Keefe had a dim recollection that she had spoken to him. In the quiet bar he picked up on her soft but unmistakable Belfast accent. She had a mischievous twinkle in her eye.

'Grand.'

Fife recognized her. 'You're staying with Martha McGinn aren't you?'

'Ay, I'm her cousin, Mary.'

'I'm Duggie Fife.'

'I know who *you* are. Doesn't everyone in Shettlestown know you – you're the hero.'

There was a challenging and amused expression on her face and Fife didn't know if she was taking the mick.

She regarded the two friends. Fife, a typical slight, sandy-haired Jock with piercing hard blue eyes and a nose that had been pummelled back into his face. His friend was broader, with an easy, happy-go-lucky laugh and softer blue eyes under dark brows. Black Irish.

'He's the Lean Mean Killing Machine,' said O'Keefe keeping a straight face.

'This is Paddy O'Keefe. He's the real hero.' Fife flicked a thumb towards his friend.

'He was a hero last night, all right. How's the head?'

'Fine.' O'Keefe found himself looking at a girl around his own age with mocking grey eyes, nice smile lines around her mouth and a strong chin. 'Would you like a drink?'

'Bacardi and Coke.'

'Are ye from the Falls?' O'Keefe thought he could place the accent.

'Can't ye tell?'

'I'm from there, too.'

'What school did you go to?'

'St Vincent's in the Falls.'

'I think I know some of your relatives. Didn't your family move to the mainland?'

'Ay. Birmingham, but I joined the army.'

'That would explain why I haven't seen you. The boys wouldn't take too kindly to that,' she said thoughtfully. 'You'd know Dominic Hogan and Brian McGirr.'

O'Keefe's face lit up. 'I was in the same form as them. Used to play football with Dom every Saturday.'

'Well you won't now. They're both doing ten apiece in the Kesh.'

Mary glanced up at him as if expecting a response but O'Keefe said nothing, his usually mobile Irish face blank and inert.

'So you're both Catholics,' concluded Fife.

'Of course he's a Catholic,' replied Mary. 'I could tell by looking at him. You too.'

She saw the look of disbelief cross Fife's face.

'In Belfast we can tell these things. If someone walks into a bar I can tell their religion instantly. We all can.'

'How?'

'You tell by the name, the accent, the look, the dress, the carriage.'

'You can honestly do that?' Fife was intrigued.

'Yes,' replied Mary as if it was the most natural thing in the world. 'You sense it somehow. It's small things. Catholic girls have their ears pierced when they are small. Proddie ones don't. Proddies are more brethren . . .'

'Brethren?' queried Fife.

'You know. Strict, like. They seem better scrubbed. I tell you. Me and a friend looked at a wedding picture of a mixed marriage. There were twenty-six faces there and we got twenty-three right. You just know.'

'I don't know Belfast.'

'There's a sadness and a roughness about it,' said Mary, suddenly thoughtful. 'The people are mad. You think they'd be talking about politics all the time. They're not. They keep having affairs in the wrong places with the wrong people and they don't care.'

She turned her attention back to O'Keefe. 'So what took you into the army?'

'Economics.'

'Was it economics that took you into the SAS?'

'Direct, aren't you?' said O'Keefe, trying to hide his surprise.

'I've been told.' O'Keefe and Mary looked at each other. Their eyes met and they smiled in mutual recognition of devilment and devilry, wild spirits capable of reckless mischief.

'I never said I was in the SAS.'

'If you hang about with that maniac Fife . . .' She nodded in his direction. 'Ye cannae be anything else. Everyone knows what Fife gets up to. Soldiers don't run about with long hair and beards. Look at you. Students at Glasgow University, are we? Sociology or anthropology, is it? And you went for a run this morning. Not natural around here, that you know, Paddy boy.'

'I've never worn a uniform in Ireland.' He chose his words carefully.

'With hair like yours, you would not be guarding the

49

palace, now would ye?' Mary stood squarely in front of him, legs spread wide for balance like a fighter. 'Don't forget, Paddy, I've seen them all. Paras, Guards, Marines and I assure you, you don't have that stamp on you. Anyway, I'm on holiday. I want to leave the troubles behind.'

Fife indicated the TV high in the corner carrying an updated report on the London bombings. 'It looks as if you've brought them with you.'

She shook her head, not willing to talk about it. 'I should be meeting a girlfriend here. I don't know where she is. I expect she'll have gone home by now.'

'Are you going to the dance at the Miners' Welfare tonight?' asked Fife.

'Might be. Are you?' Mary put on a show of polite interest.

'Not with my leg. Anyway Celtic have a pre-season friendly,' he replied.

'I'll go,' said O'Keefe quickly. 'I'll meet you outside the hall, wherever it is, at ten-thirty and take you in.'

Mary gave him a knowing look, put her head on one side and turned her earring.

'Trying to save money on me, Paddy, are you? If it's my company you'll be wanting, you can have it from now – and pay for it. I'll have another Bacardi and Coke. Now excuse me.' She picked up her handbag and marched out to the telephone in the hall.

'I reckon your leg's swelling up. Shouldn't you be away and rest it?' said O'Keefe.

'Nae sweat. I'm off to the footie. I've got a seat in the directors' box. That's what comes of being a wounded hero. You're included, too.'

'Thanks, Jimmy. But I think I'll be otherwise occupied.'

Mary returned and put her handbag on the floor. It seemed to be a statement that she intended staying.

'My friend's at home. She claims she thought we were to meet up there. I ask you.' She gave a look of mock exasperation.

An evil glint crept into Fife's eye.

'Mary, I got to tell you that Paddy is not all he seems.'

'Oh, ay.'

'Ay. If you want a real man, I'm the one. If you want a virgin, then you'd better take Paddy. He's never done a funny pee in his life.'

O'Keefe dropped his eyes and a red glow crept into his cheeks. 'I've been saving myself,' he mumbled. 'It's not important, anyway.'

'He's the only bloke I know who got a refund in a brothel. His Catholic conscience.'

Mary looked from one to another, not believing a word but curious. Never. Paddy was too good-looking. Too sure of himself. But he was blushing. Stranger things had happened. Yeh. Like what?

'I'll leave you two to it,' said Fife, standing up with some difficulty. 'Will you be all right by yourself?'

'Don't worry about me,' said Mary indignantly.

'I was talking to Jimmy Sands.'

When Fife had limped off, Mary asked uncertainly, 'Is it true you've never been with a woman?'

'It's never bothered me much. I'm away most of the time, so I don't get to meet many lassies.'

She gave him a glance which said: I don't believe a word you're saying but keep telling me anyway.

'You're very good friends with Fife, aren't you?'

'Yeh, we're good mates.'

'You know he's a head-banger. Fight anybody anytime.'

'Not any more. Not with that leg and anyway he's calmed down a lot.' Fife had to. One more fight and he'd find himself back with the Parachute Regiment, he'd been told.

'He's very serious sometimes, isn't he? You're not serious, are you?'

'No. Jimmy Sands worries for the world. I just let them get on with it. Anyway, why all the questions?'

'Maybe I'm interested in you?'

Somehow in her clipped, glass-scratching Belfast voice,

it sounded amazingly sexy. O'Keefe felt a stirring in his groin.

'You don't want to spend the night sitting in this pub. We could go for a drive.'

'Trying to save money on me again, Paddy O'Keefe?'

'No. I'll pay for the petrol.'

Much later they walked over the heather and talked and laughed and asked each other all sorts of questions as if they couldn't learn enough of each other. As the long day finally ended they sat on the warm earth and watched the sun set in a flaming orange ball. At their first kiss, Mary knew he had been lying.

They lay side by side and Paddy put his arm around her and turned her face to his.

'This is nice.'

'Ay.'

He let his hand stray to her left breast. She removed his hand wordlessly and carried on kissing him. A few minutes later he tried again.

'You *are* inexperienced, aren't you?' she murmured fondly, taking the hand away and kissing him deeply.

O'Keefe was confused. He didn't know what he was doing wrong. It had always worked before. What did she mean, inexperienced? He'd had more women than she'd had hot dinners. He stroked the back of her thigh with his fingertips and felt her quiver beneath him. He allowed his fingers to creep up a fraction at a time, sometimes withdrawing and then inching that little higher each time. She began to tense and thrust her pelvis upwards.

'You really don't have a clue, do you?' She lifted his dallying hand and put it back around her neck. O'Keefe stiffened in rejection and tried to remember those books he'd half-read about how to seduce a woman by making her tremble with pleasure. The things he'd thought he didn't need to know.

He played with her ear with his tongue, stroked her

hair and inside the crook of her elbows, which he'd read somewhere was an erogenous zone. He pressed, subtly he thought, against her so she felt the firmness in his groin. Finally she allowed him to hold her breast and, after an eternity, to fumble to undo her bra. He made his tongue perform intricate patterns over her swelling nipples, but when he put his hand between her legs she tutted in disapproval and took it away. By stealth, subterfuge and strategy he caressed her bare legs, calves and thighs until his fingers brushed against her knickers and he felt her dampness. It reassured him that he was doing something right.

In one flowing motion, she lifted up her bottom, pulled her skirt up to her hips and hooked down her knickers to her knees. 'Teeth,' she ordered, nodding towards her drawers. O'Keefe did as he was instructed looking up her lean brown legs to the fur at the top. He began to undo his flies but she took his curly head and gently but firmly pushed it down between her legs, raising herself off the ground and wrapping her thighs around his head.

Mary began to move as a swelling sea, murmuring with pleasure, her buttocks clenching and unclenching. She took his hands and pressed them over her breasts, hard and harder still. Harder and more forceful than he would ever have dared. O'Keefe felt he was diving underwater, hearing his own blood pulse around his head and feeling the pressure as her tensed thighs stopped his ears. He thought he was going to drown. His air was running out, still she did not let him surface. Finally, she shuddered and cried aloud. Then she loosened her legs and with her eyes closed, murmured: 'Now.'

Later she smiled a soft smile and said, 'You'll do. You're not right yet, but you'll do.'

O'Keefe felt a wonderful sense of floating on warm water. 'What was all that about?'

'Well, Paddy, you being so inexperienced and all, I thought I'd try to help. Most men haven't a clue. Wham bam and then forget to say thank you ma'am.' She gave a wicked grin of knowledge and power. 'That was a wee lesson, Paddy, and it was free. You got there in the end and so did I.'

They kissed again until Mary started. 'I hope you remembered to say the prayer?'

'What prayer?'

'The Sinners' Prayer of course, you ignorant Mick. Don't ye know nothing?' Mary rolled up her eyes and assumed a virtuous expression. '"Holy Mary I believe, That without sin thou didst conceive. Now I pray in thee believing, That I may sin without conceiving."'

O'Keefe burst out laughing, delighted at her brash wantonness.

'Oh Mary Mother of Jesus. Don't tell me you didn't say it. What will become of me? I know. Say it now and then maybe it'll be all right this time. You're supposed to be special forces so I'm expecting something special.'

Billy, watching from behind a gorse bush, hoped they were not going to be long because it was past his bedtime and he was going to get a lathering. But it would be worth it. He didn't want to miss anything.

Chapter Three

'Ireland stands at your bar, expectant, hopeful, almost suppliant . . .'

'For Christ's sake, get me a drink!'

'I'm trying, Jimmy, I'm trying.' Fife finally attracted the barman's attention. 'Large whisky for the groom, please. And another for the best man. Now stop panicking. The worst is over. Gladstone's last Home Rule speech to the Commons by the way. Thanks.'

'No Jimmy Sands jokes in front of Mary's relatives, the few there are, or I'll slot you.'

'Paddy, she looks lovely,' smiled wee Kate, moving past to collect her glass of champagne. 'A real picture.'

'Shuggie's quiet,' said O'Keefe, nervously regarding his whisky.

'Ay. And he'll stay that way,' replied Fife. 'Mam's told him one step out of line and he's for it. He's not afeard of any man in Glasgow, but he'll not cross our mam.'

The bar was filling up as guests arrived for the wedding reception in the country house hotel outside Worcester – just twenty-three miles from Hereford, but far enough away so those who didn't know wouldn't make the connection. Molecatcher, Seldom, Gobbo and others from their troop ordered drinks. They all had a freshly scrubbed appearance and wore dark suits and a collection of garish ties.

'What were you two fuddling about at the front? He wasn't getting cold feet, was he?'

'Jimmy asked me if I had the rings so I gave him the gears.' Fife, obviously pleased with himself, pulled out two bands of rubber from the ticket pocket of his jacket. 'I cut them from the tops of two johnnies. I thought he was going to go ballistic . . .'

'He's not got a big family and most of hers haven't come over. Maybe they disapprove of her marrying a British soldier . . .'

'Someone said he was a medic with the Engineers . . .'

'She hasn't got a father and they're not well off. They couldn't afford a posh do . . .'

'She's only known him five months. Did she have to . . . ?'

'What do you think?'

'Wasn't that bomb terrible last night in that bar in Ireland. Seventeen people killed and those poor soldiers. What a terrible Christmas for their families.'

'Billy looks the part in his kilt,' Paddy remarked to wee Kate Fife.

'Ay. The funniest thing. I caught him stuffing your Falklands bayonet down his sock instead of his skean dhu . . .'

Mary arrived in the bar from the Ladies where she had been closeted with her bridesmaid Jackie. She saw her husband laughing with Fife and felt a pang of envy. They were so comfortable together; they were like an old married couple. She wondered if she and Paddy would ever achieve a relationship like that. Paddy smiled a greeting.

'God, you're beautiful,' he murmured. 'You're shining.'

'That's because I'm so happy.' He loved the way her eyes narrowed into slits when she smiled and laughed, which was often. Now she grasped her husband's arm and squeezed, putting her head on his shoulder in an unaffected moment of open intimacy.

'Should you be drinking?'

'Away with you, Duggie Fife. It's my wedding day.'

'I trust you'll be very happy with your first husband.'

'He's not quite right yet, but he's learning.' Mary looked fondly up at O'Keefe. 'Seriously, thanks for getting him here in one piece. I had nightmares of a phone call from some barracks the other side of the world.'

56

'I promised I'd deliver him safe and sound.' He glanced at the other members of his troop, now drinking steadily. 'Although I did have some opposition.'

'And you kept your word. Paddy said you were the most single-minded man he knew. Once you set your mind to something, you'll see it through.'

'Och. He wants to be here.' Fife blushed. 'Don't worry when you spot the odd feather around his . . . um . . . parts. The glue will soak off in warm water. After twenty-four hours.'

Mary opened her mouth to protest and instead burst out laughing. 'Maybe it'll tickle my fancy.'

'You've a grand lass there,' Kate told O'Keefe. 'Look after her and she'll repay you a hundred times.'

'You're Jackie, aren't you?' said Fife. 'I've got to toast you later.'

'And I hope that's all you do.'

Why did double meanings sound so sexy in a Belfast accent?

'Are you from the Falls, too?' asked Fife, taking her reply as an invitation.

'Nothing so common. I'm from Andytown.'

'Is that different?'

'Not really,' she giggled.

'I know the Droppin' Well bar. I spent time in Ballykelly with 2 Para. Must have been slack security . . .'

'Sounds an easy target . . .'

'Provos?'

'No. INLA.'

'Doesn't show, does it?'

'She's small-boned. She'll carry it high and late like our Tracey. She didn't put on an inch until she was seven months gone and then she went up like a balloon.'

'. . . It's my duty to try to shag the bridesmaid. Ye'd not be wanting me to be in dereliction of my duty as best man would ye, Jimmy?'

'Oh, Mary. Golden Virginia sends her love.'

'She's a good old stick. Used to babysit me.'

'You all right there, Billy boy?'

'Yes thank you, Paddy. Are those men mates of yours?'

'Ay. They're in our troop.' He caught Molecatcher's eye. 'Young Billy here's going to join the Regiment.'

Molecatcher got the hint. 'You're Duggie's brother. Come and talk to us.'

Billy stood among his gods desperately trying to remember every word – but he didn't understand half of what they said.

'Ladies and Gentlemen. If you will take your seats.'

'One, just one Jimmy Sands joke and I'll drop you.'

'Dinnae worry, Jimmy.'

'And I heard Paddy behind this hedge. He was panting and puffing and sounding very breathless. "Yes, yes. You can do it. Yes, yes. Good girl. Come with Paddy." We were supposed to be on exercise but some men are luckier than others and we've all heard of the luck of the Irish. So I looked over the hedge and there he was, hard at it . . . This nanny goat had his cherry beret in her mouth. Paddy was tugging away trying to get the goat to the gate but every time he eased up, she took another bite. In the end she swallowed it.'

Fife waited until the laughter had died away.

'To Mary I say, you are a unique person. You have tamed the fire in a man I can only describe as a warrior. I trust you'll have a large family and bring them up in the true faith as loyal Celtic supporters. Paddy. What can I say? You took me under your wing when I was just a young lad. You introduced me to the odd drink – numbers eleven, thirteen and fifteen – but even then you always made sure I was in chapel on Sunday mornings. I hope you are as strict with your family as you were with me. I remember one Sunday morning in Cyprus. You made me do altar boy with Father Beattie here. As we were saying Mass, a dove flew out of the rafters. Father Beattie just said "The Holy Ghost" and carried on. Isn't that right, Father?'

The grey-haired priest smiled and nodded.

'It's my duty to embarrass the groom by telling tales of his disreputable past. But I cannot do it. I could stand here all day and tell stories of Paddy, but you just can't embarrass the man. It's impossible. This is the man who somersaults from high time to high time with never a hangover. Under that devil-may-care exterior, there's a devil-may-care interior just the same. When he was in Aldershot his party piece was to finish the night swinging from the wagon wheel which hangs from the mess bar ceiling with his trews around his ankles. Does he blush? No. Remind him of the time he dropped the Colonel's wife's goldfish in her bottle of wine . . .' A loud cheer went up from the troop's table. 'Or when he put the prawn in the Squadron Commander's shaving soap; the negligent discharge in the Far East which left a working girl lying on her stomach for six weeks. And ruined her trade . . . And he doesn't bat an eyelid. He is shameless.

'If you want to embarrass Paddy, you have to tell of the good he has done. I've carried him home a few times, but he carried me home when it mattered most. In case anyone here doesn't know, Paddy saved my life in the Falklands. He carried me for a night and a day and did he complain? Of course he did. Kept on saying he wished I was someone called Jimmy Sands. Don't understand it myself.'

Fife looked directly at his best friend. O'Keefe bent his head so the others could not see his blushes. Mary glowed with pride and reached for his hand under the table.

'Paddy, ye saved my life. You stuck with me when I thought I was a goner and you kept me alive when I thought I was going to die. Mary, I hope he keeps you as warm as he kept me.' Fife raised his glass. 'I thank Father Beattie for being here today. The bridesmaid Jackie, who looks lovely. Paddy and Mary. Bless their union.'

Chapter Four

O'Keefe winced as the cold clammy trousers squelched around his bollocks. He was always reluctant to get out of his snug, dry sleeping bag and pull on sodden clothes in the pre-dawn darkness. He steeled himself to tuck the sodden shirt into the damp trousers. This was the worst part. This and the first half-hour on the march when the dank material rubbed against all the bites and sores covering his body. He beat his boots upside down to knock out anything nesting there overnight and laced them up with para cord.

He sat on his bergen, waiting for first light to move out, and pulled a long Irish face. I wasn't there for Liam's birth and I'm not going to be there for this one. No wonder Mary is an unhappy bunny. O'Keefe felt an insect stop to breakfast on his forehead and he squeezed it to death against his dirt-ingrained skin. The night was beginning to give way to the permanent twilight world that passed for daylight under the canopy of treetops. Something rustled in the undergrowth away to his left and he heard the shrill squeal and cry of an animal in pain. The cry ended abruptly.

The jungle gave off a decaying, fusty smell as the heat increased. Soon the humidity would be eighty per cent and it would be difficult to breathe. In the brown gloom he could make out the shapes of the three other members of the patrol, including Fife, sitting motionless, each facing inwards, automatic weapons in hand.

Mary wanted a girl this time. He didn't care as long as it was healthy and whole. He still found it hard to believe the depth of his feelings towards his son. When

Liam smiled that lovely slow smile of sheer happiness, it melted his heart. He could watch Liam for hours and when he tried to walk with O'Keefe holding his tiny hands, he thought he was going to burst with pride.

But Mary wasn't happy. She was lonely when he was away on jobs. And he was away a lot. The longest trip had been six months. The shortest a week. They had been married almost two years and he had not been home more than twenty-four weeks in total. Every homecoming was like a honeymoon for the first few days. Nights of passion and sexual excitement, lots of things to talk about, catching up to do. Then you wanted to see your mates and have a pint and a fuddle. Mary didn't understand that. She'd be craving attention – or even reassurance – and he'd be in the pub talking about the job done or the next job to do.

He wasn't a bad husband. On the contrary, he was faithful, generous and caring. His legendary drinking bouts were in the past. But wives couldn't understand the comradeship that existed between the men. They regarded it as a rival. They wanted civilian lives with civilian values. They envied other families whose husbands had every weekend off; a fortnight a year on the Costa del Sol and a nice saloon car in the garage. A poor substitute for what he did.

Mary was homesick. That was the root of her problems. She wouldn't confess it and O'Keefe was scared to talk about it, fearing what dark emotions might be stirred or words spoken which couldn't be ignored. He knew she had this yearning to be able to pop in to see her mother and hear the raw breaking of the Belfast voice and smell the peat. This fearsome tribal longing that was calling her home.

It was light enough now to see the four-inch black centipede undulate over the piece of rotting wood by his foot. The jungle floor teemed with centipedes, millipedes, ants, beetles, scorpions and God knows what else. The insects were firing up, like a band warming up in beetle music, all whirring and clicking in a growing cacophony of sound.

A tree assumed shape in front of him as though someone had turned up a lamp behind it and the first bead of sweat trickled down O'Keefe's backbone.

Mary was a good mother and wife. She always put freshly cooked food on the table and they ate together as a family. A lot of army wives lived on frozen convenience food and forgot how to cook. Others were worse. They put packets of OMO in the kitchen window. Old Man Out.

Fife's filthy features became visible and O'Keefe wondered what he was thinking. He was going through a rough time living with that Vicky. She was older than he was, divorced and caught up in an angry coven of vociferous harpies who spent hours gobbing off with stories of men's bestiality and cruelty.

A leaf suddenly flicked as a droplet of water fell from the one above. O'Keefe nodded and soundlessly the four men rose, inched their way into their bergens, brushed away traces of their stay and moved into the shades of the dawn forest.

An hour later they dog-legged back on themselves and stopped for a brew. By now rivulets of sweat were running down O'Keefe's face washing the mosquito repellent into his eyes so that they watered and stung. He had not washed his hair for four weeks and it hung long and greasy. He smelled like the jungle – as was the intention.

'You all right, Jimmy Sands?'

It was the first time anyone had spoken.

'If this mossie rep can melt fucking plastic, how come it doesn't affect mossies?' Fife grumbled, swatting at his face with his filthy hand and trying not to pick the three angry red sores which had joined up to form a volcano on his forehead.

O'Keefe knelt down to break up more hexy blocks to keep the fire going. They'd each had a mug of hot sweet tea; now came breakfast of rehydrated curry. Molecatcher was urinating into the plastic container used to carry liquid human waste. They defecated into plastic bags which they also carried back to camp.

'How can a stick insect like you piss that much?' growled Fife. 'I've got to carry that.'

He fell quiet and his hand slowly reached for the kukri on his belt.

'Don't move, Jimmy,' he hissed quietly. 'Don't fucking move.'

He glided on the balls of his feet towards O'Keefe, still crouching motionless by the flickering flames.

There was a whistle as the curved blade flashed through the air and a snake's head dropped into O'Keefe's mug with a splash. Slowly, a two-foot-long body unravelled off the moss-covered branch just above O'Keefe's head.

'Jesus!'

'You want to watch that, Jimmy Sands.'

The men gathered around looking at the green and black diamond-shaped head floating in the water with a thin grey tongue protruding between its fangs.

O'Keefe touched the body gingerly with the toe of his boot. 'What sort is it?'

'Christ knows. We should take it back to identify it.'

'Bollocks to that. I'm not picking it up,' shuddered O'Keefe. 'Anyway it's ruined my bloody brew.'

'The way you make tea, Jimmy, it's improved it.'

The four marched into the basha early afternoon on schedule. Others in the troop lay in their camouflaged A-frames cleaning their kit or sat around the fire enjoying a brew-up, their reddish brown faces contrasting with the whiteness of their bodies. All wore belt kit and carried their weapon and a gulock or kukri attached by para cord. Their arrival coincided with Fred, the troop sergeant, striding out of the admin hut, two signals in his hand.

'Right. On me, everyone. On me.'

The men hurried towards the barrel-like Londoner. He waved towards O'Keefe and his party. 'Full alert. Condition

Red. No duff. The IRA has just tried to blow up the Cabinet in a Brighton hotel.'

'What the fuck's that got to do with us out here?'

Fred held up his hand for silence. He had a rearranged nose, unblinking blue eyes and a habit of nodding vehemently to reinforce his points in argument. He didn't lose many arguments.

'We're returning to the UK.'

'What! Just because the Provos tried to blow up Maggie Thatcher?' O'Keefe was incredulous.

'No, you bonehead, because Mrs Paddy has given birth to a baby girl.'

'I'm losing this,' mumbled O'Keefe.

'Look,' barked Fred. 'I'll put it in words of less than one syllable for your little Irish brain. The exercise has been terminated. We all go home. Mrs Thatcher blown up. Mrs O'Keefe delivered of baby girl. O'Keefe now father of two. Mother and baby doing well.'

O'Keefe opened and closed his mouth like a fish out of water until a huge grin divided his face and he punched the air.

'The two signals came together,' Fred grinned back. 'And as we're officially off exercise, we'd better do the decent thing and wet the baby's head.'

Fife handed O'Keefe a can of beer. 'You all right there, Jimmy Sands?'

'I've got a daughter. A baby daughter. Do you think wee Kate will be her godmother?'

'You'll have to arm wrestle her to stop her. Is there a name?'

'We thought Katie for a girl.'

Fred held his can high. 'Right, lads. Miss Katie O'Keefe.'

The fourteen members of the troop raised their cans, each still holding his automatic weapon in the other hand.

'Miss Katie O'Keefe.'

And I wasn't there for her birth, thought O'Keefe, drinking deeply.

Chapter Five

Fife swore as he turned into the road and saw the two cars parked outside Vicky's house. The Dogs of War. The coven of divorcees who met to slag off anyone who was happy and content. Painted harpies, desperate to be shagged, they turned their envy into malice and told each other it was the last thing they would do. Then they individually crept away in the dark and looked for it.

All he bloody well needed after a boring day in camp shaking down equipment and tidying up administrative loose ends. Paddy had shown still more pictures of Katie. The lads had stood around and he'd cooed with the rest. Strange how these hard men would take time out to look at pictures of each other's kids.

It was unlikely there was anything for dinner. Vicky hadn't cooked once since he'd come back from the jungle exercise. She had expected to eat out every night.

Five women in their thirties filled the white mock leather three-piece suite. Two empty wine bottles sat on the blue-tiled coffee table and Vicky was opening the third.

'Have it out with him.'

Five pairs of eyes ready to curdle concrete stared at him. He'd been made more welcome on the Argentine airfield.

'Where've you been until this hour?' Vicky asked belligerently.

'In the Paludrin Club having a few drinks with Paddy. He was showing pictures of wee Katie.'

Vicky sniffed and ran the tips of three fingers through her ash-blonde hair. 'They breed like rabbits. Anyway I don't feel safe with the Irish around. They could be spies.'

'Mary's no spy, woman.' Fife couldn't stand the super-cilious superiority of the pack. Now the pack glowered collectively in his direction.

'How do you know?'

Fife went into the kitchen without answering. He'd been right. No sign of cooking. The breakfast dishes lay in the sink. The shirts he'd washed before he'd set off were still outside on the clothes line. Another batch of shirts, neatly ironed by him, hung on the clothes horse. He took a lager from the fridge.

'What are you doing out there?'

'Reading the paper.'

'Not good enough for you, are we?' Fife grimaced and carried the can into the living room. 'You're drinking again.'

'So are you, hen.'

Vicky looked down her nose. 'There's a difference between drinking socially, which is what we're doing, and drinking for the sake of it like you lot do. So where've you been?'

'I told you, at the Paludrin Club.' Fife let the first notes of exasperation creep into his voice.

'Not been seeing anyone?' She was playing to the gallery and weren't they loving it. A domestic row before their blood-lusting eyes.

'No, hen. You know I don't play away.'

'I don't know any such thing.' The women were regard-ing him as a pack of jackals would watch a weakened prey, waiting pitilessly for the moment of the kill.

'What's this then?' Vicky reached behind the sofa and produced a shirt.

'What the bloody hell are you on about, woman?'

'Don't raise your voice to me. Attack's always the best form of defence for you lot.'

'I don't know what the fuck you're on about.'

Vicky took a delicate sip of wine, pleased with the reac-tion she had aroused. See, she said to her cohorts, I told you he was a beast.

66

'This shirt. Go on, smell it.' She bundled up the shirt and hurled it at him. 'Go on, smell it.'

The women looked expectantly. Get out of this. Caught red-handed. This is how the *tricoteuses* looked, knitting by the guillotine.

'I can't smell anything.'

'Everyone else in this room can,' jeered Vicky. 'Some old bag's perfume.'

Then suddenly Fife understood and anger swept over his face.

'What you can smell here, hen, is spray-on starch.' He spoke in a dangerously clipped and controlled way. He strode into the kitchen, returning seconds later with the spray can. Fife held the canister at arm's length and pressed the button. The women coughed and spluttered as the cloud of starch settled over them.

'Right. Smell that. It's the same as the shirt. And if any of you slags ever washed or ironed a shirt, you'd fucking well know.'

Vicky was not going to accept defeat gracefully – not in front of her friends.

'You've been playing around. Don't deny it. We know.'

She had a smug look that drove Fife to an even greater fury.

'You know jackshite,' he exploded. 'I gave my word and I meant it. I could have shagged any of your so-called friends. They're all up for it. Fucking begging for it, but I didn't. I've tried with you, hen, and I don't know why. The next time you hear I'm playing around it'll be the truth.'

The power and force surging from Fife's body filled the room. He raised his hand as if to strike her. Instead he snatched up the bottle of wine and flung it against the wall where it smashed, splattering the white paint with red liquid. The women screamed.

'Fuck the lot of you.' He stumbled to the door through the crimson haze and slammed it with such force that cheap ornaments tumbled off the shelves and crashed to the ground. Still shaking, he got into his car and drove off. He couldn't work out why he could be so calm in action and so easily wound up at home.

'Found it all right, then. Quite handy tucked behind Harrods, isn't it?'

Jolyon Rodgers looked curiously around the first floor bar in the anonymous house. The walls were full of military shields and plaques and fading, brown photographs of men with neat hair and 1940s suits.

'Not your usual watering hole is it, Simon? A bit cloak and dagger.'

'Yes please, Charles. Scotch. Civilized measure for my friend.' Simon Baines-Hickey waved to the ancient barman in his short white jacket. 'There's a certain cachet to being a member of the Special Forces Club. You'd be surprised at the people you meet here.'

Rodgers looked uneasily at an extremely tall figure in a crumpled tweed suit and desert boots haranguing a totally bald man with a black eyepatch.

'More than the Cavalry and Guards?'

'All I ever see there are my fellow officers. They can't come in here unless I invite them. Cheers.'

'You are a dreadful snob. You've started drinking early. How many have you had?'

'Elitist, old boy, and probably too many. But I've made a decision. I'm going to chuck the army.'

'I thought you were getting on well.'

'I am, but I need to work in the City for a few years.'

'Ah . . .'

'And that's where you come in.'

'Thought you wanted something, Simon. You always do.'

'Don't worry, old boy, there will be a quid pro quo.' Baines-Hickey smoothed the side of his neck with his fingertips and looked vacantly into the middle distance with his dull eyes. Despite his long face, he had the sleek air of someone well fed and well watered.

'I've got it all worked out. Army, city, politics. Not to put too fine a point on it, I need money. I can't go into politics until I've got a tidy stash behind me. No one can live properly on an MP's wages.'

He saw the amused scepticism in the other's face.

'I'm thirty years old. Proven leadership qualities. Dashing young Guards officer, pushing major, SAS and MC . . .'

'To say nothing of your family connections . . .'

'Exactly. I had a chat with one of the party's grandees, pal of the old man's. He was delighted I was taking an interest in politics. Thought my selection would be a doddle. He had some notion about cutting my teeth on some frightful inner city constituency which I didn't stand a cat's chance in hell of winning. I didn't disabuse him, but I've already chosen my seat, thank you. Next door to the family pile in bluest Wiltshire.'

'You're not usually this forthcoming, Simon. Many a slip 'twixt cup and lip, y'know.'

'No, I've told you, it's all planned. The incumbent is standing down time after this, so around 1991–92 I reckon I'll be in the House. Need a little wifey, mind. Someone to impress the selection committee and open fêtes and organize tea parties. Shit!'

He made futile efforts to dab at the whisky he had spilled on the blue, red, blue of his Guards tie and Turnbull and Asser striped shirt.

'I've even got my sights on one. Old Willoughby's youngest, Caroline. Another link with the Tory shires.'

'You *have* got it worked out, haven't you?' conceded Rodgers admiringly. 'So where do I come in?'

'Simple, old boy. I've considered property, the stock market, commodities, futures, bonds, foreign exchange. Now foreign exchange is tempting. I know one chap who had a £100,000 bonus last year on top of his salary. And they gave him a Porsche.'

'Barrow boys who've learned to wear suits. And they burn out young.'

'Quite. So in the end I've decided on merchant banking. Respectable and lucrative.'

'And you want me to smooth your path.'

'You have the right connections and you've interests in the arms industry. I could certainly help there. And I'm sure your board would appreciate a friendly MP to represent their interests.'

'You're shameless, aren't you, Simon? Bloody shameless.'

Simon Baines-Hickey gave a haughty shrug of indifference. 'Scratch my back . . .'

Chapter Six

'Paddy, give me a hand to get these Christmas decorations off the top of the tree.'

'Can't they stay up just one more day?' pleaded Liam.

'No, my lovely,' replied Mary gently. 'If we don't put them away today we'll have bad luck. They always come down on Twelfth Night. It can't be Christmas all year.'

'Why not?'

'Out of the mouths of babes and sucklings,' laughed O'Keefe.

Mary looked sideways at her husband. She had something to ask him – or rather something to tell him – and she wanted it to go as quietly as possible. Liam had been getting bad headaches recently and a domestic row wouldn't do him any good.

'Bang.'

'Aaghh.' Liam aimed his plastic M16 at his father and O'Keefe pretended to fall down.

'Why did you have to buy him a gun?' demanded Mary, testily. 'There's enough killing in the world without encouraging children to do it.'

'He asked for one,' replied O'Keefe defensively.

The phone rang in the hall.

'I'll go, I'll go.' Liam ran to answer it.

'It's bound to be your mother, your sister or one of your relatives. At least they're phoning you this time. The phone bill's going to be bloody murder.'

'Christmas is a family time and I missed them.' Mary took a deep breath. 'And I'm missing them now. I'm sorry, Paddy.'

Her tone made O'Keefe, trying to pluck a silver ball from the fir branches, pause momentarily. It portended something deep and unsettling.

'Mummy, mummy. The man wants a Chinese.' Liam looked puzzled.

'Tell them they've got a wrong number and put the phone down. If it's one of daddy's friends fooling around, it'll serve them right.'

Mary stopped taking down the Christmas cards and turned to look at her husband.

'It's different for you. You're not close to your family. You've cut yourself off. And you've been in England so long you can't remember Belfast, you don't remember what it's like.'

'I can,' said O'Keefe, reaching up for a red Santa Claus. He didn't want the conversation to take a serious turn. 'I still think about the place. Anyway you've made lots of friends here.'

'But it's not the same. It's not like you and your mates. Sometimes I think you're closer to them than you are to me. I'm not close to anyone. Sometimes I feel so alone.'

He felt a pang of guilt that he hadn't known she was lonely. He knew Mary was frequently on the phone to Belfast, but he believed she led a full life in Hereford with him and their two young children. They had a decent social life with their circle of friends. Now Mary was saying it wasn't enough and he was getting an unpleasantly hollow feeling in his stomach.

'You've got lots of friends,' he repeated.

'I've lots of acquaintances,' she replied softly. 'I'm Mrs Paddy and I have coffee with Mrs Seldom, Mrs Jockanory, Mrs Molecatcher and Mrs Sefton. You've got all these daft nicknames and we're just the female appendages to those names.'

Liam, running back into the room, caught her mood and halted uncertainly. If his mum was going to cry, then so was he.

'I didn't know you felt like this.' There was genuine concern in Paddy's voice.

'You're never home long enough to find out.' Frustration

was creeping into Mary's voice now. 'You're always away and when you're here you're down the camp or going off somewhere with the boys. It's one big game. But I'm at home with the weans all day. With no one to talk to and only the bloody TV to look at. I'm lonely and homesick and I don't like being an army wife.'

She had finally confessed.

Liam stood uncertainly changing his weight from leg to leg; Katie toddled in, dragging a rag doll behind her. She put her thumb in her mouth and looked solemnly first at her mother and then her father. She plonked herself down on the carpet.

'What do you want?' O'Keefe felt helpless in the face of his wife's admission.

'I don't know. I know I must get out of this house or I'll go mad. I need time and space to think for myself. I'd like to take the weans home to Belfast for a week or so.'

Pain crossed O'Keefe's grave face and she held up her hands, palms outwards in a pacifying gesture. 'Don't worry. I'll bring them back. Whatever I finally decide to do, I'd never run off with your kids.'

'Our kids.'

'Our kids.'

Two days later Mary and the children flew from Cardiff airport to Belfast. Except for Fife, O'Keefe didn't tell anyone where they had gone. Instead he waved them off, hoping the kids would hate it so much they'd scream to come home. Now he was getting deliberately, morosely and peevishly drunk.

'What the fuck are we doing over here, eh? Working for the English.'

'Come on, Paddy.' Fife tried to reason with him. 'We don't all hate the English.'

''Course we bloody do, but at least the Irish have their cards face up. The English cheated you out of your country, cleared you out of your homes to make room for sheep, and you tell me the Scots don't hate them? Of course you hate

73

them, but you just hint at it by resenting and resentment is really hatred turned against yourself. Our hatred is more healthy. We show it.'

It was a long and serious speech for O'Keefe and he thumped his big fist on the table so the glasses jumped. Then he slumped forward and put his head heavily in his hands.

'I don't know what's got into me. I don't understand. I thought Mary was happy.'

'I think women look for love and soldiers are incapable of giving it. At least in a way women recognize,' said Fife, who had been thinking about his own inability to form a steady relationship. 'The army teaches us to be aggressive and put up with Christ knows what without showing anything and then we go home and the women expect us to be pussycats. I try, but whatever it is women want, I can't seem to give it to them.'

'I thought me and Mary were getting on all right,' said O'Keefe in a baffled tone.

'Every time I get close to a woman, I get hurt,' confessed Fife. Each was talking about his own problems. 'I try to make it work, but they just take the piss. Maybe I try too hard.'

O'Keefe considered and thought Fife's conclusions did not apply to him. He looked into his pint.

'Will Mary be all right in Belfast?'

'She says she will. More drink. At least no one can nag me for rolling home shitfaced tonight.'

Chapter Seven

Mary didn't stop talking for two days. She stayed in the Lower Falls with an aged cousin, Annie, because her mother now only had a one-bedroom flat in one of the new blocks out in Andersonstown. It worked perfectly because after one night cousin Annie left for a fortnight to see her son in Philadelphia, leaving Mary in sole occupancy. She kept the kettle on and a stream of visitors called.

She felt at home. There was a small front room where the coffins used to be laid out and a kitchen and living area where the family spent the day. A lavatory had been built in the back and a bathroom added upstairs to go with the two small bedrooms. It was similar to the one she had grown up in, in the days when her father was alive.

Her friends were still there; most had married but few had moved far. After her time away the burnt-out shops and the big hard letters painted on the walls proclaiming FREEDOM and UP THE IRA reassured her that some things never changed. She took no notice of policemen carrying automatic weapons and wearing body armour, nor of the whirr of the cross-country tyres of the army Land-Rovers and Saracens as they patrolled the streets.

Life seemed to be getting on the same – only more so. To no one did she confess she was thinking of leaving her husband. If anyone asked about him she said, yes, he was still a medic, and swiftly changed the subject.

The only worry was Liam's headaches. Early on the third morning he woke her screaming in pain. She gave him aspirin and a cup of tea and vowed as soon as her mother made her morning appearance she would seek her advice about which doctor to call.

At ten o'clock Virginia Collins arrived. Tall, angular and prim, she was universally referred to – behind her back – as Golden Virginia because her brother Patrick John Collins was known as Old Holborn for his endless roll-up cigarettes and the aroma of the tobacco he carried with him. Neither had ever married and they still lived in the same house where they were born more than fifty years ago.

After she had critically examined Mary, she demanded to see the children.

'Liam had a bad headache about six o'clock this morning and he's asleep now,' replied Mary, putting on the kettle. 'I don't want to wake him. This is Katie. Say hello to your aunt Virginia.'

Katie was holding up her rag doll to be kissed when there was a shrill piercing scream from upstairs.

'Mum. Mum. Help.'

Mary was up the stairs three at a time closely followed by Virginia. Liam was thrashing around in the bed holding his head in his hands. He was covered in sweat and his face was blotched red, an artery pulsing in his throat.

'Mother of Jesus.' Both women crossed themselves.

Virginia was out of the bedroom and pounding down the stairs as Mary went to hold her son. Cuddling Liam, she vaguely heard Virginia giving very loud and very precise instructions on the phone and then organizing neighbours to look after Katie. She also ensured there would be no obstruction to the ambulance from any youths who fancied an impromptu street barricade. Mary was still stroking Liam's head and praying gently when the two ambulancemen arrived.

The rest of the morning passed in a blur. She remembered sobbing in the wailing ambulance as it sped to the Royal Victoria Hospital and Virginia's hissed swear words every time they were forced to slow down for traffic. Then nurses and orderlies placed Liam on a trolley, far too large for his frail little body, and hurried him away through crowded corridors. Virginia was everywhere: filling in forms, cajoling cups of tea, bullying doctors to tell Mary what was happening.

Liam was having tests, they said. They weren't sure what was wrong. It would be a time before they could tell for sure. Everything possible was being done. Please trust them.

Mary knew she had to tell Paddy, but even in her frantic state she was aware that no one in Belfast must know what her husband did.

Protect Paddy.

Late that afternoon, after the longest, most tear-stained hours of her life, a grave-looking doctor came to talk to her. He spoke with an upper-class English accent and in a way it reassured her. He told her Liam had an abscess on his brain. It had burst. He was too ill to operate. Yes, he knew it sounded paradoxical. That was the word he used, paradoxical. They were trying to stabilize Liam. As soon as they succeeded, they would operate to drain the fluid and relieve the pressure. She could see her son for a few minutes. He was unconscious. Yes, he had to be honest. There was a possibility that her son might die.

'You must call your husband,' said Virginia. 'He should be here.'

'How can a British soldier come to the Falls, even if he was born here?' Mary twisted the sodden handkerchief so tightly that the blood ceased to flow and her fingers turned white.

'Do you think the boys would do that? Shoot the father of a sick child?' demanded Virginia, her lined and leathery face impassive.

'Ay. They've done worse. They've killed fathers in front of their children. A British soldier's fair game to them, whatever he's doing. They killed children before – and apologized after.' Mary's face was as pale as starched Belfast linen, the rims of her eyes red and swollen with more tears than she knew she possessed.

Virginia took Mary's hand in her slender, ring-free fingers. 'I sent you my best wishes on your wedding day. Those weren't empty words. I've known you since you were a baby. I'll not see wrong happen to you now. If I speak to my brother and he gives his word . . .'

'Can he guarantee there'll be no problems for Paddy?'

'Oh, I think so. He's got influence. Talk of the devil.'

A tall man with a lean, learned face in a shapeless sports jacket that looked older than himself made his way along the cluttered corridor.

'Mary, how is the boy?'

'He's not at all well,' replied Virginia. 'Patrick John, a word.'

She led her brother a few paces along the drab corridor and began talking seriously in a low voice. Mary, seeing the two together, was struck how like her brother Virginia had become. As he listened Collins pulled out a tin of Old Holborn and stuck a cigarette paper on his lip while he teased apart strands of tobacco.

Patrick John Collins was well respected in the Catholic parts of the city. He'd been among the first to break away from the Official IRA to form the Provisionals. He'd served time in the early days. There had been no evidence, only an informer's slander, and he was eventually released. He'd never planted a bomb, set fire to a bus or pulled the trigger of an Armalite. He was a thinker. It was rumoured that his work went far beyond that of a Sinn Fein worker, deep into the secret councils which kept the struggle alive.

'It might be difficult. Mary's mother says he's not really a medic,' whispered Virginia.

'No. He was in 2 Para, then he joined the SAS,' replied her brother, looking sorrowful.

'You'll not indulge him then? You'll say no?'

Patrick John Collins inclined his head even closer to his sister, his long, nicotine-stained fingers rolling the cigarette.

'On the contrary, I'll say yes.'

78

Virginia gave a small smile of satisfaction.

'Go along with Mary's story. I'd like to meet O'Keefe. You have to know your enemy to fight him.' His thumb rasped over the wheel of an old petrol lighter. 'He was only recruited into the British army. He was born a Falls Road Catholic. I'll promise him safe conduct and I'll do my best to keep my word. Oh, and advise Mary's mother not to tell stories.'

Virginia waited a discreet distance from the telephone as Mary piled up the change. Collins had gone to chat to the ward sister. He seemed to know half the hospital staff and all the patients. Fife answered the phone and was explaining that Paddy had popped down the offie when he heard Mary sob.

'It's Liam. He could die. Paddy must get here.'

Fife, shocked, said the first thing that entered his head.

'I'm not sure the Regiment will let him come to Belfast.'

'Fuck the Regiment. His son's dying.'

'I'm sorry, Mary,' murmured Fife, colouring red. What a stupid thing to say! 'You're right. Of course he'll come. Hang on. Paddy's here now . . . Paddy, Mary's on the phone. It's Liam. He's ill.'

The whistling stopped and Paddy, silent and sober, reached for the phone. Fife went into the living room, his mind racing as if he was on a military exercise.

Leave. No hassle. There wasn't a job coming up. Compassionate leave. Some cock and bull story. Say Mary was in Glasgow. No problems in Belfast getting through immigration and security. They didn't look like soldiers. Which would be quicker? Flight or drive and overnight ferry? He'd find out. He thought of contacting the troop over there and instantly dismissed the idea. If anyone in power found out that O'Keefe was in Belfast on private business, the shit would hit the fan so hard . . .

'There's nothing you can do. They're going to operate as soon as he's stable enough . . .' Mary ran out of words.

'Why didn't you tell me sooner?' demanded O'Keefe.

'You couldn't have done anything. I would have had to track you down . . .' Mary hesitated, glancing at Virginia standing ten feet away '. . . where you work and that's not easy.'

In fits and starts she explained about Golden Virginia and her brother, all the time feeding in her diminishing pile of ten pence coins. As she had feared, O'Keefe exploded in wrath.

'I don't need the permission of some terrorist scumbag to visit my own son in hospital.'

'Please, Paddy, my money's running out.'

'Sorry, Mary love. I'll make the arrangements and call you back. I'll be there as soon as I can. Sooner.'

No more flights tonight, said a helpful girl at Cardiff airport. Nor from Birmingham either. The first flight was 7 AM from Heathrow. You could catch the 3 AM sailing from Holyhead to Dublin and drive up. Or there was a ferry from Stranraer. You'd get there about the same time.

O'Keefe erupted in impotent frustration. Fife carried on making phone calls while O'Keefe ranted about communications and opened a beer. Fife booked them on the first Heathrow flight.

'No way. He's my son and I'm going by myself.'

'Bollocks. He's my godson and you'll need me to watch your back.'

Twice they almost came to blows. In the end Fife only agreed to stay behind when O'Keefe convinced him he would be more useful laying a false trail towards Glasgow and dealing with inquiries.

'You'll want a tool but the one you gave me is up in Glasgow,' said Fife.

'Don't you fret, Jimmy. I've got a 9mm Browning planted on a trading estate outside Belfast for the very occasion.' O'Keefe gave an embarrassed grin. 'It was the first trip across the water after the Falklands. They were giving grief about souvenirs so it seemed a good idea to cache it. Two birds with one stone, like. Should still be there.'

And now he was sitting by Liam's bedside in the intensive care unit of the Royal Victoria Hospital. Mary had gone to fetch cups of tea. She couldn't sit still, but O'Keefe hadn't moved for hours. Waiting was one of the things the SAS did best and O'Keefe was prepared to wait until hell froze over or peace was declared in Ireland. Although his lips were still, he was praying fervently.

He'd been too late. Liam was in the operating theatre when he arrived and now he lay with an oxygen mask over his white, pinched face and his head swathed in bandages. O'Keefe's eyes followed the traces on the monitor above the bed, the two important ones recording Liam's blood pressure and heartbeat. A rubber tip on his finger recorded carbon dioxide levels. One drip went into a giving set on his right wrist, another into his left ankle because the vein on his left arm had collapsed. His eyes were closed and his little hands were curled outside the bed sheet.

The hours moved through the day. Darkness came early in January in Belfast, but O'Keefe did not notice. Sometimes Mary held his hand and sometimes he held hers, but he did not move out of the moulded plastic chair and he did not take his eyes off Liam and his life-telling monitors. Only Liam's parents were allowed at his bedside, so frequently Mary was summoned to give a progress report to Virginia, her mother or one of her relatives and neighbours who called. The flowers they brought were given to other wards. No flowers in the ITU.

The small ward baked in a dry heat that made O'Keefe's tongue stick to the roof of his mouth. Nurses changed the drips and hourly plotted Liam's battle on the chart and made encouraging noises. Doctors with stethoscopes in the pockets of their white coats came and nodded gravely. And all the time O'Keefe willed his son to live.

Do it for Paddy, boy. Do it for your da.

The day nurses left and night nurses arrived to be briefed on Liam's fight for life. The ward lights dimmed until each bed had its own pool of amber and the pert features of the ward sister at her desk were softened and blurred. Mary and O'Keefe spoke little. Occasionally they made reassuring noises to each other and once, only once, Mary had murmured very low, 'I do love you, Paddy, you know.' O'Keefe had given her an extra squeeze of her hand for that.

At midnight, nurses persuaded Mary to lie down on an empty bed next door, but O'Keefe would not be moved. Frequently on exercise he had not slept for forty-eight hours or more and this was for real. He hadn't slept the previous night as he fretted and fumed away the hours, making Fife set off for Heathrow so that they arrived with three hours to spare. And he wasn't going to sleep this night.

He was beginning to believe his vigil was the price of Liam's life. As long as he stayed by the bedside, prayed and willed his son to live, then he would live.

Do it for Paddy, boy. Do it for your da.

In the corner bed, a man died at five in the morning. The lowest time of the day. The time the old and the weak give up. There was no fuss. He just drifted away. The drips and the monitors were disconnected, the corpse put on a trolley and the bed prepared for the next patient. O'Keefe didn't even look round, but listened to the sound of his son's laboured breathing and watched the green lines on the screen moving from left to right, making jagged peaks and heart-stopping troughs.

The harsh, cold light of the new Belfast day broke cheerless and grey over the slate rooftops. Mary, again sitting next to her husband, stroked Liam's hand, brushing his damp skin with her fingertip and murmuring senseless endearments.

The day nurses came back, carrying with them the odour of fried eggs. They looked curiously at O'Keefe. The story of how he had not moved since he had arrived was spreading through the hospital. No, not even to go to the lavvy. He just sits there and stares. It's as though he's in there fighting alongside his son. Very peculiar. He's obviously devoted to the little boy.

Do it for Paddy, boy. Do it for your da.

Liam slowly, slowly, as if in a deep sleep, reached up and tried to pull off the oxygen mask.

Mary gave a strangled cry, put her hands to her mouth and felt the hot tears flow.

Liam opened his eyes: looked uncomprehendingly from his mother to his father and back again.

'Nurse. Nurse.'

The doctor with the posh English accent was pleased with himself and with Liam and made no secret of it. He positively beamed. In a respectful semicircle, three junior doctors beamed also.

'Don't thank me. It's all down to your son. He's the fighter. You know there's no such thing as an unsuccessful operation – only unsuccessful patients. In Liam's case he's exceeded all expectations. The worst is over.' He held up a cautionary hand. 'He's not out of the woods yet and it will be a slow recovery, but we hope to move him out of intensive care in the next few days. Now the best thing you can both do is get some sleep. There's nothing you can do here.'

He left, cheerfully explaining the operating technique over his shoulder to his entourage.

Mary gave a great big sigh and gazed lovingly at Liam, now sleeping again. The monitor was drawing nice regular patterns.

'Paddy, I was wrong.' She put her arm around his head and pulled him towards her. 'It takes something like this to make me appreciate just what I have. I'm not saying I'm happy in Hereford, but I've Liam and Katie and I've you and that's all that really counts.'

'It's my fault,' murmured O'Keefe. 'I had no idea how miserable you were . . .'

Mary was quick to try to make amends. 'Miserable isn't the right word. I just found Hereford . . . claustrophobic, but at the same time I'm an outsider. I don't belong. I'll try harder.'

'Things will change, I promise. We'll do more together, do more as a family. You'll not be alone so much.'

Emboldened by his response, Mary pressed on. 'To be honest, I think I was homesick more than anything. Daft, isn't it? Who could miss bloody Belfast?'

'I don't know.' O'Keefe hesitated, fumbling for words. 'I remember Jimmy Sands talking about the comradeship of those in the trenches in the First World War. If you were there you couldn't fully explain the feeling you shared; and if you weren't, then you couldn't understand it. Bit like being homesick for Belfast, I suppose.'

'We'll sort something out, Paddy. We'll be together whatever happens.' She smiled at him. 'You look a wreck and you need a shave. Go home, get some sleep. Reassure Katie we haven't deserted her.'

He was about to argue but the glint in Mary's eye told him it would be pointless.

'Just a kiss before you go.'

Chapter Eight

'Can I give you a lift, Mr O'Keefe? You must be tired. It's a long vigil you've had, but a worthwhile one.'

A silver-haired man rose from the wooden bench where he had been sitting alongside a tin full of cigarette butts. O'Keefe thought he resembled a dusty old schoolteacher with his horn-rimmed glasses and air of vague abstraction. Only the roll-up in his mahogany fingers jarred with his pensive, scholarly appearance.

'I'm Patrick John Collins.'

O'Keefe narrowed his eyes. *So I've you to thank for your gracious permission to visit my own son.*

'I'm fine, thank you, Mr Collins. I'll get a taxi.'

Collins gave a gentle, understanding smile and nodded.

'Mr O'Keefe, I gave my word to Mary that there would be no trouble while you are here. Please don't resent me for that. We don't want another Billy Best, do we?'

Collins had a formal, old-fashioned way of speaking, each phrase and sentence constructed and balanced.

'Best was killed by the Stickies and I don't need an escort.'

'Well I'll be your driver, then. Come on, man.' He turned and O'Keefe found himself following him.

'You haven't seen much of the place since you arrived, but you won't find much has changed. Why did you cross the sea, Mr O'Keefe?'

'Simple economics, Mr Collins.' The same answer he had given to Mary four and a half years ago.

'Caelum non animum mutant qui trans mare currunt.'

'What?'

'"They change the sky, not their minds, those who scour

85

across the sea,"' Old Holborn said benignly. 'Economics. The optimum utilization of scarce resources. Economics has bedevilled our people throughout the centuries. Famine, I've always thought, was relative. Especially of the soul.'

He indicated a grey Renault parked in a DOCTORS ONLY bay. O'Keefe, who hadn't had the chance to collect his pistol, hesitated.

'I am a man of my word, and if you're your father's son you could do with a drink.'

'You knew my father?'

'Ay, many years ago. You needn't rush home. Little Katie's being spoiled rotten and thinking it's Christmas again.'

O'Keefe bridled at the suggestion that Collins knew more about Katie's doings than he did – but he could murder a drink. 'I'm not going into a pub in the Falls.'

Again that wry smile. 'There'll be no trouble if I'm with you.'

O'Keefe shook his head. He was willing to take Collins's word, but he didn't want to risk being picked up by a British army raid or being clocked by someone he knew from the Det.

Collins misunderstood. 'If you like you can take the magazine out and give me your gun to carry. If anything happens, just holler. You're never far from a policeman or the British army. If I'm caught with a gun on me, I'm looking at ten years. Now isn't that Irish logic?'

'Away with ye. I haven't got a gun. I'll come for a drink, but I'm not going to the Felon's Club or any Fenian dive that could be raided at any time.'

'You choose and I will not leave your side until we're there – and not even then,' said Collins good-humouredly, and against all expectations and intentions, O'Keefe felt himself drawn to the quiet, patient man.

O'Keefe made a point of buying the first drink and the two men sat in a corner under the music speaker in the big modern hotel bar. Collins pulled out his tobacco tin and began rolling.

'We have been praying for your Liam. Ireland needs all the sons she can bear.'

O'Keefe noticed the shiny patch on the right thigh of Collins's grey trousers, caused by constantly brushing away ash which fell from the roll-ups which he smoked always on the same side of his mouth.

'To join Fianna Fail? To join the Soldiers of Destiny?'

'Don't mock, Mr O'Keefe. No, to fulfil Ireland's destiny.'

'And what's that when it's at home?'

'I believe that Britain and the British army have no part to play on Irish soil and no reason to have her hand on Ireland's soul. The sooner they are fled back to their country and the colonial apparatus dismantled, then the sooner can Ireland resolve her troubles by herself in peace and equity and harmony. As one nation.'

'That's a fine speech, Mr Collins.'

'Ay, it's the one I gave after my election the time before last.' There was just a flicker of a smile. 'You know, I was once a teacher, but then came the troubles. *Nitor in adversum*. Do you believe in history, Mr O'Keefe?' asked Collins.

'If you mean am I a communist, then no. But I'm not high Tory either.'

Collins nodded as if he had been expecting the answer. 'So tell me, what do you do in the British army of occupation?'

The inevitable question and one O'Keefe was ready for. He took a long pull of his Guinness before wiping his mouth. Collins had hardly touched his glass.

'I'm a medic and I've never worn a British army uniform in Ireland.' Both statements, he told himself were true.

'Medic, is it you are?' Collins opened his eyes wide. 'And a medic it is you'll stay.'

He unthinkingly brushed ash off his trouser leg.

* * *

O'Keefe left the hospital at nine that evening and drove the old Mini which Mary's cousin Annie had left at her disposal six or so miles out along the Whiterock road to the edge of a trading estate. After a long reconnaissance, he climbed the perimeter fence of a small steel-holding firm and disappeared into the deep shadows. He emerged twenty minutes later with a 9mm Browning automatic pistol down the back of his waistband and twenty extra rounds, tightly packed so they didn't rattle, in a box in an inside pocket of his anorak. He felt more comfortable now – just as long as he wasn't picked up in a spot search by the police. On balance, the risk was worth it.

He dozed in a chair by Liam's bed so that Mary could go home to look after Katie and have a proper night's sleep, her first in three days. He still wasn't tired.

His son was breathing easily now. The bandages, turbaned over his head, made his face look frail and vulnerable, but the monitor reported a good heart rate and a low blood pressure. He phoned Fife with the news of Liam's successful operation and Fife in turn reported that he had squared everything with the squadron and everyone in Stirling Lines sent their best wishes to O'Keefe in Glasgow. Fife was handling all enquiries in case any well-wisher wanted to know where to send flowers. No flowers, said O'Keefe.

The following morning the consultant proclaimed Liam's rate of recovery as little short of miraculous. There was only one drip attached to the little boy now and he was conscious, although very drowsy. He would be transferred to a children's ward later. O'Keefe should get some fresh air. Do him good. Doctor's orders, said the consultant avuncularly.

The Lower Falls along Grosvenor Road had suffered since O'Keefe was last there. The fire bombings and the explosions had gouged holes in the streets like missing teeth. On either side of the gutted homes, the buildings had breeze blocks in their doors and windows and yellow ragwort growing on the window sills. He recalled the petrol station that was now just a scarred concrete forecourt and the cinema which hadn't opened since a petrol bomb had exploded near the booking kiosk. The pubs had wire mesh over the windows and concrete-filled petrol drums outside to deter attacks. They still proclaimed One Hundred Thousand Welcomes. A thousand Irish bars all proclaiming one hundred thousand welcomes. One Hundred Million Welcomes in a land which distrusted strangers.

Everything was smaller and more meagre than he remembered. The only splashes of colour came from extravagant murals painted on the gable ends of the streets showing men in balaclavas posturing heroically holding AK47s aloft. He was surprised to find he had forgotten that the police wore dark bottle green uniforms and green flak jackets. They drove slate grey Land-Rovers with thick bullet-proof glass and cages to protect the sides and flaps reaching to the ground so no one could roll a bomb under them. The police stations, already barricaded and defended when he left fourteen years ago, had been turned into fortresses with high mesh fences, coils of barbed wire and gun emplacements.

O'Keefe drove along dark brick terraces bearing the names of battles from the Crimea and the Great War following well remembered routes past grim blocks of flats flying green, white and gold tricolours and into the city centre. Even here, with the broad pavements, the bustle of shoppers and the glass fronted department stores, streets had been sealed off with high metal railings and pedestrians had to pass through turnstiles manned by armed police. The army in their green Land-Rovers with the red confidential telephone numbers painted on the side and Saracen armoured personnel carriers were out in force.

He did a figure of eight and headed back along the Falls Road, the backbone linking the western Catholic villages of Belfast, past the hospital, past Clonard and Beechmount and up to Whiterock. Belfast cemetery stretched as far as the eye could see on his right. Past Milltown cemetery O'Keefe turned left down Kennedy Way into the sprawling estate of Andersonstown. He thought the modern Corporation houses were even more dismal than the old slums, with their pre-stressed grey concrete blocks and muddy grass verges littered with discarded newspapers and fish and chip wrappers.

He almost gave up then, but he steeled himself to take in the tribal areas of Turf Lodge, Dermot Hill, New Barnsley and Ballymurphy – the Murph, where the aura of mistrust lay in the air like poison gas. Men with nothing to do stood in surly groups at street corners and looked with suspicion and enmity at the Mini each time O'Keefe stopped at traffic lights.

And there was the so-called Peace Line, the twenty-foot-high barricade dividing the warring communities. It was strange to think there were still many Catholics who had never walked down the Shankill Road and Proddies who had never visited the Falls, although they were only a few hundred yards apart. It had seemed unreal in England. Here the rituals of tribalism were closely observed. You had no option. Your school, your church, your youth club, even your dances were pre-ordained by your religion and religion was only a badge of the political divide.

O'Keefe deliberately cut through Woodvale to the Shankill Road. The flags of the union and the Red Hand of Ulster flew here. There were paintings of UVF gunmen on the gable ends – the same figures in the same balaclavas as the IRA men, waving the same AK47s. But here they proclaimed: *There is no such thing as a nationalist area of Ulster; just areas of Ulster temporarily occupied by nationalists.*

O'Keefe drove through the Proddie areas to prove to himself that he was above this corroding tribalism. But he wasn't. He wasn't a member of the British army. He was a worried father who had been brought up in the Falls and who had a sick son in the RVH. He felt vaguely ashamed when he realized he was more at ease on the Catholic streets of Clonard.

He parked back at the hospital feeling depressed and on the spur of the moment decided to buy Liam a present to cheer up the both of them. Pleased with his idea, O'Keefe set off on foot towards the shops on the Grosvenor Road. He didn't know what he wanted. He only knew Mary would complain if he bought Liam a gun. In his browsing, he walked further than he intended. He was coming away from a newsagents when an Action Man doll in the window took his eye. Looking back, he saw that two men also stopped.

O'Keefe cursed himself for his carelessness. He had been too preoccupied for anti-surveillance drills. He went into the shop and, as the assistant pulled the doll out of the window, took a good look at the two men. Mid-twenties, both wearing jeans, one in a blue ski anorak, the other in a German army parka. Both hard and fit. He undid his coat buttons and touched the Browning's reassuring wooden grip. There was nowhere to lose his followers and he was asking for trouble heading into the Falls. He left the shop carrying the present in his left hand.

O'Keefe was on the wrong side of the road – the right side for a car snatch from behind. Opposite the steel front door of O'Leary's Bar, he hurried across the street and strode back towards the hospital. The two men followed him, dodging between the traffic. O'Keefe was switched on again. If the men were wired they could trigger a car into position on one of the intersections. No sign of a front tail or anyone tagging him across the road. Then he knew he'd really be in trouble. It was biting cold with a raw wind coming off the Lough, but he undid another coat button.

The two men were not from the Det. They were too bloody obvious. By now, the first two would have peeled off and been replaced, cars would have him from a distance. No. These were the Boys.

He continued walking briskly until his car was in sight. The two men held their distance. He slowed at the car park, scanning doorways and vehicles for his followers' back-up team. Nothing. He ignored his car, instead hurrying through the Accident and Emergency Department and plunging deep into the labyrinthine corridors of the hospital. O'Keefe went nowhere near his son but marched through swing doors which said No Entry into a storage area for oxygen and gas cylinders, deeper and deeper into the bowels of the vast hospital. Five minutes later he was driving away in search of Patrick John Collins.

Collins was easy to find. He was sitting in Mary's cousin's kitchen, smoking the inevitable roll-up and drinking tea.

'And shall I tell you what they were wearing?' he said calmly in reply to O'Keefe's angry outburst. 'An army parka and a blue anorak. Now, isn't that so?'

O'Keefe nodded.

'They were there for your protection, not to harm you. You're a suspicious man, Mr O'Keefe, a lot wider than I thought. I gave you my word there'll be no problems and, hopefully, no problems there'll be.'

The phone went in the hall and Mary's mother bustled away to answer it, returning to tell O'Keefe his friend Duggie was on the line.

O'Keefe picked up the phone with a sense of foreboding. They had set times and procedures for communication and this call wasn't scheduled.

'How's it going, Jimmy? How's Liam?'

'He's fine. On the mend. Comes out of ITU today. The panic's over, touch wood. How are things your end?'

'How're you fixed?'

'So so.' O'Keefe was saying that his side of the conversation might be overheard.

'There's a job coming up in two days, four-handed. Our team's been scheduled by a tosser who didn't know about Liam. Back to the trees. No longer than a fortnight. The problem is that if we're not going to do it, then it'll become official with red tape and everything that means. You follow, Jimmy?'

Yes, he was following. If he applied officially for compassionate leave the Regiment might discover that Liam wasn't in a Glasgow hospital but the Royal Victoria Hospital, Belfast. His son was out of danger. Nothing he could do here. He made a decision.

'I'll come back tomorrow.'

'Are you sure? We can still cuff it.'

'No. No sweat. Take it on and I'll bell you from the hospital.'

On the way back to Liam, O'Keefe completed his shopping and thought his decision would confirm everything Mary had thought about being married to an SAS man. Maybe he should get a nine-to-five job. If the Regiment found out where he'd been, he'd have no option.

Liam's bed in the intensive care unit was empty. He gave boxes of chocolates to the nurses and said heartfelt thanks, found Liam and Mary in a brightly painted children's ward surrounded by teddy bears and cuddly toys. Liam was wide awake and sitting up supported by pillows. O'Keefe kissed him on the forehead and gave him the present. As he struggled to open it, O'Keefe produced his last gift – a pair of gold Claddagh earrings for Mary.

'That's for being wonderful.'

They kissed. Then O'Keefe stumbled and stuttered over his news. Mary took it better, far better than he had anticipated.

'It's your job, Paddy. Liam's out of danger so you must do it. By the time Liam leaves hospital you'll be home again. Why don't you take leave then so we'll all have time together?'

Just like Mary to make the best of a bad job and to turn events to their benefit.

'Sometimes I wish I had an office job with regular hours,' muttered O'Keefe, trying to say something to make amends.

'No you don't, love. And it wouldn't be you if you did.' She saw the lingering doubts in his eyes and tried to reassure him. 'Look. It's not a question of choosing between your son and the army. You're just doing your job. I understand. Honestly.'

O'Keefe kept his head bowed, watching Liam manipulate the doll's arms.

'All I ask,' continued Mary with that smile that made her eyes narrow in merriment, 'is that the house is not a tip when we get home.'

'Did you know one man in two is out of work around here, Mr O'Keefe?' asked Collins. 'And it's not getting any better?'

'That's why I left,' murmured O'Keefe, leaning on the bar in the pub on the edge of Clonard.

'But it's the Catholic men who bear the brunt of the unemployment. The Proddies have just ten per cent out of work. Not fair is it, Mr O'Keefe?'

Old Holborn stood gallows tall and straight and there was a resigned look in his contemplative grey eyes. Ash fell from his hand-rolled cigarette like blossom in May.

'Belfast is tribal and we follow the patterns of our forefathers. You read of disturbances a hundred years ago and they seem like now. The English erected a peace line between the Falls and the Shankill in 1872 and again in 1935. The cobbles and paving stones were torn up so regularly last century that the Corporation laid down – and I quote – "a more prehensile system of paving in all argumentative areas of the town".' He paused in his lecture. 'Did you know you were in one of the more argumentative areas of the town, Mr O'Keefe?'

'Ay, I seem to remember throwing a few stones meself not so far from here.'

'Did you really now, Mr O'Keefe.'

Collins appeared amused by the idea and looked around the long dark bar with its Irish flag as if canvassing support for his humour. All conversation had stopped the second O'Keefe had stepped into the bar until the men with blank and brutal faces saw Collins behind him and the low murmured drone continued. O'Keefe, deliberately facing the door, was aware of the frequent covert glances in his direction.

'The English call our violence mindless. It is not. It is mindful of the past and hungry for the future.'

O'Keefe finished his pint and signalled for another. Collins had hardly disturbed the cream on the head of his first one. He was obviously not a drinker.

'We live in houses that are unfit for human habitation, we cannot find work for love or money and justice is something for Protestants. These things sap a community's strength, Mr O'Keefe, which is why the community must be strong. We have to look after our own.'

'Is that what you do?'

'Someone has to look after families when their men are held by the British, someone has to help put back the floor-boards when they have been ripped up by the rummage squads. I help deliver equity in an iniquitous city.'

'Don't forget it was the Catholics who invited the British army into Northern Ireland in the first place.'

'Ay. True – but times change. Don't you believe in justice, Mr O'Keefe?'

'Of course I do. I remember what it was like,' retorted O'Keefe angrily. Why was this man lecturing him like a schoolboy?

'Do you? It's hard at sixteen to appreciate the real facts. A Government which makes policy to defend the majority not the minority, and a police force which looks after the interests of that majority. Hardly fair, is it?'

'No, of course it isn't fair,' conceded O'Keefe, heatedly. 'I'd never met a Proddie until I crossed the water. I thought they had horns, but people in England don't care whether you're Proddie or Taig. Did you know two-fifths of the Parachute Regiment are Catholic?'

He stopped short, angry he had let his tongue run away with him. At that moment two men walked into the bar and halted by the door. O'Keefe felt his stomach muscles tighten. One was about thirty years old, blonde and thick-set. O'Keefe knew him from his pictures. Danny McCann. Suspected of involvement in more than thirty murders by bomb and bullet. He was definitely linked to the killing of two undercover Special Branch officers working in the docks area. He had been arrested three times and released for lack of evidence. He was too bloodthirsty and headstrong even for the IRA leadership who expelled him from the IRA in 1985. But McCann was a powerful force in Belfast and he had won reinstatement.

O'Keefe knew all about McCann. Butcher by trade. Butcher by nature. Someone who killed as much for pleasure as for the Cause.

The man with him was scrawny, with a rat face and gaunt cheekbones. O'Keefe did not recognize him. The buzz of conversation faltered and died. Collins, who must have been aware of the fall in temperature, took his time turning round.

'Patrick John,' growled McCann. 'A word with yez.'

'Danny McCann. How can I help you?'

Each stood his ground. O'Keefe looked at the lino, pitted with cigarette burns, deliberately avoiding eye contact with McCann who was staring at him while addressing Collins. He was glad he was carrying the Browning. It was really too big to conceal indoors. He would have used a Walther PPK – nicknamed the disco gun because it was easy to hide – if he'd been working. But he wasn't working and beggars couldn't be choosers. And a 9 milly Browning was a 9 milly Browning.

McCann moved from the doorway to Collins, but to make up for losing the conflict of wills he grasped the older man by his arm and led him into a corner of the bar. Ratface leaned on the counter and stared openly at O'Keefe.

Never stand out in a crowd, flake into the group. Be a grey man. Be invisible. Bloody difficult when you were being eyeballed from six feet. Deliberately and provocatively. Fuck it.

'Do I owe ye money?'

The cocky look on the other's face vanished to be replaced by one of startled surprise. It flashed across O'Keefe's mind that maybe this was one of the big boys who wasn't used to being spoken to in that way.

Then again, he might be one of the little boys who was just trying it on.

'Where ye from?'

Paddy allowed a grin to play around his lips. 'Ye don't need to know.'

There was growing uncertainty in the other's eyes now and he glanced across to McCann who was jabbing his thick forefinger in Collins's eggshell chest while Collins calmly shook his head. It was obvious that for all his menace and bulk, McCann was not getting his own way. He'd lost the argument and he was a bad loser. He turned his back on Collins and strode across in short angry movements.

'And who's this bastard?' He jerked a thumb towards O'Keefe.

'Won't say.'

'And why's that now?' There was nothing melodic or pleasing in McCann's harsh speech. The larynx grated and jarred like the rasp of a file on rusty iron. His pale eyes held as much compassion as a dead fish.

O'Keefe took his hands out of his pockets and balanced on the balls of his feet. McCann was known as a street fighter; the Provo's expert at close quarter battle. O'Keefe felt he was about to see just how good he really was.

'Strangers are generally invited. And I don't remember inviting you.'

O'Keefe would have liked to see what Collins was doing. Watching with amusement, probably, but he daren't take his eyes off McCann. He readied himself for fight or flight, in this case fight. At the same time he tried not to give off antagonistic vibes. Don't be like two snarling dogs. Put McCann off his guard.

'I didn't know it was your bar,' challenged O'Keefe.

It was said pleasantly, but a fight was inevitable. He'd shown no fear nor respect to the Butcher. O'Keefe appeared relaxed but the springs inside his body were drawn back ready to explode. Any second now. He put down his pint, eased himself away from the counter and tensed himself ready for immediate action.

McCann's eyes bulged. He opened his mouth as if to speak then took a pace forward and reared up to smash his forehead down on to the bridge of O'Keefe's nose. O'Keefe jabbed up his left arm, his palm open, in a short powerful movement. The heel of his hand caught McCann's chin, pushing it up and back.

Not too clinical. Remember your training. Start using fancy throws and moves and they'll think you're someone special. This is just a street fight.

With a bit of practice thrown in. Maybe a thousand hours of practice.

O'Keefe's right hand came up from the bar in a right cross on to the point of McCann's chin.

The first hit is worth the next ten, his instructor used to say.

McCann staggered back and O'Keefe drove his left hand like a piston into his soft solar plexus. Then he hit McCann with all his might with his right fist in a downward swing. McCann made a croaking noise and slithered to the floor. O'Keefe booted him in the head. McCann's face split and blood spurted over the worn linoleum and the fag ends. Then slowly and deliberately O'Keefe kicked him twice in his kidneys.

The head kick was for show. It would remind McCann of this beating every morning he saw himself in the mirror. The kidneys were for the Special Branch guys he'd topped in cold blood. The Butcher would be pissing blood for six weeks.

The fight had taken no more than five seconds. O'Keefe picked up his pint and moved to the end of the bar, where he had a wall behind him. The drinkers sat frozen and open-mouthed. He sneered at Ratface.

'Do ye still want to know who I am?' His voice was as harsh as McCann's had been. Falls Road coming deep from the throat and cracking and barking the unfinished words into the smoke-wreathed air.

The other stared from O'Keefe to McCann on the floor and back again like a rabbit transfixed. He made no attempt to answer.

Patrick John Collins broke the silence.

'I think we should go.'

'I'll hurry my drink for no man.'

Bravado now. For the first time he saw a note of anxiety in Collins's grey eyes. Don't push it, Paddy boy.

In the car the inevitable reaction set in and O'Keefe felt himself shiver.

'Well, they'll remember you in there for a long time.' It was said lightly, but O'Keefe could tell Collins was troubled.

'It was none of my choosing,' he replied defensively.

'Right enough, but you have to be fearsome quick to do what you did. You fight well for a medic.' Collins stopped at the traffic lights to turn right into the Falls Road.

'You've got to get them in hospital before you can treat them.' O'Keefe noticed how few street lights were working. Amber light suited neither side in their urban battle. 'I hope I haven't caused you grief.'

Old Holborn sighed deeply as if another burden had been added to his shoulders. 'Nothing I can't handle.' He made a dismissive noise. 'There's many in this city will say he deserved a lesson and that lesson was long overdue. You're going back tomorrow. That's wise. McCann will not like to be humiliated, especially on his own turf.'

All of a sudden O'Keefe felt guilty he had caused this decent, patient, caring man another problem. 'I'm sorry.'

'There's those who would thank you if they could. Don't worry – I'll not say who you are.'

O'Keefe stared through the smeared windscreen at the Belfast rain that shone in the headlights on the darkened city road.

'And who am I, Mr Collins?'

'Whoever you want to be, Mr O'Keefe.'

Chapter Nine

The six men took over an hour to assemble in the large first-floor bedroom of the grey stone guest-house. Three arrived separately on foot; one came in the back way; another, who was on the run, had arrived with the laundry. Patrick John Collins had driven up to the front door and his car was now parked on the mossy gravel under the spindly monkey-puzzle tree. The building, half hidden behind overgrown rhododendron bushes, had been chosen because it was on a main road and used to frequent comings and goings. Together the six men formed the Tasking Committee of the Northern Military Command of the Provisional IRA.

The twin-set-and-pearls spinster who owned the guest-house in Belfast's Dermot Hill had no obvious involvement with the Movement, but if the security forces investigated her thoroughly they would find she had two great-nephews in the Maze and her favourite niece had been killed by a stray round fired by a corporal from the First Battalion, the Royal Green Jackets in 1976.

The curtains had been drawn against the winter evening, foggy and bitter. And against the eavesdroppers from Special Branch's E4B with their parabolic microphones.

Collins sat in the only easy-chair and began rolling a cigarette.

'On his own manor, as well. He'll not like it. Who was it, Patrick John?' asked a thin-lipped man with a wandering left eye. Sean O'Hanlon, proud of his reputation as a fire-brand, believed his recent promotion to command the East Belfast Brigade gave him the right to question Collins.

'Just someone I know, Sean.'

'You won't know him much longer if Danny McCann

finds him. He'll wake up one morning with a bullet in the back of his head.'

'Ay, another unlicensed killing,' murmured Collins.

'So who is this man who can drop the finest street fighter in Belfast?'

'Someone I'm interested in.' The end of the roll-up flared as Collins held it in the heat above the flame. Blue smoke already hung shoulder high in the prim pink-and-white bedroom.

'You're a close one, all right,' sneered O'Hanlon.

'We've as many informers as we have heroes in Ireland and don't you forget it.' Collins leaned forward. 'To business. McCann wants to top another RUC man. I said I'd refer it back. We've done three already this month. People are tired of the same news. It's losing impact.'

'Soon no one will have the balls to wear an RUC uniform.'

'Don't you believe it. They've as many local heroes as we have,' retorted Collins softly. 'I personally think these pinprick attacks aren't worth the effort. The Chief of Staff believes in a policy of attrition, but at the same time we need the big hit that'll get the headlines again. Kieran's been investigating possible political and judicial targets. We don't want a retired octogenarian this time. Killing pensioners doesn't win sympathy. It makes us look cowardly.'

'Sir Norman Strong had been a speaker at Stormont,' insisted O'Hanlon. 'He was eighty-six years old.'

Kieran, a quiet man with brooding, deep-set eyes, coughed to clear his throat. 'That bastard Gibson looks the favourite.'

'Lord Justice Maurice Gibson? Hmm.'

Collins pursed his lips. Gibson would be a popular choice. Ulster's second most senior judge had recently acquitted three RUC constables of the murder of three of their men. In his summing-up, Gibson had said they had brought the IRA men to the final court of justice. His words had sparked off a night of rioting in West Belfast. He liked the idea of Gibson.

'We've got an in to him and he's independent, like. Doesn't allow his minders too close,' continued Kieran. 'He and his wife are planning a holiday to England in April. We could top him then.'

'Keep on it, but keep it tight.' Collins moved on to the next item on his mental agenda. 'The cowboys on the border want to do a job on a police station. They've done twelve already. I've a notion this could be unlucky thirteen. They want to use two active service units.'

He took in the looks of surprise around the room and held up his hand to still the objections before they began.

'We're trying to get them to see reason, but they do their own thing in bandit country. We've had a request for logistic and quartermaster help. They'll provide some of the weapons and explosives, but they need more. Frannie, you liaise with their quartermaster. String them along as far as possible. The Chief might get them to see sense yet.'

Frannie McFadden, the barrel-chested quartermaster, nodded. He was known as a man of few words except when drunk. Collins believed he was drunk too often.

'I'll not be giving them the crown jewels, that's for sure.' McFadden's thick lips contorted into a sour smile. 'It took a bit of persuading before I could get those weapons back last time.'

'Let's hope you won't have to break anyone's arm this time,' said Collins.

'What's wrong with a big operation?' demanded O'Hanlon.

'Nothing as such, but big operations carry big risks. Too many people in the know. If our security gets any worse, we might as well have a direct line to British army headquarters in Lisburn or Special Branch in Knock.'

'You worry too much, Patrick John.'

'Ay, it's worrying that keeps me out of the Maze.'

'Maybe you should see what it's like in there nowadays.'

Collins lowered his head and peered at him over the top of his glasses.

'Now tell me, Sean,' he began. 'What good would it do

to have me – or even you – spend just one day inside? You think that because men have been behind the wire and wrapped themselves in blankets and smeared their own excrement on their cell walls, they've fought for the Cause. Bullshite. Nine times out of ten they were careless. A soldier fights on the battlefield, not in a prisoner-of-war camp. I was inside . . .' His voice was growing harsher now. 'I was inside when you were in nappies. I was inside because one of our heroes informed on me. And I do not intend ever to go inside again. Now if you want to be a hero, go to Derry and do it. I'll arrange it for you.'

O'Hanlon coloured as pink as the eiderdown he was sitting on. How dare this bespectacled schoolmaster lecture him. Him who had killed four men with his Armalite. Fuck Collins.

'You had two boys babysitting a man over from England. Now what was that about?'

'And how do you know that, Sean?' asked Collins evenly.

'They were my boys. McCarthy told me.'

Collins ground out the stub of his cigarette and nodded thoughtfully. It was as though he was wondering the simplest way to explain how ice formed to a child.

'Sean, I know you're a loyal man. I know I can trust you with my life. But there are others, not in this room,' he added, maybe too hastily. 'Who I wouldn't trust with a dead canary.' The others murmured in agreement.

'Sean, if you will, have a word with McCarthy.' It was a direct order. 'You can tell him that when I give him a job it is a secret one, not to be blabbed to all and sundry; not even to his senior officer. Tell him that if he wants to work for me he must learn to keep his mouth shut. Tell him if he mentions that job to one more soul, he will lose his left kneecap.'

O'Hanlon, hardened to brutality, flinched. The measured, academic way in which the threat had been delivered made it a promise.

Chapter Ten

'You see, Billy, the M16's trajectory is totally different. The FN's round rises for the first 100 yards.' Fife drew lines with his knife on the tablecloth. 'This is the fall of shot and this is the killing area . . .'

'Boys and their toys,' said Mary with mock severity. 'Billy, wash your hands.'

Billy obediently rose, turned and almost fell over Katie who was holding up a glove puppet of a pirate with a hook. Katie squealed with delight as he pretended to pinch her nose with the puppet's arms.

'Paddy, don't open another beer. You know we're having wine with our Sunday dinner. Liam, where are you?'

The sound of machine gun fire indicated that Liam was in the hall. A firefight erupted as Liam and Billy exchanged imaginary shots.

'He's a good boy, your Billy,' smiled Mary, untying her apron. 'Not many twelve-year-olds would bring presents for the kids.'

'And he paid for them with his paper round money,' said Fife, pleased at Billy's good manners.

'Liam. Come and sit up.'

Fife regarded his godson critically. 'That's some scar you've got there.'

Liam self-consciously ran his hand over the fair stubble. The long scar could still be plainly seen zig-zagging across his skull to behind his right ear.

Mary carried in the joint of beef. 'Paddy, start carving. Duggie, open the wine.'

She flew in and out of the kitchen issuing commands and carrying trays of steaming food, revelling in her role as housewife and mother. A crisp white linen cloth covered the table at the garden end of the large open-plan room. The new deep-pile carpet and three-piece suite bore witness to Mary's efforts since she and Liam had returned from Belfast. Finally she surveyed the table with a warm glow. Matching plates and serving dishes and the best canteen of Sheffield cutlery, sparkling wine glasses and the joint on the stainless steel platter. Liam was on his best behaviour because of Billy, who in turn was on his best behaviour because he was trying to be grown up.

Mary felt secure, her family and friends together at Sunday dinner. It was as it should be.

'Paddy.'

O'Keefe remembered in time. 'For what we are about to receive . . .' he mumbled.

'May the Lord make us truly thankful.'

'Did you enjoy this morning?' asked Mary, heaping a mound of cabbage on Billy's plate.

'Ay, it was brilliant.'

'What did you like the best?'

Billy held his fork poised upright. 'The silver Armalite.'

'I might have known,' laughed Mary indulgently. She liked Billy. There was something frank and decent about his open face. He had an eagerness to learn and genuine willingness to please which she found refreshing. But why did he have his heart set on joining the army!

That morning Fife and O'Keefe had given Billy a treat by taking him around the less sensitive parts of Stirling Lines. Much of the camp resembled a large school campus built around 1970, but to Billy it was like walking on Calvary. He regarded the headquarters block, known as the Kremlin, as a shrine and when they bumped into Bob Doughty, now the training major, unusually for a Sunday in uniform, Billy thought he was going to burst with excitement.

'New recruit?'

'My brother, boss,' replied Fife. 'Right, Billy. Atten-shun.'

Billy snapped to attention, ramrod stiff, thumbs down

the seams of his blue jeans.

'At ease,' nodded the major.

Billy snapped out his left leg and clasped his hands behind his back.

'Very good. So you're going to try for selection?'

'Yes, sir,' he stammered.

'Need to build yourself up a bit more first. Get in training.'

Billy nodded, lost for words.

'Have you seen D squadron interest room yet? Get these to show it you. No problem.'

Billy had gawped in wonder at the silver-plated Armalite, the automatic weapons, pistols, grenades and daggers collected from operations around the world during the past twenty years. The weapons, plaques, newspaper cuttings, photographs and hand-drawn maps told of the squadron's history in souvenirs and paraphernalia. The only way his brother could get him to leave was to promise to take him again.

'Ay, brilliant,' he repeated. One day, he told himself, I'll be there. I'll be part of those exploits. Those stories will be about me.

'Katie, love. I think Captain Hook is full now. Eat your own food.'

'So, are you glad to be home?' Fife asked Mary.

'Oh ay, it's good to be in your own home. Mind you, I enjoyed Belfast once Liam was out of danger. I couldn't think of anything while he was in intensive care.'

'Do you think you could ever go back?' enquired Fife, who didn't understand homesickness.

'Easily. I think part of you always wants to return to where you grew up. Belfast is part of me.'

'I couldn't wait to get out of Glasgow and I won't ever go back there to live. You couldn't live in Belfast could you, Jimmy?'

He was expecting an adamant negative, but instead O'Keefe carried on chewing thoughtfully.

'I don't know.' He considered. 'I was surprised how much I'd missed the place. But I didn't know I'd missed it until I was back there again, if you understand.'

'Typical Irish logic.'

'Paddy's right. There's something about Belfast which draws you back,' agreed Mary.

'Even with all that violence? Nine RUC men shot in the first three months of the year and that Judge Gibson and his wife blown up yesterday morning.'

'It's a way of life,' conceded O'Keefe. 'But I bet somebody's head'll roll for that cock-up. Where was his close protection? What was he doing driving past a parked car in no man's land? It should have been cleared.'

'Please.' Mary held up her hand. 'We don't want it at the dinner table.'

'You can't get enough of it elsewhere,' rejoined Paddy quickly.

Mary turned crimson and pretended to look furious. She flicked a piece of cabbage in his face.

Fife watched Mary blush and thought how happy and relaxed she looked. The break, once the crisis was over, had done her good. And now they were on the team, Paddy could see his family every night. For a moment he wished he had a wife and family, then the desire passed.

'Oh. Look at that blasted cat after those birds,' Mary exclaimed, looking out of the french window at the small back garden. 'You're going to have to get in that garden, Paddy, it's a mess. You do the spadework and I'll take it over from there.'

'No problem. There's lots of time now I'm going to be based at home.'

'Oh yes. What's this team you started to tell me about?'

Paddy fixed Billy with a stern glare. 'This is top secret, Billy. You mustn't tell a soul.'

Billy swallowed hard. 'I promise on my mother's life.'

'There's no need to go that far, Billy,' remonstrated Mary.

'It's the squadron's turn to supply the Special Projects team,' explained O'Keefe. 'We're being trained up by A Squadron now. When we take over, we'll be based in Hereford for the next nine months or so.'

'Does that mean you do things like the men who attacked the Iranian Embassy?' Billy could not contain his curiosity. Fife nodded.

'Wow. Do you wear black and have stun grenades?'

'I'm in the assault team. Paddy's in the sniper group, but he practises assault work as well.'

'Are you trained to shoot to wound?' asked Billy.

'That only happens in the movies. If somebody's firing at you, you don't aim for his legs and his arms. You go for the biggest part of the target, probably his trunk, and hose him down.'

'Don't you aim for the head?' Billy was fascinated.

'You go for the head with aimed shots, say from a rifle. Any terrorist worth his salt is going to be wearing body armour and a man can continue to fire with a surprising number of bullets in his body. Put five bullets in his head and he's going to go down and stay down.'

'I've got more potatoes in the oven.' Mary rose from the table, rolling her eyes at the conversation.

'Do you have sniper rifles?'

'Last question. The PM7.62, uses special Lapua ammunition made in Finland. For closer work we've got the German G3. You'll find them both in that book I gave you.'

'Why's it got special ammunition?'

'I said last question. Because standard ammo may not have exactly the same number of grains of power. Snipers have to be pinpoint accurate. So what are you going to plant, Mary?'

She placed the dish on the table, sat down and looked out of the window at the April Sunday afternoon.

'I'd like a small herb garden, a lawn for the kids to play on and a flower border, but the soil is so heavy, Paddy's going to have to break it up first, aren't you, sweetheart?'

O'Keefe grinned back reluctantly. 'This time next year, the garden will be looking a treat.'

But that night two men stole a bright yellow mechanical digger from a building site in Portadown in County Armagh in Northern Ireland. They drove it along the spider's web of tiny lanes through the heart of Ulster's orchard country until they came to a derelict barn near Ballygroobany. There they concealed the excavator with tarpaulin and bales of straw. They had set in motion a chain of events which was to lead to the deaths of eight IRA terrorists and one innocent man.

Chapter Eleven

'My name's Boyle. Detective Chief Inspector Boyle.'

He said his name slowly, savouring its resonance and its depth. He made his name sound hard; as hard as he was.

'Ah yes, Special Branch.' Major Peter Taylor rose, extended his hand and winced as Boyle crushed it in an ape-like grip. The major had never seen such hair on the back of a man's hand.

It was only when he stood next to Boyle that Taylor realized just how heavy he was. Six feet two if he was an inch and built like a gun emplacement. A travelling trunk for shoulders, bulbous nose over a thick moustache and receding hair. No-nonsense eyes; eyes you would be frightened to lie to. Boyle looked what he was – an old-fashioned copper.

Major Taylor indicated the chair across the modern metal desk. They were in a small office in one of the 1960s additions to the Victorian buildings which formed the vast complex which was the Army HQ at Lisburn. 39 Brigade was housed in the original Thiepval Barracks and the various intelligence, logistical and liaison groups found shelter in the buildings which grew on demand. A huge concrete communications tower presided over the parade ground and rows of armoured Land-Rovers and Saracens.

'So you think this alleged Provo operation should go up to Intelligence and Security Group, do you?' asked the major, playing with the crown on his epaulette.

Boyle regarded the new Tasking and Co-ordination Group Liaison Officer from under bushy eyebrows. He knew Taylor had a Special Forces background or he would not have been in the sensitive job, and he was newly arrived and newly promoted. So he was willing to make allowances. Not many, just one or two. He ignored the implied doubt.

'SMIU agrees it's one for Int and Sy, but no doubt they'll tell you themselves.' Boyle looked directly at the young major. 'Special Military Intelligence Unit.'

'Yes, thank you, Chief Inspector. I did know what it meant,' said Major Taylor colouring slightly. 'I was merely surprised you knew their thinking.'

'We work together nowadays. No secret squirrelling. Intelligence is the key to success in this war,' growled Boyle, deliberately quoting the army's Land Operations manual.

It was too late by now anyway, thought Boyle, as he frequently did when having to deal with the military. The battle is lost when you see soldiers on the streets. It's all about infiltrating and manipulating infant terrorist organizations. Using informers. Jesus Christ! Nowadays informers were called human sources. And Jesus Christ knew all about informers. Boyle had run them when they had been called touts, snouts, pimps or grasses. Infiltrate – or if you couldn't infiltrate, then turn. Persuade, cajole, threaten and bribe them to betray their fellows.

'Intelligence and security must be centrally controlled to ensure the efficient and economic exploitation of resources,' Taylor quoted back at him, grinning broadly. He had been warned about Boyle and he was not about to take on this grizzled Special Branch heavyweight in his first week. 'Would you like a cup of tea?'

Boyle's eyes wandered to the steel locker in the corner where Taylor's predecessor used to keep a bottle of Black Bush whiskey.

'Um . . . I keep it in the desk drawer. Handier, actually.'

He poured two stiff measures. Peace was declared and Taylor started again.

'Don't you think it's all been too easy? The Provos have painted it in red letters on their green fields. Surely it's a deception to take our eyes off the real operation, wherever that is.'

'You can credit them with too much cunning sometimes,' replied Boyle. 'This isn't one of your streetwise Belfast units. Sophisticated tactical thinkers are in short supply on the border. This is bandit country and these are cowboys. They like soft targets: unarmed, retired or off-duty members of the security forces and rural police stations. They've attacked these isolated, undermanned nicks in the past and it's worked, so they'll do it again.'

'But you must admit, this one has fallen into our lap.' Taylor counted off the points on his fingers. 'The digger goes missing, we find the digger; we trace the explosives, we know where the bomb is being put together; we know the major players, who obligingly have a get-together and a chat; the quartermaster on the border, who happens to be under routine surveillance, suddenly gets very busy. It's all been very easy.'

'I've a tout . . .'

'Ah, a human source.'

'Tout,' he repeated. 'Grade One A. And I believe what I'm told – in this case.'

Taylor had heard all about Boyle's techniques and agent handling skills at the handover. He was said to be good. Very, very good. Too bulky to go undercover, he pulled the strings and conducted the interrogations which brought in the intelligence, the very lifeblood of counter-terrorism. Other detectives reckoned Boyle needed only seven hours to guarantee a Joe's loyalty. On a good day. Now he prepared to lock horns with this army major who, for all he knew, thought the Bogside was where the Paddies kept their lavatory brushes.

'How can a Proddie such as yourself have such good contacts among the Catholic population?' Taylor was emboldened by the whiskey.

'I see things in black and white. Either they are for law and order or they are against it.'

'So it doesn't break down into Catholics and Protestants?'

'In E3A we operate only against Republican groups.'

'And if you were in E3B operating against Loyalists, would you find it a problem?'

'Don't know. Never done it.' Boyle gave a coarse bellow.

'So this talk of collusion between RUC and loyalists is just that? Talk.'

Boyle pulled a face. 'No, I'm not saying that, major. The attack on Gerry Adams – where the police were on hand to nick the perpetrators *after* they had failed. There're a few questions there that maybe need answering. But I'm not going to ask them.'

Major Taylor also remembered why, he'd been told, Boyle was still only a chief inspector despite his success record. No glad sufferer of fools of whatever rank and deemed too close to the Unionists. He wondered if Boyle was bitter.

Boyle bent down to open his briefcase, exposing sparse straight hair pulled across his head in a vain effort to conceal his creeping baldness.

'Now let's get this moved up to Group. You'll want the Director Special Forces to oversee and the Commander Land Forces to approve. It's all happening on 3 Brigade's doorstep in Portadown, but we won't worry them yet. We'll try to ignore the Department. Their DCI at Stormont is the biggest wanker I've ever seen and Christ knows I've seen a few. No doubt their liaison at Knock already has a sniff. We'll need to step up the Det's involvement on the players . . .'

Taylor realized he was being given a lesson in the management of a counter-terrorist operation. He was also being taught how to manoeuvre through the shallows of the politics which bedevilled intelligence gathering in Northern Ireland.

*　　*　　*

Mary was still bursting with compressed fury when she opened the front door and manoeuvred the pushchair into the hall. Days like this make me hate this place. However much I reassure Paddy, I just can't help it. This is the part of the day he doesn't see.

It had all happened in the small row of shops where she went two or three days a week for her basic supplies, taking Katie in the pushchair and Liam trotting by her side. She had bumped into Barbara Molecatcher coming out of the newsagents with another woman she knew by sight. The woman, with an infuriating self-confidence, had announced herself before Barbara could make the introductions.

'I'm Staff Sergeant Donaldson's wife Anne.' There was just a whiff of condescension.

'I'm Mary O'Keefe,' she'd replied briskly.

Anne Donaldson had obviously been anticipating more information, but Mary moved on to ask Barbara about the trip to a London show she was organizing.

'I know who you are now,' interrupted Mrs Donaldson. 'I recognize the accent. You must be Corporal O'Keefe's wife.'

'Paddy O'Keefe is my husband,' corrected Mary. 'But we don't bother with ranks at home.'

She was still fuming at the pompous, overblown woman, and even angrier at herself for letting her tongue run away with her, when she reached the checkout of the small supermarket.

She loaded her few purchases into her shopping bag hanging on the back of the pushchair and removed a packet of crisps from Katie who had taken them from the trolley. Katie looked about to burst into tears. The checkout girl seemed reluctant to take Mary's offered £10 note.

'Is that all?' she asked.

'Yes, of course,' replied Mary automatically.

'Did he get that here?'

Mary turned from trying to pacify Katie to see Liam sucking a bar of chocolate. She turned beetroot red.

'Liam. You naughty boy. Where did ye get that?' In her confusion, her accent came through harsh and brisk. Liam turned sullen and silent.

'I'm sorry. I didn't see he'd taken it. You know what they're like at that age.'

The checkout girl gave her an old-fashioned look and Mary felt as if she'd been caught shoplifting.

'No better than tinkers.'

Mary looked up to see Vicky and a crony at the express checkout, two bottles of red wine, crisps and a packet of fish fingers in her basket.

'Wouldn't be surprised if she put him up to it. Don't know what they're doing over here, anyway.'

Mary felt an overpowering urge to tear out that bleached hair by the roots. She stabbed her forefinger in their direction.

'Shut yer mouth.'

'Is she talking to us?' Vicky struck a haughty pose. Too late, Mary saw she'd made a mistake in rising to their bait. Flustered, crimson and furious, she hurried home. In the kitchen she stared hard at the bottle of gin, sat down and cried.

She still felt an outsider. She yearned to tell someone about the morning's incidents, laugh at them and so stop them festering. She'd tell her mum later. Then Paddy would complain about the telephone bill when it arrived. Perhaps she would have that drink.

Chapter Twelve

The black corrugated tin barn leaned at such an angle it seemed impossible that it could remain standing. Most of the brick outbuildings on the abandoned farm had tumbled down with age, but the barn remained and someone was using it to store heavy rectangular bales of straw piled almost to the roof. A rusty plough and a broken baler stood in the field between the barn and a small copse of stunted blackthorn and whitebeam trees entwined by heavy growths of ivy.

A battered green Bedford van drove up the rutted lane. Two men got out, tucked shotguns under their arms, slowly walked around the barn, taking in the deserted fields and straggling hedges, and sauntered towards the copse. To a patrolling army helicopter, they could have been after rabbits. They inspected the narrow ditch of stagnant water and disappeared into the thicket. There in the shade, they peered into old fox holes, prodded bramble bushes and explored the mysterious darker spaces beneath fallen tree trunks where ivy and moss grew thickly. They also examined lengths of cotton hidden at ankle height between hawthorn bushes. When they were satisfied the copse was empty, they returned to the barn. They removed a few of the oblong bales and began to carry jerry cans from the van into the barn.

After ten minutes the men replaced the bales and again surveyed the empty countryside. They broke their shotguns and drove away.

In the hedge under the twisted roots of a cramped hawthorn, the man pressed the button of a miniature transmitter and muttered the van's registration and the description of the two men into the microphone. They were new faces, recruited to deliver bomb-making materials. He reckoned the bomb must be getting on for 300 pounds by now.

'Well?' Virginia Collins put down her knitting and quizzically regarded her brother. He looked tired and drawn.

'They wouldn't listen. They're going ahead with the operation. It's foolishness of the first order.' He spoke resignedly, as if he had little energy left. His sister rose and poured fresh hot water into the teapot.

'They're pushing their luck putting two ASUs together. If this lot goes wrong – and I'm convinced it will – we'll be picking up the pieces for years.'

He fumbled in his tobacco tin, his fingers pausing as he compressed the brown strands.

'It'll be fine,' said Virginia in an effort to reassure him. 'You know that good operations are the best recruiting sergeant and God knows we need new blood. I wouldn't trust your average recruit to plant a marigold let alone a bomb.'

'I understand why the council had to approve it. The cowboys would have gone off and done it on their own and then it would have been a guaranteed cock-up. But there's too many people in the know, Virginia. And you can't stop an Irishman talking.'

She handed him a large chipped mug of tea. He tore off a few strands hanging out of the end of the roll-up and dropped them back in the tin.

'The best operations have just one man. Not a bloody logistic tail the size of Halley's comet,' he concluded. 'Just one man and his controller. I just need the right man.'

'I don't think I'm going to tell Mary about this,' said O'Keefe doubtfully. 'She thinks I'm at Heathrow on exercise, not in fucking Lisburn. It's bound to be some op against the IRA. Why don't we ever do anything against loyalists?'

'No point. Hitmen from Mothercare. In the past ten years

the loyalists have managed to kill just two IRA men and two guys from the INLA. The IRA have topped more than twenty-four of their own as informers in the same time,' replied Fife.

'Out of the way, tossers.'

They turned to see Sid, part of the SAS intelligence operation at Hereford, bustling along the corridor behind them, a pile of maps under one arm.

'What the fuck are you doing across the water? Does your mother know you're out?'

'Bollocks. If I had my way I'd have given you a pair of woolly socks and a vibrator each and let you get on with it, but our masters reckoned you needed some professional help.'

Grinning, Sid hurried into a doorway guarded by two MP sergeants. Fife, O'Keefe and the others who had just landed by Chinook helicopter followed him. They found the twenty members of the reinforced Northern Ireland troop had grabbed all the chairs. Amidst the mutual slagging off, the ten men from D squadron slid down against the wall, plastic cups of coffee in their hands. The Director Special Forces, NI troop OC and his staff sergeant stood at the back of the windowless room with its dry smells of smoke, stale coffee and paper. The staff sergeant nodded to the military policemen and they pulled the door closed, standing at ease outside. Sid adjusted his half-moon glasses and picked up his wooden pointer. His briefings were popular. They were short, succinct and not cluttered with so much jargon that by the time you worked out what he was saying, you'd missed the point and had to ask some stupid question later.

A model, 18 feet by 12 feet, stood on a low table covered by a dust sheet.

'Gentlemen. Counter Revolutionary Operations defines an ambush as: "A surprise attack by a force lying in wait on a moving or temporarily halted enemy".' He paused for effect. 'And we are going to lay the mother of all ambushes.'

A crackle of tension and anticipation swept around the room.

'When we know there is going to be a terrorist attack, we have two options. We can assist the RUC to attempt an arrest with irrefutable evidence on which to base a successful prosecution. Realistically, the chances of making that arrest are minimal. The terrorists will be armed and hyped up to Saturn. As we know, confronting a terrorist during an actual attack will inevitably produce a shoot-out.'

Several men in the room nodded knowingly. They'd been there.

'Alternatively, we can stage a type A ambush. Ambushes are effective in removing a particular player or unit, but generally they give limited breathing space. This time not only are we going to give PIRA a bloody nose but we're going to black their eyes and pull their teeth out as well. As they said after the Brighton bomb, they only have to be lucky once, we have to be lucky all the time. They've had a good year. It's our turn to be lucky.'

Sid pulled a drawstring on the wall to reveal a map, pictures of a village, police mugshots of four men and another four blank rectangles.

'Last year, ASUs under the command of Patrick Kelly destroyed The Birches police station in Tyrone by putting a large explosive device into the bucket of a stolen mechanical digger and crashing it through the protective fencing.' He pointed to a face on the wall. 'It was a remarkably sophisticated operation involving around thirty-five operatives in all, including those on the diversion attack, dickers, hijackers, drivers and gunmen. Paddy Kelly is about to do the same again. The other major player is James Lynagh, the IRA commander of the Armagh and Monaghan border region.' Again he pointed to a picture on the wall. 'Both known killers. We believe they intend to deploy two units from the East Tyrone Brigade. Around eight men in the actual assault.'

Fife raised his eyebrows. There hadn't been so many

members of the Regiment together for an operation since the Falklands. Now he knew why.

'The target is the part-time police station in the Protestant village of Loughgall in northern Armagh. It's rolling terrain; what the locals call orchard country. Balleygasey Road runs through the village.' He held up the pointer. 'The road comes down the hill from the church at the highest point with a walled copse on the right. On the left, there's a row of small bungalows, the police station, a former barracks, the local football team's clubhouse and an automatic telephone exchange. There's a football pitch opposite the station.'

Sid turned away from the map and looked at the troopers over his glasses. 'The Det are watching the players. Units of the RUC's Headquarters Mobile Support Unit will provide the immediate back-up. 3 Brigade will hold the perimeter cordon sealing off the conflict area. They will also provide a Quick Reaction Force.'

He took a sip of water. 'There are two major areas of uncertainty. First, their approach to the police station. We know that they've recce'd the soccer pitch and so we'll deploy accordingly, but that is not a confirmed approach. I repeat that is *not* a confirmed approach. Secondly, we do *not* know how the device will be detonated. We don't know if it'll be set off by a timer, remote control device or something simpler. We tend to believe it will not be a remote control device. Initially they used a McGregor transmitter designed for model aircraft and boats. We jammed that on 27 mHz, so they found an area on the electronic spectrum where inhibitors would not work, the "white band". Now we've chased them off that they favour the control wire. In this instance, we simply don't know.

'There will be two killer groups. One group with two GPMGs in the copse overlooking the station to concentrate fire on the football field. The other group will be in and around the police station itself. There will of course be cut-off groups and observation posts.'

He paused and took a deep breath. 'That's the broad outline. The staff sergeant will go into the details. Everything you want to know about the players, including likely weapons, are in these files here. You get one each so there's no need to nick one.'

Sid took off his glasses and let his eyes travel around the expectant faces. 'The Provos are putting up an exceptionally heavy team of known faces. We want to remove them in one clean kill. To that end, we will set up an OP/React – an Observation Post able to react. Remember, outside this room, we do not have ambushes. Instead we have legally justifiable OP/Reacts. That, gentlemen, is Operation Judy.' He tugged at the dustsheet covering the model. 'And this is where it's all at.'

Her finger trembled so much she had trouble finding the holes in the dial. Slowly, as though the effort was causing pain, she pulled the dial around and watched as it unwound in slow motion. Six numbers. The phone rang once.

'Friday. Friday evening after work.'

Boyle's face lifted in a grim smile of satisfaction. He knew he'd been right that night those months ago. Free the little fish and you'll catch the big ones. He'd had a feeling.

The woman sat in the yellow Escort, her hands trembling too much to insert the key in the ignition. She knew she shouldn't sit outside the phone box – she was inviting attention – but she couldn't go home like this. She undid the clasp of her handbag and pulled out a mirror so she could see her white, set features. To reassure herself, she opened a box of tampons, one of them marked by an ink dot. She prayed she would never have to use it.

In the hedgerows, in the copse and from the top of the church tower, SAS men watched the Toyota Hiace van cruise down the hill past the police station. Others hidden in the station and behind drystone walls heard of its arrival over the radio net. The van had been hi-jacked at gunpoint by masked terrorists that afternoon from Mountjoy Road, Dungannon.

It was 7.15 PM. Those not watching Wogan on TV were packing into Loughgall church hall for the annual meeting of the Girls Friendly Society. Lying on his stomach in a bluebell wood, O'Keefe saw the blue van disappear only to return two minutes later. He could make out the driver and a male passenger, both wearing overalls.

Not long now.

The planners had decided to take a deliberate risk and position men in and around the station. Because it was protected by a solid low wall, they reckoned the JCB would aim for the gate. Consequently, Fife and others were crouching away from the entrance but where they had a good field of fire down the football field.

Fife claimed they were being risked for the rule of law. He'd read off his yellow card: 'Opening fire is correct only if the person is committing or about to commit an act likely to endanger life and there is no other way to prevent the danger.'

'So?' said O'Keefe, not understanding.

'Well, there's no bloody risk to life or limb in letting a bunch of hoods blast an empty nick so they have to put bodies in there, our bodies. I'm going to demand body armour.'

'Wasn't it only last night you were lecturing me that Irish chiefs considered armour ungentlemanly and they went into battle against the Normans wearing only linen shirts?'

'Yeh, but they got slotted.'

'Away with ye, ye'll love it.'

That had been two days ago and now the waiting was almost over.

Christ. There was the Toyota van. And behind it rumbled a yellow JCB. Forget the football pitch. The attack was coming by road. A man clung on to the cab of the digger carrying what looked like a G3 assault rifle. A mound of rubble in the bucket concealed the bomb.

The van suddenly braked ten yards away from the police station. Men wearing blue boiler suits and balaclavas poured out of the back. They lined up in the road and began blasting at the police station like a scene out of *Gunfight at the OK Corral*. Behind them the excavator lumbered down the hill, swerved and smashed into the gateway, the outrider leaping off.

A deadly choir of automatic weapons began singing in unison. Then the gunfire was blotted out as the 300-pound bomb exploded. Huge chunks of masonry rose slowly in the air; the digger was tossed up like a toy and one huge tyre bounced across the road, smashing through a wooden fence and into the penalty box of the football pitch where it turned a small circle and collapsed.

A shower of stones and twisted metal rained down; a player dashed out from behind the low wall into the cloud of dust. Something glinted in his hand as he ran hell for leather for the van. He made five yards before he began jerking and twitching as bullets ripped into him and he crumpled on to the road.

The terrorists did not stand a cat's chance in hell. Two general purpose machine guns, designed for the battlefields of northern Europe, capable of firing 900 rounds per minute from a disintegrating link belt and spewing out their rounds at 2,800 feet per second, added their deeper voices to the chatter of the newly issued Heckler & Koch 7.62 G3-A4K assault rifles carried by the Ulster troop, and the higher crack of the M16s fired by the reinforcements from Hereford.

The radio net was a confusing babble of shouted commands and cries of exultation.

Two players were down, another took a shot in the head in front of the van and spun round, his FN rifle clenched in his outspread arm. Two terrorists wore flak jackets – as much good as a string vest against a GPMG. The surviving gunmen were trying to pile back into the van.

Stupid thing to do, noted O'Keefe. The driver was dead,

slumped over the steering wheel and the van was going nowhere. It had no side windows so they couldn't return fire. They should have nicked something a bit cleverer. The thin metal could have been made of cardboard. Round after round pierced the van until you could have strained vegetables through its sides.

O'Keefe snarled in frustration. He was looking in on the best party in the world and he wasn't able to join in. What was the point of his stop group? No one was going to be walking away from that lot. He felt like a spare prick at a wedding.

'Delta Two. Alpha. White Citroën car moving downhill. Two pax.'

O'Keefe picked up his call sign through the clamour coming over the net.

Shit. Where'd that come from? The Citroën stopped on the hill a hundred yards short of the police station. Two men in overalls in the front seats. The back-up team?

'Alpha. Delta two. Roger. I have them visual.'

He moved aside a clump of dark green leaves, snapping bluebell stems: the white juice smeared along the barrel of his M16. The Citroën began to reverse up the hill, swerving from side to side. The passenger wound down his window. O'Keefe looked to the men around him. They knew the score. O'Keefe thumbed down the safety catch one notch to repetition and settled lower, both eyes open to look down on the car reversing erratically towards him. The tall front sight, flanked by the foresight blades, slid into the centre of the rear ring. He squeezed the trigger in short controlled bursts and the hot spent cartridge cases leaped into the bluebells.

Who said there wasn't the need for a covering party? The rear windscreen disintegrated and the car slewed to a halt in the ditch.

'And now as I lie here, my body all holes, I think of those traitors who bargained and sold . . .'

O'Keefe's voice quivered with emotion. Fife waited for the inevitable moment when he would close his eyes so he could pour another large whisky into Paddy's can of lager.

'How the hell can he sing rebel songs in British army headquarters?' asked Molecatcher, awestruck by O'Keefe's performance.

'He's Irish,' replied Fife simply.

'Just as well they're all not like that.'

'No. Some are even fatter.'

Party time. Everyone was talking loudly and drinking with a manic urgency. There was one aim tonight. Get ratshit drunk.

'I wish that my rifle had given the same, To those Quislings who sold out the Patriot Game.'

O'Keefe sat down glowing with satisfaction and drink, his blue eyes sparkling. There was only one subject of conversation.

'Did you know that one had a lighter in his hand.'

'Wondered what it was. Christ, that was a basic fuse.'

'It was fucking brave, pulling that woman and her child out of that car. He should get a gong for that.'

'I wouldn't like to be a SOCO, marking those bullet holes. Went through five mags.'

Fife let the chatter drift over him. After being in action Fife always turned introspective and analytical. It made him reappraise his life and his friends. There's Paddy now, singing the same old songs. The life and soul of every party. You know you're guaranteed a good time with Paddy O'Keefe. Every night is Saturday night, but Fife also knew how much he doted on his kids and on Mary.

Sometimes he envied Paddy his family. What did he do when he'd finished soldiering for the day? Nothing. He had no hobbies. He was obsessed with the army and all it was. He could tell you the muzzle velocity of every small-arm made since the war, how they worked and how to strip them down. The army had given him a home, good mates and a better life. It gave him discipline and purpose and kept him out of prison. He had no illusions. If he hadn't joined the army he would have ended up in a Glasgow gang. A wee hard man, drink-sodden and tattooed, dipping in and out of petty crime.

'It's the slime . . .'

Cheers and catcalls erupted as Sid, grinning broadly, made his way to the bar and held up his hand for silence.

'I just thought you'd like to know the preliminary ballistic results on the first recovered weapons.' He inspected a piece of paper. 'The Ruger Magnum pistol was originally taken from the body of RUC Reserve Constable William Clements, killed in the IRA attack on Ballygawley police station. It was used in the murders of part-time UDR man Thomas Irwin and building contractor John Kyle. In October it was used to kill businessman Kenneth Johnstone in Londonderry. One of the G3s, believed to be Kelly's own weapon, killed UDR major George Shaw. That's all we have so far.'

A great cheer went up. O'Keefe led the chant.

'We got one, we got two, We got nine more than you. With a nick nack, paddy wack, give a dog a bone, Fenian bastards fuck off home.'

Sid weaved his way between the tables to where O'Keefe was holding court. Under his ready smile he appeared troubled, but O'Keefe, flying high, did not notice.

'Have a can, slime,' he boomed, ripping the top off a lager and thrusting it towards Sid. 'We've got dozens.'

'Cheers. Just a quiet word.'

He insinuated himself next to O'Keefe. 'You were in charge of the cut-off in the bluebell wood, weren't you? You took out the white Citroën.'

O'Keefe nodded, wondering what was coming next. Only Fife, on the other side of Sid, was listening. The others were getting on with the party.

'First indications are that the occupants were not players.'

O'Keefe had difficulty absorbing the information. 'What do you mean – not players?'

'We have a positive ID. Two brothers, Anthony and Oliver Hughes. Anthony was the driver. Oliver's in intensive care in Craigavon, Portadown. Three bullets in the chest, one in the head. Anthony's dead.'

'What the fuck were they doing there? They drove down the hill after the van. They saw the firefight and tried to back out. They must have had something to do with the digger.' O'Keefe was becoming angry, not wishing to be told the men were innocent motorists.

'Found themselves in the wrong place at the wrong time. So far we have nothing to connect them.' Sid gave a lopsided smile of apology.

'They wore overalls,' insisted O'Keefe, as if that clinched the argument.

'They were builders,' replied Sid.

'Fuck.' In his mind O'Keefe saw the white car careering up the road, saw his rifle sights align and felt the judder as the three-round bursts blew the Citroën's rear screen to smithereens.

'I suppose he's got kids. All fucking Irishmen have got kids.'

'Thirty-six-year-old father of three.' Sid put a comforting hand on O'Keefe's shoulder. 'It just happens. There's no blame attached to you or anyone else in your team.'

'Will I have to go in the witness box?'

'Tell them you saw him make an abrupt movement and feared he might be drawing a weapon,' joked Fife.

'Shut it,' spat O'Keefe.

'Sorry, Jimmy.'

O'Keefe remembered he had stopped a copper getting medical help for the two men in case they were armed and capable of responding. Christ, he'd almost put a couple of rounds in each just to be on the safe side as he'd approached the car, M16 at his shoulder, his nerves screaming and adrenalin pumping. Three kids without a father. What the Christ had he done?

Sid was surprised to see O'Keefe was taking the news this

badly. He'd have thought the big, loud Irishman wouldn't have given a damn.

'You won't be called to give evidence at the inquest.' He tried to reassure O'Keefe. 'It's no one's fault. These things happen.'

'Ay,' said O'Keefe bitterly, crumpling a beer can in his fist as if it were a paper cup. The laughter ran out of his eyes. Eight terrorists and he had to go and kill an innocent man. 'Overalls. They wore blue overalls,' he mumbled to himself. 'Same as the fucking players.'

Chapter Thirteen

O'Keefe paused at the gate and made a conscious effort to put on a cheerful face as he walked up his short garden path. Nine o'clock on Saturday night. Too late to organize a babysitter. We'll get a takeaway and have a quiet night in together.

He found Mary huddled up in the corner of the sofa. She was sitting in silence and staring at the unlit gas fire. She looked pale and he could see she'd been crying.

'What's wrong, love?'

'You are.'

Great. All he needed. O'Keefe mentally ran through his recent transgressions. Nothing spectacular. In fact he had a clear conscience.

'Where're the kids?' His first priority.

'In bed where they should be.' She made no effort to rise to greet him. There was a half-empty glass of clear liquid by her side. 'Where've you been, Paddy?'

The Loughgall ambush had filled the TV and radio news all day. The airport story sounded increasingly implausible. She saw him hesitate.

'Don't bother,' she said in a dull tone. 'I know you weren't at Heathrow on exercise. You've been in Ireland.'

'And how do you know that?' he asked softly.

'Barbara Molecatcher told me.'

'Oh.'

'Why did you lie to me, Paddy?'

Why had he lied to her? He didn't know why. He just had.

'How many other lies have there been?'

'None. I swear.' He felt helpless against her silence and

130

the tears she'd shed. 'Is that what's upsetting you?'

'You were one of those who killed Colm.' She picked up her glass and stared into it, refusing to look at him.

'Mary, hen, I don't know a Colm.'

'Colm Magee. My second cousin on my mother's side. He was twenty-one and you killed him in cold blood. You murdered him.'

'Mary, I'm sorry, but if he was one of the IRA hoods then he got what he deserved,' replied O'Keefe evenly.

Mary hunched over her glass, her small body compacted in her grief and unhappiness.

'The SAS has killed innocent men before. Remember that sixteen-year-old boy at Dunloy in County Antrim in 1978? Alan Bohan and Ron Temperley shot him and they're still serving here. I know they were acquitted but you people think you can just kill and get away with it,' she said bitterly.

The memory of the Irish for slights and insults.

'No, hen. These were known players.'

'Colm was one of yours.'

'No, he wasn't.'

'He was a young Catholic lad. How could you kill your own kind like that?'

'He's not my own kind. He was a Catholic gunman.'

'And what are you?'

Her words pierced him like a lance. He had no answer.

'Leave it, Mary, please.'

He didn't know that Mary's mother had been on the phone from Belfast three times since Colm Magee's identity was revealed. She had wept down the line for her dead kin and demanded that Mary go over for his funeral. A journey she knew would be impossible. She was determined to cause mischief between her daughter and the son-in-law she had never trusted. And she was succeeding.

'Why did you shoot him?'

'I didn't. I promise you I didn't,' replied O'Keefe. That's one promise I know is true, he told himself.

'Why didn't you just arrest them?' she asked simply.

'Love, they were heavily armed faces.' He spoke patiently. 'You can't arrest eight terrorists like that. There would have been a shoot-out whatever happened.'

'It was a massacre. You should be tried for murder.'

'It's better to be tried by twelve men than carried by six.' O'Keefe couldn't take any more. 'I'm going to see the kids.'

'Don't wake them,' she said automatically. She didn't look up.

Mary didn't think she'd ever felt so alone in her life. She hated Hereford that day. She had seen the divide and knew, against all senses and reason, on which side she stood.

Her neighbour had told her the news over the garden fence.

'Didn't the boys do well!'

'Sorry?' Mary took a clothes peg out of her mouth.

'Getting those eight Irish terrorists like that.'

'Like what?'

'Oh, sorry . . .'

The wives she had met shopping had gloated over the Regiment's success. They stared in the window of the TV shop, triumphant and malignant, feasting their eyes on the corpses of the boys their husbands had slaughtered. Women had whispered behind her back once they heard her accent and looked sideways at her as if she were a dangerous freak. One woman had even shrunk away when she'd spoken. Everywhere she sensed hostility and suspicion. She was angry at the way she'd been treated and furious with herself for allowing it to happen. Then there were the others who thought she was a Proddie and wanted her to share their elation. They were worse, if anything.

She took in the fitted carpet, the floor-length curtains, the new furniture and the large TV. This was her home, but she was still an outsider in this town. She didn't belong here, but she wasn't sure she belonged in Belfast either. One thing she knew with growing certainty – stay here much longer and she wouldn't be able to go back. She would be tainted and her tribe wouldn't accept her.

O'Keefe sought sanctuary in wee Katie's bedroom. He looked lovingly down at his daughter in her innocent sleep. She had her thumb in her mouth and her other arm stretched out. Her teddy bear slumbered on her shoulder. Sweet dreams.

He was baffled by Mary's tearful reaction to the shooting. He also asked himself why he'd lied to his wife. Why hadn't he told her where he was going? Because, he realized now, he'd been uncomfortable and embarrassed by the job.

Was part of me feeling guilty for firing on fellow Catholics? Away with ye! Flights of fancy. But I did lie. Did I feel guilty? I don't know. I just don't know.

Katie fumbled for her teddy and pulled it closer.

He didn't hear Mary softly enter the room. He just felt her hand touch his and give a reassuring squeeze.

'I'm sorry I had a go at you. It's not been a good day and I took it out on you. Come downstairs, love.'

They sat on the sofa, holding hands like schoolchildren. Slowly she told him of her day, how some women had spurned her and others, thinking she must be Protestant, had come up and congratulated her.

'Shall I go back to the Paras?' asked O'Keefe, softly. 'I will if you want.'

'Do you think it'll be any better in Aldershot?'

He thought about it. 'No. Probably worse.'

Then she told him how those yobs had spat at her. O'Keefe stiffened. Part of that gang always hanging around the chip shop. Skinheads with bovver boots. Eyes narrowing, he enjoyed finding a focus for his anger. He rubbed his knuckles in anticipation.

Mary related her mother's phone calls. Apart from her cousin Colm she also knew the innocent driver who'd been killed. Anthony Hughes. One of the nicest men living. He'd helped her mam nurse her dad through the last weeks of his life. Small world.

O'Keefe shut his eyes and thought hard of Liam and Katie.

'Sure, a day like this makes you glad to be alive.'

'After what you drank yesterday, I'm surprised you are,' retorted Fife.

'Ay well, we had to celebrate the fact that you're still among us. Next time I'll fight my own battles, Jimmy Sands. Thank you very much.'

A skylark rose from the long grass, climbing vertically with frantic fluttering of its wings. Its song drenched the air. A warm, gentle breeze wafted over the firing range in the hills outside Hereford and there was a definite feeling that summer was here.

O'Keefe balanced the familiar weight of the Heckler & Koch G3 rifle and began to go through the safety drills. He'd made the mistake of telling the Lean Mean Killing Machine about the yobs who'd spat at Mary and his plans to batter them. Now one was in hospital and another three were waiting for the swellings to go down to see just how much their features had been rearranged. Bloody Jimmy Sands. He'd gone straight down the chippie and laid out the lot. The local police had been understanding. The Regiment hadn't. Fife had been warned that one, just one, more incident and he'd be back with the Paras. He was on borrowed time.

O'Keefe began thumbing rounds into the green aluminium magazine. He felt he could crush the G3's tinny mag in his fist. He preferred the solid pressed steel of the FN. He held the weapon by its pistol grip and inserted the mag with his left hand, clicking it into position.

In the minibus on the way up from the camp, Molecatcher had admitted that his marriage was over. He was looking forward to joining the singlies again for nights on the town and reliving his youth. It was always the same, thought

O'Keefe, blokes divorcing, remarrying, re-divorcing. The divorce rate in the army was high, but the rate in the Regiment was spectacular.

He pulled the cocking handle back with his left hand, pushed it into the cocking handle receiver and gave the handle a hefty bang to send forward the working parts.

'At your target in front, five rounds in your own time.'

He pulled on his earmuffs. Five yards to his left, Fife was also making himself comfortable on the ground. O'Keefe brought up the rifle to his shoulder feeling the touch of cold metal against his cheek. Three hundred yards at the circle inside the Figure 12 target of a soldier's head.

Mary was unhappy and the children sensed it. He'd hoped her homesickness was behind them. They'd been like newlyweds again when she came back from Belfast, but now the shadow over them had returned. Unspoken, obscurely defined and vaguely conceived, and all the more terrifying because of its dark ominous threat. If he was honest, he knew he couldn't bear the thought of losing Mary.

O'Keefe breathed easily and flipped off the safety catch with his thumb. It's Liam's check-up next week. He's coming on grand. And Katie's a stunner. She'll break some man's heart. Probably mine. I want to see them grow up.

Breathe in, line up the sight picture, squeeze the trigger, expel the air. It felt good. He knew he was on target. He fired four more times and then cocked his right leg in the air and turned his weapon on its side to show he had finished. When all was silent, a man with a white stick pointed out O'Keefe's group. A tight group inside the circle. Fife next. O'Keefe pulled off his earmuffs so he could hear Fife swearing. Two in the ring and three low to the right. That would teach him to get drunk the night before a firing exercise. Me? Well, drink never affected Paddy, did it?

Chapter Fourteen

'I'm not staying long. Not after what's happened. I won't feel right.'

Mary held Liam's hand and O'Keefe carried Katie, trying to make sure she didn't get any of her red lollipop on his full dress uniform. Billy was walking ten yards behind, in a dream. Remembrance Sunday. The day Stirling Lines opened its gates to wives and families to commemorate the dead. The gym was turned into a chapel for the morning and everyone gathered to watch the parade as the squadrons and associated units laid poppy wreaths under the names of the Regiment's dead on the clock tower. It was a day not just of remembrance but also of reunion as the old and the bold gathered to relive their exploits.

But this morning the IRA had exploded a bomb in the Ulster Protestant town of Enniskillen. It was their reply to the Loughgall ambush six months before. There were at least ten dead and many injured and already the humility and courage of Gordon Wilson, who held the hand of his daughter Marie as she died under the rubble, had touched the nation.

The two minutes' silence after the Last Post seemed an eternity to Mary. But now every day seemed like a week and every week a year. The months since the ambush were bleak, arctic expanses. She clung on for the sake of Paddy and their children, but knew she couldn't go on.

I know it's not fair but I can't help it.

They paid their respects at the Regiment's graves in St Martin's churchyard and now they strolled back past the clock tower to the buffet. Liam, in some game of his own, broke away and ran off across the parade ground.

'Liam. Liam. Come back here.'

Mary's Belfast accent cut the air. A woman wearing a black astrakhan coat and a look of haughty disdain recoiled as if she'd been physically struck.

'Is she allowed in here?' the woman brayed loudly to a group of dignitaries. 'What's she *doing* here? It's ridiculous having someone like that in the camp. Really!'

Mary stood open-mouthed in hurt amazement. She had no chance to recover before Paddy thrust Katie into her arms. He had a strange and angry look on his face.

'Caroline, darling.' Simon Baines-Hickey, oozing smugness in an immaculate pinstripe suit, embraced the woman.

It was the first time O'Keefe had seen Baines-Hickey since that night in the Falklands. His face was as smooth and pink as ever. He appeared sleek and prosperous, repulsively so in O'Keefe's eyes. O'Keefe had to speak to him. He didn't know what he was going to say, but he had to get the man to acknowledge him.

But first he had to take his eyes off the medal hanging from the blue and white ribbon on Baines-Hickey's right breast. The Military Cross. What a fucking travesty.

'Ah . . . O'Kane, isn't it?' said Baines-Hickey, after a moment. He turned to the woman who glanced at O'Keefe's three stripes and dismissed him. 'Darling, this chap was with me on that raid when I won my gong.'

'O'Keefe. My name's O'Keefe. And I didn't think you'd have the balls to show your face here.'

'Oh really?' He affected puzzled amusement. 'And why's that?'

Paddy was about to reply when suddenly Fife was standing between them. He hadn't changed out of the jeans and anorak he'd worn on protection duty around the churchyard. His eyes were glassy in fury and his top lip was drawn back like a wild animal's. He wasn't about to take prisoners.

'You wanking coward,' he snarled at Baines-Hickey. 'If it hadn't been for Paddy, my name would be up there.'

137

He pointed to the list of names below the clock with a trembling finger.

'What are they *talking* about, Simon?' drawled the woman looking at Fife as though he'd crawled out from under a stone. 'Tell that scruffy little man to go away. He's a disgrace.'

Her overweening arrogance served to pour kerosene on the flames of Fife's anger.

'You're yellow. You should have won the Nobel Peace Prize for your fucking soldiering. You got an MC for cowardice and Paddy who saved me almost got the sack. Take off that fucking medal.' Fife went to rip the medal off Baines-Hickey's chest.

'Simon,' snapped the woman. 'Call the military police and have this obnoxious man thrown out of the camp.'

'You stuck-up, ignorant cow. I belong here. I'm guarding the likes of you.'

Fife's anger was travelling at the speed of gun cord. There was going to be an almighty explosion.

O'Keefe's eyes creased and he gave a smile of resignation and regret. This was going to solve all their problems in one blow. Literally. He was about to say goodbye to the army.

'You're a coward and a liar,' he told Baines-Hickey in a surprisingly soft tone. He gathered a mouthful of phlegm and spat directly in his face. 'That's what I think of ye.'

There was a moment's silence when no one moved. Baines-Hickey put his hand to his cheek and looked with repugnance at the spittle.

'You insolent swine. I'll have you court-martialled.'

'No, you won't.'

O'Keefe saw the white Citroën break up under the rifle fire, the two men in the front seats, their bodies all holes; he heard the whispered row in the darkness in the Falklands when Baines-Hickey had refused to meet his eye, felt again his legs buckling under Fife's dead weight and smelled the vomit; he remembered his leper-like treatment when they told him he'd been wrong to disobey an officer to save a life.

The injustices of years culminated in the punch. Just the one punch, directly to the point of the jaw.

As Baines-Hickey fell, his outstretched arm dislodged the wreaths, so that they tumbled and circled and rearranged themselves around his unconscious body. In the silence, O'Keefe picked up the poppies and painstakingly replaced them around the base of the cenotaph.

'I want you to know I intended no disrespect to the dead, sir,' O'Keefe told the CO. 'In fact, I reckon those blokes up there would have done the same.'

Part Two

Chapter Fifteen

Six staggered Land-Rovers funnelled the dual carriageway heading north out of Belfast into one lane. Paddy O'Keefe inched forward, mentally noting he wouldn't have parked the Land-Rovers like that. Too exposed to a hit and run attack from the other lane and slow to respond to any threat. He opened the car boot for a sullen-faced policeman to inspect its emptiness. The policeman poked under the carpet and the spare wheel watched by two absurdly young gunners from the Royal Artillery. Others lay on the grass verge, their new SA80 rifles covering the oncoming traffic. They'd experimented with the SA80 in the Regiment. Bloody awful weapon. You had to use your trigger finger to release the safety catch. Give me an M16 any time. Stop it. It's the past. He pulled away, telling himself to concentrate on the future and getting a job.

He thought of little else. He'd tried the security companies and now he was trying security departments of the bigger firms. And he was running out of places to go. He was the provider and he wasn't providing. They'd come to Ireland as Mary had wanted and found they had jumped straight from the army frying pan into the Belfast fire. They'd got what they paid for their home in Hereford, but the money wasn't going to last for ever. Hell. It wasn't going to last for long.

Every time he applied for a job there was that same bloody question. What school did you go to? What did it bloody matter? He pulled out to overtake a lorry with a smiling cow on its rear door. That bloody former corporal in the Royal Corps of Transport that morning, questioning his ability to guard a building site. He'd forced himself to listen to the crap-hat describing how he'd travelled the world, killed with his bare hands and all his coy hints about Special Forces. And he still hadn't got the job. He knew he hadn't.

A Mercedes screamed up to within a foot of O'Keefe's rear bumper and started flashing its headlights. Must have been doing a good 110mph. O'Keefe jabbed his middle finger in the air and took his time. He felt a flash of resentment and anger. He couldn't say who he was or what he'd done. He was fighting with one hand tied behind his back. This call from the copper had come out of the blue. He had no idea what it was about, but in his situation he wasn't going to leave any stone unturned.

He overtook the lorry and prepared to move in to the inner lane. The Mercedes gave an impatient barp on its twin horns. It crossed O'Keefe's mind to touch the brakes, but he knew he couldn't afford to get his car repaired and he had to stay out of trouble. As soon as the gap opened, the Mercedes swung inside him to undertake, the driver mouthing obscenities.

Fuck it. O'Keefe hit the accelerator and jerked down on the wheel. The Mercedes bucked like a frightened hare and swerved on to the hard shoulder. For a moment it appeared as if the driver had lost it, then he regained control and pulled away, giving one last V-sign.

That'll teach the bastard.

Shit. What is happening to me? Paddy O'Keefe, road rage merchant. A few months ago I'd have laughed at the local hero, but somehow there's not much laughter around any more. He turned off the road for Holywood, unthinkingly checking in his mirror to see who else left the main road. Old habits die hard. The pub was the first on the left. He pulled into the car park and shook his head at his own madness.

Boyle sat at the bar with a hot Powers in front of him. He felt bloody awful and he knew he was going down with a cold. His joints were aching, there were wads of cotton wool behind his eyes and he had a throbbing headache. Could be 'flu. People didn't go sick with colds any more. They all had 'flu. The pub was quietly busy at lunchtime. Enough drinkers so they wouldn't stand out; not so many as to be overheard. He didn't know how the DSF would react to one of his former men being tapped, so he hadn't told him. In fact he'd told no one about the meet. He'd booked it out to a tout in Bangor. Right area and near enough if he was tagged.

Boyle and O'Keefe carried their drinks to a secluded table and took stock of each other. The detective had clocked O'Keefe as soon as he walked through the door. His shock of curly black hair was unmistakable but, Boyle thought, his face was fuller than in his pictures. He'd put on some weight. Many men did when they left the army, but in O'Keefe's case it was an indication that his self-discipline was wavering. No one made SAS men stay fit. They did it because they wanted to.

O'Keefe in turn registered the dour bulk of the policeman and decided to do away with pleasantries.

'What can I do for you?'

'It might be a question of what I can do for you,' replied Boyle in his nutcracker voice. 'How're you and the family settling down?'

'Fine. How'd you find me?'

'You've worked with us. An ant doesn't fart but we know.' He took a sip of hot toddy. 'You haven't asked for my ID.'

'I know who you are.' It had been easy to get a description of Boyle from one of the lads who'd been on the NI team. In fact the detective was bigger than his description. A thick neck rising directly from his powerful shoulders. Tufts of hair coming out of his ears. Running a little to seed, though, with a paunch straining against his perfectly ironed white shirt.

'You've chosen a nice part of east Belfast to live. You're off Ormeau Road, aren't you?'

O'Keefe grunted. He didn't know for how much longer.

145

'Good schools for the kids. That's important,' continued Boyle. 'Leased though, the house, isn't it?'

They were like two fighters circling each other, neither willing to make the first move in case it left them vulnerable to counterattack. Boyle popped two aspirins out of their wrapper and washed them down with warm whiskey.

'So how's the job hunting going?'

'Okay.' O'Keefe was noncommittal.

'Can't be easy for someone like you.' Boyle cursed himself for his clumsiness. His head was splitting.

'What's that supposed to mean?' O'Keefe was ready to take offence.

'I mean your abilities are very unusual, but I don't suppose you have any paper qualifications?' He answered his own question. 'No, you left school too early for those. It's not easy getting a job locally even if you've a degree. I suppose you've tried the security companies. Run by failed and fading coppers. Wouldn't give them a beery fart, myself. But you'd give any firm a touch of class – if they knew who you were. And that's the problem, isn't it? You can't tell them, can you?'

O'Keefe finished his Guinness and wondered where the pitch was headed.

'Maybe I could help you there. Put in a word, like. Not say exactly who you are but let them know your worth.' He flexed his aching shoulders.

'That's very kind of you, Mr Boyle. Can I get you a drink?'

As O'Keefe went to the bar, Boyle pulled a sour face. The meet wasn't going as he would have liked. He didn't have the control he needed and O'Keefe wasn't playing the role of supplicant. He should have left it until he felt sharper and more alert. Still, if O'Keefe thought he could buy his help for the price of a hot toddy, he'd a lot to learn.

O'Keefe returned with the drinks. He appeared to have been thinking.

'Do you know, Mr Boyle, until I came back, I had no idea

how important schooling was in getting a job. Not how far you went in school, just which school you went to. I went to a wrong one.'

'You mean to a Catholic one.'

'Ay.' O'Keefe's eyes swept round the carpeted bar with its small groups of businessmen eating toasted sandwiches, a gaggle of secretaries and a couple of drivers. All in work.

'I'm not here to compromise you. I'm here to help you, if you wish,' said Boyle, misinterpreting his glances.

'And what would you want in return?' At last O'Keefe had acknowledged that there was a bargain to be struck.

'Just keep your eyes and ears open. Use your training.' Boyle shrugged so as to belittle his suggestion.

'And where am I supposed to hear anything interesting that you would want to know about? I'm not involved in any movement and I've no intention of joining one.'

Two rosy-cheeked young men in well-cut sports jackets and shiny brown brogues entered the pub. O'Keefe recognized them and sneered inwardly: ruperts.

'It's surprising what you see and hear. You've still relatives in the Province . . .'

'Not many. They're out of Belfast and I don't see them.'

'Your wife's side has connections . . .'

'Christ, there's not a Catholic family in Belfast that doesn't have connections somewhere,' O'Keefe exclaimed angrily.

'Colm Magee was quite a connection. Shot by your former colleagues at Loughgall.'

So he doesn't know I was there. Good. The bastard doesn't know everything. Just thinks he does.

'I'd say the McGinn family had more connections than most, wouldn't you?' insisted Boyle.

'You wouldn't be asking me to inform on my wife's family, would you?'

'I'd never ask you to harm your kith and kin. But you could help keep the peace . . .' He was about to add '. . . and prevent British troops being murdered.' But he wasn't allowed to finish the sentence.

'Crap. You want me to grass up my fellow Catholics,' exploded O'Keefe.

Boyle gave a wry grin. 'Oh. It's a Catholic you are now, is it? It's a soldier you were before.'

Heat flooded into O'Keefe's cheeks. 'I was born a Catholic and I'll die a Catholic and it's my business and no one else's.' He jabbed his thick forefinger at Boyle in short, angry gestures. 'Let me tell you, I had no reason to know I was a Catholic until I came back to this blighted land. Now every one wants to know my bloody religion before they'll even look at a job application form.'

He regretted that his angry outburst had led the conversation back to employment.

'I can get you a job tomorrow . . .'

'Ay, if I become a tout.'

Boyle shivered. His arms and legs were one racking ache. He made one last effort.

'I don't envy you, O'Keefe. You're a bit of a piggy in the middle, aren't you? You might be finding difficulty finding work with Proddie companies, but I'd be careful about venturing too deep into the workplaces of your fellow Catholics – just in case they find out you were SAS.' He held up his hand. 'Oh, I'll not tell them. I'll sign no man's death warrant – unless he be a terrorist – but if they sus you, you'll be dead in an hour.'

As he saw O'Keefe's eyes harden, Boyle knew he had got it wrong.

He finished his drink alone. He would go home and nurse himself before his head burst. But first he had to make a few phone calls. To reinforce the ones he had already made. O'Keefe might try to cast his net wider than the obvious security firms and Boyle had to ensure that wherever he went the door would always be closed.

He'll be back, forecast Boyle. Two weans and a lease on a fine house. He'll be back. But I did handle it badly. Too crass. The subtlety of a steamroller. He sneezed.

*　　*　　*

'So you kill him? What good will that do, eh?' Patrick John Collins paused from teasing strands of tobacco from his tin and put his head on one side like a quizzical schoolmaster.

'He was in the British army. It'd be one for the boys in Gibraltar.'

Collins regarded Sean O'Hanlon as if he was a particularly dense pupil.

'Don't you learn any lessons from Enniskillen – about killing unarmed civilians?' Old Holborn slowly shook his head.

'Our three on Gibraltar were unarmed when they were slaughtered in cold blood,' snapped O'Hanlon. There was a growl of agreement around the drab room. The smell of hot vinegar rose from the fish and chip shop beneath and Collins for once almost felt hunger.

'They were on active service. They knew the risks. Don't confuse what we tell the world's press with what we tell ourselves.'

Collins was losing patience with Sean O'Hanlon's simplistic views. Kill, kill, bomb, shoot, kill. O'Hanlon's rise was symbolic of the calibre of recruits nowadays. It was a concern he shared with the inner cabinet. The level of capability, morale and training dictated their activities. More bullet than ballot box.

'If there was a lesson to be learned from Gibraltar,' continued Collins. 'It is that we have the security of a tea bag.'

The Northern Military Command had discussed the difficulty of striking the right balance only last night, though he wasn't about to tell the others in the room. Give the Active Service Units complete autonomy and they came up with Enniskillen – the greatest public relations cock-up since the Brits shot the wounded after the 1916 Rising. Even in Moscow they queued to sign the book of condolences. But the alternative – to run operations from the centre – ran the risk of security leaks. Gibraltar had been a perfect operation – betrayed.

They still didn't know the traitor. So you turn in on yourself. Trusting no one and doing nothing while you chase your own tail. And wasn't British intelligence loving it. A hint in this newspaper, a seeming indiscretion in that one. They want us to tie ourselves in a knot and that's precisely what we're doing. Collins brought himself back to the present and found Sean glowering at him. He turned slightly to look him directly in the steady right eye and O'Hanlon dropped his gaze.

'He'd be an easy target,' he muttered, not wanting to give up the argument.

'Easy targets are not always the best ones,' replied Collins. Then he raised his voice to make sure he had the attention of the area commanders. 'But I'll say this. If he's anyone's target, he's mine. And I'll not have a hair of his head harmed, unless or until I say so.'

Mary looked up from sewing Liam's name tags on his school shirts as she heard the front door open and close softly. She listened as Paddy took off his coat, walked along the hall and began to climb the stairs. He didn't call out.

It meant he hadn't got the job. He always went upstairs when he came back disappointed and defeated. It was as if he needed to delay confessing his failure to her. Instead he would go and play with the children in their bedrooms, handing out the little treats he brought home, even though he knew they couldn't afford them; symbolic of his refusal to admit his failure even to himself.

'I hope you didn't wake the weans. They wanted to wait up for you.'

'No, they're both sound asleep.'

Mary pulled a casserole dish out of the oven with the remains of a congealed shepherd's pie in one corner. She regarded it apologetically.

'It's a bit dried out. I expected you a few hours ago.'

'I stopped for a drink, hen.'

The worry and frustration inside Mary boiled over.

'There's not enough money to go around without you drinking it,' she shouted. 'How am I supposed to feed and clothe the weans? I know to the penny how much I need to see us through the week and it doesn't include you getting drunk . . .'

'I only had two pints. Christ, hen, it was the first drink I've had for a week.' O'Keefe was hurt and indignant.

Mary's anger evaporated in an instant. It was wrong to take out her fears on him.

'I'm sorry, love. There's a lager in the fridge. Would you like it with your food?'

He nodded gratefully. Mary crossed to the large fridge freezer, took out the can and returned to the table. She liked this kitchen. She could walk around in it. It was the biggest she had ever known, but the lease on the Victorian semi-detached was up soon and they wouldn't be able to afford to renew it. They even had an option to buy. Mary loved it here. It was in a leafy suburb – far enough away from the tight streets and tower blocks of West Belfast to be divorced from the troubles; close enough to her mother, sister and relatives to feel she was home. But they were going to have to move – and Paddy just wouldn't talk about it.

'Don't drown it. It's not my fault it's dried out.'

Paddy ignored her and continued to pour brown sauce over the pie.

At first, Paddy hadn't been in a hurry to get a job. They'd had a marvellous three weeks' holiday in Florida together, but then back in Belfast the reality slowly sunk in – like an unpleasant stain spreading over hopeful white linen. The Belfast they saw last year had been a snapshot taken on a rosy day when everyone was kind and cheerful and wanting to help. A community pulling together to help in time of crisis. Liam's illness had distracted her attention from the underlying permanent rottenness that blighted the city.

They'd spent a small fortune moving, bringing everything

151

from Hereford – most of which, including the car, they were still paying for. Although Mary had heard the stories of how difficult it was to get work, somehow she hadn't thought it would apply to Paddy. At least he kept trying. But one day he would give up, they all did. That was a day she feared. Already the remorseless search was sapping Paddy's pride; his eyes didn't smile as often as they used to. Quick words were creeping in between them and she hoped the children didn't notice.

Paddy seemed to divine her thoughts. He paused in his steady eating. 'I can get a job abroad easily enough.'

'And why would you want to do that?' Mary kept her voice as light as she knew how.

'Cos I can't get a fucking one here.'

'Don't swear,' she chided automatically.

'It makes sense. I'm the best qualified soldier in the world, but it means bugger all in civvy street. I haven't got a trade or any type of skill. I can't repair a TV set or fix the central heating. All I can do is soldier. I can get a job tomorrow body guarding or training. They need people in Sri Lanka and there's always work out in the Gulf.'

He picked up his can and drank from it.

'Use a glass. How long would you be away?'

'Maybe six months, but there's usually leave in the middle.'

Mary regarded him with her deep, calm eyes.

'*I* could always get a job. They're looking for part-time workers in the clothing factories. Maybe I could do a few mornings a week.' It was a plan she had worked out. 'You could look after the weans, or if you were busy then my mother or sister would help out.'

'I don't want you working. Your place is with the children and the home.' The matter was closed. He was the provider: she was the homemaker. It was a reflection on his inadequacy that she should even suggest it.

'Well, I don't want you going abroad. Stay here and be a father to your children.'

152

'I'm not being much of a father now, am I?' In his anger, he sprayed half chewed pieces of mince and potato over the square wooden table. 'Why did we come back to this bloody place? Just so you could be near your family.'

'It wasn't just my idea,' replied Mary sharply.

''Course it was. You were going on about how much you hated Hereford and how great it would be back in Belfast. Well, it's not. It's shit.' He picked up the sauce bottle and shook it viciously so that dollops of thick brown fluid splattered over his plate.

'I suppose you didn't get that job.'

'No.'

'Well, you could have told me. What am I supposed to do. Guess?'

'Of course I didn't get the job – or any other fucking job . . .'

The kitchen door opened and Katie stood gazing solemnly from one to the other. She was rubbing her eye and looked about to burst into tears.

'Don't cry, sweetheart.' Mary swept her up in her arms. 'Now look what you've done.'

'There, there,' comforted her father, rising from the table. Mary pushed him back into his chair.

'Back to bed with you, young lady.'

She returned to find O'Keefe staring at the yellow and white check cloth that covered half the table. Mary rested her hand lightly on his shoulder.

'She's asleep now. Probably won't even remember in the morning.' O'Keefe put his large red hand over hers and squeezed.

'I know,' said Mary. 'It's not easy but these quarrels don't help . . .'

There was a gentle tapping at the back door and they exchanged puzzled glances. Mary's family were their only regular callers and they were daytime visitors.

Mary led Patrick John Collins into the kitchen.

'Virginia said you'd had the results of Liam's final check-up.

153

I found myself out in these parts, so I thought I'd call in.'

'That's kind of you,' said Mary. 'Would you like a drink?'

'Just a cup of tea. Do you mind if I . . .' He produced his tobacco tin while Mary fussed around him as she would at a pastoral visit from her priest.

It was the first time O'Keefe had seen Collins since their return. He looked more worn and tired than last time they'd met. O'Keefe noticed his right sideburns were stained brown with nicotine where he held his roll-up.

'You'd never tell Liam had been ill,' concluded Mary, pouring out the cup of tea. 'How are you keeping?'

'I've never been so busy. Do you know, when I first became a councillor I tried to have clinics at certain times of the week, but I soon gave that up, there was simply too much to do. That's why we set up the Sinn Fein community aid centre. And how about yourself,' asked Old Holborn, turning to O'Keefe. 'No regrets?'

'Too early to say yet,' replied O'Keefe noncommittally.

'It'd be fine if he could get work,' said Mary, abruptly. O'Keefe flashed her a bitter look of betrayal. She was treating the man like a bloody father confessor. It was none of Collins's business if he couldn't get a job.

'Ah.' Collins made the sound explain everything. 'You said it was economics which drove you to join the army in the first place. Well, you've chosen a wrong time to leave it. The shipyards are closing, aircraft factories on hold, heavy industry is failing. You're fine if you're a housewife who wants to work a few mornings a week to earn pin money . . .' Again O'Keefe looked at Mary. 'But it's not easy – especially for a Catholic man. So you've been trying?'

'He's spent the last few months trying,' Mary answered for him.

'Maybe I could help.' Collins made it sound as if they would be doing him a favour. 'There's always vacancies in the building trade if you know where to look. Do you know anything about building?'

O'Keefe shook his head.

'Plastering, electrics, bricklaying, that sort of thing?'

'No.'

'Perhaps I could get you something driving. Only a few days a week, like. Nothing that would interfere with your dole money.'

Mary made a noise like a steaming kettle coming to the boil.

'He won't claim it. He's too proud.'

'I don't want others knowing my business,' explained O'Keefe lamely.

'Don't you now?' said Old Holborn softly.

Thirty minutes later O'Keefe was finally persuaded that he wasn't sponging off the state; that he was entitled to unemployment benefit, income support and goodness knows what else. He accepted he had to put his children before his pride. That it was nothing to be ashamed of. He had paid into the system. Time for the system to pay back.

Collins left knowing that O'Keefe was at last willing to be dependent on others. He promised to be in touch.

Chapter Sixteen

Next morning O'Keefe put on his old tracksuit and went for a long run for the first time in weeks. He was letting himself go and the weight was piling on. He hadn't heard from Fife for a while: probably he was away on a job. He didn't want to be the one to phone when he had nothing but bad news. Maybe things would improve now. Be positive.

His new mood lasted until he walked in through the door of the dole office. Christ! The arrogance of those snot-gobbling clerks. The receptionist didn't even bother to look up when O'Keefe spoke to her. He was just another claimant, another form, another waster. The drab green paint, the permeating odour of old tobacco and stale, unwashed bodies slumped lethargically on the hard benches under peeling posters, created an atmosphere of debilitating indifference.

The clerks sat behind thick glass at high desks so they looked down at the claimant. Part of the psychology of the system, O'Keefe recognized. For whose benefit? To make the claimant feel smaller or the clerk larger. He came out of the office shaking with suppressed fury at the humiliating ritual of signing on and the smug, spotty pen-pushers who left a man with no self-respect. God, he'd like to get a few of those little bastards on a parade ground. He felt dirty, cheapened and belittled.

He stopped on the pavement to let his hurt and his temper abate. There, across the road, was Boyle. He was standing by himself, looking down the road. O'Keefe thought about his offer. As he did so, Boyle turned and caught sight of O'Keefe in the entrance of the social security office. An expression of knowledge and contempt flickered across the policeman's face for a microsecond before his features resumed their heavy lugubriousness. It was long enough to send O'Keefe's blood again seething round his head in a moment of pure hate. Boyle stood for the establishment, the system. Protestant and English. And he hated it for the way it made him feel soiled and second class.

Stuff your offer, Mr Boyle. I'll play on my own side.

He returned home to find that Collins had left the name and telephone number of a delivery company. Twenty-five pounds a day – but nothing permanent, he'd understand. With renewed hope, he sat down and wrote off to a fresh round of firms inquiring about security work.

For two or three days a week, O'Keefe drove around Belfast dropping off carburettors, oil filters, pistons and brake pads to various garages. He was stopped daily at checkpoints and road blocks, each day fearing he'd see someone he knew and grateful there wasn't a Parachute Regiment battalion currently in Belfast. The family were treading water financially, but Mary's plans to buy the house were dead. No building society was going to give an unemployed man a mortgage.

Periodically, O'Keefe built up his hopes about better work – only to see them dashed. Even when he tried outside the world of security for employment, it seemed the fates conspired against him.

'I don't understand,' he told Mary bitterly one morning, holding out a letter from a major manufacturing company. 'That interview next week for the job as a sales rep. They've cancelled it. They say the sales team is being restructured and there are no vacancies. Last week, they said they were expanding.'

At the end of the sixth week he was leaving a garage in The Glen when he saw a man in the timber yard next door put up a sign advertising for a driver. He shook hands on the job on the spot. Start on Monday. He quit his part-time job that night and went home to tell a delighted Mary.

Patrick John Collins, who had somehow heard that he had handed in his notice, seemed equally pleased for them.

'Well? Anything on him?'

The brigade intelligence officer shook his head. 'He's not political. Never been involved.'

'Everyone's involved.'

'I mean he's never done any work for the army or the government. He's not a member of any party.'

'He's a Catholic?'

'Of course.'

'Then have a quiet word. He should listen to reason. If he doesn't, then torch the fucking building yard and make sure you destroy the vans.'

'Why?'

'Ye don't need to know. And ye should know better than to ask.'

'Sorry, Patrick John.'

Mary ran her fingertips through the beads of condensation on the metal window frame and looked down to the potholed walks and bare grass where pinched-faced kids with snotty noses lingered in their thin anoraks and wellies one size too large. The smells were distilled from her childhood. Urine and beer in the metallic lift with its ugly graffiti; vinegar and stale cooking oil in the corridors. She had returned to her ghetto roots and she wept tears of bitter defeat.

The corporation tower block wasn't in the Lower Falls, but it wasn't far away. Mary knew she was being sucked backwards and downwards and she feared for her children and for her hopes for them. Old Holborn had used his influence and by some standards the flat wasn't too bad, but they'd had to sell some of their furniture because there was no room. The neighbours had been welcoming and the community association helped them move in – supervised by the ubiquitous Golden Virginia. Mary thought she sensed in her mother a smug satisfaction that her aspirations had been thwarted – although maybe it was just that sort of day.

The first night, when the children were finally in their bunks sharing the same bedroom, Paddy and Mary sat and reflected each other's hollow sadness. She reached out and held his hand across the dirty plates smeared with the traces of fried egg yolks in silent apology.

'Do you know, Mary hen, I've been thinking. I've not sung one Irish rebel song since I've been back.'

The part-time driving job had been given to someone else. He was losing interest in life, watching television in the daytime, trying to fill his empty hours. He had given up training and his gut hung over his belt. All he had to do was to get the kids' breakfast the four mornings a week she worked in the clothing factory – and that's about all he managed to do.

Patrick John Collins waited almost a fortnight before he came to fetch O'Keefe to meet the foreman of a site a mile away in Springfield where they were building a new supermarket.

'Ah, Mickey. This here's Paddy. He's a good friend of mine. You mentioned you could use a hand this week.'

Mickey had puckered scar tissue around his left eye and only half a left ear. 'What can you do?' he asked.

'Push a wheelbarrow as well as the next man,' retorted O'Keefe.

Mickey grinned. 'Okay. Tomorrow. Can't guarantee how long, though.'

O'Keefe became aware in the first hour how little he knew about building work. There was an easy way and a hard way to do everything and O'Keefe didn't know the difference. He was a willing worker, buckling down to fetch and carry on command. Pushing a wheelbarrow full of bricks up a plank the front wheel slipped and the barrow went over spilling its load on to wet, levelled concrete and clipping the elbow of Black Barry Kennedy, the big loudmouth who dominated the site with his coarse voice and threats.

'You stupid bastard.'

'Sorry. Sorry about that,' replied O'Keefe, looking helplessly at the bricks.

'You will be fucking sorry if you do it again.'

The others were idly watching, clocking how the new man was going to cope with Black Barry's bullying.

'Chuck them bricks back up to me,' said O'Keefe.

'Fuck off. Get them yourself and don't step on the concrete.'

It was obvious he had to step on the concrete to retrieve the bricks. He took two steps and crouched to pick up the nearest bricks. With a roar, Black Barry launched himself on him – just as O'Keefe knew he would. Ten seconds later he was filling a bucket with cold water to throw over the unconscious builder. After that, others became willing to show him the short cuts and his gaffes were forgiven. At the end of the day they went for a pint and he made a point of buying Barry the first drink to show there were no hard feelings.

All week the weather was glorious and O'Keefe revelled in the physical outdoor life. If he wasn't using his brain at least he was regaining his fitness and earning money. Friday was cloudless and the temperature was soon in the high seventies. In the early afternoon, they heard the crump of an explosion and saw a cloud of dust and smoke rise over the Murph. Minutes later there was the wail of sirens travelling up the Springfield Road. He lost interest when he saw Mickey coming around the site carrying envelopes containing the week's wages.

He'd heard there was overtime to be had on Saturday morning – time and a half. Steady work and a few Saturdays over the next few weeks and they might even have enough for a week's holiday somewhere with the kids.

Mickey handed him his envelope. 'Thanks, Paddy, but I can't use you next week. Getting a bit ahead of ourselves. Last in, first out. Ye understand.'

O'Keefe didn't understand. How could there be overtime on one hand and cutbacks on the other.

'Come by in a week or so's time. Things might be different then.'

He nodded his thanks and went back to work without saying a word.

He was first aware of Patrick John Collins when he heard Mickey's voice calling for him and, looking over the first-floor brick wall, he saw the two men standing conspiratorially close next to the pile of sand. Collins took O'Keefe's arm and led him to a quiet corner of the site. He looked worried and his movements denoted urgency.

'Need a word with you. Need a favour also. Did you hear that bang a while ago? That was a man called O'Riordan being careless for the last time. The trouble with O'Riordan was that he was never satisfied with a simple device. He always had to go one better. This time the device went one better than him.' For a moment his face lost its anxious edge and he looked regretful. 'Still, he was a good man and he'll be missed by many.'

O'Keefe wondered what this had to do with him. Old Holborn seemed to be struggling to say something.

'The problem is that he made another . . . device. We think it's on a timer. It's in the middle of a block of flats and an awful lot of people are going to get hurt if it goes off. When it goes off.'

'So disarm it.'

Collins made a gesture of annoyance as though waving away a wasp. 'And who's going to do that? The British army? And how do we ask them? We'd lose face. There's no one in Belfast at the moment . . . Did you handle explosives, Paddy boy?'

'A bit,' admitted O'Keefe reluctantly.

'That's what I was thinking.' Collins suddenly lost patience.

He swung round to stare directly at the labourer's sun-burned face. 'The bloody bomb's going to go off and there's nothing *we* can do. I know who you are, Paddy boy. I know who you are. Look at the bloody thing.'

O'Keefe had never seen Collins this agitated. Still he stood his ground, uncertain what to do. He knew he owed Collins, but he didn't want to get mixed up with the IRA. On the other hand he wasn't going to harm anyone. He was protecting life.

Collins sensed his hesitation. 'O'Riordan's brother was blown up last month. O'Riordan just found out it was down to two INLA headbangers. He was planting the second bomb when it went off. The first is in an empty flat under where he believed one of his brother's killers lives. He was wrong; the man moved a week ago. That's all I can tell you and all you want to know.'

'What about leaving here?'

'No problems.'

O'Keefe turned to see Mickey giving him an encouraging thumbs-up.

Chapter Seventeen

There were large damp stains across the aggregate of the block of flats and you didn't have to be a building expert to know they wouldn't see the millennium. Two hard-faced men tried to be inconspicuous at the entrance of the block and another two waited on the first landing. The skylight over the front door of the flat was smashed and the flat itself looked as if it had been abandoned.

Gingerly O'Keefe peered into the darkened living room. As his eyes became used to the gloom he saw a solid wooden box in the middle of bare, dusty floorboards.

He caught the sweet smell of marzipan.

And he heard the steady tick tock tick tock of a clock.

Collins handed him a powerful torch. In its beam O'Keefe saw that the room was empty apart from a ripped easy-chair, a three-legged plywood table in the corner – and the box measuring around fifteen inches by twelve and eight inches deep. Peering out of the top was an old-fashioned alarm clock with two bells and hammers. It was ticking loudly. A carpet had been nailed over the window.

O'Keefe checked there were no wires between the box and the door before stepping into the humid, airless room. He was grateful for the bare floorboards which prevented any hidden pressure switches. He ran the torch around the box and its cord handles to ensure it was isolated and then turned his attention to the carpet. When he was certain it was just nailed to the ceiling, he gave a sharp tug and it fell into his arms.

'What was that there for?' asked Collins, from the door-way.

'To direct the blast upwards.'

Oh Christ. The box was full of six-inch sticks of Nobels 808. Not as stylish as Semtex and indicative of an older hand at work. There was nothing wrong with the 808 – just wasn't fashionable. It'd do the job just as well. It had probably been stolen from a British army base in the 1960s and kept by O'Riordan as his private store.

There was enough plastic explosive here to bring down the whole bloody block. The first trickle of sweat ran down his back.

The brown greaseproof wrappings were transparent in patches, showing the moisture oozing through. The heat of the flat was causing a chemical reaction separating the nitroglycerine from the plastic compound of the explosive. The PE was unstable.

'You'll have to evacuate the building,' rasped O'Keefe in charge now. 'I might need three hands so I'll want a volunteer. But everyone else has to get out. Say it's a fucking community picnic, but get them out and well away in case the windows blow.'

'I'll stay with ye,' said Collins in little more than a whisper. He left to give orders to clear the building and returned as O'Keefe opened his Leatherman, a superior Swiss Army knife favoured by special forces, and tested the blades of the wire cutters.

Collins put a hand on O'Keefe's arm. 'You be careful now. O'Riordan was an awful tricky man.'

He stood behind O'Keefe feeling utterly helpless. Their own bomb disposal man was in the South and there wasn't time to summon help from Derry or the borders. He had to trust O'Keefe, and to demonstrate that trust he had to stay with him. If they survived he would build on O'Keefe's willingness to help to his later advantage. If they didn't – it wouldn't matter anyway.

As O'Keefe sat on his heels and stared at the rubber-lined box, he heard urgent hammerings on front doors and raised voices. The small alarm in the clock face pointed to just after three o'clock. He had no more than ten minutes. The clock, embedded in the top layer of the damp explosive, was connected by two wires to the detonator and by another two wires to a rectangular nine volt battery. The detonator needed only a charge of one and a half volts, so O'Riordan had believed in P for Plenty. It sat under the clock, firmly inserted into an explosive candle.

O'Keefe tried to put himself in the mind of the dead bombmaker. What would he do? The alarm clock suggested something primitive but effective. Yet Collins had stressed the devious mind of O'Riordan. Never overlook the simple ways, his explosives instructors used to say. Radio frequencies and lasers are all very well, but a good mechanical spring can trigger a bomb just as well and probably more surely. O'Riordan would have approved of the lectures.

He considered the options. The bombmaker could have glued a piece of wood with a wire to one of the bells so that when the alarm went off, the hammer striking the wire would complete the electrical circuit. There was no sign that the bell had been tampered with.

He could have broken off the minute hand and attached the wood and the wire to the face of the clock so that the hour hand made the connection, but the clock face was intact.

O'Keefe inspected the back of the clock. There. A tiny block of wood and a thin piece of wire fixed to the key which wound the alarm. When the alarm went off, the wire on the turning key would come in contact with the other metal key and complete the circuit.

He had six minutes.

O'Keefe carefully pulled apart the two wires leading from the detonator to the clock and snipped one, making sure the cutters did not touch the other wire. He bent the first wire away and cut the second one before gently withdrawing the slim, cigar-shaped detonator from the explosive and laying it on the floorboards. If the clock went off early, there would be nothing worse than scorched wood. He cut the wires leading from the ignition set to the detonator.

Then he rocked back on his heels, breathed out deeply and turned to grin at Collins. He realized for the first time that his head was pounding.

'Done?'

'Ay. For the moment.' O'Keefe stood up. His head swam because his blood pressure had fallen due to the fumes coming off the explosive. He needed a drink of water and time to let his head clear before he took the explosive out of the box. In the kitchen he splashed water over his head and neck before wiping his hands and face on a roll of kitchen towel left behind.

'I thought you said this guy was tricky. That was almost too easy.'

He threw the crumpled-up towel into a cardboard box in the corner and as he did so caught sight of a piece of pink nylon cord. He delicately removed the paper to expose the cord. On the end was a small, round split pin.

That's why it had been so easy. He'd disarmed the one he was supposed to find.

He held up the pin to show Collins.

'Booby trap.'

'Can you disarm it?' asked Collins bleakly. He had believed the crisis was over. He didn't want to go back into that humid room with the sweet smell of sudden death.

'I only make mess, I don't clean it up,' replied O'Keefe. 'But . . .'

The split pin could have come from a variety of switches; pressure, pressure release, pull, push, tilt, time. But which one and where was it?

Back on the floor, O'Keefe shone the torch around the clock. With greater tenderness than he had ever held even his own baby son, he slid his fingers in the crevices between the PE sticks. They had softened in the heat, giving slightly under his fingers. Gently. He could hear Collins breathing as he stood directly behind him. Brave man. They would

166

both be blown to kingdom come if he cocked up. With infinite patience he delved, a fingertip at a time. At one end of the box his fingers, moving as lightly as a butterfly's wings, brushed a taut, thin cord.

Something told him not to touch the clock. Instead, O'Keefe removed sticks around it so he could see the top of a metal switch. A pull switch stapled to the hard rubber lining of the box. He delicately traced the string with his fingertips until he came to one leg of the clock.

If he had lifted the clock he would have released a compressed spring driving a needle into the .22 explosive charge of the detonator and setting off the explosive. The detonator passed vertically through at least two rows. He stared intently at the cord before grasping it between his thumb and forefinger; pulled to ensure there was slack around the clip of the switch and picked up the Leatherman placed at his right hand. He snipped once. So far so good.

Delicately O'Keefe picked off the stick on top of the pull switch. He took three deep breaths, wiped his right hand on his shirt, put the split pin between his lips and his thumb over the end of the pencil-like switch, turning it until the hole pointed outwards. He squeezed the pin together and, like threading a needle, inserted it in the switch to retain the spring. He prised the switch off the side of the box and gently teased the detonator free of the explosive. He placed the joint detonator and switch under the heel of his right work boot and prised the two apart.

Triumphantly O'Keefe held up the two parts, one in each hand.

'Well done,' breathed Collins, wiping his sweating palms on a large white handkerchief. 'Why did you put them under your heel?'

'To minimize the explosion if the detonator had gone off. The heel would have absorbed most of it.'

'Jesus.'

'Your Mr O'Riordan was quite a boy.'

O'Keefe felt empty and drained and someone was beating a bass drum inside his head.

Slowly, carefully, he lifted away the clock and methodically began removing stick after stick. When there were four layers left, he began to concentrate on the end away from the pull switch. Close to the bottom he became aware that the rows were fractionally uneven. Concentrate.

'Torch.' Collins passed him the torch like a theatre nurse handing a surgeon a scalpel. He shone the beam directly diagonally downwards and something glinted. Something green and metallic. Something like a pressure switch.

Then O'Keefe understood.

O'Riordan had planed the inside of the box, but the bottom hadn't been thick enough to hide the three-quarters-of-an-inch-deep switch completely.

Someone was looking after him that day. If he had continued to remove the sticks evenly he would have taken the weight off the pressure trip. Less than one and a half pounds and there would have been an almighty bang.

O'Riordan's last card.

'God's a Catholic after all,' he told Collins.

Concentrate. Accidents happened when you relaxed. It wasn't over yet.

He began to remove the sticks around the top of the switch, applying downward pressure on the spring-loaded lever at the same time.

'Take the split pin out of the pull switch,' he commanded. 'Be ready to hand it me.'

O'Keefe gingerly lifted one stick and was pushing down with his left hand when there was a sharp crack behind him and a muffled curse. In pulling out the pin, Collins had snagged the cord, tripping the spring. The switch clattered onto the floorboards.

O'Keefe, his two hands inside the box, froze.

'Sorry,' mumbled Collins.

O'Keefe continued to take out stick after stick. When it came to the last layer, he inserted his left thumb between the explosives, while sliding out the sticks with his right thumb and forefinger. At last he could see the hole for the retaining pin. He held out his hand, took the pin, glistening with sweat from Collins's fingers, and slipped it into the side of the pressure switch.

Finally, gratefully, he sat back on his heels and appreciated the true courage of the bomb disposal teams.

In the kitchen he crumbled a couple of the sweating sticks in the metal sink and lit them.

They flared up with a bluish white flame, giving out the cloying smell of marzipan. O'Keefe ran the tap to flush the sink with cold water and crumbled the next lot into the dying flames. When every stick had been burned, he rubbed his eyes and leaned against the wall, momentarily spent.

His face and body were covered in a cold sweat. He felt lethargic, as limp as a dish-rag. His hand was shaking, but only he would have noticed.

'Get me away from here and get me into a pub and get me a fucking drink.'

He didn't speak until they were in a small bar off the Whiterock road. O'Keefe downed a triple whiskey in one and held out his glass for a refill. He swallowed that and then looked hard at the wall.

'Thank you. Not many men could have done that.' Collins sipped a half of Guinness and looked as though he would have preferred a cup of tea.

'If I'd known what I was starting, I'd have left it to the tick-tock men.' O'Keefe took a pull of the pint that appeared before him. 'What was he thinking of, putting that in the middle of that block? He'd have taken out God knows how many.'

Collins grimaced. 'Ay, O'Riordan wasn't thinking clearly. Not after his brother died. That's what war does to you, you see.'

O'Keefe opened his mouth to protest, but Collins spoke first.

'It is a war and we're all involved.'

'I'm not.' O'Keefe gave a resolute shake of his head.

'We're all part of it whether we like it or not,' repeated Collins with sibilant insistence. The man fell silent. Then O'Keefe told him what he had realized the first night in the flat.

'Do you know, Mr Collins. I've not sung an Irish song since I came back to Belfast. It's not the same when you're here. It's not romantic, it's just grim and grimy. Life's not about bravery and sacrifice. It's about denial and having no dignity and poverty and being second class and being held in contempt. And it's hard to sing about those things.'

'I think you already have, Mr O'Keefe,' said Collins looking at the burly man in a respectful way. 'You're face to face with reality, but you still feel on the outside. You're a victim of the system as much as any Catholic man in Belfast but you don't believe yet that it's your fight. Don't you feel a tightly bound rage that the Protestants hold the best jobs, the best land, the best houses? They hold power. To whom do you think the UDR man owes his primary allegiance? Not to Westminster or the English officers who change every few years. But to his own Protestant community.'

'I don't hate, Mr Collins. Life's too short to hate.'

'*Veritas odium parit.* I'm sorry. Truth begets hatred,' he explained. 'But you're starting to resent, though, aren't you? Resent the fact that you are a second-class citizen?'

O'Keefe could only nod.

'Fanatics make bad soldiers, Mr O'Keefe. They die well, but fight with one eye. Irish Republicanism is not fighting a sectarian war,' preached Collins. 'The IRA doesn't kill people because they are Protestant but because they support the Crown. Republicans like myself believe that a United Ireland is an intrinsic good. Some of us are ready to pursue this goal at all costs. Tell me, do you believe that violence can be justified for a cause?'

Of course he did, Collins knew that. O'Keefe was used to obeying orders – and giving orders – that resulted in men's deaths. He was used to dealing in absolutes. When he was told to fire, he aimed and fired. He was used to killing. He would only have to accept the legitimacy of the order to kill. Or the legitimacy of the cause.

'The majority has no right to be wrong,' said Collins, quoting Eamon de Valera.

As soon as he saw Collins's car draw up, Mickey came hurrying over, hand outstretched.

'A grand thing you did there. A grand thing. I'm glad you came back.' Mickey pulled an envelope from his back pocket. It looked fatter than the earlier weekly wage packet.

'This is for tomorrow's overtime, but I don't expect to see you. The way I look at it, if I was you I'd have a bloody drink and a half tonight and the last thing I'd want to do in the morning would be to go to work with a sore head. So don't. I'll see you Monday.'

'But I thought I was laid off,' stuttered O'Keefe.

'Bollocks. Monday morning. Okay?'

Mary was still putting away the food when she heard the front door open. She involuntarily glanced at the clock. Just before five. Her heart, which had been buoyant a moment before, sank. Paddy coming home at this time meant something was wrong. The sack?

But he walked in the room with a huge grin on his brown face and parcels under his arm. He crouched down to kiss Katie and Liam and produced a farm complete with animals for his daughter and a Wild West fort for his son. Standing up, he planted a smacking great kiss on Mary's lips.

'So you've not been fired then?'

'No. Early cut and a bonus – and work next week. Get a babysitter. I'll take you out for a meal tonight.'

'We don't need to go out. Look at this.' She stood aside to reveal a table laden with groceries. 'We won the Community Association's summer raffle. Golden Virginia

171

brought it up not half hour ago. Or at least two of her helpers did. Virginia couldn't lift it. You should see how much meat there was. That's all in the freezer.' Mary bubbled on happily. 'There's tins of ham, chocolates, wines, beers, sherry, dates, fruit, biscuits, cakes, I don't know what. There's a good £300-worth if there's a penny. Maybe our luck's changing.'

'Maybe,' agreed O'Keefe, who couldn't remember buying a raffle ticket.

It was Patrick John's idea. The Community Association ceilidh was an opportunity for a rare night out for Mary and Paddy together and a chance for O'Keefe to air his larynx, if he chose. Babysitters were no problem. O'Keefe had hesitated, but seeing the expectant pleasure in Mary's face told himself he would have to start mixing some time. Now was as good a time as any.

The ceilidh was held in a red-brick hall with a bar along one side draped in the inevitable green, white and gold tricolour with tables arranged around a small dance floor. One or two groups of men had given him the hard eye when he walked in, especially a younger crowd at one corner of the bar. Messengers and errand boys; the cannon fodder of next year. Collins made a big fuss of them, buying them drinks and sitting them at his table with Golden Virginia.

O'Keefe enjoyed the songs even though he didn't know the new ones about helicopters and Armalites. He joined in the old ones, not giving his all, just showing he knew the words. He and Mary danced together, holding each other as lovers do and they found themselves laughing more in those few hours than they had done in the past few months.

He was still laughing as, arm in arm, they walked out of the hall into the still not dark summer night. Then he froze. Two yobs in jeans, bomber jackets and trainers were eating chips on the pavement twenty yards away waiting for a bus. Their greasy hair was lank and long at the sides.

O'Keefe took one look, grabbed Mary's arm and pulled her abruptly back out of the street lighting back into the entrance.

'What's wrong?'

'We could have another drink.' He couldn't think of an excuse for his behaviour.

Mary was puzzled. 'We told the babysitter we'd be back by eleven. We should go.'

He inched his way back into the hall to be met by a quizzical Collins.

'Just thought I'd go to the lavatory,' explained O'Keefe lamely.

He stood staring at the white tiled wall trying to think. A man came in and he went through the motions of urinating. What the hell were those two doing outside? He'd clocked them instantly. They were from the Det. And they were good. He'd been on a secret squirrel course with the pair of them at Pontralis. O'Keefe did up his flies and wondered how to get out of the building without being seen or arousing suspicion. He didn't think they'd seen him. He was doing nothing wrong, but he didn't want to appear in their reports.

He couldn't tell Collins or anyone else about the blokes outside. That would be tantamount to ordering their execution. In the passageway, O'Keefe caught the sleeve of the club steward. He was going to have to be blatant.

'Tell me.' He made his voice sound rough Falls. 'Is there a back way out of here?'

The steward nodded calmly. 'You're with Patrick John, aren't you? Come with me.'

'My missus . . .'

'In the black skirt and cream blouse, right? I'll fetch her.'

O'Keefe waited in the cellar room behind the bar. The old steward returned with a worried-looking Mary. The man unlocked the fire exit, turned off the light and pushed open the door. They found themselves in a narrow alley at the side of the club, shielded from the road by a brick wall specially built for the purpose.

'Bottom of the lane, turn left and a taxi will pick you up. Good night to you.'

O'Keefe was surprised at the efficiency, then realized the well-oiled route existed for the benefit of any player not wanting to be caught up in an army raid. Not ten paces around the corner, a taxi slowed up behind them and flashed its lights. They drove home in style; Mary, bless her, asked no questions.

Chapter Eighteen

'Jimmy Sands, how are ye?'

Fife's voice over their new telephone took O'Keefe by surprise. He hadn't spoken to his mate for months. He hadn't wanted to confess things were going badly. Better not to speak than have to openly admit he was a failure – or tell pointless lies of his successes.

'How're you doing?'

'I've been away. An unnamed Asiatic country. I can't tell you where over the phone, but it's got a triangle. At last I've found a place where even I can look down on the locals.'

O'Keefe guessed it must be Thailand, where the Regiment were training up local forces in the struggle against the drugs warlords.

The initial reserve fell away and within minutes they were chatting as if they had been in the Paludrin Club the night before. O'Keefe couldn't help himself, he wanted all the gossip from the Regiment and Fife was happy to oblige.

'Peter the Plank's been born again,' chuckled Fife. 'He came back from Delta Force in the States a reborn Christian. He's walking around with a Bible in his back pocket. Dodger Green's got made up to sergeant, B Squadron's gone to the trees. Two new guys from selection joined the squadron, one from the Black Mafia, the other from Green Howards. They seem okay.'

'No paras?' interrupted O'Keefe.

'No. The Green Jacket's joined Air Troop. Typical. Oh, Donald the Ditch, you know, the rupert in 17 Troop. He's got the MC. He told the lads he'd won it on their behalf, so they've organized a rota to wear it. Give him his due, he thinks it's great . . .'

Fife had returned after three months to find Vicky had let his clothes go mouldy. That was the final straw. He'd gone back to live in the bunks. Molecatcher had a steady bird. For all his talk of joining the singlies, he'd shacked up with the first bird he'd gone out with. Best of luck, said O'Keefe. He was never cut out for the single life. He needed a roof to fix or a living room to paper.

Kate and Shug were fine. Billy was doing well in the Cadet Force and showing no signs of becoming less army barmy. He seemed destined for the Paras.

'I gave a paper on why there should be twenty-four men in the troop rather than sixteen. More flexibility, more combinations. Went down well, but nothing will happen. By the way, everyone's using the Heckler and Koch MP5 over the water.'

'What's wrong with the M16?' asked O'Keefe.

'Need a heavier round. You need the 7.62 for cutting engine blocks. Same furniture as the G3.'

'Never liked them, too tinny for me. Why don't you use the SLR?'

'Can't get the folding stocks. Oh, Digger was casivacced out of your neck of the woods.'

'What happened?'

Fife burst into laughter. 'He got the clap. No duff. What's happening with you?'

In turn, O'Keefe told Fife that Mary and the children were fine. Liam had no long-term effects from his brain operation.

But Fife detected something in O'Keefe's tone.

'You sound a bit flat.'

'Ay, sometimes this place gets to me,' admitted O'Keefe.

'Are you working?'

O'Keefe took a deep breath. He'd been fearing this moment of truth. 'I'm in the construction industry.'

'What? Security work?'

'No, on the construction side.'

It slowly sunk in. 'Labouring!'

'Leave it.'

'What the fuck are you doing that for?' Fife was outraged.

'It's not easy to get a job over here,' replied O'Keefe slowly.

'Come on, Jimmy Sands, with your connections, it'd be a walk-over.'

'What connections?' demanded O'Keefe, sourly and Fife suddenly understood.

There was a clicking on the line.

'Is this secure?' asked Fife.

'I reckoned so,' replied O'Keefe, uncertainty creeping into his voice. The line went dead, crackled and came back to life.

'Are you there, Jimmy Sands? Hello. Are you there, Jimmy?' Hereford sounded a thousand miles away.

O'Keefe hesitated. 'Ay, Jimmy Sands. I'm still here.'

Chapter Nineteen

'Where all your rights have become an accumulated wrong, where men must beg with bated breath for leave to subsist in their own land, to think their own thoughts, to sing their own songs, to gather the fruits of their own labours, and, even while they beg, to see things inexorably withdrawn from them – then, surely, it is a braver, a saner and a truer thing to be a rebel, in act and deed, against such circumstances as these, than to tamely accept it as the natural lot of men.'

O'Keefe, flushed and vibrant, sat down to loud cheers and applause.

'Very pretty, Paddy. I didn't know Roger Casement's speech from the dock of the Old Bailey was in your repertoire.'

Patrick John Collins had been looking for O'Keefe for the past hour and the last place he had expected to find him was the Republican community hall. He'd called at the flat and found a subdued Mary.

'I don't know where he is,' she said truthfully. 'He goes out some nights. I assume it's for a drink, but I don't know where.' In her eyes was the fear that Paddy was seeing another woman. For the moment, at least, she didn't want to know. She just sat in front of the TV and wondered. 'I'm sorry, Patrick John, I can't help you.'

Collins's men trawled the local bars and he was coming to the same conclusion as Mary when they tried the community centre as their last chance – and found him.

'Is this where you've been coming at nights?' asked Old Holborn, incredulously. If O'Keefe thought he was safe and accepted here because he had defused the bomb, he was wrong. That was as closely guarded a secret as it could be in the circumstances. Collins had encouraged O'Keefe to bring Mary here, in his presence, on three separate occasions, but he had not intended O'Keefe to visit by himself – and certainly not to become the starring turn.

'Ay, I like it here,' replied O'Keefe simply.

'Why didn't you tell Mary where you were going?'

O'Keefe opened out his shovel-sized hands in a helpless plea. He wanted someone to explain to him why he hadn't told his wife. It was the same when he'd been on the Loughgall job. He'd been embarrassed, ashamed and confused then as well. He knew that one wrong question and he could be blown away, but he enjoyed the craic and he was among his own. His rendition of Casement's speech was becoming a regular request. He knew you always felt most comfortable with those who reinforce your own self: your beliefs, prejudices, tribal adhesions. Was he becoming one of the tribe? One of the underclass fighting against the Crown and all it stood for? So why didn't he tell Mary?

He'd first come by himself when he was still smarting over Detective Chief Inspector Boyle. The Special Branch man had driven up in his unmarked police car and just sat watching O'Keefe work, pushing wheelbarrows, carrying planks and pails of water. He had returned the next two afternoons as well, each time making sure O'Keefe saw him. The message was clear: You can do better than this, Paddy boy. He didn't know the depth of Paddy's pride and how each wordless visit was pushing him further across the divide; a divide from which it was becoming harder and harder to return.

Collins sat so his head was close to O'Keefe's and O'Keefe could smell the stale smoke and redolence of Old Holborn. 'I remember you telling me you were a medic, Paddy. And a medic I took you for. Well, we've use of a medical man this very night.'

'What's up?' O'Keefe instinctively became wary.

'It's nothing too serious and normally we could cope with

it, but there's a problem at the moment with holidays and that. It's a small bullet wound – not received from the authorities, I hasten to add – but it needs attention.'

'I can't perform a major operation, I haven't the tools nor the skills. If it's serious, then he should go to hospital,' whispered O'Keefe.

'He will, but not around here. Just patch him up so he can travel.'

'I'll need my medical pack.'

Collins gave him a grateful smile. 'It's in the car. I took the liberty when I called at your home. But you're a devilish hard man to find . . .'

From the man's musculature, O'Keefe reckoned he was in his forties. He couldn't see his face. The man sat naked to the waist and wore a black balaclava. He had forearms like hams with old tattoos deliberately defaced to prevent identification. A bullet had gone straight through his meaty left upper forearm behind the bone. There was a small round entrance wound and a larger jagged rectangular hole where the bullet had exited. O'Keefe looked at it with interest. He'd seen wounds like it before, but he didn't expect to see one in Northern Ireland.

He was somewhere in the prosperous tree-lined Protestant suburbs of northern Belfast, somewhere off the Malone Road, he thought. A large detached house with its own drive. Good cover. Better than a flat in the Ardoyne with army surveillance looking in through your front windows and the shorts – the armoured Land-Rovers – whirring past every few minutes.

The man sat on a hard chair in the bathroom.

'Anaesthetic?' queried O'Keefe.

The fourth man in the room held up a half-drunk bottle of brandy.

O'Keefe took off his jacket, undid the wishbone clip on the green medical pack and unrolled it on top of the bathroom chest of drawers. He scrubbed his hands and gently inserted his forefingers in both sides of the hole in the arm. They touched.

Never assume, he'd been taught. Others before had assumed they were treating the same wound until it was too late. He folded the man's arm so his left hand rested on his right shoulder.

On the way he'd made Collins find a late night chemist and sent the driver in for a pack of sanitary towels, hydrogen peroxide and a bottle of surgical spirit. Now he splashed the surgical spirit around the wound. He needed to debride it, cleansing it of the dirt and fibres from the man's shirt and jacket that had been carried into the wound. Bacteria were already at work bringing the risk of anaerobic infection which could result in gangrene.

'Are you left-handed?' asked O'Keefe, drawing an imaginary line under the arm joining the two holes.

'Nah.'

'That's all right because you won't be using this arm in a hurry,' said O'Keefe. He was intrigued at the angle of the wound. As far as he could make out, the man must have had his left arm raised above his head and the round had travelled across his face from right to left, missing his mouth and chin by no more than two or three inches. Strange.

'Get on with it,' growled the man.

O'Keefe splashed the clear spirit over the forearm, picked up a scalpel and sliced through the skin into the fleshy underpart of the arm.

The man gasped, tensed and clutched his shoulder with his left hand.

'Don't,' instructed O'Keefe, tapping the hand. 'You're making it worse. Try to relax. Give him a slug of brandy and a belt to bite on.'

'Fuck off. I'm all right.' The accent was the hard flatness of Northern Ireland but not Belfast. He guessed at Derry.

'Don't argue, arsehole.' O'Keefe thought it was time to show who was boss. He stood back and stared hard into the man's eyes – emotionless pools of mud. 'This is going to hurt like hell and I don't want you leaping around when I'm cutting. Fucking well do what you're told or do it your fucking self.'

'He'll have the belt,' said Collins in a placatory manner and nodded to the minder, who handed his thick belt to the seated man. He took a hefty swig of brandy, coughed and put the folded belt between his teeth. He nodded to show his readiness.

O'Keefe again ran the scalpel along the reddening wound, his forefinger guiding the shining, blood-flecked blade deeper and deeper until it entered the channel gouged by the bullet. With forceps in his left hand, he gently opened out the wound so the tunnel became a trench. The man did not flinch.

As he thought, the dead grey flesh started about two-thirds of the way along the bullet's passage. With blade and forceps he picked out the tiny shreds of cloth and shrivelled skin from the raw wound, wiping the instruments on a sanitary towel. He used another freshly opened towel to sponge up the blood behind the blade. When he reached the dead tissue, he stopped, checked that the hydrogen peroxide was less than six per cent and filled a syringe with the bleach. It fizzled as it came in contact with the flesh.

The man's eyes were cracked stone. He had neither moved nor murmured.

'Give him another drink. Not much longer,' reassured O'Keefe. The man had lost his bravado and he nodded stoically. 'The hydrogen peroxide is anti-microbial. It'll kill the surface bacteria. Now I've got to remove the dead tissue.'

O'Keefe wiped the scalpel and sluiced more surgical spirit over the blade. The amount of dead tissue increased near the jagged exit wound. Intricately, O'Keefe sliced and sliced again until he came to living flesh. The man put his hand inside his balaclava and wiped away the sweat running into his eye. O'Keefe motioned to the minder to hold a sanitary towel in place to staunch the oozing blood. He put his nose to the wound and sniffed. No foul smell. No infection yet. He dropped the scalpel into the basin, washed his hands and threaded the needle with Dacron.

'We didn't do needlework at school so this isn't going to be pretty, but it'll hold.'

O'Keefe pulled together the two edges of the wound with the forceps and inserted the needle. The man winced as he felt the thin plastic thread hauled through his muscle. O'Keefe tied the knot, cut the suture and repeated the procedure a further nine times.

He took the belt out of the man's mouth and inclined his head in appreciation of the man's bravery. His teeth were firmly imprinted on the leather. Enough for him to be identified by his dental records. Collins obviously had the same thought, for he set to bending and twisting the belt.

'Drink,' ordered O'Keefe. The minder thrust the bottle towards the wounded man, now slouched like an empty sack, but O'Keefe grabbed it and took a hefty swig from its neck. He took another pull and passed it to the man. Collins opened his tin of Old Holborn and started to prepare a roll-up.

'Keep your arm in that position and take whatever pain-killers you want. Reaction is going to set in and you'll feel like a pile of shit.' He reclaimed the bottle. 'I've done a butcher's job. He needs to see a doctor in twenty-four hours or you could end up with a one-armed hero.'

The man briefly mumbled his gratitude. He wasn't being supercilious now. He was whacked and words were too much of an effort.

'I'm obliged to you,' said Collins when they were back in the car. 'You said you were a medic and you are. That's what happens when you trust people. Now tell me, do you think he'll pull through?'

'I reckon so. He's got the constitution of a bull. And the courage of one.' O'Keefe paused. 'Anyone who's got his hands up to an AK47 and lives to tell the tale deserves to fight another day.'

'What!' Old Holborn turned sharply to stare at O'Keefe, who was savouring his moment as a detective.

'The way I see it, he was standing there with his hands up so they, whoever they are, had the drop on him with an assault rifle up his nose. Not many men would get out of that.'

Collins inhaled deeply. 'Remind me never, but never, to underestimate you.'

'Was I right?' O'Keefe was pleased with his deductions.

'More or less. I was telling the truth when I said the authorities were not involved. But how did you work it out? How did you know it was an AK47?'

'The shape of the exit wound and the position of the dead flesh,' explained O'Keefe. 'With the British army's SA80 or M16 with a 5.56 round, the morbidity is near the entrance wound because the round yaws when it hits the body. With the 7.62 of the FN, the dead flesh is around the exit wound because it's a larger, heavier round. The AK47 fires a 7.62 intermediate cartridge. It's the only weapon I've come across where the bullet exits sidewards. But I won't ask you what happened.'

'I think you know already, but listen. For your own good, stay away from the community centre for a while. I've a shrewd suspicion British intelligence has frozen the area. You don't want to be swept up in something that doesn't concern you – or even pictured at the end of a long lens, do you?'

'Here you are, Mary. I've brought the wandering laddie home.'

'I can smell the drink.' She looked directly at her husband putting down the medical pack on the table. The chill in the air in the room told Collins he should leave.

'Well . . . ?'

'Patrick John had a friend who needed stitching . . .'

'So where were you, Paddy?'

'I told you. Patrick John had a friend . . .'

'I mean before. Where did Patrick John find you?'

Mary folded her arms over her blue quilted housecoat and looked very small and vulnerable.

'He looked in all the pubs for you,' she prompted.

'I was in the community club,' O'Keefe finally replied.

She looked at him blankly and he repeated: 'I was in the Republican club having a few drinks.'

He was like a small boy caught picking his nose. He looked at the floor and became aware of her thin white calves over her flat slippers.

'Oh, Paddy!' She didn't know whether to laugh or cry. Finally she did both. 'Here's me been thinking you were out with the girls and all the time you were out with the Boys.'

She halted, trying to absorb this new information. Then her relief turned to concern. 'Paddy, Paddy, what have you been doing?' She spoke to him as she would to her son when he came back filthy from a day's play.

'Nothing,' he replied, as innocently as he knew how. 'Nothing.'

'You're not to get involved with them, do you hear? You're not.' She felt a shiver of anxiety for her man. 'You of all people. Ye've seen it from the other side.'

'Whist, woman. I'm not involved.'

'And what were you doing tonight?'

'Patching up someone who'd been hurt in an accident.'

'Accident my eye. There's hospitals for that sort of thing. See, already you're lying to me. Look at me now.'

'It was a bullet wound,' he confessed. 'But not one from the authorities.'

She thrust out her chin pugnaciously. 'And what'll become of you? You want to be a hero so they'll write songs about ye, is that what ye want? Songs with short verses and an even shorter chorus so the boys can remember them on Saturday nights when they've had a bevy. Let's have Paddy O'Keefe's song. How the brave hero was shot down and left Mary and his two weans.'

'Christ, woman!'

He kissed her forehead and she clung to him, a pathetic small creature who came up to his chin.

In bed she stayed awake a long time, staring in the blackness. On balance she wished he was seeing another woman. She would fight for her man against any female rival; how did she fight against Oglaigh na hEireann? She had done her best not to get personally involved, but her kith and kin had been drawn into the troubles in 1969. Her grandmother – the matriarch of their family – lived in Percy Street, a few doors down from the Finucane brothers and just the wrong side of the Falls Road. The family home had been bombed and burned by the rampaging Proddie mob while the B Specials had clustered on the corners smoking and watching. Her gran had been given an hour to get out and leave behind everything. Thirty years of her life hijacked in sixty minutes.

She had cousins who'd done time in the Kesh – one had been on the blanket for four and a half years – two others had died, one shot by the army, the other blown up. There was even an informer who had been executed by the IRA. But all the time she had tried to keep her distance and now this flesh-eating, blood-sucking monster had its talons into her man. So soft that he probably didn't feel them.

Two days later, she learned that they had won a week's holiday for four in Majorca. She wasn't surprised.

Boyle, wearing a dark suit and a Queen's College tie, to which he was not entitled, dawdled on the edge of the queue passing through the strict security procedures at Belfast's Crumlin Road courthouse. He clutched a battered black briefcase and did his best to look like a country solicitor. Ahead of him, Frannie McFadden, almost as broad as he was tall and his face mottled purple by drink, filed through the anti-rocket fence.

Police and court officials had their own separate entrance, but Boyle had his own reason for mixing with the public.

He didn't believe McFadden was just an unemployed steel erector who had been caught using a stolen credit card. He believed the man was a Provo quartermaster who liked to gamble and drink to excess. Boyle also believed Frannie had had his sticky fingers in the IRA's till and now he'd been nicked as he tried to make good his pilfering. If the Boys found out he'd lose his kneecaps.

Frannie's phone had been tapped for a fortnight now – and revealed nothing. Phone taps rarely did any longer. Everyone expected it. He had been watched periodically, but Boyle could not yet make out a case for the round-the-clock observation he would have liked. A few whispers and his gut told him he was right to be interested in Frannie, but he needed more than that. He wanted to see how he coped in the dock, and most of all he wanted to see his behaviour as he waited for his case to be called. Boyle had arranged the committal to be late in the morning session so Frannie had lots of time to sweat.

McFadden looked tense. Good. The more he sweated the more amenable he'd be to do business. Boyle was ready to help. He could weaken the prosecution case and give him a few thousand quid to pay his debts – if he played ball.

He passed through the fence under the hard stare of two policemen carrying submachine guns. He walked through the metal detector and put his briefcase through the scanner. His sergeant was already in the courthouse waiting to return his Smith and Wesson pistol. He held his arms away from his body for a brisk but efficient body search and entered the airlock between the two cordons.

Other undercover detectives, better trained at close surveillance and certainly less conspicuous than Boyle, could keep tabs on Frannie, but they could only report what they saw. Boyle would feel the accused's fears and emotions. He passed through the second separate screen, again showing bogus identity to an old sergeant who looked at the photograph of the solicitor from Bangor, compared it with

Boyle's face and returned it with a perfunctory nod. He and Boyle had sat opposite each other at a police dinner the previous Friday, but they were used to strange games here.

McFadden headed up the stairs straight for the public cafeteria, probably to meet his solicitor. As Boyle went to follow him his bleeper went off. At the same time the public address system crackled into life.

'PC Withers to the police room. PC Withers to the police room.'

It had to be a real emergency for his office to use his code name. Indicating to his sergeant to keep an eye on Frannie, Boyle made his way to the police room and dialled his direct line at Special Branch headquarters.

'Sir, she's pressed the tit.'

'Shit. When?'

'Ten minutes or so ago, sir.'

Hell and damnation. Boyle had been fearing this moment since that Chief Superintendent and his Inspector had been ambushed in South Armagh. He suspected that they'd been carrying copies of documents they shouldn't have. Documents which had fallen into the hands of their IRA killers. It hadn't taken the Provos' intelligence men long to add those bits to their jigsaw. A jigsaw which when completed gave a clear picture of the woman who had made the vital phone call just before the Loughgall ambush.

'Where was she lifted?'

'We think her house, sir.'

'Get an army chopper up, pronto. They'll probably head for Coalisland, but there're more lanes around there than there are people. Ask 3 Brigade to get their QRF to cordon the town. As much presence on the ground as possible without it looking as if we are mounting a major op. I'm on my way back.

'Hang on, sir, there's something coming in.'

Boyle chewed his lip with impatience. They owed it to the woman to get her out unscathed. It would deny PIRA a propaganda victory and send the message to other touts that SB would look after them.

'They've taken her in her own car, sir.'

'Yellow two-door Escort ELY 517,' said Boyle automatically.

As he sat in the police car speeding back to Knock he cursed being forced to leave the court. One tout less meant one more tout needed. He'd return to Frannie.

The woman gibbered in terror in the sweltering blackness. They had bound her hands behind her back and tied her ankles with wide brown tape. A third strip covered her mouth. She lay cramped and sweating on the car floor under a pile of coats. Her panic at suffocating made her breathe all the faster and she gave out small whimpers of animal fear.

They had come for her when she returned from taking her daughters to school. The big man was said to be the IRA boss in Coalisland – and Dom Maguire, thin and raw-boned, she knew as the younger brother of one of those killed in the Loughgall ambush. They had hard eyes and they looked grim as they barged their way into the house.

'Are ye alone?'

'Yes,' she gulped.

'Ye'll know why we've come.'

'No. No I don't. What is it? What do ye want?'

To her own ears, her voice sounded shallow and unconvincing.

'We have some questions to ask you, missus.' The big man had the unrelenting voice of command, but when Maguire spoke it was softer and more dangerous. The voice of someone who wasn't sure of himself or what his next actions would be.

'What sort of questions? I don't know what you mean.'

Maguire hit her, back-handed and hard; his knuckles crashed into her unprepared mouth making her bite her tongue. She reeled across the kitchen, knocking over two yellow chairs and slid down the wall. She tasted the saltiness and put up the tips of her fingers to catch the blood trickling over her cut lip.

'You do, you bitch.'

She didn't ask why he had struck her. Instead, she slowly rose to her feet and reached for her brown handbag on the sideboard. Maguire was there before her, shaking out its contents. Her purse, key ring, make-up, mirror, shamrock handkerchief and a packet of tampons. She picked up the handkerchief and dabbed at her mouth.

'You're coming with us, missus.'

'No. No. No.' She recoiled from the two men in horror. 'My daughters, they're only little. I've got to be here when they come home from school.'

'You can do this the hard way or the easy way, missus, but you're coming.'

She decided then that her only chance was to bluff it out. Screaming or fighting wouldn't do her any good. Outside the kerbstones of the small council estate were painted green, white and gold. Her neighbours wouldn't help her against the Provos. If they got wind of what was happening, they'd be off to establish alibis elsewhere.

'All right, I've nothing to fear. I'll come with you.'

Her positive reaction caught the men off guard. As naturally as she knew how, she began replacing her possessions back in her handbag, cursing her hands which betrayed her by shaking uncontrollably.

'You don't need that,' spat Maguire.

She clutched her bag before her in both hands like a shield. 'I don't know how long you'll want to ask me questions, but I'll need these.'

She held up the packet of tampons. 'It's my time of month.'

'All right, missus, all right.' The big man made a dismissive gesture and turned away in embarrassment.

She opened the flap of the box to check how many there

were – the most natural action of a woman setting off on a holiday – and moved them around with her fingers. The one with the red dot on top, she pressed as hard as she could without it becoming obvious.

Her mobile panic button. The one her handlers had given her in case of something like this happening. The small transmitter sent a signal to a relay hidden in the junction box of her home. The boosted signal was picked up by one of the many antennae on the 120-foot-high communications tower rising over the black concrete military police fortress dominating the centre of Coalisland.

'Christ, get a move on,' snarled the big man. 'We'll take your car.'

Maguire collected all the coats hanging on pegs in the hall.

'What do you want them for?'

'Just get on, missus.'

Opposite her semi-detached house, the driver of a local butcher's van watched as the two men escorted the woman down the cracked concrete path to her car. She was put in the back seat; Maguire sat next to her. The big man nodded to the van driver who drove away.

The woman looked out of the back window as they left her street, wondering if she would ever see her home again. Her daughters would return from school and find the house empty. Bile rose in her throat. She suddenly remembered that her mother was due to come round that morning to go shopping together. Her tongue was swollen and she gently rubbed it against her teeth to test the pain.

Beside her Maguire fidgeted nervously. As they left the last house behind and green hedgerows began to flash past, he erupted.

'You killed my brother, you bitch. You killed Fergus.' Suddenly he was on her, hitting her with both hands, trying to drive his fist into her nose. When she put up her arms over her face to protect herself, he punched her hard in her left breast and then in the ear, pulling her hair and biting her scalp in his frenzy.

'I didn't, I didn't. I swear I didn't,' she shrieked.

'Leave it,' growled the big man to Maguire. 'Fucking leave it, I say.'

Maguire pulled back, flushed and breathing deeply. He spat in her face.

They pulled off the road into a rutted farm track. She feared they were going to execute her then and there, but the big man tied her hands and feet and Maguire ripped off a third piece of tape with his teeth and pulled it tightly over her mouth. When she was trussed and helpless, he grabbed her ears and pulled her face towards him.

'By the time I've finished with ye, ye'll wish you was dead.'

He pushed her into the gap behind the passenger seat and piled the coats over her. She began to sob, snorting and snuffling through her nose. From the way she felt herself being thrown about, she reckoned they were travelling the back lanes. There was a helicopter somewhere overhead, but army helicopters were as common as sparrows and she thought no more of it. They were taking her to a safe house for interrogation and she didn't believe she would ever leave there alive. Her poor daughters. The thought of them made her wail deep in her throat. The car stopped and she was thrown against the seat in front. It slewed round, leapt forward and then braked sharply once more. The men swore. The doors were pulled open and she heard deep voices raised in anger. The coats were removed and she found herself looking directly at the muzzle of a big pistol and behind it the bulk of a stern policeman in a flak jacket. He pulled the tape off her mouth and she dissolved into hysterical tears.

'So how are you enjoying your job?'

'Fine, thank you. Is that why you stop and watch me?'

'I just wanted to see how you were getting on, Paddy.'

'Paddy was the man who dug the canals and built the railways. O'Keefe's the name. Mick O'Keefe. Mister O'Keefe to you, Mr Boyle.'

Boyle took the rebuke in silence and turned on to the coastal road. He drove quickly and lightly, like a ballroom dancer.

'There's a job going I thought you might be interested in.'

'I'm not talking about anything in this car. I am not an informer. I have never been an informer and I shall never be an informer for the RUC Special Branch.'

Boyle gave him a twisted grin. 'There's no tape recorder in this car, but if there was we could cut, splice and edit so that you would say exactly what we wanted.'

He parked next to a slipway and they walked a little way to lean on the sea wall watching the small dinghies fill their white sails in the soft afternoon light.

'I'll not take the Crown's pieces of silver,' said O'Keefe, aware of his dusty labourer's clothes compared with the other's suit.

'You already have,' said Boyle in his corncrake voice.

'Bollocks.'

'You're too good a man to waste himself. Look, I'm not prepared to see a fine soldier end up performing Casement's speech for pints in a Fenian club.'

The butter of flattery mixed with the vinegar of omniscience.

'Know everything, don't you?'

'"Where all your rights have become an accumulated wrong, where men must beg with bated breath for leave to subsist in their own land, to think their own thoughts, to sing their own songs . . ."' quoted Boyle. 'It's a fine, fine speech and one every right-thinking person would agree with, but I think it's being used under false pretences by the wrong people.'

'Maybe they're my people.'

Boyle turned away from the sea and the wind caught his sparse hair. He looked tired.

'Be logical. How can they be *your* people? Not long ago you were involved in military operations against them.'

'Maybe I didn't know what it was like to be a Catholic in Belfast then.'

'Crap. There's a whole lot of Catholics in Belfast and Northern Ireland – forty-three per cent of the population to be exact – but they don't all go around killing and bombing those who disagree with their views. Face the facts, O'Keefe, Sinn Fein is a minority party in the north and in Dublin it's regarded as an irrelevance at the best and an embarrassment most other times. Sinn Fein commands about fourteen per cent of the total electoral vote in the north and about forty per cent of the Catholic vote.'

O'Keefe watched the yachts scudding over the blue waves. He'd done some sailing with the Regiment. He wondered if Liam would enjoy it.

'And do you think the people of Eire want a united Ireland? They pay lip service to the ideal, but the IRA is illegal in the south and less than two per cent support Sinn Fein. Hardly a burning issue, is it?' He glanced at O'Keefe gazing out to sea and continued. 'There's no economic sense in reunification. Northern Ireland might be a poor country, but the south is even poorer. Did you know the British Government subsidizes the Province to the tune of around £2,000 per British citizen per year? In the past twenty years more than 17,000 new houses have been built, largely in Catholic West Belfast. If England's a colonial oppressor, she's an extremely benign one. It would be cheaper for her to cut her losses and run. What I'm trying to say is that you can be a Catholic in the north without having to join Sinn Fein or the Republican movement.'

'You can't be a Catholic and work, though,' rejoined O'Keefe.

'Yes, you can,' argued Boyle, lifting his large head to challenge the assertion. 'It's not easy for Proddies and it's worse for Catholics, but it is getting better. Each time a Catholic gets a job it should encourage his mates to look for work and not sit on their arses at home. Sometimes I think ghettos are in the mind.'

O'Keefe regarded the tall policeman with interest.

'You probably weren't here when the Provos had a campaign of burning down businesses, throwing Catholics out of work. It became hard for them to explain demanding Government investment in new businesses while they were torching existing ones. So the IRA tried to rationalize it with a poster with two pictures showing a gutted shop and a housewife being searched by two bored Jock soldiers. The caption read: "This (the burned out shop) is necessary to prevent this (the street search)." The disparity of violence seemed to have escaped the IRA.'

A dinghy close to shore went about, its sails flapping as she lost the wind. Boyle's deep, measured tones continued. 'The vast majority of Provos are local hoodlums turned community warriors. When you were in the Regiment you believed the IRA were cowardly, murdering thugs who you'd have taken out in one night if you had been allowed to. Why've you changed your mind? Have you seen any particularly heroic deeds in your time here?'

O'Keefe held up his hands to say enough. 'What do you want?'

'There's a job going which would suit you down to the ground.'

O'Keefe was suspicious. 'Oh, yeh?'

'There's an outward bound college being set up in Carrowkeel on Lough Foyle for deprived teenagers of both religions. They want someone with leadership qualities and enthusiasm to organize and oversee the outdoor activities. It doesn't pay a fortune, but it's living in and maybe Mary would get involved as well. I can put a word in.'

'Why would you do this for me?'

'The RUC are involved on the community side of the project. A mate of mine's in charge and you're perfect for the job. Believe it or not, Mr O'Keefe, I don't care a toss about your religion. As long as you are on the side of law and order, you're all right by me.'

Boyle would want something; there would have to be a quid pro quo, thought O'Keefe. But the offer was tempting. He looked again at the sailing yachts. Must be wonderful to have the freedom of the wind like that. To get away from the land and all its dusty problems.

Boyle followed his gaze.

'And you honestly think a Catholic could get that job?' demanded O'Keefe.

'They're looking for a Catholic. They want to attract teachers and instructors from both religions.'

Liam would enjoy the outdoor life. He tried to keep the enthusiasm out of his voice.

'So what does it involve, then?'

'It's very much what you want to make it. Sailing, climbing, orienteering, whatever.'

All second nature to him. And it would get the family out of West Belfast. A place in the country by the sea. A helmsman on a Mirror class dinghy was leaning so far over that his shoulders were brushing the waves. He would teach Liam to sail, swim; he could run survival courses, long hikes in the hills.

'So who would these kids be?'

'Inner city thugs. You'll have your hands full. When a local hero from the Falls meets his reflection from the Shankill, things get heavy. It'll probably be the first time they'll have met someone not from their tribe. That's why whoever's in charge has to be able to command respect, share enthusiasms and impose discipline when needed.'

Boyle could see O'Keefe's eyes coming alive with the challenge.

'The idea is they'll go home fitter and healthier and knowing that neither Proddies nor Catholics grow horns.'

'And what will you be expecting in return?'

'Nothing,' said Boyle, slowly and deliberately. A rare,

thin, unexpectedly daunting smile burst on to his severe face. 'What good do you think you'll be as an informer in Lough Foyle?'

That made sense, but O'Keefe still sensed a trap. In his experience policemen, especially Special Branch men, did nothing for nothing.

Boyle sensed his reservations. 'Talk it over with Mary and phone in the next few days.'

He could pull a few strings. Shouldn't be a problem. The conversation as they returned to Belfast was positively animated and amicable.

Chapter Twenty

Mary looked up from the kitchen sink as the rotors of an army helicopter began to play a tattoo above the flats, sending washing lines on the balconies billowing in its downwash. Two Saracens and a hardened Land-Rover swung into the square; squaddies piled out of the backs, SA80s strapped to their wrists, and took up firing positions pointing at the block on Mary's left. It was the first time in her tenure that the army had invaded the housing estate. She instinctively thought of the children. Katie was having tea at her friend Annie's and Liam was kicking a football with his crowd on the playing field. Soldiers were crouching behind low walls and the APCs, taut anxious faces beneath their helmets. Just young kids, thought Mary. Younger than Paddy when I met him that summer in Glasgow. She felt a sliver of pity for the soldiers. Mere targets, Paddy said. They never shot anyone, they were there to be shot. There was only one unit who killed on behalf of the Crown: the Regiment. She moved from the window and prepared to tackle the ironing, idly wondering why her period was late.

If she had stayed five seconds longer she would have seen Katie and Annie, hand in hand, toddle around the corner into Hamel Square and stop to stare solemnly at a corporal kneeling behind the Saracen, rifle to his shoulder. The girls had become bored playing with Annie's little ponies so they'd gone to buy sweets at the estate shop. Annie wanted to run home when the patrol arrived, but Katie was used to men in camouflage smocks and khaki trousers. They were nice to her and gave her bars of chocolate. These men, however, did not smile. They looked tense and frightened.

'Get off the streets, pet. Go home,' the corporal commanded in a Liverpool accent. Annie tugged at Katie's hand, but she stood her ground.

'My daddy's got one of those,' Katie chirped up, pointing to the rifle.

The hum and crackle of the radio came from the back of the Saracen. 'Alpha romeo has a negative on the sniper, Corp. The chopper's thermal imaging is on the blink. They're visual. Could be a come on.'

The corporal grunted. 'What did you say?'

'My daddy's got one of those,' Katie repeated uncertainly now. 'But I don't think it's the same.'

'How do you know your daddy's got one?' The corporal held her wrist and tried to sound unconcerned and friendly.

Katie knew her daddy had a gun. She'd seen him carrying it that day he hit the man in the barracks. And she had seen Daddy's friends with guns lots of times.

'I've seen it.'

'Hey, corp, maybe her old man is the sniper.'

'Shut it and pass the word for Sergeant Riley.' He reached in his pocket for chewing gum. 'What's your name?'

'Katie.' She examined the gum doubtfully.

'Where do you live, pet?'

'Alpha romeo's scrubbing.'

The helicopter lifted and wheeled away north-east towards Aldergrove as a scowling sergeant arrived with a stick of squaddies and Katie suddenly felt scared.

'Where do you live, pet?' the corporal quietly repeated.

'Number fifty-one Frank House,' replied Katie promptly, pointing to her home.

'Try it,' the sergeant instructed the radio operator.

'Five One Frank – Foxtrot Romeo Alpha November Kilo – House.' At army HQ Lisburn, a private tapped the address into a computer.

'Patrick Michael O'Keefe, 31 years of age; Mary Flora, 31; Liam, 5 and Katie, 3. Been there two months. No form.'

'He's not likely to work on his own turf, is he?'

'Where does he keep his rifle, sweetheart. Eh?' But Katie had clammed up. Her lower lip trembled and she presented a frail figure in her blue print dress and plastic sandals.

'Come on, pet, you can tell us.' The sergeant turned back to the radio operator. 'Patch me through to Brigade. We'll need the okay to go in.'

In the inquiry later, the evidence given by the soldiers of the Queen's Regiment and by the residents of Hamel Square differed sharply. However, they were agreed that three events now took place almost simultaneously, although it was pointed out they must have occurred in sequence because they provide a causal link.

Firstly, Liam and his friends heard that the army were in the square and ran back to see what was happening. Liam saw his sister standing in the middle of a group of soldiers. She was in tears. As he watched, she tried to run away but one of the soldiers held her by her thin wrist. Katie screamed in fear. Witnesses agreed that Liam tore into the middle of the group, kicking and hitting out to try to rescue his little sister.

A single shot echoed around the square. A soldier fell, blood spouting from his neck.

O'Keefe drove in to Hamel Square. He did not hear the shot, nor did he see his children, who were on the far side of a Saracen.

The testimony of the soldiers and the residents is now contradictory. The troops were united in their statements that, in deploying to react to the single shot and in their haste to get their wounded comrade to hospital, Liam was knocked over and trampled as they bomb-burst away from the open space. No one actually saw him fall.

Residents claim that when the shot was fired the sergeant swung at Liam with his rifle butt and then deliberately kicked him in the head as he lay on the floor.

The sergeant said in evidence that he believed at the

time that the girl had either been a come-on or the shot had been fired to delay the raid so the Provos could move the weapon believed hidden in 51 Frank House. He agreed he summoned reinforcements, recalled the helicopter and on his own initiative sent half the patrol to seal off the flats and raid number 51. He alleged he did not see the little boy lying on the pavement, blood seeping out of his nose and ears.

But Mary did when she looked out after the shot. She thought Liam had been hit. She was out of the door of the flat and running hard when the first soldiers turned into the corridor. It appeared as though she was fleeing. Three of them picked up Mary and manhandled her back into the flat. She fought like a wildcat. Only the visor saved the eyes of one soldier. Nothing saved another's groin and he went down vomiting. Then one caught her with the barrel of his rifle, breaking two teeth and splitting her lip. With difficulty they put plasti-cuffs on her.

Paddy saw Liam when he got out of his car. The boy lay on the pavement with his head lolling in the gutter. A small pool of blood was collecting around his cheek in the gravel. He heard a woman scream in fury and the sound of a man's voice raised in anger. Ignoring the troops crouched in their firing positions, he ran to his son. As he did so, one Saracen roared away in a cloud of blue diesel smoke and two armoured Land-Rovers swung into the square, blocking the entrance. Soldiers dashed to their fire positions, calling hoarsely.

'Liam.' The boy had turned putty grey. O'Keefe cradled his son in his arms.

'Get on the net. Get an ambulance,' ordered O'Keefe.

'Fuck off out of here,' screamed a squaddie.

Paddy began to pick up Liam when the soldier, eyes glazed in fright, pushed him away. 'Fucking leave him, I tell you.'

'Use your comms to get Brigade to summon an ambulance,' shouted O'Keefe.

'Who the fuck are you to give orders?'

'I'm his father.'

The young soldier tensed; his eyes flicked around searching for his mates.

'Your son?' He jerked his rifle at O'Keefe. 'Right, you Mick bastard. In the back.'

O'Keefe's jaw dropped in amazement as the soldier waved his gun barrel towards the back of the APC. 'My son needs help.'

'Get in the fucking back or I'll blow your fucking Taig head off.'

'My son . . .'

'Fuck your son. He won't grow up to be a fucking IRA gunman now, will he?'

O'Keefe went as cold and detached as he had ever been in his life. Liam needed skilled medical help and needed it quickly. He was going to pick up his son, put him in his car and drive him to the Royal Victoria Hospital.

'I've got the fucking father, sarge,' the soldier sang out triumphantly, digging the muzzle into O'Keefe's neck.

Never do that, sunshine. I can turn before you can pull the trigger. It only takes a couple of degrees either way and you've missed. As soon as Paddy felt the barrel against his neck, he began to rise slowly, leaning back to keep contact with the cold metal, until he was balanced and coiled like a spring, then he exploded up and backwards, knocking the rifle to one side. The flak jacket and protective helmet offered few targets so O'Keefe struck the soldier with his fist on the side of the neck and then again on the point of the jaw. The soldier crumbled; his rifle, tied to his wrist, clattering to the ground by his side.

As he picked up his limp son, Katie emerged from behind a Land-Rover and flew to his side, her face streaked with tears.

'Daddy, daddy.'

She clung to him as he walked to his car. He was at the passenger door when three wide-eyed, frightened soldiers, breathing heavily, caught up with him. The first hit him in the kidneys with the butt of his rifle, the second struck him in the back of the neck. O'Keefe, still carrying his unconscious son in his arms, roared with pain and fell to his knees. The third squaddie lashed out with his boot into O'Keefe's unprotected face. He fell back and Liam spilled from his arms. More soldiers ran up and O'Keefe, his hands cuffed behind his back, was dragged towards the APC.

'I want my da. I want my da,' screamed Katie, trying to touch her father.

'Fuck off, you mick brat.'

O'Keefe was thrown into the dark interior, two squaddies jumped in on top of him, the doors clanged and the Pig rolled away.

'Well, sergeant?'

'A British army medical pack, sir, but it's not a standard one. Lots of extra bits and pieces including a trauma pack. Our own medic is green with envy. Wants one like it.'

'No sign of a weapon?'

'No, sir, and we've had everything up. Looked everywhere. There's no weapon concealed. Stake my life on it.'

'What does the wife say?'

'Nothing printable, sir. She clobbered young Wilson a treat, though.'

'Tell him to put it down to experience. Right. Get the men together and let's get out of this dump. There's a full-scale riot brewing and I don't want to be caught here with these high-rise blocks around. How's the boy?'

'The ambulance is about to leave, sir. Perhaps we should exfil with that.'

'All right, sergeant. Make your report as soon as you get back. Make sure everyone in the initial contact has a good look at it. How long was that boy lying there in that condition?'

'Difficult to say, sir. There was a contact on and we were following a hot lead to a potential illegal weapon.'

'Yes, yes, I know all that, sergeant, but there'll be shit flying on this one. Make sure everyone understands.'

'Excuse me, sir.' The corporal approached with a piece of paper. 'British army discharge papers, sir. Sergeant Patrick O'Keefe was discharged from Para Reg in November last year.'

The officer closed his eyes. 'Oh fuck.'

The first stones rattled against the front mesh screen of the Land-Rover.

Golden Virginia surveyed the wreckage of the flat with grim satisfaction. The bastards had done a thorough job. Floorboards pulled up and splintered, the ceiling ripped open in the search for false cavities. Wardrobes knocked over and hacked to pieces. And the soldiers had found nothing because there was nothing to find. She waited until the first volunteer arrived to begin putting the place back together and then set off for the hospital.

'You're lucky you didn't get the beating of your life after what you did to that soldier. What's your fucking game, Paddy?'

'How's my son? Where is he?'

The battalion intelligence officer sneered coldly at O'Keefe.

'I don't know how your son is and I don't care. This special British army medical pack was found in your home. Where did you get it?'

O'Keefe couldn't believe this was happening. A twathead, tossing crap-hat asking him about a fucking medical pack while Liam was lying unconscious somewhere.

'The quicker you answer my questions, the sooner you may have access to your son, Paddy.'

'Paddy was the man who dug your canals and built your railways. My name is O'Keefe. Mick O'Keefe, Mister

O'Keefe to you.' He remembered he had used the same speech some time recently. He couldn't recall when.

'When did you last use this pack, Paddy?'

'I'll have you for this. I'll fucking have you.' O'Keefe eyes burned like a wild animal's.

The room was windowless and bare apart from three folding chairs and the trestle table with two telephones. He was in one of the heavily fortified British bases. He didn't know which.

'Why would a building labourer in a council flat in West Belfast need a trauma pack?'

O'Keefe had never hated anyone as much as he hated that rupert then. He felt his right eye closing from the beating in the back of the Saracen, saw his Liam lying in the gutter, and his hatred swept over the whole fucking British army. He set about freeing his hands cuffed behind his back.

'What have you murdering bastards done to my son?'

'All in good time. Where did you steal this pack? When did you last use it?'

His silence infuriated the battalion officer, hoping for a quick result before he had to hand his prisoner over to the central interrogation unit.

'Get it into your fucking head, I don't give a toss about your son. I want to know how you got this?'

I am going to kill you, vowed O'Keefe, silently. You and the bastard who injured Liam. I am going to find him and kill him for what he did to Liam and then I am going to kill you for being a cold-hearted bastard who can't understand a father's love for his son.

'You assaulted a British soldier. So did your wife. We'll hand you over to the RUC, but first I want to know who you killed for this go faster pack.'

There was a soft knock at the door. The captain rose and went into the passageway. An MP carrying a baton and wearing a pistol, uselessly in a buttoned-down holster, stood against the wall by the door glowering at the prisoner. O'Keefe, who was almost out of his plasti-cuffs, thought about breaking the man's neck.

The captain returned. There was an angry flush on his smooth cheeks.

'You've been wasting our time, haven't you?'

'I thought you'd been wasting mine,' snarled O'Keefe.

'You kept that medical pack as a souvenir when you left the British army . . .'

The white phone rang.

'Hereford!' The captain looked daggers at O'Keefe. 'Fucking little macho men.'

He put down the phone. 'You've done a lot with your life since you left the so-called élite, haven't you?'

'Failed selection, did you?'

The captain snarled and O'Keefe knew he'd hit home. 'Mind your fucking manners. You're still looking at six months for assaulting that squaddie and so is your slag of a missus.'

O'Keefe refused to rise to the bait. Instead, he slipped off the cuffs and rose to lean his large fists on the table in front of the startled captain, who swallowed nervously.

'I want an inquiry into what your men did to my son. They're a disgrace.'

The captain was feeling his way towards the panic button under the table when the phone rang again. Not taking his eyes off O'Keefe, he picked it up. From the change in his demeanour, O'Keefe knew he was listening to a superior officer.

'But . . . yes, sir . . . but . . . yes, sir.'

He put down the phone and glared at O'Keefe. 'You can go. I'm sure you know the procedure should you wish to make a formal complaint.'

'Where's my son?'

'I'm informed he's at the Royal Victoria Hospital.' The captain had one last laugh. 'Rioting mobs have been on the streets because of an incident in the locality of Hamel Square. The buses are off the streets. You'll have to walk.'

* * *

206

It was long gone midnight and O'Keefe slumped at the scrubbed kitchen table, the dregs of a bottle of whiskey in front of him. He ran his hand through his thick hair and his eyes were reddened, tired and inflamed as a smoky sunset.

'I prayed over that boy,' he murmured as he stared sightlessly deep into his glass.

'I know,' said Collins, resting his hands around a large mug of tea.

'I wish to God I'd never come back to this place.'

'You mustn't blame yourself.' Collins was aware all he could offer were clichés of comfort and sympathy. He found room in the overflowing ashtray for another butt. *'Ira furor brevis est.'*

O'Keefe's flat had been duly photographed in its wrecked state and then a company of volunteer carpenters, glaziers, electricians and plasterers had descended. Mary had had two teeth removed, another capped and the inside of her mouth stitched. She was being kept at the RVH overnight for observation. There was nothing more to do at the hospital.

'I'm going to get those bastards. I'm going to get them if it's the last thing I do.'

O'Keefe felt he would never sleep again. Neighbours had eagerly told how Liam had been felled by a rifle butt after he bravely went to his little sister's aid. Now his brain was racing and sometimes his anger ran away with his tongue and he became incoherent, raging at the cruelty and the callousness of the British army. He placed the blame squarely on the sergeant who had struck down Liam and the intelligence captain who refused to help O'Keefe see his son.

'I'm going to kill them,' he said with an air of finality. He took another drink and decided to share his secret with Old Holborn.

'I've got a gun hidden.'

'What sort of gun would that be?' asked Collins in an indulgent tone.

'A nine milly Browning.'

'A pistol's not going to be a lot of good against a general purpose machine gun, is it?'

'It's better than nothing.' O'Keefe emptied the bottle into his glass. 'I might be drunk, Mr Collins, and I am certainly angry, but I give you my word that I will kill those men. I shall show them the same mercy and compassion as they showed my Liam.'

His eyes came up and held Collins's patient grey ones and they were empty of pity.

'Believe me,' he hissed with a fierce intensity.

'I believe you, but tell me tomorrow when you're sober.'

'I'll tell you tonight, tomorrow and every day until eternity. They were Queen's Regiment. You'll know where they're based.'

Collins nodded. 'But I don't think you'll do much good with a pistol.'

'I'll do my best.' O'Keefe glared at Collins, daring him to contradict him. Collins took his glasses off and gave them a polish. The action made him appear all the more like an academic.

'I've something better than a 9mm pistol,' he confided in a conversational tone. 'It'd be no good in the hands of an amateur, but then you're not an amateur, are you, Mr O'Keefe?'

Part Three

Chapter Twenty-one

There wasn't another house in sight; just the deserted fields, seamed by drystone walls and the odd copse, rolling away towards the blue-tinged foothills of Slieve Gullion in the far distance. From the bungalow, set on a small hill, Mary O'Keefe could see for miles. To the west the silver of Muckno Lake across the border in Eire and to the south the stream which would grow into the Creggan river. Soon it would be dusk and not a light would be seen. Mary watched from the french windows as the local co-operative milk tanker trundled along the narrow lane at the bottom of her large, steeply rising garden. A pale blue car which had been following the tanker turned into the gateway, rattled over the cattle grid and carefully negotiated the two deep potholes in the winding drive. Mary waved and went into the kitchen to put on the kettle.

'You must do something about those potholes.' Yvonne Hogan bustled in, arms full of bags and packages.

'I'm sorry. I keep meaning to,' lied Mary. 'Thanks for doing the shopping.'

'No problem. I was going myself so it wasn't a big deal.' Yvonne lived at the farm a half a mile away over the hill. She was plump, ruddy, always busy and always had time for a cup of tea and a chat. 'And what have I got for my little treasure?'

Bridie, hearing Yvonne's voice, came flying into the room to be picked up. She sat in Yvonne's arms happily sucking on an ice lolly.

'Look at that mess on your tee-shirt. You only put it on half an hour ago,' said her mother despairingly.

'They're into everything at that age. Aren't you, Boo?'

Bridie, known as Boo because of her early efforts to pronounce her name, simpered with pleasure.

'Boo was confined to her room because she threw her cereal over the cat.'

'They talk about the terrible twos but now she's four she's become a right little scamp.' Yvonne stroked Boo's straight blonde hair. 'She's got your eyes, you know, Mary.'

'Well, she didn't get her temper from me.'

'Oh no?' laughed Yvonne. 'I was there when that potato lorry blocked you in, remember?'

'She's too used to getting her own way, aren't you, madam?' Boo hid her face in Yvonne's red, wrinkled neck, delighted to be the centre of attention.

'It's inevitable when you don't have a man about the house. You have to spoil them a bit.'

Mary paused from unpacking her shopping to stir the teapot.

'Katie's good with her, isn't she?'

'Katie's old for her age. Eight going on forty-eight.'

'It's a shame there aren't more little girls for her to play with. I still think you're very brave, living out here all by yourself.'

'I've told you, Yvonne. I wanted to get away from Belfast.'

Yvonne made sympathetic noises. 'Of course, after the explosion and everything. Will you be putting a memorial notice in the papers for the anniversary this year?'

'No. Not this time. I'll never forget but it does no good dwelling on the past,' murmured Mary. 'You see the notices year after year and you wonder why they do it. Some people seem to need to make a public show of grief. I don't.'

'Of course.' Yvonne struggled to pick up her tea with Boo still clinging to her neck. 'And you'll always have the little one.'

'Yes, I'll always have Boo,' began Mary and stopped with a haunted far away look in her eye. 'But then I thought I'd always have . . .'

212

She tailed away in her own thoughts. Yvonne sipped her cup of tea. Life had dealt Mary O'Keefe some cruel blows, to be sure it had.

'You set out your stall there, old chap. Most impressive.'

Simon Baines-Hickey leaned nonchalantly against the counter in Annie's Bar and straightened his blue silk tie. He had invited Jolyon Rodgers to hear his maiden speech and now received the congratulations as his due.

'Well done, Simon.'

'Thank you, Sir Eric.' He nodded deferentially to the senior party whip.

'Not many youngsters are willing to dabble in Northern Ireland. Something of a minefield, but then I suppose with your military background you can speak with first-hand knowledge. A little controversial for your maiden speech, eh?'

'That Devlin woman could do it – it shows our side are not afraid to confront the issues.'

'Quite. Quite. Keep it up.' The whip drifted off.

'You've chosen Northern Ireland because no one else will touch it,' accused Rodgers.

'It's an easy way to get noticed in a short time. As you know, I'm in a hurry.' Baines-Hickey ordered a half of Federation beer for himself and a large scotch for his guest.

'And you're not going to give up your connections in the arms trade or that murky private security world in which you dabble?'

Baines-Hickey looked aghast. 'Of course not. Why should I?'

'Conflict of interest, maybe?'

'Rubbish. I'm merely availing myself of the opportunity to study the arms industry at first hand. I'm planning to get on the Defence subcommittee.'

'Ah yes, we have a favour to ask.' Baines-Hickey took a mental step backwards. 'We understand there's going to be a Select Committee on merchant banking.'

'Then you know more than I do.' The MP bristled.

'The bank's intelligence has always been first class as you know from your time there.' Baines-Hickey nodded warily. 'It would be helpful if you could be on that committee. After all you have worked for a merchant bank.'

'Ye-es.' The politician sounded doubtful. 'Can't apply for *too* many committees. Looks pushy. I am a new boy after all, remember.'

Rodgers had expected this reaction. He took a sip of whisky and waited as two florid, corpulent men shook Baines-Hickey's hand.

'Sorry, old boy.'

It wasn't clear if Baines-Hickey was apologizing for the interruption or turning down Rodgers's suggestion.

'The time spent in committee won't harm your outside business interests. Now you've completed the end user certificates, you'll want financing for those Stingers for Zagreb. We could probably knock half a point off for a good friend.'

Baines-Hickey wondered how Rodgers knew about the surface to air missiles deal. The carrot and the stick. He put a brave face on the situation.

'No, no. You misunderstand. I'll be delighted to help the bank in any way I can. I was just wondering how to get on the committee. Still, I'm sure it won't be a problem.'

'I'm sure it won't be,' agreed Rodgers.

Jenny Dove had been instructed to park no closer than 300 yards from the block of flats and to save time she made the mistake of trying to carry the heavy sports bag and the small vacuum cleaner in one journey. As she entered the block's grimy hallway with its scrawled graffiti, the lift doors were just closing. She started to run, the doors opened again and the vacuum cleaner spilled from her gloved hands. A pimply young man with a shock of blond hair helped her to pick it up.

'Thank you.'

'Which floor do yer want?'

'Seventh please.'

As she spoke, she realized he would spot her accent as an outsider. She kept her eyes down, but she could feel him staring at her in open curiosity. Jenny deliberately wore cheap, ill-fitting jeans and an anorak, but there was no disguising her Slavic cheek bones nor her amber-copper hair. He would remember her. She dawdled until the lift doors closed, then hurried along the corridor and let herself into flat 39.

Jenny approved of the lace curtains and pulled them back to peer at the heavy black gate in the distance. She plugged in the vacuum cleaner and thoroughly cleaned the living room before pulling an old table near the window and erecting a screen using a large piece of black cloth and two long telescopic aerials. The sports bag she left at the bottom of the wardrobe under a pile of old blankets. When she left twenty minutes later, she double-locked the flat door.

She had intended to walk down the back stairs to avoid meeting people in the lift, but as she approached the stairwell she made out a dark figure standing motionless behind the frosted glass door. Changing her mind, she continued on to the lift.

Once outside the block she walked briskly to her car, frequently looking over her shoulder. Once the vacuum cleaner was in the boot she breathed more freely. You're becoming scared of shadows, she chided herself. That's what a couple of weeks away does for your nerves.

'He's killed at least a dozen men and we still don't have a clue who he is. It cannot continue.' Brigadier Bob Doughty, newly appointed Director Special Forces, Northern Ireland, looked around the conference table. 'Surely someone in the intelligence community must have a sniff of him.'

'The sniper doesn't match any known profile, but I'd bet

you a pound to a penny that Collins is involved some-where.' DCI Boyle leaned back in the chair and played with his pencil.

'Why do you say that?' demanded Doughty.

'New information, reliable information, suggests that Collins runs some form of special operations executive.' Boyle chose his words carefully. 'This would explain why he's not shown up before. We should give his Community Aid Centre a higher priority.'

'Jack, does the Department know anything they're not sharing?' Brigadier Doughty turned to MI5's representative from the Security Liaison Office at Lisburn.

'Certainly not.' The plump young man with wavy hair was most indignant. 'We've nothing on him. Tapped his phone a few times, but he's always been clean. There's never been anything to connect him with any PIRA oper-ation and nothing to link him to the gunman.'

'Why aren't the touts doing the business?' asked the brigadier.

Boyle finally broke the silence around the table. 'It's because they're not that leads me to suspect Old Holborn.'

'Irish logic,' laughed Doughty. The others chuckled. Boyle's nationality was in a minority among the eight men. 'Though I take the chief inspector's point. The sniper's becoming the stuff of legends, but that's all he is – myth and legend. He cannot be allowed to continue to kill our top men seemingly at will.'

Boyle cleared his throat. 'I'd like to put Collins under surveillance using the Branch's E4A and the eavesdrop-pers from E4B. We should have a permanent phone tap – though I don't expect much from that – and buzzword intercepts on his known associates and every phone within half a mile of his house. I'll work out the trigger words.'

'It's not an easy house for the watchers,' warned the major in charge of 14 Intelligence Company. 'You have to walk men through and you're looking at a lot of manpower and for a long time.'

'Chief Inspector?' The DSF was prepared to hold the ring.

Boyle looked slowly around the table at the counter-terrorist chiefs. 'It's the best lead we have. Collins is known to be security conscious to the level of paranoia. That would account for the lack of information about the marksman. There are men on the Provos' Northern Council who don't know who he is. I believe Old Holborn has an independent command of some kind and he's running the hitman. But if you were to ask me for proof, I couldn't give it. It's just my gut feeling.'

'We all know your gut feelings, so if everyone's agreed . . .' said Doughty. 'Good.'

'Hands off cocks. Hands on socks. Move it. Move it. Zero dark thirty.' The door crashed open, lights blazed on and the two corporals screamed through the small barrack room like banshees. 'Up. Up. Move it.'

The beginning of another day's training at Browning Barracks, Aldershot. Billy, who had been sleeping like a baby, leapt out of bed. His first waking thought was hunger. He was always hungry. He was eating for three and he was still starving. He'd put on a stone in training. His hair was cut to the wood. He was permanently knackered.

He'd never been so happy in his life.

Billy hurried through the room jobs, sweeping around his bed space, making his bed with geometric precision and helping his scruffy, cack-handed mate get his bed up to standard before going off for scoff. The platoon corporal, giving his lads the once over before they went on muster parade, nodded with approval at Billy's black army boots. Billy had spent the previous evening scratching the paint off the eyeholes to expose the brass; he had worked away for hours ironing polish into his boots to burn out the creases and then worked away with cotton wool and water at the leather until it shone.

'Where'd you learn that trick, son?' asked the training screw, indicating the gleaming eyeholes.

'My brother, corp.'

'Good lad. Follow him and you won't go far wrong.'

'Thanks, corp.' Billy swelled with pride.

The parade ground was as grey as the sky – and about as large. It was cold and looked like rain. The sergeant glowered at the neat ranks of young soldiers, immaculate in their olive drab sweaters and peaked caps, and filled his lungs.

'At the cautionary word of command, brace up, shoulder movement, gain height. Stand upright. Get your neck back in your collar.'

Sixty recruits pretended to be soldiers.

'On the command Attention you will bend the knee, bend it sharply and drive the foot in flat and hard. Squad . . . Atten-shun.'

At last it's for real, thought Billy, straining to gain an inch and staring straight ahead from under his peaked cap. Years of dreaming. Now here I am.

'On the command Stand At Ease, the left foot will be driven out approximately thirty inches and the hands placed behind the back. In this position you will not relax. You are not standing easy. You are stood at ease. Right. Gentlemen. Stand . . . at . . . Ease.'

Rear rank instructors moved like sharks along the lines of the young soldiers, tweaking shoulders, moving a leg further out, adjusting head positions. No one had to adjust Billy's stance or correct his uniform. He was turned out like a Guardsman. After all the hours playing soldiers and Fife's instruction, it was second nature to him. He felt he had come home.

'Corporal, march them off. About turn. By the left, quick march. Left right left right.'

The sergeant crossed to the slight, sandy-haired man watching from the edge of the parade ground. His beret was folded in his pocket and he wore no rank but there was an air about the man which said he belonged here.

'Jimmy Sands, the Lean Mean Killing Machine. How're you doing?' greeted the sergeant, shaking hands.

Fife was surprised his nicknames had reached his parent regiment. 'Just come down to pick up some kit.' He didn't elaborate.

'Your nipper's doing well. Coming for a brew?'

'Ay, grand. So he bloody well should. He's wanted to do this since he was toddling.'

'The screws say he doesn't stop talking about you.' The two men walked towards the sergeants' mess. 'You've got a good lad there. Willing to help others. A natural leader. He'll end up with a commission. How d'you fancy your nipper as your rupert?'

'Bollocks. He wouldn't fucking dare. Anyway I've warned him the last thing he ever wants to do is to get himself noticed,' laughed Fife, delighted at Billy's progress but determined not to show it.

'He'll win the Best Recruit Shield hands down. If anything he's too eager. He's trying to catch you up.'

'Tell him about the two bulls.'

'What?'

'You know. The young bull said to the old bull: Let's run down to the field and screw a few heifers. The old bull said: Let's walk down and screw them all.'

'The temporary ceasefire ends at midday. The same time as that scumbag finishes his shift. It'll be a timely reminder the war's still on. As chiefie his car is closest to the gate, but he stops to talk to other warders,' said Jenny Dove, closing the wardrobe door.

'One shot is all I need.'

'This one is an absolute swine. He's a big noise in his local Orange Lodge and he gives our boys a hell of a time of it. They've only to look at him sidewards and they're in solitary.'

Jenny repeated the briefing she'd been given. She passed the sports bag to her colleague, who began unpacking it.

Tense and focused, they'd hardly spoken since they met that morning for the first time for two weeks.

The Robar 50 BMG weighed 25 pounds when fully assembled. The rifle was used by US Special Forces snipers and it must have been stolen from them for it was camouflaged in their colours, useless in this room but handy in the field.

The gunman clipped the 29-inch-long chrome molly barrel on to the composite stock and attached the telescopic sight. The distance from the flat to the prison gates was 600 yards. A good sniper's range. Someone had been clever spotting this shot. Buildings either side formed an urban canyon so that he could see only the prison gate and thirty yards of the warders' car park. It was perfect. By the time the authorities worked out where the shot had come from they'd be well away.

'How was Washington?'

'Academic conferences are always a bore,' said Jenny, adjusting the back screen so the marksman would not be seen from outside. 'But I had to go. You understand don't you?'

'Did you give your lecture or whatever you call it?'

'My paper. Yes, it went down well. A Princeton dean suggested I might apply for an assistant professorship there.'

'Did you shag him?' he demanded brutally.

Jenny crossed the room and squeezed his balls. 'And what's it to you when I'm away?' She narrowed her eyes in sexy invitation and released him. 'No. But it wasn't for want of him trying.'

He didn't know whether to believe her. He slid in the trigger group and inserted the bolt before selecting one of the specially made .50 cartridges, weighed to the exact number of grains, and thumbed it into the magazine in his left hand. He added two more and clipped the magazine on to the rifle.

Jenny pulled the table closer to the window and opened the casement. The gunman ran his fingers over the sill to check for the dust that would billow outwards with the explosion, betraying their position. He trusted Jenny to have cleaned thoroughly, but he checked anyway. The door was locked and bolted and a chair wedged under the handle. He rested the bipod supporting the heavy barrel on the table, being careful it did not protrude out of the window. He was invisible against the black back screen.

Behind him Jenny swept the surrounding area with her binoculars. There were few people about the streets. Sunday morning hangovers were keeping them at home. The sniper settled over the weapon, pointing at the green Volvo estate geometrically parked in its bay. As midday approached the need for sexual release began to surge through Jenny. She rubbed her hand over her breasts and felt her nipples harden and rise, slowly she slid her hand between her legs and suppressed a groan of pleasure. God! How much she wanted to be fucked while he pulled the trigger or better still, pull the trigger herself while he took her from the back. Jenny bit her lip at the sublime agony of the thought.

A clock struck twelve. The end of the ceasefire. No one could say they didn't keep their word. No one could say the Movement was spent, either. Relax, get comfortable. This was a good shot. No breeze, cold clear day. Nice gentle downward angle. A group of men wearing raincoats over their dark uniforms came out of the gate. They'd finished their shift promptly. In a hurry to get away. Well, one wasn't going far. There he was. Red-faced, short, bull-chested. His body language said he was the boss.

The warders drifted towards their cars. In the flat the killers pulled on their ear defenders. The Chief Prison Officer detached himself and halted at the car door, keys in hand. His head moved in slow motion into the cross hairs. The sniper exhaled gently, his finger tightening around the trigger set to a feather-light two and a half pounds.

The dull boom filled the room and echoed around the thin walls. Dust rose from the floor and drifted down from the ceiling despite Jenny's efforts. Through the sight, the gunman saw the warder's head explode in a cloud of bloody miasma. He was out of his boiler suit, worn to reduce the possibility of leaving forensic evidence, and stripping down the Robar before he turned to find Jenny standing flushed and open-mouthed, her lips heavy with promise and her pupils dilated.

'Come on.'

Jenny snapped out of her sexual trance, placed the rifle parts in the large sports bag and hurried out. The lift was waiting. They were half a mile away before the first police sirens could be heard.

Chapter Twenty-two

Patrick John Collins paused, holding the blue flame of the petrol lighter an inch from the end of his roll-up, and stared hard at the commander of the East Belfast Brigade who, against all his expectations, was still alive.

'No. No. No.'

'The orders come directly from the Chief of Staff.' Sean O'Hanlon did not try to keep the victory out of his voice.

'If he wants Boyle taken out, then we can do it our way.'

'The Chief wants a showcase execution. Plenty of publicity. They're going to make a video of it to show around the clubs. Be good for recruiting.'

O'Hanlon's left eye was still wandering, Collins was glad to see.

'My man is successful because he works independently of the ASUs. He keeps away from the cowboys.'

'Whacking British army officers, RUC men and chief prison officers like the one last month. Not very sexy, is it?' sneered O'Hanlon.

Collins was not prepared to let O'Hanlon see how angry he was, nor could he bother to explain that the targets were strategic, hitting infrequently but where they did the most damage. He left the fireworks up to the others. Their hits had as much long-term impact as a roman candle. An incandescent whoosh, a lot of noise and light, and then you found nothing had changed.

'The ASU won't like having an outsider put in to lead them.'

'They'll do as they are told,' snapped O'Hanlon. 'I don't know why the Chief is so keen for your man to lead this operation. The boys are perfectly capable.'

Collins knew. He was successful as director of special operations because he was careful, very careful; always working with small groups or individuals; always in tightly sealed compartments. No one knew what he did. No one except the Chief of Staff. But the stories were already being repeated in the clubs and bars of the marksman who killed with a single shot and never hurt innocent women and children. He was becoming a cross between Robin Hood and the Jackal.

Collins knew the more talk, the more his man would find himself in the spotlight – and he didn't want that. His man was a special resource to be used sparingly. Boyle was a worthwhile target, he agreed; a walking memory bank and a hardened pro. But don't kill him this way.

'Boyle drives home to see his mother outside Limavady on the north coast in County Derry almost every other Sunday. He changes his route, but there's a twelve-mile stretch he can't avoid without a long detour.'

'Okay. Make sure the next few Fridays and Saturdays are quiet. You don't want him having to work over the weekend because some local hero wants to make a name for himself.' The smell of warm bread from the bakery beneath made Collins feel hungry. Why did the meetings always take place around food? 'How many people know about this operation?'

'Only the Chief of Staff, you and me,' replied O'Hanlon promptly. He felt important to be included in such exclusive company.

'Rubbish,' exclaimed Collins. 'What about the council who've sanctioned the operation? Those who have done a recce on the roads, those who've clocked Boyle's movements.'

'You're paranoid, Collins. Do ye know that? You're paranoid.'

'Ay,' replied Old Holborn, ruefully. 'It's being paranoid what keeps me alive.'

* * *

'I have spread my dreams under your feet; Tread softly, because you tread on my dreams.'

'Dunno.'

'Right, get them off.'

'Jenny, you're mad.'

'You agreed to play strip Irish knowledge.'

'But you keep finding things I don't know.'

'I don't think there's anything you do know. Yeats, and you should have known that. Get 'em off.'

'You have an advantage over me.'

'Yeh, I went to school.'

And the rest. One of Collins's talent spotters, a former pupil from his teaching days, now a senior lecturer at Trinity College, Dublin, had recommended he cast an eye over Jenny Dove. Collins recognized the neurotic febrility in the beautiful Anglo-Irish scholar; divined a rebel heart looking for a cause and kept her lily-white, working away at Trinity until he had a use for her.

Paddy O'Keefe was infatuated, although he tried hard not to show it. She was ten years younger and from a different social world. She came from a class where women weren't scared to take the lead or play sex games. She was full of imagination and he was intrigued by her intelligence and her beauty.

He looked from the flickering blue flames at the woman kneeling above him. He had to admit she was beautiful. She had the pale golden complexion and serenity of an eleventh-century icon found in a small monastery outside Kiev. Pale, golden and elusive, with a patina which glowed and was unreal. Her tumbling amber and copper hair framed her high cheekbones. Only her green eyes betrayed her fanaticism. Sometimes they sparkled in merriment; sometimes they shone in amusement; but frequently they crackled, burned and seared in the corrosive intensity of their beliefs. She smiled, exposing white teeth which looked as if they could shear through a man's forearm. It was a dangerous smile, a predator's smile; it promised passion and instability and looked as if it could consume not just the forearm but the torso and the whole being as well.

'I'm just a bit of rough to you.'

He rolled over in front of the peat fire.

'Christ, why are you so sexy?' purred Jenny, her face shining in the firelight. It had been a master stroke by Collins to team them together. O'Keefe had wanted to work totally alone, but snipers were vulnerable when lining up their target. A sniper needed a spotter; a number two to keep guard while he concentrated through the telescopic sight. After he had once almost been caught, Collins had suggested Jenny Dove. At first O'Keefe had serious reservations, but Jenny's commitment and willingness to learn made her ideal for the task.

'You should have played this game with Jimmy Sands. He was boned up on Irish history and the Troubles – just like you.'

'Who?'

'My best mate. We used to do everything together.'

'Everything?' Jenny raised an eyebrow in suggestive interrogation.

'Everything.'

'Strange name.'

'Should have been Bobby Sands, but we got it wrong.'

'Oh.' Jenny slowly understood. 'Unionist bastards thought it was funny when a martyr died. I'm surprised you did.'

'It's amazing what's funny in the army. It's what keeps you sane.'

Jenny acted as a back-up, cover and lover. O'Keefe didn't know if Collins was aware that her greatest strength was also her weakness. Jenny, witty, sane, laughing Jenny, had a dark streak running through her. She had a macabre fascination with killing. Her love-making after each shooting had an unnerving, jagged feverishness when her climaxing took her to the very edge of her being.

For him killing was a job like punching bus tickets, but

one day he knew she would demand to kill – to taste her ultimate thrill.

He looked up from his book. 'Okay, what's a galloglass?'

'Easy. A retainer or the family of a professional soldier from *galló gláigh*. Get them off.'

She looked hungrily at O'Keefe's broad torso.

Initially, O'Keefe's conscience made him feel guilty about sleeping with Jenny. He confessed his sins to the God in his head and convinced himself that sex with Jenny didn't mean that he no longer loved his wife. In his dislocated existence, he was two different men, each in a self-contained life with a different woman. Bloody guilt.

'Ireland has outlived the failure of all her hopes and yet she still hopes.'

'Um.'

'You don't know, do you!' Jenny was triumphant. 'Let go. Let go. Be honourable. There. Look he's standing up to say hello. He wants to see me if you don't.'

'You've got all your clothes on. Ouch. Gently.'

'And whose fault's that? Roger Casement, by the way.'

'Didn't your mother ever tell you not to talk with your mouth full?'

The idea of a lovely large gin and tonic formed in Mary's mind and consumed her with anticipatory pleasure. No, she told herself sternly. It's only five o'clock. Not yet. Wait until dark. Don't think about it. Yesterday she'd caught herself mixing a drink while she made Katie's tea after school. The problem was that she had little to do and she was bored. She'd had morning coffee with Yvonne; taken Boo to play school and brought her back; flicked over the housework. Modern houses needed so little work. She never thought she'd hear herself bemoaning the fact that there wasn't enough housework. She should do something. The Open University, maybe. She didn't go and see her mother so much now. She couldn't find much to talk about. There was a coolness between them, caused on her mother's side, Mary sensed, by jealousy. Jealousy of what!

A red light blinked on a distant hillside. She rose, walked to the french windows and regarded the shadowed land-scape hiding God knows who or what in the way of armed men: freedom fighters, terrorists, British soldiers, oppressors, call them what you will. The light was a long way off, coming from near the small lake at Cullyhanna. Someone signalling, perhaps. Too far away for anyone to be signalling to her. It was so peaceful here; strange to think of these funny goings-on under her nose. A good place to bring up the girls, if only there were more children their age. Boo didn't seem to mind, she chattered away to herself and her dolls and twice a week Mary drove her to the play school in Crossmaglen so she would have company. Katie spent her free time at the riding stables a couple of miles away, happy to muck out, groom and generally pitch in. The stables said Katie had a natural affinity for horses. Perhaps she'd buy Katie a pony when she was a little older. She'd ask Yvonne, she knew about these sort of things.

The red light blinked again and moved upwards. A UFO? That might be one way of getting a ceasefire. Another set of three letters. IRA, UVF, UDA, RUC, UDR, now UFO. She giggled. The light was heading diagonally towards her. She heard the distant drumbeat of the helicopter's rotor blades as the phone rang.

'How are ye, hen? How're you doing?' Duggie Fife's voice caught her unawares.

'Fine thanks, and how are you?'

'Och, ay, grand.'

The two fumbled for their first few sentences until their natural amity asserted itself. Fife was short on small talk, so after he'd asked how things were and Mary had told him, as always, that they didn't need anything and they were well provided for, it was generally up to her to chatter on. She asked about Billy. Yes, Billy was training to join 2 Para. He was doing well. There was the hint of pride in his voice. Fife finally got round to the point of his phone call.

'I've some news for ye.' Having got so far, he hesitated and then said in a rush: 'I've met a girl and I'm engaged.'

'Congratulations,' said Mary, warmly. 'It's about time you settled down. Anyone I know?'

'No. Lassie called Lizzie. She's English, but very nice. Not like the usual slags I end up with. We're sort of living together already. I'd like you to meet her if you're ever in England. I reckon you'd get on.'

I hope she copes better as an army wife than I did, thought Mary, realizing he was asking for her approval. Married to Fife's best friend, she'd become like an older sister and confidante. She knew how much he had enjoyed sharing their family life in Hereford. It would be good for him to settle down.

'I was wondering what Liam wants for Christmas.'

'You needn't bother.'

'Don't be daft, he's my godson.' He paused. 'No change, is there?'

'The speech therapists are pleased with him. They reckon he's trying to talk more. But it's a slow business. He'll be home for the holidays. Oh, I don't know. Something colourful. Something to help his co-ordination. But only something small.'

'I'm coming over the water for a wee while. I'd like to come and see you, but you're really in bandit country down there.'

'It depends which side you're on,' she retorted sharply.

'I can get to Dundalk to visit Liam. Gi' us the address again, will ye, hen?'

Mary gave him the address of the special home where her brain-damaged son now lived in his own dislocated world; the Peter Pan world of someone who would never grow up.

She returned to the windows and reached for the curtains to close them. She stood as if being crucified. Perhaps she was. At each dusk, she thought of Liam. No, that wasn't true. She thought of him all the time – but especially at dusk; the dimming of the light, when the day's hope was extinguished to be replaced by ignorance and incomprehension. Liam had possessed so much light in his life and it had been put out. At least for others the sun will rise again tomorrow, but for Liam it will always be dusk.

Her eyes saw nothing then her vision cleared and she was looking back at that Christmas in Breedon Hill with Paddy and Liam and Katie. The perfect Christmas with her husband and her children. Liam would be here this Christmas. He and Boo would play together. They were the same mental age after all. Fuck it, bugger it and bollocks to it. She would have that drink and a bloody big one.

The weasel-faced man with the green and white bobble cap emerged from the newsagent with the copy of the *Sun* in his right hand. The winter morning was grey and hard and he turned up the collar of his donkey jacket against the rain in the wind coming off the lough. An onlooker might have wondered why the man didn't shove the newspaper deep in his pocket to keep his hand warm. At the crossroads, he suddenly changed the paper to his left hand and trotted across.

'All right, all right,' muttered Boyle to himself. 'Don't make a bloody meal of it.'

Boyle let him turn the next corner then pulled out into the rush-hour traffic. He found a gap in the oncoming stream, made a last-minute right turn and circled round the side roads so he was facing wee Dermot. He was marching along, waving the bloody paper like a baton – and he was on the wrong side of the road. Just in time he remembered and skipped across. Boyle pulled to a halt, threw open the rear door and Dermot leapt in, burrowing under the raincoat behind the passenger seat.

'Whisky one, whisky two. Persil.'

'Whisky one, whisky three. Persil.'

'Roger.'

Boyle's support vehicles either end of the street gave him a clean bill of health and he set off through Protestant north Belfast on the Ballymena road towards the open country. A dark green van with white letters proclaiming *St Francis Society for Sick Animals* followed him.

Only when they were on the outskirts did Boyle speak.

'Well, wee Dermot. You asked for the emergency meet. What do you want?'

'It's what I have that you'll want,' came the satisfied wheedle from under the coat.

'You have something on our man?' Boyle failed to keep the interest out of his voice.

'It's not that easy, Mr Boyle,' whined Dermot, emerging.

Boyle glanced over his shoulder at the man crouched behind him, frowned at the dandruff on his left shoulder and unthinkingly brushed it off over Dermot.

In a country lane, Boyle halted. Dermot stiffened as he saw the green van stop fifty yards away.

'No one's going to top you,' reassured Boyle. 'Right, what've you got on the big man?'

'It's not him exactly,' replied Dermot, screwing up his thin face. 'But I've something I know you'll want; something you'll pay a lot for. Shall we say £5,000?'

'Shall we say bollocks, Dermot.' The wee man is too cocky, thought Boyle. Time to shake him up. 'Dermot, you're not doing me favours, I'm doing you one.'

He reached into his left hand overcoat pocket and produced a single typewritten sheet.

'Do you know what this is, Dermot? It's part of the police report into the goings-on at the children's home where you work at weekends. You know, the results of the investigation into those rumours about the young boys.'

Dermot licked his lips nervously. Boyle handed him the page and turned away to look at two rooks cawing against each other from the top branches of a bare tree. Dermot's

231

face had turned crimson with embarrassment and shame.

Boyle held out his hand for the sheet. 'You'll be daft enough to show it to another of your sad bunch. That's only the draft of a provisional report. What it finally says and when it's finally handed over to the prosecutor's office is up to me. Maybe that page – and a few others – might get lost. Get my drift, Dermot?'

The little man nodded vigorously. 'There's going to be an ambush,' he blurted out.

'That's better. Now try to remember Kipling's five faithful servants.'

'Eh?'

'Where, why, how, when and who.'

'I don't know when or where.' Wee Dermot put up a hand as if to fend off a blow. 'But I know who. I know who the target is.'

'All right. Who?'

'You,' crowed Dermot.

Boyle already knew. He had thought for a while that his turn must be coming in the killings of high-ranking army and RUC officers which had crippled their intelligence capability. Then two weeks ago a teenage girl had committed suicide while nominally in his custody. Wallop. That's me in their sights. Goes with the turf. And all on a bloody DCI's salary. There'll be few to shed a tear, even in the Branch. But I'm not going to die yet and not by the hand of any bead-rattling scumbag. The sour thoughts sped through his brain as he nodded sagely. But he already knew.

'Who's going to set the ambush, Dermot?'

Dermot was disappointed at the heavy man's reaction.

'Boys from the Derry Brigade and someone else, I don't know who. Honest,' he snivelled.

Boyle frowned. He had no dealings with Londonderry. He seldom went there and if he did, it was invariably in connection to a case. His presence there could not be guaranteed. Then again, he did go to Limavady just twenty miles away . . .

'All right, Dermot boy, I'll tell you what we'll do. I'll trust you with my life. I'll put a document authorizing the release of this report and outlining the criminal charges in my office safe. Every morning, I'll not send it. But if anything happens to me, those who'll tidy up will find it and act on it.'

'Oh Jesus, Mr Boyle. You'll not do that.' Dermot was horrified.

'Life inside isn't very pleasant for offenders like you. Even segregated under rule 43. The cons always get the perverts. Makes them feel manly. You know, a boiling pan of fat, the quick knife in the shower, the screws who are more than willing to turn a blind eye.'

The colour drained out of Dermot's foxy features; his eyes darted around as if searching for a means of escape.

'I'll also leave a letter for Declan Higgins and Sean McGrady. They're still northern command's judge and jury, aren't they? *I* don't care how many Catholic orphans you bugger on your weekends, but I reckon they might. You'll probably never even get to see the inside of a prison.'

'Oh no, please, Mr Boyle.'

Boyle sensed rather than saw the merest glimmer of hope in the small, cunning eyes. He walked over to the waiting van and leaned in the driver's window. Dermot sat uncertainly by himself, not knowing where to look or what to do.

'You don't have a passport,' said Boyle when he returned. 'Don't think of applying for one, either here or in the Republic. You won't get one. By the time I've dropped you off, your picture will be at the ports and airports. You have nowhere to go, Dermot boy, nowhere to run.'

Boyle saw the last dregs of hope flicker and die in Dermot's curdled eyes. 'You'd better do your best to keep me alive, hadn't you?'

The rain drummed on the glass panes; the ill-fitting windows rattling in the gusts as outside the storm surged and rumbled. The dusty upstairs room of the lonely pub in the dark countryside was bare apart from a damp upright piano and a pile of metal and canvas chairs stacked under a dust sheet. Collins used an old saucer as an ashtray and surveyed the three red-faced, raw-boned agricultural workers as they pulled their shapeless winter coats closer around them and huddled around the single electric bar. Kevin Fitzgerald, Eamon McManus and Jim O'Neill called themselves the spearhead of the West Derry Brigade. Collins considered them more of a blunt club. They were used to stiffing aged, part-time UDR men who worked as dustmen or dog catchers. Their target this time was tough, trained and shrewd. The three had been swigging bottles of Guinness by the neck for almost half an hour now and they were getting impatient.

'Why do we want this big-time operator? We don't need anyone to teach us our trade,' griped Fitzgerald, turning up his collar as the thin, stained curtains billowed with the draught.

'We'd no problems stiffing those two bastards in summer, that's for sure,' crowed O'Neill, just twenty but already with a face of a peeled beetroot. 'This fucking BTO can't even get to a fucking meeting on time.'

From under the dust sheet rose an apparition in black balaclava and combat jacket with an Armalite rifle at his shoulder. Only Collins facing the men could see him as he soundlessly made his way, testing each floorboard until he was just five feet behind them.

'I'll give him two more minutes,' growled Fitzgerald, the leader by virtue of his age and wanton willingness to kill. 'Then I'm going.'

There was the telltale snick of a safety catch being removed. The three spun round as Collins moved out of the field of fire. The man leaned into the stock of the rifle, both eyes open.

'It's the fucking SAS,' cried McManus.

'If it was you'd be fucking dead.'

'How long have you been there?' demanded Fitzgerald.

'Long enough, sunshine.'

'Christ, you're the big man. We thought we were waiting for you and all the time you were here. Christ, that's brilliant,' gasped O'Neill enthusiastically.

'Very fucking clever.' Fitzgerald resented being outwitted in front of the others.

Collins decided it was time to defuse the situation. 'This is Kevin Fitzgerald,' he said to the hooded man. 'He was on hunger strike in the Kesh with Bobby Sands. You were on the blanket as well, if I remember, Mr Fitzgerald.'

Fitzgerald, who had an angular, mottled face and large ears, was instantly mollified. 'Ay, that's right enough. If we hadn't been ordered to call off our hunger strikes after Michael Devine died, I wouldn't be here now. Mind you, I personally had no say in the matter, I was in a coma at the time. I was ready to follow Bobby Sands all the way.'

'You're a brave man, Mr Fitzgerald.' Collins spoke with respect.

'Are ye going to let us see your face now? You're among friends you know,' said Fitzgerald.

'It's better if you didn't. If you get captured and tortured, you can tell the truth and say you don't know who I am.'

'But you've seen our faces.'

'I'm not going to get caught,' said O'Keefe in a slow, matter-of-fact voice.

'Right.' Collins became businesslike. 'This copper has been targeted by Northern Command, so there must be no mistakes. The attack is going to be videotaped, so make sure you are well covered. The cameraman doesn't need to see your faces. Remember that.'

O'Keefe stepped forward. 'Boyle will leave his home around ten Sunday morning to drive to Limavady. He changes his route, but he has to turn off at Dungiven and there's one stretch he can't avoid unless he's going to take a long detour. He normally drives a metallic silver Rover, but we'll get a call when he leaves home to confirm that.'

He spread a large-scale Ordnance Survey map on the floor and indicated with the front sight of the Armalite.

'Here's a long straight, but then the road enters a series of bends as it follows the river. I recce'd the route last Sunday and Boyle should be there around 11.10. Certainly not before 10.55 unless he's going like a bat out of hell. Traffic will be light on a Sunday morning. A dicker up here on this escarpment can see along the straight and down to the series of bends. I intend to put a block across the road here, at the second bend.' The three men studied the map closely. 'A farm cart with hay would be good. Make it look as if it was stuck going into this unmade lane.'

Collins sensed resistance growing in the men.

'We can get a hay cart, no problem,' said Fitzgerald slowly. 'But around here we're used to making our own plans.'

'Yeh. Let's just fucking do it. None of this fucking talk,' jeered McManus.

'And what would you do?' asked Collins politely.

'What would I do?' yelled McManus. 'I'd fill a van with the boys and blast the bastard. That's what I would do.'

The hooded man looked at him with steady unblinking eyes and McManus suddenly wished he hadn't spoken.

'And what happens when the bastard turns round and blasts you? You do it my way or not at all. Now either fuck off or get on with it.'

The hard, unforgiving eyes told McManus he would not leave the room alive. He folded his arms in defeat and dropped his head on to his chest.

'No problem,' he managed in a surly mutter.

'One of you will be in the road making like you're directing traffic. He will have a long coat and a concealed weapon. The other two will be in the hedgerow on the driver's side.'

'Where will you be?' asked Fitzgerald.

'The road's too windy to reverse easily. The target's train-ing will be to try to get around the obstacle. In case he does,

I'll be beyond the ambush to ram him. I'll be driving a blue Opel saloon. Don't shoot me. Have a good look at the area tomorrow, but don't make it obvious. The forecast is for more rain, which'll be good for us. Any questions?'

The three men sat dumbly.

'There fucking well should be,' shouted the hooded man angrily. 'If the shit hits the fan, make for the scrub between the road and the river. If it goes well, you'll have at least ten minutes clear. Lay on change cars towards the west. Don't nick anything on Saturday night which'll blow the whistle. Organize two safe houses within ten miles. Boyle doesn't usually have a bodyguard, but he might if he gets a sniff of trouble. Leave the bodyguard to me and go after the target.'

'Make sure the dicker is someone you can trust with your life, because that's what you'll be doing,' added Collins. 'Work out what you'll need in the way of weapons. It'll be better if you didn't use your own for forensic reasons.'

He caught the greedy glitter in McManus's eyes and thought Frannie McFadden might have problems getting his guns back. But then McFadden was used to such problems and had his own way of solving them.

The hooded man walked lightly to the door. 'I'll be in touch. There'll be no move before Saturday morning. Now if you'll wait five minutes until I'm clear, I'll wish you all a good night.'

He slipped into the darkened car, putting the Armalite under a coat on the back seat. Jenny negotiated the first quarter-mile of the twisting lane before switching on the headlights. Anyone driving up behind them now would have seen a BMW with English number plates.

'How was it?'

'A lot of tosspots. Great at knocking over haystacks. Fucking fools at anything else.'

'But not *the* fools.'

'Huh?' O'Keefe's mind was on the operation.

'"The fools, the fools. They think they have pacified Ireland. But they have left us our Fenian dead. And while Ireland holds their graves, Ireland unfree will never be at peace."'

'Padraig Pearse.'

'You're learning, Paddy,' she laughed. 'But it's not a lecture on Irish poets you'll be getting from me tonight. I've a fire and a drink for you.'

'He's not for me. He ran to his death. What sort of man is that?'

Jenny divined he was talking of Pearse. 'A martyr.'

'Bollocks to martyrs. Ireland has too many martyrs – it's our word for blundering failures.'

'Shall I be coming with you on Sunday?' she asked softly.

'No, Jenny.'

She walked her fingers up O'Keefe's leg into his groin until she felt his stiffness and then in one vicious movement seized a handful and squeezed as hard as she could.

'Does that mean you're open to persuasion?'

'No,' he grunted through gritted teeth.

Chapter Twenty-three

'That's me passing Lisabuck Inn.'

'Tango, delta. Roger.'

'Tango, bravo. Yellow and green tractor. One pax. Passing Rectory Lane on right.'

'Bravo, roger.'

'Delta, tango. That's me passed the tractor. My Sierra 50-55.'

'Roger that.'

Duggie Fife squinted through the windscreen as the wipers battled to cope with the downpour. Alongside him, Boyle's body armour strained the seams of his blue topcoat. Fife had tried on the lightest Kevlar, but it inhibited his movements and he wanted to be able to move quickly if the shit hit the fan. According to Int and Sy group, the shit was definitely going to hit the fan.

'Bravo passing Cloonkeen crossroads.'

Fife had difficulty reading the signposts in the torrential rain. 'Tango passing Cloonkeen crossroads. My Sierra 45.'

'Roger and delta's at the crossroads.'

Ahead he caught a glimpse of the battered Ford Transit van, the sweep vehicle in the three-strong convoy. That should have been Fife's command, but two new blokes had just joined the troop straight from selection and it wouldn't have been right to ask one of them to drive the target. They might panic or fuck up. Duggie Fife, the Lean Mean Killing Machine, never fucked up. The eight men in the vehicles before and after the target car carried Heckler & Koch MP5s, HK53s, M16s and G3s with the collapsible stock – a combination chosen for ease of handling in confined spaces and firepower.

Fife just had his 9mm Browning pistol and an intense wish to stay alive.

'Delta, alpha. Players are *not* repeat *not* at their homes. All believed to have left early morning.'

'Alpha, delta. Roger. Call signs acknowledge.'

'Tango, roger.'

'Bravo, roger.'

Fife cast a glance at Boyle who sat impassively at the news that the three gunmen had gone off radar.

'Tango, delta. Stand by. Stand by. Red saloon coming up very fast. Possible contact.' The calm voice of Molecatcher in the back-up vehicle made Fife's hair crackle with apprehension. 'Red saloon is a VW Golf. Two pax, possibly more. Still coming.'

'Okay?' Fife asked Boyle.

'No problems.' The detective stared directly ahead through the bleared windscreen.

'The VW is overtaking us . . . now. Two pax. Male. Acknowledge, tango.'

'Tango, roger.'

'Alpha, delta. Red VW Golf. Registration yankee lima mike niner five two.'

'Copied, delta.'

The army computer at Lisburn could identify ownership of the VW inside thirty seconds. Fife accelerated to catch up with the lead Transit to gain some of those seconds. In his mirror he saw the red car surging behind him, sending up a tidal wave on the road. They were closing rapidly. Fife touched the goggles hanging loosely around his neck with his gloved left hand. Goggles and gloves were to protect him when the windows blew out in the firefight.

'This could be it, sir,' he warned, instinctively loosening his Browning from his shoulder holster. 'Please remember, don't get involved. Just keep your head down and do whatever I tell you.'

'You mean you don't want to have to worry about being shot from your own side. What are you going to do?'

'Depends on him,' said Fife, his eyes flicking to his mirror. 'If he tries to blast us when he's alongside, I'll shunt him and then get out of the way. The boys will close front and back and do the business. If he gets ahead and stops, I'll ram him.'

'Saloon is closing, closing. My Sierra 60.'

Fife was driving dangerously fast for the conditions, but the red car was overhauling them. He came to a long right-hand bend and maintained his speed, letting the Rover drift slightly across the treacherous surface. He was within sixty yards of the battered Transit. Inside the boys would be hands on, the specially modified doors ready to fly wide open.

The red car filled his wing mirror.

'Here they come.' He braced himself for the clatter of an automatic weapon and the thump and thud as the bullets struck home. The red car drew alongside. The car's windows were closed. Fife eyeballed the passenger. He was looking ahead.

The rear of the VW was level with the Rover's bonnet. Fife braked, sponging the pedal to prevent skidding. The red car cut back in front sending a wall of water crashing over the windscreen and washing out the road ahead.

On the net Fife heard the head shed giving the owners of the car a clean bill of health. He changed down to third gear and continued to brake. The VW was pulling away.

'That's the VW past me. No action. Sierra down to 35. Repeat 35.'

A wave of nausea swept over Fife. He was tempted to yawn.

'Two local heroes,' concluded Boyle. He sounded disappointed. 'You wish they'd get it over with.'

Fife nodded vigorously. 'Yeh. You get this with so many jobs. You get psyched up, fired up and then they blow out. It's a pisser.'

The three vehicles spread out again to avoid looking like a convoy. They didn't want to deter the attack: they wanted to trigger it. At the same time the lead vehicle and the back-up had to be close enough to provide support when the bullets started flying. It was a delicate balance.

'Tango, bravo. Green Commer van approaching.'

'Roger, bravo. I have the van.'

'Tango, bravo. That's me at Barna crossroads.'

'Roger, bravo. Now approaching the crossroads. Shit.'

An ancient pickup truck with two calves standing roped in the back pulled out on to the main road without looking. Fife hit the brake and the car slewed to within feet of the pickup's tailgate.

'They're like that in the country,' grunted Boyle by way of apology as they entered a short straight. The pickup was indicating right.

'That's me behind an old farm pickup. Sierra 20.'

'Delta's backing you, tango. Have you visual.'

'That's me approaching Killgreen crossroads.'

'Roger, tango.'

Fife knew from the recce the previous day that the next stretch was winding and narrow. Good ambush country. He could feel his nerves jangling. For Christ's sake get it over with.

The pickup turned off right up a lane leading to high ground, the two calves swaying in unison. Fife put his foot down going into the bend and then braked immediately. A large farm trailer loaded with hay was trying to turn into a narrow track in the high hedgerow.

'What now!' Fife's first reaction was that of exasperation.

'Tango, bravo. Blue Opel saloon. One pax.'

Fife coasted towards the trailer, judging whether there was room for him to slip past when his face suddenly creased in concentration. Why hadn't the sweep car reported the farm trailer?

Because it hadn't been there twenty seconds ago. Shit.

'Stand by. Stand by. Possible contact. Trailer blocking road on bend.'

A tall, rawboned man wearing an old shapeless raincoat stood in the middle of the road to direct traffic. He was wearing a flat hat and his collar was turned up against the driving rain. His hands were plunged deep in his pockets. As he walked towards the car, Fife spotted he had new blue overalls under his coat. That was enough. He hit the accelerator and the car leapt forward as the trailer rolled back to block the road. Fife braked again, pulled on his goggles and slammed the car into reverse. The man whipped out a sawn-off shotgun from under his coat and at the same time Fife heard the distinctive bark of an AK47. The offside rear window shattered into a thousand sharp pieces.

'Contact. Contact. Two players. One in hedgerow to north.'

He thrust the gear lever into forward and aimed the car at the man with the shotgun. He dived behind the trailer. Fife felt the car judder as it began to take hits. The windscreen starred as a bullet passed between them and Fife flinched instinctively.

'Correction three players. Get down,' he cried to Boyle who had also brought out his pistol. He pushed Boyle into the passenger footwell.

He heard the calm voice of Molecatcher. 'Alpha, delta. Contact. Quarter mile south of Killgreen crossroads. I am at Grid 643870.'

That would bring the big boys running.

Fife punched out the starred and cracked glass with his gloved fist and fired twice through the windscreen at a man who appeared in the hedge with a rifle. The man disappeared.

The front wing of the blue Opel appeared past the end of the trailer. Fife caught sight of a man in a black balaclava clutching an AK47; then he ducked as more glass exploded over him.

'Out. Out.' Boyle tumbled out on to the soaking road and Fife followed him to sprawl flat on the tarmac, pressed against the side of the car. Short bursts of automatic fire from round the corner told him the back-up team had joined the party. A bullet ricocheted off the tarmac six inches from his nose and he jerked back, ripping out his communications earpiece. Thirty yards away a man in a blue boiler suit, carrying what looked like a video camera, began to run in slow motion across the road. After three long steps he reached up on tip toe, shuddered, spun and fell to the ground where he lay twitching.

Fire was coming from both sides now as the SAS parties converged on the ambushers. A high-pitched scream pierced the rain and there was a moment's stillness, then the firing built up to a crescendo before all fell quiet once more.

'Rear area secure,' someone called.

Fife, from years of training, turned his head to look in the opposite direction. As he did so, he saw the slender wands of whitebeam and hazel in the hedge bend against the wind.

'Stay here,' he ordered Boyle.

He scuttled across the road to the shelter of the bank and wiped the rain from his eyes. Inch by inch, he rose to peer through the bare twigs at the dismal scrubland which he knew fell away to a narrow river. He made his eyes inspect every inch of ground and finally he was rewarded by a droplet of dark blood under a holly tree.

Through the hedge, he paused. Behind him he heard harsh, victorious shouts. The RUC specialist Headquarters Mobile Support Unit would soon arrive to seal off the area, but it would be too late then. The stunted trees with twisted holly bushes and dense, tangled brambles offered perfect cover and the relentless drenching rain would obliterate all tracks. Fife wrapped both hands around the grip of his Browning and, with his arms stretched out in front of him, cautiously advanced. He was rewarded almost immediately by a footprint in the soft earth. The gunman was heading to cross the river and escape in the spider's web of tracks and lanes on the far side.

Fife, his leather jacket buttoned up to his neck, set off on a parallel track. Eighty yards on, in a small clearing on his right, he caught sight of the player. The man was kneeling. He had removed his balaclava and he was holding it to his right ear trying to staunch the blood dripping like a tap from his lobe while at the same time examining a dark stain on his left thigh. The shoulders of his combat jacket were sodden and his short dark hair stuck flat to his head. An AK47 lay within arm's reach. The man's broad back was towards Fife as he advanced out of the eye of the storm. He was within six feet before the man sensed his presence.

Fife bent into a firing crouch, both eyes open. He reckoned he'd fired maybe five times; another eight rounds left.

He waited for the man to make a move; to reach for his weapon to give Fife the chance to pump three or four bullets in his back and then a final one to the head. But the man knelt motionless.

'All right, laddie. Nice and slow.'

Others in the Regiment would have slotted him. The head sheds wouldn't be too happy about a survivor. Made the operation untidy. There had never been an arrest made in an SAS ambush in Northern Ireland. But Fife had never killed in cold blood and he wasn't going to start now.

He was four feet away. Close enough not to miss; far enough not to be jumped.

'Turn a-fucking-round. It's your last chance.' Fife's voice grated.

Slowly the man turned his head and then his body followed.

'What's wrong, Duggie? Haven't you learned to shoot a man in the back yet?'

A blackness engulfed Fife. When he could see again, Paddy O'Keefe still crouched in front of him. A different Paddy, but the same one. Fife's jaw sagged and his eyes stared in disbelief at the ghost in the rain.

'But you're dead. You're supposed to be dead. The explosion . . .'

'I'm a hard man to kill, Duggie boy.'

O'Keefe looked steadily at his old friend whose face was now as pale and washed as the winter's day.

Thoughts and emotions surged and churned through Fife's mind; confusing him, baffling him. Paddy. My best mate. My mentor. The man who saved my life. Jimmy Sands. Here. Now. Kneeling in front of me. Fife was engulfed by a wave of sadness and finally of incomprehension.

'What the fuck are you doing here?'

'Trying to get away from you lot.'

Paddy's eyes were different. Even squinting against the rain, they were sombre. The blue sparkle had been replaced by the dullness of the sea on an overcast day. The curly hair was cut short and he had a dark beard. The beard was the last thing Fife noticed.

'You're part of that . . .'

'Get it over with,' rasped O'Keefe. 'Otherwise I'll die of cold here.'

Jimmy Sands. Jimmy Sands. The man who saved his life.

Fife thumbed up the safety catch and lowered his Browning to his side. He turned with the heaviest step of his life and began to make his way ponderously back towards the road. The rain washed away the tears.

After five leaden paces he halted and looked again at O'Keefe who was limping away, his weapon in his hand.

'I didn't forget you,' called Fife. 'I didn't forget you, Jimmy Sands.'

'Bobby. The name was Bobby Sands.'

Chapter Twenty-four

Seldom did Collins remind others how often he was right, but in his anger and his relief he could not contain himself.

Ted Daly, a special emissary from Dublin, suffered the full scorn of Collins's tongue. He held his peace but Sean O'Hanlon, who had been ordered to escort Daly to the meeting above the bakery, was losing his temper.

'Your man got away didn't he? None of those SAS bastards were injured. If your man is as good as you claim why didn't he stiff one or two of them instead of legging it?' he sneered.

The public urbanity slipped from Collins like a pristine shroud exposing the gaunt bones of a misshapen monster.

'Why did he run away? I'll tell you why he ran away. Because he was caught in a deadly ambush through the treachery of his so-called comrades in arms. At least he's alive to fight another time. Christ, you make me sick, O'Hanlon. Why don't you go and wrap yourself in a tricolour and go and lie under a bus. Then we can say it was a Crown assassination and you'll be a martyr and no use to anyone. In your case it'll be a fucking improvement.'

'Patrick John, it's about treachery that I want to talk to you . . .' Daly had never seen Collins in such a temper. 'The Chief wants you to find the leak. We don't know whether it was in Derry, Dublin or here. We don't know for certain that we have a traitor in our ranks . . .' Collins gave a sarcastic bark. '. . . or whether the Brits picked it up electronically. You have absolute powers to question anyone you wish, irrespective of rank. Do whatever you want. Go wherever you want . . .'

'A Witchfinder General,' mused Collins. About bloody time.

'Use O'Hanlon's men,' continued Daly.

O'Hanlon opened his mouth to object, but Daly held up his hand to still him. 'Orders. They weren't involved. They knew nothing of the operation. They're to report directly to Patrick John.'

'And no one else,' said Collins quickly.

'The Chief says we're going to need your man soon. We have to show the Crown we can hit back.'

'One to put on the scales against this fuck-up, you mean,' agreed Collins, sardonically. 'Ireland is well versed in turning her defeats into mythical victories, but I can see four funerals will not have the same propaganda impact as a real success.'

The two men opened the rear door of the council house with a duplicate key and paused. The smell of yesterday's chip fat hung in the air. Dirty bastards. Going on holiday and leaving the pan still on the stove. The men locked the door behind them and bolted it. A red light blinked in the darkness of the living room and they froze. No one said anything about a bloody alarm. A pencil torch showed a video flashing. The men relaxed. That would have been caused when the power was cut to the whole street so they could enter in total blackness.

In the front bedroom they unpacked the camera lenses and the parabolic microphone and tested their communications. They made themselves comfortable. The family had only gone away the previous day and they were not back for a fortnight. Two solid weeks of staring at Patrick John Collins's front door.

'You're quiet tonight. Is your leg hurting?'

'It's just a scratch, Jenny.'

'Are you sure you're not just being brave?'

'I'm sure, thank you.'

Her middle-class English accent with its long vowels and inbred confidence annoyed him. Cultured and knowing, like Jenny herself. Usually she was welcome, but the flames of the peat fire were transporting him to other times and other places and he resented her intrusion.

Bloody Jimmy Sands.

'That's what happens when you go on a job without me to look after you.'

'Bollocks. That's what happens when you work with a load of tosspots and someone talks.'

He felt nothing for the dead men. He'd hardly known them and the little he'd known he'd despised. But he couldn't stop thinking of Fife.

'What was Collins thinking of?' asked Jenny.

'Collins argued against it.'

'I think Patrick John is a genius.'

It hadn't taken the scene of crime officers long to deduce there were four, five counting the cameraman, on the ambush. The local RUC had already called at the isolated cottage. Jenny had been magnificent. The English car, the accent and her poise dissipated any suspicions.

'I'm by myself, officer. My sister and her brood are arriving on Tuesday. They should have been here yesterday, but the youngest isn't well. I was in Belfast on business so I came on ahead. Do you want to come in for a cup of tea or a drink? Yes, of course I'll lock all the doors and windows. Thank you, officer.'

She sensed something was troubling O'Keefe.

'Tell me,' she said softly.

'I was thinking of Jimmy Sands. My best mate.'

'Was he as good a fuck as me?'

Jenny let her robe fall open showing her full breasts and the shaven diamond of pubic hair. He smelled her heat, but tonight her beauty and her wanton availability bounced off him like slush off blue ice.

The tip of her tongue slipped along his neck into his ear, but he wasn't there. He was drinking alongside Fife in the Rat Pit, the Havelock, the Globetrotters and a dozen other pubs in Aldershot, doing the Saturday night runner from the Indian, laughing in the Paludrin Club in Hereford, watching the snake's head splash in his mug, scooping up Fife from that ditch in the Falklands, carrying his unconscious body through that never ending night.

There was the time in Botswana when the troop had carried their canoes in single file down the track to the river. He and Fife had been last. They'd heard shouts up ahead and saw the guys throw down the canoes and belt for the trees, scrambling up like demented chimps. They'd looked at each other and shrugged. Then they'd seen the charging rhino and he'd broken the 100 metres record – to find Jimmy Sands already hanging from the first branch.

Then there was that time – on the same exercise – when that hippo had come up under Molecatcher's canoe. Molie had been thrown in the water. Everyone had done a Sanders of the River in double time apart from Fife who had tried to calm the panic by shouting: 'Don't worry. They're herbivores.'

In spite of himself, O'Keefe burst out laughing at the memory.

And the lioness who had come prowling through their camp when they were all in their sleeping bags. She'd stood in the middle and roared and everyone had tried to pick up their weapons without moving. Christ they could have shot shit out of each other.

The sad, reflective smile on O'Keefe's face gave way to anger. Why Fife? Of all the fucking blokes in the fucking Regiment, why fucking Fife? Fuck him. Fuck Jimmy Sands. Fuck Bobby Sands. Fuck the whole lot of them.

Jenny's fingers began to play around his groin. Fuck Jenny.

'So they didn't get you, Mr Boyle. Is there a reward?'

'Blood money, you mean, wee Dermot.'

Dermot screwed up his piggy eyes into an obstinate stare. 'I saved your life.'

'Ay, Dermot. But if I gave you money, you'd go and spend it and then the boys would come asking where you got it and you wouldn't want that, now would you?'

'I wouldn't, honest, Mr Boyle.' Boyle shuddered as Dermot extracted a nasal hair with difficulty. 'But I'm scared, Mr Boyle. They've got some general witch in to find out who talked about the ambush and I'm scared.'

Boyle pulled a thoughtful face. Interesting. With a little luck he could help PIRA tie itself in knots.

'Don't fret, I'll point the finger in another direction. Do you know who this witchfinder is?'

'No, Mr Boyle. Not yet.' Dermot hesitated. Boyle let him struggle to unwrap a packet of Players Weights and light one before he spoke again.

'That report's well buried, Dermot, but you might think about giving up your weekend job. I told you, stick by me and I'll see you all right.'

'I'll tell you something.' This was Dermot's moment of victory, the moment when he pricked the bubble of Boyle's complacency. 'You didn't get the big man. You got the four boyos, but the big man escaped. Your lot aren't that good.'

'Which big man?' demanded Boyle.

'The one you're always on about. The one who's been knocking over the brass with his long gun.'

'But he works by himself,' objected Boyle. 'He wouldn't get mixed up in a two-bit ambush. It's not his style.'

'They roped him in to make sure it went right. That's why there was a video camera there, to record it.'

'But it didn't go right, did it?' pointed out Boyle. 'As I said, stick with us, Dermot boy.'

'The Republican press are having a go about the death of the cameraman,' said Brigadier Bob Doughty, sliding the video into the machine.

'Fuck them,' growled Boyle.

'Quite,' agreed Doughty. 'Now, it's not everyone who gets to star in their own death.'

'Your lads were grand. But I'm concerned about the one that got away.'

Doughty pressed the play button. The screen filled with flickering black and white lines, then a pale picture of a desolate rain-drenched road slowly formed. The camera focused on a hay cart and a man standing in the pouring rain. It panned to two figures in boiler suits and balaclavas crouching behind the hedge, AK47s to their shoulders, before tracking the silver Rover as it approached the cart. The camera zoomed in on a gunman as he opened fire and then followed the line of fire to the car. A rear window shattered and Fife could be clearly seen coolly aiming two shots before disappearing out of view. A line of bullet holes perforated the driver's door.

'There,' pointed Boyle. 'There's the bonnet of the blue Opel just arriving.'

'Seeing this, it's a bloody miracle anyone's here to tell the tale.'

'SOCOs counted fifty-four bullet holes,' said Boyle dourly. 'By the time they'd stuck their wires in the holes to plot the trajectories, the car looked like a porcupine.'

The camera suddenly spun round in a blur of hedgerow and picked up two men in uniform with rifles to their shoulders. The frame jerked as if the cameraman was running and the picture became a whirling maelstrom of sky, grass, tarmac and hedgerow before freezing on a car tyre.

'The end,' grunted Doughty. 'So what exactly are you saying?'

'The word is that the big man was brought in to oversee the operation and he escaped.'

'You mean the sniper.' Bob Doughty looked doubtful. 'It's not his MO. His fingerprints were all over those thirteen killings. Single shot, long range with a .50 calibre and all

252

aimed at vital targets apart from the first two. This is a completely different type of operation.'

'The SOCOs believe they found the fifth player's escape route towards the river. He was wounded. Remember it stopped raining soon after the ambush. From the footprints and the blood spoor they think the player stopped for a time in a clearing. He knelt, turned and then went on. There were two sets of footprints. The second set goes as far as the clearing.'

'You don't know the men were there at the same time,' pointed out Doughty.

'My bodyguard disappeared in that direction as the shooting was dying down. When he came back he looked as if he'd seen a ghost. He was very quiet afterwards. I thought it was just reaction . . .'

'Fife saved your life.'

'That's what he was there to do.' Boyle saw he had gone too far. 'I'm not ungrateful, Brigadier, but a major player has escaped. If he turns out to be the sniper then it's a disaster. I'd like to know how it happened.'

Hard, uncompromising bastard, thought Doughty. We got four terrorists in a perfect operation with no casualties on our side and this copper wants to open what could be a can of worms. No wonder the Provos target him and his own colleagues keep their distance.

Fife stood ramrod straight to attention, fixing his eyes on a map of South Armagh above Doughty's head.

'I've no reply, sir,' he repeated for the third time.

Doughty ran his fingers through his hair and snatched off his half-moon glasses in a gesture of exasperation.

'For fuck's sake, Fife. This is not a hostile interrogation. You'll be giving me the big four next. And stand easy.'

Fife didn't move a muscle. His demeanour was that of a keen and decent schoolboy who'd let the side down but for his own good reasons. Doughty rose from behind his desk and paced his small office.

'Jimmy Sands. Listen to me. We've served a lot together. Seen a lot together. I've known you for – what? Ten, twelve years? You're one of the finest soldiers I've ever come across. I had you down for SSM when Andy goes next year and then RSM after that. That's the way most people in the Regiment see it. So stop fucking around and tell me what happened.'

Muscles twitched around Fife's jaw and his eyes pleaded silently for understanding. Doughty indicated the three folders scattering his desk.

'Something happened there. SOCO reports indicate a fifth player who escaped down by the stream. You went in that direction telling DCI Boyle to wait. You returned empty-handed. Now Boyle is honking because the player who got away is the one believed to be responsible for the sniper killings.' Doughty opened out his hands in a gesture of incomprehension. 'What happened?'

Fife turned to face Doughty. He liked and respected the officer. They were both professional and that counted for a lot in Fife's book. He knew he should give Doughty an answer, but he could not bring himself to lie. He'd told officers enough lies in the past – somehow this was different. This was a secret he could never share or defile by lying.

'I . . . I lost my nerve, sir.' In a way, he told himself, that was the truth.

'And . . .'

'That's it, sir.'

'Bollocks.' Doughty looked at him shrewdly. 'Boyle said you came back looking as if you'd seen a ghost.'

'No reply, sir.'

'The troop say you were very quiet that night. In fact, you've been very subdued since the contact.'

'I've no reply, sir.'

'I don't believe you've lost your nerve.' Silence again filled the room. Fife again stared at the map of South Armagh while Doughty fiddled with the folders.

'You're not making it easy for me, Duggie. *If* you have lost it, and I don't believe for a minute that you have, then there's no place for you in the Regiment.'

'Yes, sir.' There was an awful resignation in those two words. 'I'll leave the army, sir. I've done my time.'

Doughty sighed. 'All right. If that's what you want. I do not like to lose a good soldier, but you're leaving me no option. You won't want to go back to the Paras while all the bumph is being sorted out, so you're officially on leave from twelve hundred today. Make sure someone knows where you can be contacted.'

He came round the desk, his hand extended. Fife took the hand but refused to meet Doughty's eyes.

'You're throwing away your career. I'm truly sorry. I'll put the word out. You'll not be short of work.'

Chapter Twenty-five

The hard-faced woman towered over the two little girls giggling nervously before her.

'When did you last see your daddy?'

Boo looked uncertainly up at Katie and tugged at the top button on her cardigan. The woman's stern features softened into a confiding smile.

'Come on. You can tell me. When did you see daddy?'

Katie squeezed her lips together and clasped her little sister's hand tighter. Boo opened her mouth and took a deep breath. The woman inclined towards her expectantly.

'Daddy is dead,' she piped up. 'Dead, dead, dead.'

Virginia Collins beamed proudly. 'There's a clever girl. Now remember you must always say that if anyone, it doesn't matter who it is, asks you about your daddy.'

Boo beamed, delighted she'd given the correct answer.

'You'll remember that too, won't you, Katie?'

'Yes, Aunt Ginny,' Katie replied patiently.

In the corner of the living room, Liam rocked himself to and fro, a small dribble of saliva trickling from his mouth. Katie gently dabbed it dry with her pocket handkerchief.

'You all right there, Liam?'

He made a porcine grunt of assent and leered.

'Are we all ready then?' Golden Virginia brushed away Mary's last-minute thanks. 'It's nothing. We enjoy having the children, especially at Christmas time. It'll do you good to have some days alone.'

Paddy O'Keefe, who had been observing the children's farewells from the depth of the hallway, knelt down to offer farewell kisses. 'Now, Katie. You look after Boo and Liam, all right?'

'Yes, daddy.' She threw her arms around his neck. 'Thank you for being here at Christmas. It was lovely.'

O'Keefe winced. He could have taken a hit from an M16 and felt it less. Children knew how to hurt – even when it wasn't said deliberately.

He wrapped her in his arms. 'Have a lovely time and be good. And I'll see you again really soon.'

'Now don't lose that watch, Boo,' fretted her mother. 'Are you sure you don't want to leave it here for safe keeping?'

Boo made a small mouth and stubbornly clasped her right hand around her left wrist. She had never had a watch before and this one, a present from her daddy, was a lady's watch with jewels. Mary saw Boo's determined look and knew she'd scream the house down if they tried to remove the watch.

'Come and wave us goodbye, daddy.'

'I'll kiss you goodbye here.' O'Keefe never went near the windows or outside in the daylight, but he couldn't tell his children that.

'Your beard tickles,' complained Boo. To her this strange man, whom she was told to call daddy, was an outsider who called at irregular intervals bringing presents like her watch and telling her off for her table manners.

Mary waved them off down the long drive with its two potholes while O'Keefe watched from the gloom of the living room. It was early afternoon on 27 December and he had been home just three days. As Mary came back, he saw her brush away a tear.

'What's wrong?' There were so many things wrong that he was scared to hazard a guess. Mary began pouring herself a gin and tonic. Not too long ago it would have been a cup of tea.

'You shouldn't have bought Boo that watch. It's too old for her. And too expensive. A jewelled watch for a four-year-old. I don't know!'

'What's really wrong?'

She finished pressing out ice cubes into her glass before she spoke again.

'This is no way to live, Paddy.'

'You've got a lovely home,' he said defensively, waving his hand to encompass the well furnished bungalow.

'I've got a lovely house,' Mary corrected. 'But I didn't have the final say in choosing it. It had to be in such and such a place, by itself, not overlooked, close to the border. I was told to live here.'

He felt aggrieved. He'd personally chosen the family home. But to meet his needs rather than the family's. Mary didn't know of his two escape routes over the hill to the Republic less than one and a half miles as the fugitive ran, nor of the trusted lookouts in the derelict barn on the high ground to the east who monitored all movement around the bungalow and were ready to give covering fire if he had to flee on the cross country three-wheeler. The large holes in the drive were dug deliberately to prevent him being surprised. And the cattle grid, which covered a deceptively deep hole, could be dropped electronically by a panic button in the house. Only from the air could he be taken and the sentries were under orders to fire on a helicopter. Here he was well protected.

'But you like it here. The movement has done you proud.'

Mary rounded on him, eyes blazing. 'How proud can you be when you can't spend more than four days with your own children in case they blab that they really do have a daddy.'

'The kids love it at Virginia's. She spoils them rotten. It gives us time together. To do exactly what we want.'

Jenny's image swam before him and for a second he hated himself for his hypocrisy. Slim, elegant Jenny was in England with her posh family in Royal Berkshire. It was impossible not to make comparisons. Mary was shorter; she'd put on some weight around her hips and her breasts were fuller and more pendulous. For a mother of three she was in good shape. Mother of my three. He felt a wave of admiration and love for her. She had never questioned his motives or his actions. She refused to judge him and when it had been necessary for him to fake his death, she had accepted it with an almost oriental resignation.

He wasn't to know that out here in the country the struggle and the aims, and the means towards those aims, had acquired a different set of values. The rioting screams of the Lower Falls had hushed to the rustling of the trees on the lonely hillsides.

'Come to bed?'

Mary saw in Paddy's eyes a vestige of the old laughter. She looked fondly at the crinkles radiating from his eyes and felt a warm egg break inside her.

'You know I can't afford to get pregnant,' she said in a stage Irish accent. 'What would the neighbours say and me a poor widder woman.'

But later in bed as they lay on their backs, contained in their own world, Mary asked, 'How long is this going to go on for, Paddy?'

'Until we've driven the Crown out of Ireland and the six counties are free. We're wearing down their will. We're winning the fight.'

'Fight! What fight! What are you fighting for?'

'For freedom,' he replied simply.

Mary squirmed to hear her husband spout the inanities of the politically correct line and exploded in pent-up anger.

'Freedom from what? Freedom from fear? I'm frightened all the bloody time. Freedom of speech? I'm so worried about saying the wrong word that I daren't mention your name. Freedom to be a family? Freedom! huh!'

She rolled over and held him.

'Why can't you live at home?' she begged softly.

'You know I don't exist.'

That's the sadness, Paddy, she thought. You don't exist. She held him as tightly as she would a frightened child and let her tears trickle on to the pillows as the bleak December afternoon grew dark and finally died.

'Och, away with ye, Billy. Your screws in Para Reg know jack shite about reconnaissance. Look. Go to a target area, put in a CTR. When you've got what you want, move back and stop at an easily identifiable FRV, say a thousand metres away. Your LUP will be to the rear of this. Remember your seven Ps?'

'Ay. Proper planning and preparation prevent piss poor performance.'

'Will you two please stop talking about the army. I don't know what I expected in Glasgow on New Year's Eve, but it certainly wasn't a lecture on infantry tactics. Really!'

'Sorry, Lizzie.' Billy was instantly apologetic and Lizzie felt a pang of regret that she had protested at all. Billy was such a nice lad, she'd decided. Tall, with wide-apart hazel eyes and regular features, including a straight, unbroken nose, he didn't look at all like his elder brother. Shame about the cropped army haircut which made his ears stick out.

'Hey, Billy, that bird over there is giving you the eye. Why don't you go and say hello?'

Lizzie brushed her long tumbling brown hair out of her face and turned to look across the smoke-filled, crowded pub at three girls laughing together. Duggie Fife waved a greeting.

Billy blushed and looked into his drink. 'I'm okay here, honest.'

Lizzie realized Billy was shy. He could talk to her because she was Duggie's girlfriend and almost one of the family, but he was too embarrassed to try to chat up girls.

'Go on, Billy,' urged Fife. 'Get yourself a poke for Hogmanay.'

Billy finally looked up from his pint and a large, fiercely blonde girl beckoned. He dropped his head, his cheeks flaming.

'Och away with ye, Billy. Will you go and get bloody laid. Big Sal's doing everything but putting it in for you.'

Lizzie excused herself, but when she returned from the lavatory she found Billy sitting by himself. Fife was talking earnestly to the blonde girl and she was laughing. Lizzie saw Fife reach in his back pocket and pull out some money, then dancers started leaping up and down in the middle of the bar and they were blocked from view. When the music ended, Fife had disappeared.

A Beatles record started up and, feeling she might well make the best of a bad job, Lizzie coaxed a reluctant Billy on to the dance floor. He danced self-consciously and woodenly and at the end of the record she decided she shouldn't prolong his torture any longer.

Three sullen-eyed men were sitting in their chairs and there was no sign of Fife. Lizzie reached the table first.

'Excuse me. Those are our seats. We were dancing.' The men pointedly ignored her, staring at the dancers, drinks in hand. 'I said those are our seats.'

Billy moved in front of her. 'You heard the lady. Those seats are taken.'

'Yeh. By us,' sneered one with bottle shoulders.

'Are you going to move?'

'Nah. What're you going to do about it, laddie?'

'Outside. The three of you.'

'Big man, yeh?'

'Up,' commanded Billy, gesturing with his index finger. The men sniggered unpleasantly and put down their pints.

'Leave it, Billy,' pleaded Lizzie. 'It's all right. We'll sit somewhere else.'

She was close to tears. Fine New Year's Eve this was turning out to be. A rough pub in Glasgow; her bloke had deserted her for a tart and now his brother was about to get beaten up on her behalf.

Then she saw Fife across the room. He was grinning in triumph at the big blonde. He glanced in their direction; the smile fell from his face and he was moving across the crowded pub like a shark through water.

Bottle shoulders stood up and lunged for Billy's lapel. Billy grabbed his wrist.

'Turn around, scum, or I'll drop ye here and now.'

The man turned slowly and extended a hand, palm outwards as though to fend off Fife.

'This ain't your quarrel. Nothing to do with you, Duggie.'

Fife appeared slight against the man's bulk, but there was a gleam in his eye that the other couldn't match.

'That's my bird, that's my brother and that's my chair.'

The colour drained out of bottle-shoulders' face. He swallowed nervously and the other two suddenly found their shoes fascinating.

'No . . . Ay . . . Didn't know that. No offence meant. No harm, eh? Okay, Duggie. We'll move. All right, Duggie? Eh?' His cronies rose, making placatory noises. They grinned in embarrassment and faded into the crowd.

Billy felt cheated. Lizzie found she was shaking.

'What was that about?'

'Och, just some of the lads wanting a bit of fun.'

'Dance.' The big blonde girl stood over Billy. He began to stutter an excuse, but she lifted him bodily to his feet, flung her arms around him and began smooching.

Fife gave a delighted chuckle and leaned to peck Lizzie on the cheek. She jerked away.

'What's wrong, hen?'

'It's not very nice to leave someone like that. I don't know anyone and Billy almost got into a fight for my sake.'

'Och, hen.' Once again Fife was attracted by Lizzie's softness and vulnerability. She didn't nag him or goad him like Vicky had done. He still bitterly recalled the final scenes with Vicky. She had gone on and on at him until even her

262

friends had told her to stop. 'Bollocks,' she'd replied. 'It's the only language he understands.'

Lizzie was proving that he responded to another, altogether softer language.

'Did you think I was running off with Big Sal?'

A tear rose in the corner of a large brown eye. 'Now you're making fun of me.'

Fife hurriedly pulled out a clean handkerchief and decided he'd gone far enough.

'It's not easy to get a hotel room in Glasgow at Hogmanay. Everyone's too drunk to answer the phone.'

'What?'

'It's a wee present for our Billy.' Fife took her hands in his. 'You saw how shy he is.'

Lizzie was flabbergasted. 'But how can you . . . ?'

'Och, she owes me.' Fife saw suspicion flood over Lizzie's face. 'She had a fellow who used to batter her rotten. I just stopped him, that's all. There's nothing wrong with our Billy. He's as good as any bloke here. Big Sal will end up with somebody, so why not Billy? I told her he's dead fit and his training will give him the stamina of ten so they'll have a grand time. You wouldn't want him being a virgin soldier, would you now?'

'You mean she's agreed?'

'Ay. I've booked them into a doss house near here and given her the money for the room. Don't tell Billy. It's the sort of thing brothers do for each other, hen.'

'Maybe in Scotland they do.' She was relieved and happy all of a sudden. 'You know he was willing to fight those three men.'

'Ay, he's a good lad.'

'They wouldn't move for him. Why did they move for you?'

'Och, hen, they know me.' Fife shrugged. 'They don't know Billy yet, but they will. Do you want to dance? I promise you no one will take our seats.'

On the tiny, packed floor, they passed close to Billy. Big

Sal had her tongue firmly down his throat and she was holding his buttocks, pressing his groin into hers. Billy had his eyes closed and he looked happy.

Chapter Twenty-six

DCI Boyle admired the plump fish he had drawn on the notebook in front of him. The open-mouthed fish was complete with tail, fins, gills and even scales. The scales had taken a time, but he was thinking. Boyle had read through the stack of files on his desk and started to write his thoughts and conclusions, but somehow the fish had appeared and grown in detail over the past thirty minutes.

It was worth a go. Totally unsubstantiated, totally without even collateral evidence – but worth a go. Why had the Big Man changed his modus operandi? Had he volunteered to lead the attack on him or had he been ordered? If he'd volunteered, did he have a personal grudge against him? Enough people with those. Either way, it showed the player was highly skilled and versatile. Not just a good shot but a good operator. What part had Collins played in setting up the ambush? He wished he knew more about Old Holborn, but the fortnight's surveillance had drawn a blank and the phone taps had produced exactly what he'd expected – the square root of sod all.

He thought of the man he'd almost landed, but for those blundering heavy-booted squaddies. Collins had known him because Collins made it his business to know everyone. That explosion had never been satisfactorily explained. Word was the boys had cocked up in a big way with a 400-pound home-made car bomb which had become unstable. Paddy O'Keefe had volunteered to try to defuse it. There was little left of the car and very little left of him when it exploded as he was bending over the bonnet. No teeth, no finger tips. Just the heel of a boot and a battered medallion alleged to belong to O'Keefe. Neat and vague at the same time. And Boyle didn't like that.

Boyle drew a worm on a hook just before the fish's gaping mouth. He appreciated the symbolism. Definitely worth a try. He would task it in the meeting this afternoon. It took for ever to set these bloody things up.

The smell inside the RAF Hercules was a unique cocktail of aircraft fuel and sweaty bodies with a large dash of fear. Dull red bulbs cast distorted shadows in a world of half-light where only the whites of the men's eyes shone. The wind howled in through the gaping side doors from the night sky outside. In the midst of the cramped, vibrating fuselage an eerie silence surrounded each man. Some pretended to sleep, others stared bleakly ahead, mentally running through the jump to come.

Knowledge Dispels Fear was the motto of the RAF Parachute School. No it bloody well didn't.

Billy thought back to the gypsy's warning before they'd boarded the Hercules.

'The green light constitutes a direct command. Failure to jump on this command is a court martial offence and will result in court martial.'

Failure to jump. Just let them try to stop him jumping. This was the last hurdle. His second night jump and then he would be a fully fledged paratrooper. His training would be over. He knew he was favourite for the champion recruit award. Just this one more jump. A trickle of sweat ran down his back. Despite the swirling cold air, he was roasting.

'Action Stations.' The air quartermaster at the rear pointed with outstretched arms at the two doors. Billy rose and began shuffling awkwardly forward, bumping into the man in front and in turn being jostled by the one behind. His left hand was wrapped round the 70-pound metal container attached to the front of his parachute harness. His mates looked drawn and as nervous as he felt. Billy touched the medal of Saint Michael hanging around his neck under his uniform. Saint Michael. Patron saint of parachutists. God's warrior. Duggie's own medal. The one he'd worn in the Falklands and through all his years in the SAS. He'd given it to Billy and it was one of Billy's proudest possessions.

The two rows swayed as the C130 banked to come over the Drop Zone. Billy ran through his checks. Static line hooked up to the strong point, container attached to the lower D rings; the reserve chute to the upper D rings; top hook and pin secure; static line clear to the left; helmet, quick release box and leg pin.

'Thirty okay. Twenty-nine okay . . .'

Billy waited until he felt the man behind slap him on the shoulder.

'Two okay. One okay. Port stick okay.'

The taut face at the head of the starboard stick was suddenly bathed in a sickly green.

'Go, go, go.'

Billy shuffled to the door and flung himself through the opening, head down to make himself as compact as possible. A rush of wind and then falling, falling in the blackness. One thousand, two thousand, three thousand, four thousand. A crack, a tremendous jerk on his shoulders and someone lifted Billy with a giant hand and scooped him skywards. Billy looked up and saw his big circular canopy, black against the crisp February night. Checking there was no one beneath him, he released the container on its fourteen feet of rope. He reached up for the lift webs to steer away from the solid shape which suddenly loomed out of the darkness on his left. On the ground he could see the white beacon of the DZ. He was moving away and to the right. He turned to assess his drift. As he did so another canopy passed below him. Christ. That was a near one. He tugged viciously on the left riser, overcompensated and swung across the sky. He was facing the light now, but he didn't seem to be getting any nearer.

The Hercules trundled on through the dark sky, nine tons lighter.

He had just forty seconds between leaving the aircraft and hitting the ground and it was falling apart. He was yawing, the heavy container acting like a pendulum. In a flash, he realized that while he'd thought he'd been moving forwards, he had in fact been drifting backwards. He tried to re-orientate himself.

Shit. The ground. Turn. Turn. He was going in the wrong way. He was halfway around when his container smashed into the earth. Billy bent his legs but he was tense; mentally preparing to fall in one direction, he was pulled towards his load. He landed on top of the metal container; there was a crack as his left tibia broke and he let out an involuntary scream of pain.

Duggie Fife, in his blue blazer, crisp white shirt and grey trousers with a knife-edge crease, leaned forward in the deep armchair looking alert and eager. He was ill at ease but hid it under a cloud of belligerent professionalism.

'I'd prefer to choose my own men,' he repeated.

Baines-Hickey glanced sideways at the swarthy, squat man who claimed to be a special forces colonel in the Colombian army. The officer shook his head regretfully.

'Señor Fife. You may train the men up to your standards. If there are any who do not make it, bin them. No problems.' He spoke army slang with a thick accent. 'You will be dealing with some shit hot men. Paramilitaries, yes. But shit hot. And you will have the final selection.'

Fife again inspected the glossy fourteen by twelve aerial pictures of the fortified hacienda with its cordon of barbed wire and the armed watch towers at each corner.

'I suppose these are the barracks.' He indicated a rectangular building at one end of the compound. 'Any idea how many men?'

'Maybe, forty, maybe sixty.'

'There's a big difference between forty and sixty.'

'These are preliminary intelligence estimates,' said Baines-Hickey soothingly. 'We can harden the intelligence when you're on the ground. No problem there, is there, Almaro?'

'None at all. And any equipment you want is yours for the asking.'

'Look, maybe I'm being thick, but why can't you just get a load of your paras to blast this villain?'

'No, you're not being thick, Señor Fife. My country is very complicated. It is not like in Britain.' He looked to Baines-Hickey to explain.

Baines-Hickey poured himself a large whisky from the drinks cabinet in the hotel suite and added a dash of soda. Fife decided it must be one of his calculated mannerisms and remembered how much he disliked the man. But work is work. Baines-Hickey had not mentioned their run-in at Hereford. Instead he had been flattering about Fife's soldiering qualities in front of the colonel, with just the hint of the patronizing rupert which so infuriated Fife.

'Our American cousins want Gabriel Marcia Gacha taken out because he is deliberately targeting the US for his cocaine. The CIA believe that the Drugs Enforcement Agency in the region has been infiltrated and they know a large part of the Colombian armed forces are corrupt. The money these drugs barons have to splash about is unbelievable – more than the wealth of many small countries.'

The colonel nodded his head in agreement. 'There have been known cases of helicopter pilots flying over cocaine factories to warn them as they went to pick up the special forces who were to destroy the factory. That's why it has to be a small, self-contained group. We need your expertise to train them and lead them, but when the firing stops it has to be a Colombian victory. You understand. You will not be in any team photographs.'

Fife could accept that. A training job like so many he'd done in the Regiment – but normally they didn't work alone. He looked directly at Baines-Hickey.

'I don't understand your part in this. I thought you were an MP.'

Baines-Hickey gave what Fife described as 'an SAS smirk'.

'You know what it's like. Once you've been part of it, you never really leave it.'

Yes, I know what it's like, thought Fife. Security companies run by former special forces officers moved in a twilight world where the British government and others paid generously for dirty jobs which were deniable and unattributable. Skulduggery by proxy. With MI5's and MI6's permission, and frequently encouragement, they worked for foreign governments, Arab royal families and multinational companies.

'It's worth £50,000. The duration should not exceed two months. It will depend on how long you need to train up the men, but we don't believe we can hold security on the operation longer than that. The actual raid will depend on Gacha's presence, of course, but we'll feed you all the intelligence we can. Almaro will be your liaison inside the country.'

Fifty thousand pounds. Lot of money. But it wasn't Baines-Hickey's balls in the grinder if anything went pearshaped. It was his own. What the hell.

'I'll do it,' said Fife.

Almaro rose out of the Knowle sofa and gave him a meaningful look of gratitude and a firm, manly handshake. Baines-Hickey also smiled and shook his hand and he felt he had been kissed by Judas Iscariot.

Fife left the Cumberland Hotel, took the underground to Charing Cross, did a little ducking and diving around the station to make sure he hadn't been followed and caught a train to Woolwich.

The prospect of work excited him. He wasn't sure how Lizzie was going to handle it, but he was a soldier and his trade was soldiering. She knew that when she'd taken him on. He'd moved into her small flat in south-east London. Well away from Hereford. Too many faces who left the Regiment still hung around the town; the old and the bold, trying to be part of something they no longer belonged to.

Fife stopped at the reception desk on the second floor of the Queen Elizabeth Hospital and asked a young nurse for directions to Billy's bed.

'You're Billy's brother, aren't you? He doesn't stop talking about you.'

'How is he?'

The nurse pulled a face. 'The leg will mend in time – although he may have a limp. But he's taking it so personally. He's a smashing bloke, a really nice guy. Everyone here makes a fuss of him, but he seems to have given up. We can only help him so far, he's got to help himself as well.'

Billy lay in the corner of the ward looking listlessly at the wall, a cage over his left leg. Military magazines lay untouched on his bedside cabinet.

'You're a tosser. What were you doing landing on your bloody container? Didn't you look down?'

Billy sat up in bed in his maroon Parachute Regiment tee-shirt and tried to appear indignant.

''Course I did. It was dark.' His hazel eyes were clouded in regret. 'To be honest, Duggie, I cocked it up from zero to the DZ. It just fell apart on me.'

'It happens,' Fife replied laconically. 'So what do the doctors say?'

'Not a lot.' Billy did not want to talk about the future – or lack of it.

'Mam says they told her you may never walk again.'

'Och, you know what she's like,' Billy retorted briskly. 'They say I'm going to have to have a couple of pins through my leg and Lord knows what else.'

'That's all right.'

'No, it's not. They reckon I'll never be able to jump again in case the pins snap.'

'Cheer up. It's not the end of the world. The Paras'll give you a job. You've got your wings. You did your eight jumps. You went out of that plane and landed on the ground – okay, you broke your leg, but you did it. Don't worry.'

'Don't take the piss.' Billy wouldn't meet his eyes, looking down the largely empty ward. 'I'm not being a bloody remf.'

'There's nothing wrong with being a rear echelon mother fucker. We'd guys in the Regiment with one arm, one eye, God knows what, but they're still in.'

'You don't understand. They'd been there, seen it, done it. I've done nothing.' Billy picked at the white sheet covering his useless leg.

'Don't give up.'

'I was going to get the Best Recruit Shield. One stupid accident . . .' Billy's open features contracted in bitterness and frustration.

'The army isn't the be-all and end-all, you know, Billy,' objected Fife, thinking that for him it had been just that.

'It is for me,' Billy replied angrily.

'Look at me.' There was steel in the command. Fife focused on Billy's empty eyes. 'You want to be like me. Right. I don't give up. Ever. You want to be like me. You don't give up. Ever. You can do it if you want. Only you can do it. No one else. You hear me. No one else.'

Fife leaned forward, grasped Billy's arms and held his eyes, pouring his own strength and power into him. He seemed to be staring into Billy's soul, imbuing the youngster with his own indomitable will. Billy began to feel the flicker of a flame being ignited inside him. A very small flame.

'You do not give up. You never give up. Even when you're dead you don't give up. You hear me. You wanted to fight. Okay. Well you've got a fight now and there'll be no medals at the end. You've got to fight yourself, Billy. And it'll be the hardest fight of your fucking life.'

Billy nodded, mesmerized by the force and energy surging out of Fife's pale blue eyes. 'You do not give up. We'll see you in the army yet.'

'Okay,' said Billy, and for the first time in weeks he found himself smiling.

*   *   *

'We had to write a story about our daddies today,' said Katie, sitting down to her plate of fish fingers and chips. 'You could either write about a day out with your daddy or write about what his job is. The best is going to get a gold star.'

It was normal for Katie to give Mary a full report on her day at school as she ate her tea.

'What did you tell Mrs O'Connor,' asked Mary, as nonchalantly as possible.

'Oh, it wasn't Mrs O'Connor. She's away for a few days. It was another lady.' Katie screwed up her face in concentration. 'Mrs Mullen. She's nice. She talks to me a lot.'

Was she getting paranoid or was there something suspicious in this?

'And what did you say about daddy?'

'Well.' Katie spiked a chip with her fork and held it upright to examine it closely. 'Clare and Carol and me hadn't finished our big painting and we had all the painting pots out and things so she said we could do our story in the morning. What shall I say, mummy?'

'Have you told her you don't have a daddy?'

'Ye-es.' Katie was puzzled. 'But mum, I do have a daddy, don't I? But I mustn't say I do, must I?'

'That's right, pet.'

'That's all right because Mrs Mullen asked me daddy's name and I said I didn't have one.' Katie, relieved that she had said the right thing, finally popped the chip in her mouth.

'What did she say, pet?' Mary tried very hard not to let a note of anxiety creep into her voice.

Katie swallowed. 'She said she was sorry but I could make up one if I liked. I did right, didn't I, mummy? Only it's so difficult remembering.'

'Of course you did, pet. If anyone asks, you must always say daddy's gone to heaven,' said Mary, idly stroking her hair.

'She asked when I last saw daddy.'

'Yes?' God, this was terrible.

'I said yonks and yonks ago.' Katie dabbed a piece of fish finger in a pool of tomato sauce.

Mary felt a cold chill down her spine. 'I think you'd better stay at home for a few days. We'll say you've got a cold. We'll have lessons here and you can ride and we can go shopping. Would you like that?'

'Yes, mum. Can we go and see Liam as well?'

'Of course. Yes, we'll take Liam out for the day.'

Time for a very large gin and tonic, Mary told herself.

Dear Duggie,

I know you are overseas on a job so I'm having this letter forwarded to let you know how I am getting on. I'm fine. The doctors are pleased with me. They said I wouldn't walk for at least six months even with crutches, but I can already get across the ward – with a bit of help from the nurse. I'm using weights so my upper body is like Mighty Mouse while my lower half is like Mickey Mouse. I've stomach muscles like walnuts inside rubber gloves. I've got a great physiotherapist and we do lots of hydro treatment to strengthen the leg. I'm going to prove them wrong when they say I'll never parachute. I've proved them wrong on everything else. I've sweated cobs but I'll sweat more. I'll be jumping out of a Fat Albert yet. I don't know what you're doing but when you get back, come and tell me all about it. Take care of yourself.

Your brother, Billy.

PS You told me not to give up. And I haven't. You'll be proud of me yet.

Fife folded the letter and put the envelope in a side pocket of his canvas bag. He checked the rest of his pockets to make sure he was carrying nothing which could identify him. He heard the choppers coming in low over the mountain forest

274

to their base in the loop of the broad river. Gacha must be confirmed at the hacienda. His men were trained and fired up to go. The arrival of the choppers indicated the attack was on. Time to earn his corn.

Jenny Dove glided over the trim lawn radiating sex like heat from the sun. Men paused as she passed, responding to primeval instincts. She was vivacious, almost frenetically so, and one or two of the senior police officers present at the high-powered reception, especially those who had served with the drugs squad, wondered if she was on cocaine or speed. A blood test would have proved negative. Naturally highly sexed, Jenny was hovering just below the peak of climax. The Japanese businessmen, who were going to run the projected car factory, bowed low to her and she smiled graciously back. She wore a severe grey silk suit with a skirt that was almost too short. The muted colour, a deliberate play on her name, served to highlight her hair with its streaks of copper and rust. Her full lips were pursed and if anyone had watched her closely, they would have noticed her glance once or twice at the wooded hill almost half a mile away and occasionally at her watch.

Tall men with buttoned-up jackets to conceal their Smith & Wesson revolvers stood facing outwards at the perimeter of the gathering, and other policemen with flak jackets and rifles watched from the parapets of the Georgian mansion set in its own large grounds on the edge of Belfast.

Jenny had already spoken to Assistant Commissioner Duncan, a thin, humourless man in uniform carrying brown leather gloves and a cane, and had promised to talk to him again. As four o'clock approached, Jenny excused herself from a senior civil servant in the Northern Ireland Office and, holding her half-full glass of white Burgundy, drifted back towards where Duncan was towering over two bespectacled Japanese. It was unseasonably warm, the earlier breeze had dropped and a few high, fluffy clouds broke up the blue sky. Waitresses in black dresses and small white pinafores circulated with silver trays of vol au vents and glasses of champagne, wines and orange juice. A string quartet played Boccherini on the terrace. All in all a perfect afternoon to flirt with death.

The Japanese smiled in greeting and Jenny manoeuvred so she stood obliquely between Duncan and the wood and smiled serenely. Her loins tingled with anticipatory pleasure.

The sharp crack as the heavy bullet sped less than a yard from her head made her jump. There was a dull boom and the policeman's head exploded in a cloud of blood, tissue and bone, splattering her suit, her hair and her face. She put out her tongue and tasted the saltiness of the vaporized blood. As women screamed, men shouted and the sack that had been Assistant Commissioner (Intelligence) Duncan sank deflated on to the manicured grass Jenny enjoyed the deepest orgasm of her life.

Patrick John Collins took the cup of tea from his sister and stirred it meticulously and slowly six times. The habit drove Virginia mad, but she had long ceased complaining.

'The violence is unfocused. It's clouding the real issues. We've nothing against the Proddies, Virginia. Our battle is with the Crown,' complained Collins. 'Ten dead, including children, at the fish shop bombing in the Shankill, the seven the UFF did at the Rising Sun in Greysteel. These tit-for-tat killings are just driving the politicians closer together. Look at this so-called Downing Street Agreement.'

'We've got too many leaders who believe they're TV celebrities,' sniffed Virginia. 'All they want to do is have their pictures taken shaking hands in Washington. They're losing touch.'

'We'll hear what the Brits have to offer at the peace talks. We must observe the ceasefire up to and during the negotiations to demonstrate we can control the rank and file, but there's no way we'll give up our arms this time. Last time we did that, we were betrayed and massacred.' Collins automatically brushed cigarette ash off his right trouser leg and reached for a pile of housing grant applications.

'While I remember,' said Virginia, beginning to peel vegetables for that night's meal. 'Mary's hoping to see Paddy. She asked if we'd have Katie and Boo for a weekend soon.'

'Not on the phone, I trust.'

'Of course not. She sent a message.'

Collins appeared thoughtful. 'Do you think she knows or suspects about Jenny Dove?'

Virginia stopped to think, knife in one hand, potato in the other. 'I don't see how she can. I think she's reacting to that scare. It must have been Special Branch. What a terrible thing to do, asking a wee lassie about her dead father.'

'I've been wondering about resting Paddy for a while. He's too popular. Too many bloody boozed-up boyos want to sing about him. Too many ASUs want to task him. I think on balance I'll not jeopardize him with this ceasefire looming.'

'He's become a hero among the rank and file, especially the wilder elements,' agreed Virginia, sounding as if she disapproved of O'Keefe's cult status. A knock on the door interrupted her. Collins put down the forms and went to answer it.

When he came back he was frowning.

'He's killed Duncan, the Assistant Commissioner (Intelligence), at a government reception for the Japanese.'

'Did you task him for the hit?'

'No.' Collins looked drawn and tired. 'Duncan wasn't any good. Why kill him and have him replaced by someone better? I was trying to preserve the man, not kill him.'

'Does this mean Paddy's working for someone else or has he decided to go off by himself?' demanded Virginia, drying her hands.

'*Homo alieni juris* or *homo sui juris*?' More and more Collins

277

wished he was back in the classroom doing what he had enjoyed most – teaching. 'I don't know.'

'It'll be a popular hit. Great publicity. The shot'll go around the world.'

God, he felt weary. He felt like a smear of margarine trying to cover a slice of bread. Too little, too thinly spread. An endless grind of problems, day after day, week after week, year after long year. It was making him tired and tetchy. It also carried the risk of making him careless. He'd been working all hours trying to find the informers on top of his Sinn Fein duties. At least the allegations of financial irregularities against Frannie McFadden had been cleared up. He'd been acquitted of stealing that credit card on very slim prosecution evidence and he'd presented balance sheets of the command's accounts to halt the wagging tongues. Collins had had his suspicions that McFadden's gambling was out of control, but he seemed to have cleaned up his act. Collins was glad. But now Paddy was going off the rails. If it wasn't one thing, it was another.

'That's not the point. You can't have him taking pot shots at whoever he fancies. It's bound to affect the run-up to the peace talks,' he told his sister. 'Still, in the short term it'll take attention off that business down south.'

'He's confessed, then?'

'Yes. Named his handlers as well.' Collins lit another cigarette. 'You know, Virginia, I still have a feeling that we were fed O'Rourke. We were meant to find him. I believe in cock-up not conspiracy, but the way the defence was allowed to see evidence which showed he hadn't put batteries into the timing device was either downright careless or bloody deliberate. And I think it was deliberate.'

'But he's guilty?'

'Guilty as sin. They're executing him tonight.'

'Well then. And you got that slag in Antrim. You've done well.' She put a comforting arm around his shoulders.

'Those touts we've found couldn't have blown the Boyle job. There's one still out there, maybe two.'

'Couldn't it have been electronic surveillance? It's not every house that can be swept and kept clean from listening bugs like this one.'

'Ay, it could be. That's the problem. I could be looking for something that isn't there and it's tying us in knots. And now it looks as if we have a loose cannon on our hands.'

'I think you are probably the most evil person alive. I'm scared of you.'

Jenny's lips parted in a ravenous smile, her green eyes turning into spearheads above her high cheek bones.

'You and me together, there's nothing we can't do.'

She slid down his naked body and sank her teeth into his soft inner thigh. O'Keefe gasped and pulled at her hair to raise her head. It became a contest of pain and endurance. When he couldn't stand any more, he screwed the knuckle of his forefinger into the nerve in the small of Jenny's back.

'Whip me.'

It was a command and a challenge. See if you can break me, her eyes taunted. She rolled on her stomach and grasped the brass bedhead with her hands, provocatively raising her bare buttocks and spreading her legs. O'Keefe, at a loss for a moment, pulled his leather belt out of the loops of his trousers. He curled the buckle end of the belt in his fist and uncertainly brought it down across her backside. She grunted softly and raised herself higher in defiance. He struck her again and again. Red weals appeared on her soft skin. Tears welled in her eyes and she clung to the brass rails as the leather descended time and time again until her upper thighs, buttocks and lower back were a criss-cross of livid lines and bruises.

As O'Keefe thought he dare not continue, she turned over. Her face was streaked with tears and her lower lip was swollen where she had been biting it to prevent herself calling out. Again she grasped the bedhead and defied him to strike. After the first two stinging blows, she opened her legs in arrogant defiance of the pain he was inflicting. She gazed directly into O'Keefe's eyes and braced herself for the next blow. He struck her across the flatness of her stomach and gradually worked up until he made the belt whistle down hard across her nipples, once, twice. Jenny's neck muscles knotted with the pain, but she still held his eyes with her own, dropping her gaze only to glance at his erection as he kneeled over her. She returned to his eyes, this time with the hint of victory. O'Keefe slashed her across her pubic bone and again at the diamond of auburn pubic hair. Then suddenly he flicked his wrist and caught her between her outspread legs. She opened her mouth but swallowed her cry. She was stinging, scorching in heat and on fire. O'Keefe whipped her again in exactly the same place. She cried out as the white pain seared up through her belly.

Then she was on him, a whirl of teeth and nails. O'Keefe pinioned her, using his greater strength, held both her hands in one of his, parted her legs and gently, tenderly began to make love to Jenny.

'I tasted his blood, you know.'

Their mutual consent of death bound them together as no wedding ring could have done.

'You smiled at him just as I pulled the trigger.'

'I tried to stand as close as possible so I could feel the wind of the bullet. I was turned on by the idea that you could see me through the sight, you could line me up in the cross-hairs. Now you know how much I trust you.'

O'Keefe remembered he had indeed framed her head in the scope, had studied her flaming mane with the cross-hairs on her forehead and, for more than a passing moment, thought about squeezing the trigger.

Chapter Twenty-seven

Billy took a swig of lager from the can and frowned impatiently at the tanned, emaciated figure of his brother sprawled on the sofa. There were as many versions of Fife's escapade as there were pubs in Aldershot, but all Fife wanted to do was talk about Billy.

'Para Reg were willing to keep me on as a storeman armourer but there was no way they were going to let me jump, so I thought bugger it,' explained Billy. 'I've worked on my leg so I can tab for miles and it's getting stronger all the time.'

'So you quit?' demanded Fife. He was trying not to take the next painkiller until at least 5 PM – a few minutes later each day. The amoebic dysentery and the infection had left him limp and spent; his face had lost so much flesh it resembled a living skull.

'I've quit the Paras but . . .' Billy stood up and began pacing the floor of the Lewisham flat as if to show his leg was better, his pent-up nervous energy preventing him from sitting still any longer. '. . . but I've joined the Royal Highland Fusiliers.'

'You've done what!'

'You told me not to give up and I didn't. The last doctor reckoned there was no reason why I shouldn't join the infantry. Just not the bloody Paras.' There was a hint of bitterness in his voice. 'The Jocks were glad to have me. I report at Redford barracks at 0900 Monday.'

'Billy, that's bloody marvellous. Good for you.' Fife's face flushed with pride at his younger brother. He struggled to pull himself upright. 'Bloody good for you, kid.'

Lizzie brought in the hillock of corned beef sandwiches,

281

put two rounds on a plate and placed them beside Fife, regarding him with tender concern.

'Here you are, Billy. Help yourself.'

'I can't eat all that, hen.' Fife looked at the food with distaste.

'There's a battalion in Northern Ireland. I want to get out there as fast as possible,' continued Billy.

'You'd better hurry up. It looks like peace is breaking out,' Lizzie chimed in.

'So what happened to you?' Billy addressed his older brother. 'There's stories that you were set up.'

'Set-up. Fuck-up. Call it what you want.' Fife pulled a wry face. 'We were ten Ks from the war RV when we heard on the radio that Gacha had left. We scrubbed and as we turned back, my command chopper's engine began coughing and spluttering. We were in the mountains and we couldn't maintain altitude. Finally we just fell into the jungle. The two in the back got a rotor blade across their heads and the pilot died the next day, so I was the only survivor. I had no radio, four cracked ribs, a twisted ankle and not a lot of water. It took me fourteen days to hack back.'

It was a long speech and it left Fife almost as exhausted as he'd been the day he crawled out of the jungle to that startled peon's hut. Billy began asking questions, but Lizzie was quick was step in.

'You mustn't tire him, Billy.'

'He's all right. The Regiment wants me to give a lecture on my escape when I'm stronger. I'll get you in on that.'

'Was it sabotage?'

Fife shrugged. 'The pilot seemed to think it was dirty petrol. Who knows? No one bust a gut to come looking for me, that's for sure. They were surprised to see me when I finally got out.'

'Word is you got £75,000 for the job.'

Fife laughed weakly while Lizzie made a noise like a kettle boiling over. Billy looked uncertainly from one to the other.

'Typical bloody army. It's no one's business how much it was, but as it happens it was £50,000 and he won't touch a penny of it.'

Fife made a dismissive gesture with his hand.

'I'm not taking money from one hood to wipe out another, I've told you, hen. We're not hard up.' Fife saw Billy looking puzzled. 'Keep it to yourself, Billy. It *was* a set-up.'

'What!'

'The Escobar family put up the money to rub out the rival Gacha clan. The CIA and MI6 knew about it; they were happy to let it happen. One drugs baron less. I wasn't meant to come back.'

'How d'you know?'

'I had a visit from the suits. If the attack had gone ahead and I survived, they were going to shoot down my chopper on the way out. In a way the accident saved my life.'

'What about the guy who gave you the job?'

'Colonel Almaro was certainly in on the double cross. If I see him again I'll drop him on the spot. Don't know about Baines-Hickey. I intend to pay him a visit when I'm stronger. If I thought . . .'

He erupted in a burst of coughing, pulling his knees into his chest to ease the pain on his ribs. Lizzie decided enough was enough.

As she saw Billy to the front door she said proudly, 'A couple of blokes from the Regiment called in to see him. They said it was a miracle he made it out of the jungle. They reckoned no one but the Mean Machine could have done it.'

'He doesn't look well,' said Billy.

'You should have seen him when he first came back.'

Boyle looked out through the windscreen at the dark clouds building over the Irish Sea. There was a storm coming. The sea sensed it, sending up steep angry waves with white peaks. He could smell the fear on the wee man sitting behind him. The heat was still on to find the killer of AC Duncan. While leaders and diplomats talked, on the street the IRA was having its balls squeezed.

'So, what's the word, Dermot?'

'They say the big man's got a bird.'

'What do you mean? A girlfriend?'

'No. A bird who helps him.' Dermot ran his fingernails down the back of his hand. 'There's something funny about her. Talks posh.'

'Where's this from?'

'Some bloke who was supposed to secure the flat the prison warder was shot from. He was curious to see the big man so he hung around and there was a good-looking bird with red hair. She was carrying things into the flat. This bloke held the lift and she said thanks or something, but it was a strange accent.'

The words came out in a breathless, whining rush. Dermot ceaselessly peered through the car windows at the deserted promenade and wriggled lower in his seat.

Boyle recalled a report from the watchers of E4A which crossed his desk and he'd stored away in his mental filing cabinet. They'd seen Patrick John Collins meet an attractive auburn-haired woman at the Lansdowne Hotel. They'd been following Old Holborn and it had not been possible to take photographs of her. Perhaps she was the same woman.

And what if the killer did not have a woman but was in fact a woman. Christ. They'd never even played with the idea.

'Has there ever been word that the hit man could be a woman?' he asked.

Dermot shook his head in brief jerking movements. 'Not even a whisper, Mr Boyle.'

'What about Patrick John?'

Wee Dermot twitched visibly. 'I'm scared, Mr Boyle. Patrick John's the devil. They say he's this witchfinder bloke. He'll have me like he had Porky O'Rourke down south. Christ, they shot him in the head and executed him.' His voice rose to a squeak.

Boyle discerned two strands in Dermot's disconnected ramblings, confirmation of something he'd heard elsewhere. Collins was coming out of the woodwork. He'd known there had to be more to Old Holborn than just the scholarly Sinn Fein councillor and Republican intellectual. Recent activity was proving him right. Collins behaved every minute of every day as if he expected to be watched, bugged and followed, and he acted accordingly. They'd lost him totally for three days and another time he'd surfaced in Dublin after going missing for two days. Despite his witchhunting he'd led them to no one.

Secondly, wee Dermot was on the verge of cracking up.

'They were meant to find O'Rourke,' lied Boyle. 'I gave him to them to protect you. I told you I would and I have.'

Dermot summoned up all his courage. 'I don't want to do this any more, Mr Boyle.'

His forehead was covered with sweat and his eyes rolled around like a terrified racehorse. It had to come, acknowledged Boyle. The moment when the informer judged the risks outweighed the rewards, the threats or whatever motivated him.

Tough. Fucking tough. He did not reply and Dermot felt obliged to fill the silence.

'They're going to know it was me who told you about the ambush. Collins'll put two and two together and find me. He's very clever.'

'How's he going to find you? You're one of the many, Dermot. That's your strength. A messenger and a carrier, that's all.' Boyle made an effort to reassure the man.

'But the bakery . . .' Dermot won an internal struggle. 'I'm sorry, Mr Boyle. I'm grateful. Don't think I'm not, but I've had enough. If there's a ceasefire you won't be needing me, will you?' he said with forlorn hope.

'Calm down. Don't do anything hasty.' Boyle had known

touts who'd gone to the IRA and confessed, implicating their handlers and blowing the whole bloody operation. He didn't need that. 'I'll not bother you for a while.'

'For ever, Mr Boyle,' wheedled Dermot.

'For ever's a long time, Dermot. Don't forget that report from the children's home.'

'I don't go there any more.'

'Too late, Dermot.'

'That's blackmail.'

'Yes,' agreed DCI Boyle.

'Take your time. Exhale gently, now squeeze the trigger.' Jenny tried to do as O'Keefe instructed. 'You're too tense and you're holding your breath. Just breathe normally. Get your eye closer to the sight.'

Jenny tried to come to terms with the big gun. Three hundred yards away on a cliff edge, a supermarket frozen chicken sat on a rock in front of two large black sheets of artist's paper, stuck together to make a backdrop. The tufts of coarse grass, the heather and the wheeling gulls and gannets took O'Keefe back to the Falklands.

After much badgering and cajoling, he had finally agreed to teach Jenny to fire the Robar. He'd chosen an inaccessible length of cliff outside Schull in West Cork where they were posing as holidaymakers, hiding the rifle in a specially constructed recess in the chassis of Jenny's BMW with the English number plates. They had parked on a lonely headland and scrambled over rocks for almost an hour before O'Keefe set up the target facing the sea.

Yesterday, they'd spent two hours pretending to fire the unloaded gun out of the bedroom window of the rented farmhouse at cows in the nearby field. He'd made her strip the rifle and reassemble it until she could do it blindfold.

'Spread your legs more. You should be used to that.' He was rewarded by an index finger jerked skywards. 'Make a firm fire base.'

With the bipod supporting the long barrel, Jenny pressed

the stock into her shoulder and wriggled until she felt comfortable. O'Keefe adjusted her body position. 'Put your right arm and elbow out at more of an angle to help form the shoulder pocket. That's it. The right hand must hold the stock firmly, thumb over the top forming a spot weld against your cheek. Don't slacken your hold on the trigger. A loose grip can make you jerk at the last moment. Keep the eye still relative to the sight before and after firing. Breathe easily. The rise and fall of your chest will spoil the shot. Don't hold your breath for too long. You must fire so that you do not disturb the way the weapon is lined up with the target.'

All second nature for Paddy – and a hell of a lot for her to absorb. The cross-hairs drifted on to the chicken. She remembered to partly exhale and squeezed the trigger. Click.

'Better. This time's for real.' He slipped a long cartridge into the breech and pulled back the bolt. She felt a tingle of nervous anticipation.

'Take your time.' She didn't. She snatched at the trigger and closed her eyes as the boom of the gun startled her. O'Keefe looking through binoculars shook his head. The next time Jenny made herself relax and breathe easily, bracing herself against the recoil of the rifle.

'High and to the right,' announced O'Keefe. Her next shot was two feet away in the same quadrant. O'Keefe adjusted the sights for windage and elevation. Jenny's hands were trembling, but she was enjoying cradling the awesome power of the heavy gun. That Freudian crap about the weapon in the hand as the extension of the organ maybe wasn't so much crap after all.

The next two shots were level with the target but to the left. Seagulls rose, whirling and screeching in protest at each explosion and out to sea a small fishing boat had appeared on the horizon.

Jenny looked serious and determined as she pushed her hair aside and felt the cool of the gunmetal against her cheek. Her ears were ringing as she exhaled and pulled the trigger. The chicken disintegrated in an exploding mass of pulp.

'Wow. Jesus. Look at that.'

The thrill of the hit surged through her like a sexual current. She leapt to her feet and did a little dance of joy. Soon, soon she would have a real target in her sights.

'You'll not get anywhere in the army unless you can get a vindaloo down your neck,' grinned Fife, ripping off a piece of nan bread and dipping it in the dark, pungent sauce.

Billy wiped the sweat off his forehead with his sleeve and took a gulp of lager.

'That's what you're doing wrong,' lectured Fife. 'Drinking lager on top of curries is like throwing kerosene on a fire. Use the rice or the yoghurt to cool it down. Mind you, this isn't a real vindaloo. We had one in Goa once, pork pickled in vinegar. Now that was a ring sting. Had to keep the loo paper in the fridge.'

Billy was quietly drunk. He was having trouble keeping his eyes open, but he wasn't going to admit it in front of Duggie. Not long ago, Fife had been an emaciated wreck. Now the Lean Mean Killing Machine was back to almost full health and fitness – a testimony to his natural strength and resilience.

'Och, it runs in the family,' he said when Billy complimented him. 'Look how you came back after that injury. Here's to you. You deserved your award for best recruit. Your mam was full of it. Proudest day of her life, watching you pass out at Redford Barracks. Enjoy this meal, you'll not be having many of these in South Armagh. You never get to leave the basha there. We lived on egg banjos. Bloody awful place. Four days a time out in the cuds. I don't know why you're so anxious to get there.'

'It's somewhere to start,' replied Billy. The red flock

wallpaper began to swim before his eyes. An Indian waiter peered anxiously at him. He told himself he was not going to be sick.

'It's a shame we've stopped using the FNs.'

Fife was quick to agree. 'Yeh, the SA80's a bloody awful weapon. Does too much for what you want it for.'

'Yeh. But . . .' Billy hoped he was not going to sound childish. 'I could have used Paddy's bayonet.'

'Have you still got that?' Duggie Fife's face broke into a delighted beam. 'The one he brought you back from the Falklands?'

'It's going to Ireland. I used it on my rifle in the Cadets. It's my good luck charm. That and your Saint Michael.'

Fife didn't point out that the Saint Michael hadn't prevented Billy from breaking his leg and he suddenly felt a pang of fear for the future.

'You take care down there. It's bad country.'

'I'll be all right. What with Paddy's bayonet and your medal, what can happen to me?'

'Don't be cocky. And don't be mouthy. No one likes a gobby nigg. Stay quiet and learn. Pick one soldier who's a professional, watch what he does and copy him.'

Fife felt absurdly protective towards his younger brother. Billy was in the army because he had been in the army. Billy had followed in his footsteps.

'Hello, hen. You're on time. Have a drink.'

Lizzie inspected the two men. Billy looked the worse for wear and Duggie had spots of high colour on his cheeks, a sure sign he'd been drinking heavily. It was Billy's last night on leave. He flew to Scotland on the first shuttle and then left to join his battalion in Northern Ireland.

'What's the point of me having a drink when I've come to drive you home,' she laughed. 'A coffee, please.'

'It's Billy's last supper. Eat, drink and be merry for tomorrow you die.'

Billy mumbled some indistinct words of apology, rose and did his best not to run towards the lavatories.

'He idolizes you, you know,' scolded Lizzie. 'You shouldn't make fun of him.'

'Och. I mean no harm. And he'll have the piss taken out of him enough in the army. He's a good lad and he's going to make a grand soldier.'

'He's worked hard to get where he is. Be easy on him. He's got a difficult act to follow.'

'Of course I'm proud of him, but we're Scots, Lizzie. We don't express our feelings.'

Billy returned looking better. He began toying with his food.

'Hopefully these peace talks will come off and then there'll be no risk,' smiled Lizzie.

'Och. I don't want them to happen yet. I'm hoping to see some action. I've dreamed of this.' Billy's eyes lit up. 'Lizzie, all my life I've been the boy who listened while Duggie and Paddy and others told stories. No more. Now I'm going to be the man who tells the stories.'

Chapter Twenty-eight

'You've not been responding to my calls.'

'I'm here now.'

'Well?'

'Well what?'

Patrick John Collins gave Jenny the sad reproachful look that a teacher would give his favourite pupil who'd failed an examination.

'AC Duncan.'

'Good hit, wasn't it?'

'Untasked and unasked-for. Some of our masters were not best pleased.'

Jenny impatiently flicked back her hair with her long fingers, showing off her burnished copper nails.

'People will say hard things of us now, but we shall be remembered by posterity and blessed by unborn generations.' She stared defiantly at Collins, who did not meet her gaze but concentrated on rolling a cigarette.

'I've always thought Pearse's poem casting himself as Jesus and his mother as Mary sums up so much of what is wrong with Ireland. Irish women think their sons are saints and Irish men believe their mothers are virgins.'

'You're not a fan of Pearse's! You surprise me.' There was a definite coolness in her tone. She had expected praise for the killing and here she was being told off.

'Pearse's overall military and political ends were undefined. Leading a raggle-taggle army to seize Dublin's Post Office and declaring independence – what was that supposed to achieve? There was no clear end and he certainly didn't possess the means to carry out the end.'

'Pearse's end was his own death and I believe he sought

that death.' How dare Collins insult one of her heroes, one of the great leaders of the 1916 Rising.

'That was the only clear intention about him,' retorted Collins.

'What are you saying, Mr Collins?'

'I'm saying there is no room for the flamboyant gesture.'

'Not even if it is successful?' shot back Jenny. 'The hit made news around the world. Our masters may not have been happy, but the foot soldiers were all for it.'

'Sometimes, especially if it's successful. The shooting jeopardized our place at the negotiating table. It put our leaders in the uncomfortable position of being asked to dissociate themselves from the killing and to condemn violence. They didn't want to be asked those questions. Don't you understand?'

Jenny reddened and looked away at others in the tea room of the large Belfast department store. Collins pressed on. 'It would have been better if the trigger had not been pulled. I haven't been able to get a message to you because of the storm you brought down around our heads. The organization has been paralysed. We have an unspoken understanding not to take out their very top men. Don't you think we could have killed the GOC or the RUC's Chief Constable if we wanted to? The assassin will always get through, but killing can be counter-productive.'

Collins idly inspected the tea room's clientele which consisted largely of middle-class, middle-aged women resting in the middle of their shopping; exactly why he had chosen the rendezvous. But there were two young men loitering by the Danish pastry selection. He believed he'd lost his watchers with the help of the dustcart which had blocked their car. Maybe they had summoned a back-up team. He didn't know. That was the problem. Nowadays, he never knew. And he was tired of it.

'Once I got word to you, you didn't respond.' Collins sighed. 'Whose idea was it?'

'We decided he was an ideal target,' declared Jenny in a bold voice. She wanted to make it clear to Collins that she did not regret the killing. 'I heard of the reception and got myself an invitation.'

Collins was quick to pick up on her slip.

'So, you weren't even spotting.'

'Duncan and other senior officers in the RUC didn't believe we should have a voice at the peace conference.' Her eyes blazed directly into his. 'How dare they? It's our lives, our souls, and they ignore us. We showed them that they exclude us at their peril.'

There was no deference, no apology for what had happened. Only stubborn disobedience and the burning belief that she was right.

'The killing of Duncan was a mistake,' repeated Collins. He had to make her see that she was wrong. But instead she mocked.

'What would you have me do? Go round intoning "Out, out damned spot"?'

Intriguing comparison, thought Collins. Jenny Dove as Lady Macbeth, with her ambition sustaining the physically courageous but morally weaker Paddy O'Keefe.

'No, but I wish you'd remember that all our yesterdays have lighted fools the way to dusty death.'

'Very clever,' said Jenny sardonically. Macbeth's speech on hearing of the death of his wife. Is Collins threatening me in some abstruse way?

With a flash of intuition, Collins demanded, 'Did Paddy know he was freelancing?'

'He was comfortable with the target. He thought Duncan should die.'

'Only because his wife told him so,' replied Old Holborn, again lapsing into the Macbeth analogy. 'Vaulting ambition can o'erstep itself, you know.'

Jenny glared at him. Why should Collins be the only one to nominate the target? What gave him the right to tell her what to do? He was nothing but an old has-been, unable to keep pace with the movement's future. Let him spout Macbeth to his heart's content in the dull and dusty corners of forgotten rooms. We'll fight in sunshine and the glow of burning buildings.

Collins gave up trying to make Jenny see sense. Instead he leaned forward and smiled.

'It's just as well you seem to enjoy difficult targets because the next one is in a class of its own.'

Jenny, assuming that Old Holborn was offering an olive branch, softened and raised an eyebrow in interest.

'He's one of ours. A traitor. These are delicate times, but the Brits won't object to us dealing with one of our own. They'll know what it's about and they'll know that if they make a fuss, then we can embarrass them by revealing their agent-running techniques.'

The two men had sat down at a nearby table. They didn't have the stamp of watchers, but then they didn't have any shopping with them either.

Jenny leaned forward, straining to pick up Collins's deliberately mumbled words.

'His name is Roddy Donlan and he's privy to the inner councils. Donlan can give the Brits a daily feedback of our reactions to the negotiations. The Brits think they've turned him. He claims to be playing a double game, but I've a growing notion Donlan could actually be handing over the crown jewels. We're going to bait a trap and this is where you come in. He meets his handler in a clever way. First he signals that he has information by the position of his bedroom curtains. Then by a combination of curtains and windows open or closed he nominates one of four roads where there's a standing vehicle checkpoint. He's stopped at the checkpoint, made to get out of his car and enter the bunker, seemingly to have his driving documents examined. In reality, that's when he meets his handler.

'We're going to feed Donlan information which, if he's a traitor, he'll want to pass on promptly. At the same time we'll summon him to a meeting in Monaghan. Donlan lives in Armagh, so he can tell the Brits to pick him up at the checkpoint outside Middletown near the border. It's one of his regular stops. We want you at the VCP. If Donlan gets out of his car and begins to walk to the command bunker, it means he's a traitor. Kill him. If he stays in his car or isn't stopped, it'll mean our fears are groundless.' Collins drew on his roll-up. 'I rather feel Donlan'll walk.'

'When?'

'Four or five days. No longer. Avoid the road. Everyone is filmed at the checkpoint and they keep the tapes. Don't put yourself in the frame.'

Collins thought the two men had been lingering too long over their coffee. Keeping his voice level, he continued. 'There're two men sitting behind you who I don't fancy. I want you to leave now and I'll see if you're followed. If you are, or if you even suspect you are, walk into the Lansdowne Hotel in twenty-five minutes from now and the cavalry will come to the rescue. Don't go near your car and don't take any chances.'

At that moment, the two men rose to their feet, smiled at each other and prepared to squeeze between the crowded tables. The first man reached back and discreetly pressed the other's hand in an intimate gesture.

'Patrick John. I don't know what the target looks like.' Jenny knew she'd been right. The man was losing his grip.

'There's an envelope with Donlan's picture tucked in the map book lying on the back seat of your car which, if you remember, is parked in bay D116 level four in the multistorey around the corner. Don't look at it until you're clear of the city.'

Jenny Dove was both bored and nervous. She had been in her sniper's hide for nine hours now and the excitement had given way to tedium. She was beginning to understand Paddy's phrase: Hurry up and wait.

The slit trench was covered by scrim netting entangled

with leaves and branches. More scraps of netting and foliage were fixed to the long barrel of the rifle by rubber bands to soften its straight lines. She had taken off her rings and wristwatch in case they reflected the sunlight. From her position on the spur of high ground the .50 round would carry over the two lush fields and a small wood to where a tributary of the Blackwater river followed the road and where the British army had built a checkpoint just half a mile from the border with the Irish Republic.

As the sun rose her dank, earthy pit turned hot and airless and for hours now she had fought down the panic of claustrophobia. Looking through the sight, Jenny had come to recognize the soldiers dealing with the steady stream of cars, vans, lorries and tractors as individuals; the fat jolly corporal; the eager youngster who seemed to be everywhere, busy on one chore or another; the thin, grumpy one with the glasses who hadn't smiled in the hours she'd been watching.

Mid-morning, Jenny used the Redfield telescopic sight to re-measure the distance to the checkpoint. She set the sight on three to give the widest field of vision and adjusted the magnification power until the difference between the two horizontal lines at the top of the lens bridged a soldier's torso, estimated at eighteen inches from waist to neck. She read off 500 metres from the lower right-hand corner and agreed that the sight was set accordingly. She increased the magnification to its maximum of nine so that the cross-hairs were only just visible.

The leaves on the trees were constantly moving, indicating a wind speed of around five miles an hour. The wind was from directly behind her so she didn't need to alter the windage on the sight. She forced herself to finish the Mars bar and took a swig of water, grateful that Paddy had insisted she carry at least two pints. She put the chocolate wrapper in her pocket. Never leave anything behind. A blackbird fussed in the hedgerow behind her.

Fifty yards up the slope, a growing nervousness that he had been wrong to let Jenny make the hit was gnawing away at Paddy O'Keefe. She had gone on and on at him, wheedling, beseeching, arguing and throwing tantrums until he had finally given way. She had desperately wanted the opportunity to prove herself. She argued that Donlan was the ideal opportunity; a low-grade target, a mere messenger in the Monaghan Brigade. Jenny said Collins wanted Donlan killed because he would lead the Brits to arms dumps during the ceasefire. The shooting would have fewer repercussions than the hit on Assistant Commissioner Duncan. That had been a beauty. The High Command had been delighted, said Jenny. One day they would congratulate him in person.

O'Keefe heard the bells of the convent in Middletown to the east. The angelus. To his left, down their escape route along the sunken lane, he could see a silver glint of the waters of Glasloch in the Republic. No one was stirring, not even a rabbit.

His silenced mobile phone on the grass flashed.

The target was on his way. Jenny extended a gloved hand and gave the thumbs up to show she too had received the message. The target would park his car and walk in a straight line away from Jenny to the protected door of the bunker, so she wouldn't need to judge the lead-in. It was all going to be so simple.

Jenny wriggled her toes and suppressed a nervous yawn. Patience. Patience.

A civilian car drew up at the checkpoint. An officer escorted two men in suits through the barbed wire entanglements into the concrete command post. Jenny felt herself tighten like a turned screw. She became intoxicatingly aware of the smell of the warm grass and the buzz of insects. She checked the range and the elevation for the last time. Three and a half minutes for 200 metres, nine minutes for 400. Stop it. It's all set up.

She fidgeted when she should have been still.

A red Montego was at the barrier. She let the air escape between her lips like a tyre deflating. The Robar rested on its bipod, steadied by her left hand, her left elbow under the receiver. She pulled the butt into her neck and squared her shoulders. Head, arm, hand and weapon acted as a single unit. The soldiers appeared huge through the sight. Paddy told her to always shoot on the lowest magnification. She'd ignored him today. Nine gave her a larger target but made the movement of the cross-hairs more pronounced. Perhaps she should lessen it.

Jenny moved unnecessarily to get more comfortable and in doing so put herself off balance. Through the scope, she saw the willing squaddie directing the car into a parking bay. The driver got out. Tall with short cropped hair, late 30s. Donlan.

A crescent-shaped shadow appeared on the left side of the sight telling Jenny she was not looking directly through the scope. Donlan locked his car and walked towards the bunker. She pressed her right eye closer to the sight as the young fusilier drifted between her and her target, blocking her shot. Shit.

Jenny held her breath for too long. She exhaled with a gasp and the cross-hairs lurched across the carpark and through the barbed wire. She took a steadying breath and found she had canted the rifle, tipping it to one side so that the muzzle was no longer vertical with the sights.

Jesus. Get it right.

Donlan stood with his back to her but the cross-hairs were to the left of the target now. Somehow she had pivoted around, only fractionally but enough to throw the shot. She readjusted and found she was over-correcting. Chasing her target. The stock was growing heavier. She was finding it difficult to hold the rifle still. Concentrate on hand-eye co-ordination. Easier said than done.

Donlan was at the door. The hairs lined up on his back as the soldier stood to one side. Her finger tightened around the trigger. Her last chance. The cross drifted seemingly by

298

itself on to the back of Donlan's neck; hair curling almost to the collar of his green jacket. Yes, oh, yes.

Jenny squeezed the trigger.

Nothing.

She cried out in anger. She'd forgotten to take off the safety catch. The safety catch Paddy had put on when loading the rifle all those bloody hours ago.

Jenny fumbled and knocked off the catch. The door was closing. She was seized by rage and frustration. Her one and only chance – gone. Her face contorted into a grotesque mask of hate and resentment.

No. No. No. Jenny kicked the trench in impotent fury. This bloody peace would spoil everything. She'd never again have the chance to fire the Robar in anger. She'd never fire at a living target. She would never kill a man.

Hell and damnation.

That squaddie. The one who seemed to be everywhere, stood by the door laughing. Laughing at her. Mocking her failure. Her lips drew back in an animal snarl. The cross-hairs were steady now. Jenny Dove pulled the trigger.

Part Four

Chapter Twenty-nine

The bloody chips were soggy. Typical Belfast chips. Couldn't get a decent bag of chips south of Leeds. Certainly not here on the edge of The Markets. The pub door opened and a warm cloud of stale beer and cigarette smoke billowed out. The player had been in there for twenty-two minutes. He was going to have to go in and make sure chummy hadn't slipped out the back. No big deal. It wasn't one of the shitholes down the Falls or in the Murph where you wouldn't walk in because you knew you'd never walk out again. The brewery had tarted it up with dark green paint and gold harps and shamrocks to make it look like an American's idea of an Irish pub. An Irish theme pub in Ireland. The thin, scruffy man with the long lank hair covering his earpiece grinned to himself.

Two army Land-Rovers whirred past. You didn't see them so often now. The peace talks were about to begin; the ceasefire was in place and the city was slowly moving back to normality after so many years.

It didn't mean the IRA rested. Nor did he.

He scrunched up the chip paper and tossed it in the gutter. It would have been out of character to look for a litter bin. He wiped his greasy palms on his stonewashed jeans and booted the wrapping towards the drain. As he leaned forward, his body communication harness cut into his armpits. The harness could restrict him if he got into a bundle. He was going to have to adjust it. A damp breeze came off the Irish Sea and he pulled his windcheater around him, grateful for the unseasonal weather. It was difficult to conceal even a Walther when everyone was wearing shorts and tee-shirt.

He pressed the transmit button taped to the inside of his left wrist.

'Romeo. Golf.'

'Golf. Go.'

'Golf's entering the bar.'

'Roger, golf. Romeo's backing you foxtrot.'

'Lima's mobile.'

'November's mobile. Have you visual.'

'Roger.'

One of the team would take his place at the bus stop while the other two cruised locally.

Okay. Relax. Just flake into the scene. Here comes Mr Grey Man doing a fair impersonation of Mr Bag O'Shite.

Saturday night and the pub was crowded. He found a place at the end of the bar and ordered a Guinness in an accent that was convincing enough if he didn't have to get into a prolonged conversation. He looked around the bar without making eye contact, giving it just the mildly inquisitive once-over you'd give a strange pub. O'Hanlon was sitting in the corner with a couple of known faces. Thin-lipped, wandering left eye. Intelligence suspected he would be moving a large quantity of Semtex to a long-term hiding place in the next few days. He looked settled for the night. His missus and his kids were away and this was play time.

And in another half an hour it would be dark enough to break into his pebble-dashed council house in Short Strand, have a look see and leave a little something behind.

'Golf, romeo. Confirm bravo.'

He pressed his wrist mic sending two bursts of squelch as an affirmative.

'What did I have, said the fine old woman, What did I have, this fine old woman did say. I had four green fields and each of them a jewel, But strangers came and tried to take them from me . . .'

A reedy Irish tenor pierced the babble of conversation.

Shit! Who's that small bloke sitting near the door, singing

with gusto. He stopped himself frowning with concentration. He'd seen him before. Where? In a photograph or in person. There was something different. The glasses? Had his hair been shorter? He saw so many photographs every day. He put his training into play and mentally recalled the mug shots on the board of the briefing room in the hangar at Aldergrove airport. No. He was certain the face wasn't on the hit parade. The B League? The pack of pix they all flicked through every couple of days or so. He didn't think so. God. It was infuriating. He stole another glance. A player? A suspect? A BTO?

If he's not from a pic, then he's from real life. From where? From Newcastle, where he came from? He let his mind roam around his old haunts. Had they served together in the Light Infantry? He tried to imagine the man wearing khaki and then tried to see him on parade or in the NAAFI. Again the pieces of memory just wouldn't form a cohesive picture.

'There was war and death, plundering and pillage . . .'

Try in Ireland. He'd been in Derry for six months before it was feared he'd been compromised. The cold grey terraced houses stretching up the hill towards the Creggan? No. Down in the Bogside? Shantello? The face remained elusive. He'd seen it more than once.

'But my sons have sons as brave as were their fathers. My four green fields will bloom once again, said she.'

The singing ended on a rousing cheer and he tore himself away from his puzzle to become aware that two men against the far wall were giving him the eye. Soon they'd want a word. Time to move. O'Hanlon had just been bought a pint. He wasn't going anywhere. The other man was making his drink last. Who the bloody hell was he?

A thin, viscous film had spread over wee Dermot's upper lip.

'Honest, Mr Collins. Honest.'

Collins believed wee Dermot was a snivelling, amoral

wretch who would have difficulty defining the word. He had obviously been terrified, but was it the terror of an innocent man facing the executioner's bullet or had Dermot something to hide?

'Remember, Dermot. Confession is good for the soul. Only through confession can you find redemption.'

Tears welled in Dermot's pleading eyes. Tears of pity for himself. There's something there, mused Collins. Something hidden deep. Some terror greater than I can wield, some secret more deadful than that of informing.

He took a cup of tea from his sister and sat in his armchair still thinking of the interview. Dermot was back at work in the bakery with two new hands who were obviously Provo heavies just there to turn the screw.

'Take a biscuit. You're not eating enough to keep a sparrow alive. Here.'

Virginia piled three custard creams on a plate and gave her brother a concerned sideways look.

Collins recalled one of his failures in the early days. There had been a leak and the finger had pointed at one man who had guilt written all over him. He hadn't protested and they executed him. Two months later, the truth emerged. He wasn't a traitor. He had been sexually abusing his daughter. Perhaps he saw his death as an atonement. The hard men would have shot him for incest anyway. He returned to the present. He had narrowed the leak in the Boyle ambush down to one of three, with Dermot as the prime suspect. Collins would find the man, ceasefire or no ceasefire.

'Is it today Paddy and Jenny move into the farmhouse?'

Virginia brought him unwillingly on to yet another problem. He didn't feel well and he'd lost weight – not that he had any to lose. He was sleeping badly and a couple of nights he'd woken up drenched in sweat – and not the sweat of nightmares. He'd go and see a doctor for a check-up when he had time. He never had time. He'd make time tomorrow. Let others enjoy their ceasefire, his problems continued unabated.

'It should be, although they've become so erratic that I don't know anymore.'

Golden Virginia scowled. 'You're going to have to rein him in.'

'Easier said than done.' Collins methodically stirred his tea and she gritted her teeth. 'I've thought it might be better to dispense with him altogether after the last shooting. The Crown came within an inch of cancelling the talks. The Loyalists loved it. It gave them the chance to say we couldn't control our men. No, it might be better to dispense with him.'

'What do you mean, "dispense with him"?' Virginia was alert and prepared to do battle. 'He's done you and the movement proud. If you feel he doesn't have a role any longer, then pension him off. You've done that before.'

Collins bit into the biscuit, pieces falling on his grey sleeveless pullover. Virginia hovered anxiously. She considered O'Keefe as much her protégé as Patrick John's and she was not willing to see him harmed.

'The ceasefire won't last,' she prophesied. 'You'll need him again.'

'I think it's in our interest to make the ceasefire last,' replied Collins evenly. 'It's got us to the negotiating table. It's got us recognition as a legitimate voice . . .'

Virginia snorted. 'If you call our so-called leaders posing in dinner jackets in front of the TV cameras recognition. And you can't tell me you believe in giving up our arms while the British are still in Ireland.'

'Of course not.' Collins was impatient. 'But there'll be no place for O'Keefe if the ceasefire sticks. He'll be an embarrassment to both sides. Sometimes, Virginia, it's difficult to pension off gunmen. They become dependent upon killing. They need the excitement. It's like a drug which feeds them. Remember Danny McCann, he was an adrenalin junkie. If he hadn't been killed on the Rock, he would have got it somewhere else.'

'O'Keefe's too professional to let that happen to him.'

Collins stretched out for his tobacco tin, spilling crumbs on the carpet. His sister tutted in disapproval and bent down to brush them up with her hand.

'How do you explain the killing of the squaddie?'

'Why don't you ask them?'

'I'm not going to change standard operating procedure. I'll see Jenny the day after tomorrow.'

Virginia pulled a sour face. It had been an inspiration to give O'Keefe a lily-white woman as a spotter and liaison, but on a personal level she regarded it as unfair on Mary.

'Still, good did come out of it.'

'Yes, we won't have to worry about Donlan's loyalty for a while.' Collins gave a wry smile while turning the roll-up in his fingers. 'He believes the killing was a warning. Now he's falling over himself to pump out whatever bilge we want. We'll use his handlers' questions as indicators of the Crown's areas of uncertainty.'

'So O'Keefe did you a favour.'

'No.' Old Holborn was not willing to let it go that far. 'It was a cock-up and I made the best of a bad job.'

'What do you reckon to this INLA talk?'

'About O'Keefe? Wishful thinking. *Fama nihil est celerius.*' He took the proffered new cup of tea and flicked ash into the saucer. 'They'd love to have him. It would give them the standing they need. At the moment they're just a marginalized bunch of violent, unfocused psychopaths.'

Still, the thought of O'Keefe throwing in his lot with the Irish National Liberation Army made Collins wince. He didn't need any more problems.

'So what will you do about Paddy?'

'I don't know yet.'

He drew on his cigarette and the wreathing smoke prevented him seeing Virginia's sharp look of disbelief. This wasn't like her brother. He always knew what he was doing three or four moves ahead – certainly two more than anyone else.

* * *

O'Keefe glanced in his driving mirror to ensure the B143 was empty before turning into the unmarked lane which skirted the high ground on the right. As he climbed he saw the sun glistening on the myriad lakes and watercourses to the south and west. He hit the A34. There was not another vehicle to be seen and within 300 yards he turned off again, still tacking south. He drove through Aghnahinch and Clonkee, marking the single bar in the row of low cottages and the newer bungalows back from the road in the rolling farmland. At Kilgarrow Lake he turned right and he saw the blue-tinged hills and the heights of Slieve Rushden across the border in the Republic.

He passed the rickety wooden milk stand and the un-metalled track, driving almost a mile until he pulled into a lay-by with a panoramic view over the waters of Upper Lough Erne. O'Keefe glanced at the lough, then turned his back and climbed the hill on the other side of the road. At the top he pulled out binoculars and lay in the grass for an hour, inspecting the square grey farmhouse at the end of the track from the milk stand. His safe house.

The front door opened on to what had once been a lawn running down to a broad, grassy field before the lane. At the back the land rose more steeply and the remains of a grass track led through the banked hedgerow to the fields beyond. O'Keefe approved of the hideaway, situated amidst the maze of lakes, inlets and rivers.

Once he was sure the house was secure, he worked out his escape routes and concealed the car in the open-sided barn at the side of the house. He let himself in with the hidden key. The building was cheerless. Not much laughter or happiness had ever filled its walls. Sunshine streamed in through the windows, but somehow it was cold sunshine. Bleak House.

He hoped they wouldn't be there long. Not now his mind was made up. He'd told Jenny that morning as they were preparing to leave the safe house outside Strabane.

He stopped in the window, taking care to stand well back,

and regarded Cavan across the border. Jenny didn't believe me, I could tell. She should have done. That's it. All over. The ceasefire will be just that on my part. I've ceased firing. She'll have to like it or lump it.

Bitch. If there'd been just one flicker of regret or remorse . . .

Slotting Toms was never part of my act.

A young lad from a Scottish regiment, the TV news had said. There had been no reason to kill that squaddie. He'd been one himself. He had nothing against them. Jenny had pulled the trigger purely to experience the thrill of killing. The second she fired that shot she ceased to be exciting and fun and instead became a murderess. It was strange how easily what had passed for infatuation soured into contempt.

He assessed the security of the farmhouse even as he thought about Jenny. The thin hedgerow in the southern corner of the field offered an obvious approach to intruders. He'd put a trap or two there. A few trip wires out in the fields. When Jenny went to Belfast she could buy security cameras to put among the roof tiles. A mixture of high tech and low animal cunning. He saw Jenny's blue BMW hesitate at the end of the track and then turn towards him.

'Choose your bedroom. The front left is mine. It's got the best field of fire.'

'What!' Jenny's hopes of making the peace in bed were dashed and she spun round and stared at him in fear and in anger. 'You sanctimonious shit. I have one hit and you treat me like a piece of rotting flesh. You've killed dozens.'

O'Keefe didn't reply. He'd got into the habit of not bothering to reply. His self-sufficient silences drove her mad.

'Just because I killed once.' She'd had enough of his bloody righteousness. She clawed his arm and thrust her face into his.

'You killed the wrong man. You fannied about until the

'target had disappeared and then you let fly at a poor bloody squaddie.' Calmly, he picked her hand off his biceps.

'You should have that speech taped,' she spat. Stupid man. 'If you've said it once, you've said it a hundred times. They're all legitimate targets, Crown lackeys. One's as good as the next.'

'No, they're not. You killed needlessly and you killed without orders. It's nothing to be proud of.' Jenny could not understand that he took out a selected target. Always with a purpose. He concentrated on putting away the groceries Jenny had bought.

'So it's all right to blow someone away when you are told to. I vas only obeying orders,' she sneered in a German accent.

The row had gone on for almost two weeks now and it was too late to apologize. Hell can be other people. This morning's declaration that he wouldn't fight any more was the last straw. As far as she was concerned, he'd lost his stomach for the struggle and was trying to blame it on her.

'This is getting us nowhere. Let it be.' He walked out of the back door to the cars.

'Wimp. Coward. Nancy boy. ' She taunted him, helpless in her frustration. Bog-thick Irish bastard.

Yet Jenny knew she needed him. She might despise him, but only Paddy could give her the ultimate pleasure; the opportunity to kill. And for that chance she was willing to put up with his bucket of shit.

O'Keefe returned carrying the canvas holdall containing the Robar, an AK47 and his 9mm Browning. Jenny glanced covetously at the guns. She had spent hours stripping and cleaning the weapons with loving, painstaking care. They were her guns. As much hers as his.

'It won't happen again,' she managed in a conciliatory tone.

'I know,' replied O'Keefe.

'You're a legend, Paddy. A thing of myth and fable. You can't stop now.'

311

'Myth and legend is made of flesh and blood. I'll not take another life.'

In his bedroom O'Keefe slid the pistol down the waistband of his trousers. He left the other weapons in the bag at the bottom of the wardrobe. When he was sure Jenny was occupied, he extracted the bolt from the Robar and the firing pin from the AK, placed them in an envelope and taped it to the inside of the wardrobe. He didn't trust Jenny any further than he could throw her – and that wasn't very far at all.

Chapter Thirty

Morning prayers were over and the 14 Int operatives dispersed around their hangar in the restricted part of Aldergrove airport. Mr Bag O'Shite had a job monitoring a bomb factory in a council house kitchen in Turf Lodge that afternoon, then he was off for a couple of days. He planned to wash his hair.

He knew he should adjust his communications harness, but the bloke in the bar last night kept troubling him and he went into the operations room to consult the rogues' gallery. First he looked at the noticeboard full of head and shoulders of that week's star players. No, he'd known the face hadn't been there. He pulled out half a dozen playing-card-size books of faces and made himself comfortable, filthy trainers up on one of the metal desks. Concentrate on the shape of the face, the ears, the slant of the eyes. The features the punter couldn't change easily. Outside aircraft landed and took off, but he was lost in concentration. Face after face. Player after player. Police mug shots, prison pictures, snatches in the street, happy snaps copied from family albums, long lens jobs, blurred and almost useless, even snaps taken in automatic photo booths.

Current most wanted players, those on the run, known major players, lamplighters, messengers, drivers, dickers, the American connection, drugs dealers, front men who ran taxi companies and fruit machines. Nothing.

Then he did the same with the Derry file and again drew a blank.

His head was swimming by now. Take a rest or you won't see for looking. There were faces around him on the walls from their own team, pictures of various jobs. He let his gaze settle on the one taken after the Boyle ambush at Killgreen. He'd been on attachment to a call sign of the RUC's Headquarters Mobile Support Unit – a six-week swap to see how the other half lived. He arrived at the ambush scene just as the SAS men were pulling out. They'd all met up later in the Det's bar for a monumental piss-up – the guys from 22, the SB men, the Det lads who'd tailed the players. Even the watchers from E4A had come out to play. It had been a hell of a night.

Shit!

The problem with women was that they didn't under-stand the concept of honour. Perhaps honour was a male prerogative.

'You just can't bear to be safe, can you?' Her parting words. Safety or excitement had nothing to do with it. It was a debt.

Yes, he assured the salesman alongside him, the saloon handled very nicely. Just a little run out to Lisburn. Want to feel her on the open road. It had been a choice between home and honour. No contest. Yes, good acceleration. He liked that. Sportier than she looked. How much off for cash? Cash cash. He was going to be in Northern Ireland for some time and he needed wheels. He'd cast some bread on the waters. Let's see what the tide brings in. If that failed there was always one starting point – and he had all the time in the world. The Italians reckoned vengeance was a dish best eaten cold. And they were the experts.

Yes, this car would do fine. He wasn't expecting to have to outrun the Bill and she had a bit of poke if he needed to put his foot down. Best of all, there were a thousand cars exactly like this one on the roads of Ireland. He needed to go to the wood near Maghereagh Cross south of the border to collect one or two things and there was the bungalow to stake out. He needed wheels. How much off for cash? Cash cash.

*　　*　　*

'So what's he doing here?'

'Perhaps he fancies a holiday.'

Boyle gave Major Taylor a look of utter contempt and the officer coloured. 'No one comes to Belfast on holiday. Your man is certain?'

'Yes. He was in the QRF call sign and they drank together later. You would have seen him.'

Boyle pulled at a tuft of hair that protruded from his left ear and stared at the grey drizzle that fell over the fortress-like Special Branch Headquarters at Knock. Boyle didn't like loose ends and he didn't like puzzles; now he was confronted by both.

'Do we know how long he's been here?'

'No. He was spotted last night by accident, but it was only this morning he was positively identified. No one had a clue he was over here. He's grown his hair and he's wearing glasses. Don't know if it's an attempt at a disguise or just ageing.'

'No idea where he's staying?'

'No.'

'Could he be seeing old mates in the Northern Ireland troop?'

'I asked the staff sergeant if they had any old friends over at the moment. He looked blankly at me. I'll have to be more specific.'

'Could he be lying?'

'Could be.'

'It still doesn't explain why he was in a Republican bar singing rebel songs . . .'

The green phone rang. Boyle picked it up and Taylor found time to look around the sparsely furnished office. It was strictly functional. Just a computer terminal, a screen and a printer, a paper shredder, three filing cabinets and three phones including one with a does-not-exist number. Maps, lists and rotas filled the walls. There were no trophies, no framed citations, although he knew Boyle had several, no press cuttings, no family photos on the desk. The only human touch was a print of Botticelli's Venus. Taylor began to analyse the psychological import of the picture when he became aware Boyle was staring directly at him.

'Yeh. Yeh.' Boyle began scribbling furiously. 'And how did he manage to do that without them noticing . . . you mean a cock-up. Fucking Mets couldn't monitor grass growing without getting it wrong . . . Oh, I see. Down to the Regional Crime Squad, was it? I'm so sorry.' The heavy irony in his voice carried no apology. 'Thank you anyway.'

Boyle put down the phone and lifted his eyes to the ceiling in exasperation. 'Our friend has drawn ten thousand from his bank account. There should have been an alert on it, but someone's cocked up. He withdrew it . . .' he looked at the calendar on the wall behind him '. . . six days ago.'

'You wouldn't need £10,000 just to see friends,' mused the major. 'Drugs?'

'He'd be a brave man to try to muscle in here. The Provos and the UVF have the city sewn up. The only time they talk to each other is to settle drug distribution deals.' Boyle picked up a pencil and twirled it between his thick fingers. 'I suppose he may have brought a message from his former chums in South America. Setting up new supply lines.'

'Not probable, is it?' objected Taylor.

'No,' conceded Boyle. 'But I've been wrong before.'

'What about a bit of freelancing? Security work or body-guarding?'

Boyle felt he would have heard if there was a new kid on the block. 'Don't think so, but I'll make some calls.'

'Could he have been put in by another agency? Five or Six playing games.'

'Shit.' Boyle's face hardened. 'I wouldn't put anything past them. He could have been drafted in on licence by one of your cupboard MoD mobs trying to justify their existence now the Cold War's over. I'll pass it through the clearing house to make sure we're not treading on anyone's toes.

If some crackpot agency has inserted him unofficially, I'll have their guts for garters.'

'Of course, it could be something completely unconnected with his past. Maybe, he's got a job here. Maybe he's putting money into some company, setting up business.'

'I don't see him as an entrepreneurial type. But you're right. We look for conspiracies when there could be an innocent explanation. Still . . .'

'We could ask him what he's doing here,' suggested Taylor mildly. 'As you say, we can't ignore his presence, especially now everyone's walking on eggshells.'

'We'll bring him in softly softly and have a chat with him. If nothing else, I want to find out how he knows the words to those songs.'

Mary pushed open the living room windows to blow away the dust particles hanging in the stale musty air.

'Yeuk. It smells like a grave,' complained Boo, holding her nose in an exaggerated gesture of distaste.

'No it doesn't and you don't know what a grave smells like.' Katie was quick to contradict her.

'Yes I do.'

'Stop it, you two. Katie, turn on the immersion.'

The girls were tired and fractious. It had been a ridiculously early flight back from Gran Canaria, but now they were home and they had most of the day ahead of them to get organized, do the washing, buy food. All the boring things one did at the end of a holiday.

She would go and see Liam this afternoon. She felt bad about not taking him with them, but she had wanted the girls to have a fun time before starting the autumn school term. Katie had volunteered to look after him, but Mary had decided, for right or wrong, that Katie deserved to be a little girl once in a while, not a carer for her handicapped brother. Poor Liam. He probably hadn't remembered that they had not been to visit him. Mary told herself she would find a way to make it up to him. She'd take him out for day trips. As long as he didn't have those awful tantrums. That's where Katie was so good . . .

God bless Yvonne. Milk in the fridge and a loaf of bread. Mary put the kettle on.

'And where do you think you're going?'

Mary stared in astonishment at Katie standing at the kitchen door in her jodhpurs.

'Over to the farm to see Willow. She'll have been missing me.'

'Ponies do not miss people and you're not going anywhere until you've sorted out your washing and helped Boo make her bed.'

Katie put out her tongue, wrinkled her nose to show she wasn't really being cheeky and returned to her bedroom. Back to reality. Mary had thought a lot about the family and Paddy as she'd sat on the beach watching the girls play.

If this ceasefire works . . . please God make it work . . . they might be able to become a family again. Not in Northern Ireland. But they could emigrate. Maybe begin a new life in Canada or Australia. New Zealand, even. Somewhere far far away where no one knew them and they could be safe together.

Mary tested the thought of being away from Northern Ireland and Belfast and found it held little pain now. She had outgrown her homesickness. The raucous call of her tribe had subsided to a murmur which could be disregarded. There were other, stronger, imperatives.

'I haven't got it. Honest.'

'You have, you have. I hate you.' Boo dashed into the kitchen, tears streaming down her face. An angry-looking Katie ran in after her. Both were talking at the same time.

'She's got it. She's hiding it.'

'I haven't! I haven't!'

'What?' Mary tried to make sense of the commotion.

'She's got my watch,' sobbed Boo.

Oh, no. She hasn't lost her treasured wristwatch that

daddy gave her for Christmas, that she wore even in bed. Then Mary's head cleared.

'Silly thing. I've got it for safe keeping.'

Every morning on holiday Mary had made Boo hand it over and every evening she reclaimed the watch to wear at supper. Last night, with the excitement of the farewell party and the fireworks, Boo had forgotten to take it back. Mary produced the watch from her handbag. Boo's tears dried instantly and she set about putting it on.

Boo was like Paddy, thought Mary. There was a wicked devilment in those eyes and she had his smile. She'll break someone's heart one day. Katie is more like me. Life for Katie was serious, a succession of self-imposed tests.

'Remember to put it back an hour,' advised Katie.

'Why?'

Katie launched into a detailed and individual explanation as Mary thought how much she'd like to see her husband.

Chapter Thirty-one

'I'm not here for an inquest.' Inviting confrontation, Jenny
Dove leaned forward into the shaft of sunlight which fell
through the high window of the Botanical Gardens tea
room, turning her amber hair as translucent as her skin.
'There were reasons why it was impossible. We did what
we could.'

Get your retaliation in first.

Collins viewed her with his patient grey eyes and reckoned she was using her pugnacity as a cloak to hide something. Everyone's hiding something. What? He sought to
placate her – for the moment.

'Operations don't always go smoothly. You have a brilliant
track record. It's inevitable things go wrong sometimes,' he
said to mollify her. 'Anyway you'll have the chance of a
rest now – with this ceasefire.'

It was his turn to bend forward; only his gesture implied
confidentiality and sincerity. 'We'll observe that, you know.'

Jenny recognized it as Old Holborn's way of telling her
they were being put out to grass. Not that simple, Patrick
John. I have a couple of games of my own to play yet.

She was a walking spaghetti ball of emotions. Before
meeting Collins she had sat on a bench in the Botanical
Gardens for a good half-hour trying to unravel them. It
hadn't been easy.

First, there was the insult to her *amour propre*. No one
had ever dumped Jenny Dove. No one. She was the one
who did the walking.

Hell hath no fury like a woman scorned. Crap. Me, I don't
get angry. I get even. If I can get Paddy on my own for one
month I know I can make him mine again. I'm not sure I

want him, but if anyone's saying goodbye it's going to be me. See how he likes it.

Petty, vengeful, spiteful. Yeh. Bitter, twisted, vindictive. You bet.

And that leaves the way open for another opportunity to fire the Robar; another chance to kill. A month away should see the peace talks collapse – if history was anything to go by. Then they would be needed again. In the meantime, I'll let Collins think that others, like INLA, want us to join them or even that O'Keefe might fight on single-handed. I'll encourage Old Holborn to keep us sweet and send us off somewhere nice, sunny and romantic for a month so I can work my wiles.

'And how do you know *we'll* accept this ceasefire? Just because you're embracing the coward's way out, it doesn't necessarily follow that we will.'

'Is that how Paddy sees it?' asked Collins mildly. He picked up his tea cup and held it in a particularly effeminate way, his little finger sticking out at right angles. '*Si vis pacem, para bellum.*'

Jenny ignored the Latin tag. Perhaps, mused Collins sadly, she did not understand it.

'Do you think his public would allow him to retire?' Jenny spoke lightly but with menace.

She's making it sound as if O'Keefe was an ageing pop star, thought Collins. Is she including him in her fanaticism or do they march hand in hand?

'He has a following. If he put the word out to carry on the fight, they'd fight.'

'Would they?'

'You know they would.'

Some would, he conceded. The hard-liners, the wild wing, would fall into step behind this legend. They were looking for a new champion. They felt betrayed by their own leaders who had changed from firebrand rebels to namby-pamby politicians. They needed a hero. Would O'Keefe dare come into the open? Not very likely in a rational world – but when had Northern Ireland been part of the rational world?

Collins knew that Jenny did not believe in decommissioning so much as a catapult until the British were out of Northern Ireland for good. On a personal level, he guessed that the idea of returning to Trinity College and her doctorate had lost its appeal. She'd tasted the heady champagne of adventure and she wasn't willing to return to the sour grapes of academe.

Jenny played with her scone and tried to outguess Collins. So far so good.

'After all, you are not the only sponsor interested.'

So now it was a business proposition, was it? Was this a reference to the INLA, he wondered. He nodded slowly. Silence was an inquisitional tool Collins wielded like a scalpel. Normally it would have unsettled Jenny, but she was fortified by her other purpose, the tangential aim which Collins, for all his intuition, could not guess. The month alone with O'Keefe.

'So what do you suggest?' Collins was first to speak.

'Perhaps it would be best if we went away.'

'Yes.'

'Away away. Abroad. Out of temptation, if you like.'

'Out of the eddies and flows of the current.'

'Exactly.'

Jenny did not plan to spend weeks of shortening days in a succession of damp, cheerless houses heated by peat fires, where to go to buy a packet of cornflakes or a gin and tonic invited one's life history.

'Can you arrange that? Not America or Europe. Somewhere where the police have other priorities and we could pass as tourists. The Far East. Thailand, maybe.'

'That shouldn't be a problem,' conceded Collins.

Now she was getting her own way, Jenny looked at Collins in kindly concern. 'You look worn out. Sorry, it's our fault.'

Collins stifled a cough. 'Tell me. When did you last go to confession?'

The question startled Jenny and she floundered, her mouth open in surprise as she sought for a reply. What was this to do with anything? She felt a stab of fear as she realized she did not know what Collins was thinking. Here she was, steering him so cleverly towards getting what she wanted and all the time part of him was going his own way.

For Collins, her hesitation and uncertainty confirmed earlier suspicions. It was his fault. He should have found out before.

'You're not a Catholic, are you, Jenny?'

Her blush answered for her.

A bloody Janissary. Ready to storm the walls and lay down her life for an alien cause – as long as she took others with her. An awful tiredness seeped into his bones. Yet another problem.

Fife held the uncomfortable swivel chair and spun it round so he sat with his arms resting on its back. Boyle burst into the Portakabin, a heavy folder under his arm. He swept off his jacket and dismissed the two guards with a wave of his hand. His bulk filled the prefabricated office, his head almost brushing the ceiling.

'Right.' The single gravelly word echoed off the partition walls. No pleasantries for old times' sake. 'What are you doing here?'

'Some of your blokes suggested I might like to pop in for a chat.'

Boyle flashed a mirthless grin which vanished the second it appeared.

'You've been around since you left the army, but I didn't think you'd wash up here. So?'

'I'm minding my own business.'

'Someone suggested you might be carrying messages from your old friends in South America. Not a good idea. The drugs scene is strictly controlled in the city. The last thing we'd be wanting is a turf war. Well?'

Fife was indignant. 'Away with ye. Do you honestly think I'd be involved in drugs?'

'You were in South America,' replied Boyle evenly.

'That was different and you know it.' He struggled to keep his temper. This was just another exercise in hostile interrogation, he told himself. Rule number one: don't let the questioner get under your skin.

'Okay. Say I believe you.' Boyle scratched under his armpit. 'Why are you here?'

'Just having a look round. Maybe see old friends.'

'You don't have old friends in Belfast. You have old enemies. It's not healthy for you here. Go to somewhere like Blackpool. There it's healthy.'

A large van slowly backed past the small window blocking out the light. They both watched in silence as the eclipse passed.

'All right, you're working for the Department or some cockeyed mob.' Boyle jabbed a sausage-sized finger at Fife. 'I don't know what *they* told you, but I'm telling you that you won't survive a week on the streets by yourself. Look, I don't care if you get yourself killed, but don't do it now. Now is not the right time.'

'There's never a right time to get killed and I promise you I intend to stay alive. Remember, I helped you stay alive once.'

He had spent more than an hour in a car with this copper waiting for the bullets to arrive. They had been under fire together. In the army that would count for a lot. Here, there was as much camaraderie as you'd find in a shoal of herrings.

'That was yesterday. I want to know what you're doing on my patch today.'

'I've told you. Just looking around.'

'Not working for Five or Six?'

'No.'

'Not helping out Military Intelligence?'

'No.'

'How long have you been here?'

'Five days.'

'Where are you staying?'

Fife told him the name of a guest house off Wellington Park, a genteel Catholic area so far untouched by the Troubles.

'How long do you intend to stay?'

'That depends. Not long, I hope.'

Boyle was becoming frustrated. He watched Fife's face closely and it was giving nothing away. He was awesomely self-contained; compressed and stolid in his answers. He showed no trace of the explosive power Boyle had seen him demonstrate at the ambush.

'Look.' He tried a different approach, spreading out his large hands in a gesture of openness. 'This interview is not official. If it was you'd be in an interrogation cell in Castlereagh, not in this bloody Portakabin. This is all off the record. It's a difficult time at the moment. Everyone's jumpy. Just put my mind at rest.'

'I feel at home in a divided city. I'm from Glasgow, remember.'

'Bullshit you do,' exploded Boyle. 'If you've something going down against the bead rattlers, tell me. Maybe I can help. Unofficially of course.'

Fife remembered that Boyle was a staunch Loyalist. He didn't know whether to believe him or not. Not that it mattered.

'You haven't done your homework, have you? I'm from the smoking handbag brigade myself. A Mick who couldn't swim. Maybe that's why I feel at home here.'

Boyle withdrew the hand of friendship. 'Give me your glasses,' he commanded. Fife handed them over the desk.

'Plain glass,' snorted Boyle.

'They're not, I've an astigmatism in the left eye.'

He reclaimed the glasses before Boyle could examine the left lens.

'What were you doing in Fenian bars singing rebel songs? Strange thing for a former squaddie to do.'

'I was singing those songs in Glasgow before I knew what IRA stood for. The English have nursery rhymes. We have rebel songs. It's not personal.'

Boyle rose out of the chair and Fife admired the knife edge creases along his shirt sleeves.

'What have you done with the ten thousand?'

The question surprised Fife. They had been monitoring him much more closely than he'd suspected. He'd be doubly careful from now on.

'If it's any concern of yours, I've gone in with a mate who's expanding his ice cream vans. Selling ice cream. Not drugs,' he added.

'And you can prove this?' sneered Boyle.

'Not to the Inland Revenue's satisfaction. No.'

Chapter Thirty-two

Paddy O'Keefe threaded the 0.15mm through the eye of the skewer embedded in the earth, securing the end to a bracket on the old gatepost. Primitive but effective. The trip wires to the north and north-east entered the house with the TV aerial; those to the east and south – the direction of the track – came in with the electricity supply, while the two lines on the west ran diagonally along a field hidden from view by the falling land and the stone wall. P for Plenty. They came together in the kitchen with a relay in his bedroom. Anyone touching or breaking a wire completed an electrical circuit setting off an alarm clock.

But ground level alarms were prone to be set off by animals, and at seven that morning O'Keefe had tumbled out of bed and to the window, where he'd seen a dog fox stare indignantly at the unexpected wire before arrogantly resuming his morning patrol.

O'Keefe had also dug foot-deep holes at weak points in the hedgerow and where the wall had tumbled down. In the holes he had inserted sharpened sticks smeared with cows' excrement. He'd covered the holes with a latticework of twigs and dead leaves and then moved old cowpats around them to channel an intruder into the traps.

Jenny had not returned from Belfast last night. She'd warned she might stay with friends. O'Keefe didn't know whether she'd had a man or not and he didn't really care. If she had slept with a bloke it disturbed him only because she was prepared to lie to him about it. Between them as a team there had to be trust and mutual confidence. Destroy that and you destroyed the team.

He wound the fishing line around the bracket and turned

the screw to increase the tension on the wire. Nice and taut. If Jenny had been able to find what he wanted in Belfast, he could build a more sophisticated system. He saw her BMW turning up the long track towards the farmhouse.

'Sorry I didn't make it back last night. I was running so late,' apologized Jenny lightly, giving him a peck on the cheek before he could turn away. This was how she'd decided to play it. Friendly, fun and available.

'They only had three cameras. I hope they're the right sort. The man in the shop wasn't a lot of help. I've decided to treat us. I've bought a couple of Dover sole and a bottle of Sancerre. It's how the other half lives.'

She twirled in front of him, a sparkle in her eyes. O'Keefe wondered dully whether her good humour was the result of a night of sex. She did look good, he had to admit. Tight jeans and a shirt which showed her figure off to her best advantage. He refused to be moved by her beauty or her humour.

'What did Collins say?'

'He was brilliant. He said, and I quote, "It's impossible for every operation to go exactly as planned" . . .'

'Then he's never heard of the seven Ps,' interrupted O'Keefe sourly.

'. . . And that we'd, you'd, done superbly well and it was time for a rest – with full honours.'

Jenny was clearly wiping clean the slate after the days of bickering and silence. And she was inviting O'Keefe to do the same.

He saw she'd bought the *Belfast Telegraph* and he reached for it, not wanting to appear too eager.

'Collins wants us to go away somewhere nice for a month's break. Maybe the Far East. Just while the talks are on. He says we deserve it.'

O'Keefe looked through section 12-3 of the classified ads. Personal messages. Nothing. He felt a pang of disappointment. He'd hoped Mary would want to see him when she and the girls returned from holidays.

Jenny was regaling him with a full account of her Monday evening in Belfast, how she'd got together with a few friends, they'd shared a takeaway and watched TV together and then she'd gone to bed early – by herself. O'Keefe folded the paper and began to examine the cameras. Collins's offer of a month in the sun was tempting. Maybe, just maybe, if the passport was good enough, he'd never come back. It could be the first step to a new life. If Old Holborn could get them to Thailand, then he'd go. He watched Jenny bending provocatively, flaunting the curve of her buttocks. A month ago he'd have taken her on the ground then and there. Now lust had given way to a feeling of distaste.

A plan was forming in his mind. What if he could lose Jenny in Thailand and meet up with Mary and the kids? They'd be halfway to Australia. They could all go off together. To a new life.

Jenny, glancing round, saw him looking pensively at her behind. She'd win him back yet.

'Chief Inspector. Come in. Take a pew. Move those papers. God, if I'd known how much bumph was involved in this job, I'd have stayed a captain.'

Boyle sat down heavily. 'I have to admit I'm totally at a loss over Fife. He's not here on holiday. He's not that sort. He's too intense. He'd get bored or shitfaced inside a day. He's here with a purpose – but what that purpose is, Christ only knows. That's why the profile could prove helpful.'

'I'm afraid I don't have the profile yet,' apologized Brigadier Doughty. 'But I think I can tell you why Jimmy Sands is in Northern Ireland.'

'Who?'

'Sorry. Duggie Fife.' The officer leaned back in his chair and made needless adjustments to the symmetrically rolled-up sleeves of his khaki shirt while he waited for Boyle's question. Doughty was enjoying the interview. It wasn't often he could tell Special Branch something they didn't know.

'Why?'

'He wants the man who killed Private William Agnew.'

Boyle waited for more information.

'The Fusilier who was shot at the checkpoint near Middletown. The last British soldier to be killed in Ulster.'

'It had the sniper's fingerprints all over it,' recalled Boyle. 'But we didn't understand why he'd killed a squaddie. He'd never done that before. Why should Fife be interested in Agnew's death?'

'Because Billy Agnew was his younger brother.'

Boyle's eyebrows rose in surprise.

'I don't believe he was a blood relation,' continued Doughty. 'I think Fife's mother took in Billy when he was a small child, probably not even a legal adoption. Billy worshipped Fife. He was desperate to follow in his footsteps. I met him once in Hereford. Nice lad. He was badly injured training for the Paras so he joined the Royal Highland Fusiliers. Gets to Ulster and he's killed in the first week. Jimmy Sands is taking it very personally.'

'What can he hope to achieve?'

'Fife has been here on Regiment business a few times so he knows his way around. He'll be pulling in a few favours from people on the security side.'

'No one in the Northern Ireland troop admits to hearing from him.'

'They wouldn't, would they,' replied Doughty drily.

'What can he do?' sneered Boyle. 'One vengeful squaddie isn't too much to worry about. Not in the larger scope of things.'

Doughty did not agree. 'You only met Fife at Killgreen, didn't you? You don't know him. He's remorseless, implacable. He will simply never give up. One of his nicknames was the Lean Mean Killing Machine and it sums him up. If I was that sniper, I'd give up my job, change my name and take up sheep farming in Australia. Even then, I'd put money on Fife finding and killing him.'

'But how's he going to get near him?'

'There's many in the Army and the RUC who would be delighted if Fife could get the Provos' top gunman.'

Boyle was thinking. 'Of course, there may be a reason why Fife feels he can find the sniper. If they served together, say . . .'

'Yes, chief inspector.' Doughty was curt to the point of rudeness. 'I know your theory on the identity of the sniper. Your ideas have been canvassed at the highest level. They are plausible but without any real evidence, and until you can furnish that evidence I will not be persuaded.'

'What will happen if Fife does find the sniper?'

'He'll kill him and in doing so kill the peace talks.'

Boyle made a rapid decision. 'We'll use the Prevention of Terrorism Act to put him on a plane back to the mainland.'

Doughty grinned. 'You do not understand this man. You could transport Fife to Tierra del Fuego and he'd still get back to Belfast.'

'We're staking out his digs. We'll pick him up.'

Doughty indicated the direct link to Knock. Boyle called his sergeant and gave instructions for Fife to be brought in.

'We can hold him for seven days without charge if necessary, but if he's as determined as you say, then perhaps we'll do him on illegal possession of a firearm.'

'You don't know he's carrying one,' said Doughty.

'Yes I do,' replied Boyle, his face a blank.

'You mean fit him up.' Doughty scowled his disapproval.

'Not permanently. Just to keep him out of the way.'

The black phone rang and Doughty picked it up. 'It's for you. From a mobile unit.'

'Yes . . . what . . . when . . . how do you know? Shit. Go over the place with a fine toothcomb. Get in a search team and see if the garden's been disturbed. He may have cached arms there. And put look-outs at the end of the road just in case he comes back.'

He turned to Doughty. 'Fife has done a runner. Seems he never returned after the interview yesterday evening. He left a bag behind, but his bed's not been slept in. I suppose he may have had a night on the tiles.'

Doughty shook his head. 'Fife wouldn't drink when he's working and he's working now.'

'He headed for the hills as soon as he knew he was clocked. Shit.' Boyle looked disgusted with himself.

'There's nothing you could have done,' reassured Doughty. 'I'll put out the heavy word that he's poison. The Northern Ireland troop will be told to report any contact. I don't think they will because they've got their own loyalties, but they'll know they'll be RTU'd if they help him.'

Boyle stood up, eager to get to Fife's digs.

'This will have to go to the Collator,' continued Doughty. 'I can see it ending up at JIC. No one farts at the moment but they want to know what he had for breakfast.'

'Come on, you two. Hurry up. Boo, where are you?'

'I'm just getting my watch.'

Mary lifted her eyes to Heaven. That blasted watch. It had stopped soon after Boo had put it back an hour. From Boo's behaviour you'd have thought the world had stopped as well. Mary reckoned she'd probably got sand in it.

'We'll drop the watch in that new place and then we'll go and see Liam. Have you got his present?'

'Yes, mum.' Katie held up a brightly wrapped parcel.

Mary chivvied the girls into the car and stood for a moment mentally checking she had locked the doors and secured the windows.

She'd put on a little weight, become a little matronly, although her jaw line was as firm and determined as ever, observed Fife as he lay motionless in the sweet-smelling grass in the back field.

He had been watching the bungalow since an hour before dawn, having left his car two miles away and tabbed through the darkness. He had seen no one and no one had seen him. The first lightening in the eastern sky over Slieve Gullion found him exploring the derelict stone barn on the nearby hillock. Others had spent some time there from the number of cigarette butts and torn pieces of chocolate wrappers. Nothing recent. He spent two slow hours circling the bungalow, examining it from all angles until he was satisfied.

A small girl he hadn't seen before drew the curtains in her bedroom just before 8 AM and half an hour later Katie came out to talk to a pony in the field where he was now hiding. He had watched with interest as Mary hung washing on the line. A seemingly innocent line of washing could provide a signal to a watcher miles away. Fife drank from his water bottle and failed to deduce any pattern in the sheets and pillow cases. Just before ten, Mary set off with the girls in her small Volvo.

He waited another thirty minutes before he crawled on his elbows and toes up to the garden and then sprinted for the cover of the back wall. From the side pockets of his camouflage trousers he produced a thirteen-piece cylinder lock picking kit. He inserted a thin three-inch tension bar into the patio door lock, wound an elastic band around the bar and attached it to a drawing pin he stuck into the wooden surround. He selected a rake and pushed it in and out of the lock. Within two minutes he was inside the house.

Fife stayed stock still listening to the silence. The room was neutral, neat and feminine. He recognized the wooden standard lamp and nest of tables from Hereford. The other furniture was new. The bungalow was carpeted throughout and everything seemed to be newly painted. It must have cost a lot of money. He moved swiftly and purposefully. He opened the wooden bureau and examined well organized sheaves of household bills, insurance policies, the girls' passports and medical records. There was no personal correspondence or memorabilia of any kind. On the kitchen noticeboard he found a few postcards written by friends on holiday. One from Mary's mother from Galway. The bathroom was cluttered by cans, bottles and tubes, and all very female. There was no sign of a man's razor or deodorant. According to the bathroom, only women lived in the house. In the girls' bedrooms he swiftly looked through their desks and bedside cabinets for a Christmas card or a birthday card. Again he drew a blank.

He padded into Mary's bedroom and knelt before the bedside chest of drawers. The top drawer was full of trinkets, costume jewellery, one or two leather belts. Nothing else. No letters. Paddy and Mary used to write to each other. Why hadn't she kept his letters?

There was something missing. Something, somewhere wasn't quite right. He stopped to think. Slowly, it dawned on him that it wasn't what he'd found, but what he hadn't found. There was absolutely nothing of Paddy's in the house. No wedding picture on the dressing table, no family groups with Paddy grinning broadly. The house in Hereford had been littered with them. There were pictures of the girls and one of Liam, but not a single likeness of O'Keefe. Not even a photograph by Mary's bed. It was as though he had never existed.

The second drawer held Mary's underwear. He carefully picked up a handful, checked nothing was hidden at the back and replaced the underwear. He was not enjoying doing this but he pressed on. The third drawer held rolled-up socks and tights. He was about to close the drawer when a pair of blue socks took his eye. They looked bigger than the others. Men's socks. He opened them out. Definitely men's socks and well worn. Then he saw another pair of grey socks. These were newer and he could make out the SIZE 9-11 still on them. Paddy, he knew, was size ten. He replaced everything as he found it and went back to the underwear drawer.

Skiddies. In the middle of the pile. Maroon skiddies. So, some man kept a pair of underpants and two pairs of socks here. An overnight change of clothing.

He inspected the shirts and blouses hanging in the wardrobe. There was a dark green denim man's shirt. It could be Mary's, but Fife knew Paddy's weakness for green. He stood on a chair and put his hand on to the top shelf, stretching up to feel in among the folded jumpers and sweaters. There, on the side, his hand touched a small packet.

A packet of condoms. One left in the pack of three. Either Mary was seeing another man – which Fife did not believe – or she was prepared for the occasional visit from her husband.

Fife was well pleased. He'd lie up until dark and then tab back to the car for more supplies. It could be a long wait.

The shop was more than a jewellers. It was a warehouse of electronic goods. There was a variety of clocks and watches together with all sorts of electronic devices from handheld digital games and computerized personal organizers to electric and mechanical timers, calculators, radios, stereos and remote control racing cars and power boats.

Mary left it to Katie and Boo to explain what they wanted and the girls, feeling very important, approached the counter as Mary drifted off to look at the electrical kitchen equipment.

'Please,' said the smaller, blonde one. 'My watch won't go.'

'She's broken it,' chimed in Katie.

'No I haven't. Mummy says there could be sand in it.'

'We'll see what we can do, shall we?' said the young male shop assistant, bending down to take the watch.

'We've just come back from holiday,' explained Katie.

'You didn't buy this on holiday?' said the man, thinking the watch was too expensive to belong to a little girl.

'No, my daddy gave it to me,' volunteered Boo before she could think. 'Ouch.'

Katie kicked her in the shin. Boo turned as red as her tee-shirt and bit her lip to hold back her tears of pain and embarrassment.

'Can you mend it?' asked the older girl.

'Oh, I expect so. We'll have to take the back off and have a look. Give me your address and telephone number. Now what's your name?'

Boo proudly recited her address and newly memorized phone number.

'It should only be a few days. We'll give you a call when it's ready.'

O'Keefe? O'Keefe? Something in the back of his mind bothered the shop assistant. Why had that girl kicked her little sister like that? When they closed for lunch he went to the secret room at the end of the warehouse, opened the steel-lined door by pressing a daily changing combination of numbers and switched on the computer.

There had been some debate in the Security Service about setting up the store. Its critics claimed it encouraged and aided the bombmaker and there were enough of those around Armagh and the borders. But its supporters pointed out that it sold nothing you couldn't buy in Belfast if you knew where to look, and this way they could identify the purchaser of any equipment later found to have been used in explosive devices. To this end, the store issued surprisingly old-fashioned hand-written bills with the customer's name and address while a very modern video camera secretly recorded every transaction. It was the latest in a line of Intelligence stings in Northern Ireland which had included a betting shop and a dry cleaner's.

The operative wanted to see what the super new intelligence computer Crucible made of the name – if it made anything at all. He typed in the day's code, his out station number and finally his password. Then he typed in O'Keefe and the address and waited.

Access Denied.

That was no great surprise on this bloody system where you could spend hours feeding it only to be told you didn't have sufficient grade of access to get anything out. But he was intrigued that such an innocuous request would be denied. The screen flashed up another message.

Urgent. All requests and data to be referred to DCI Boyle, Knock.

The operative thought about ignoring the instruction – he was Army Intelligence not SB. But he knew his attempt at access would have been logged by the computer and soon he would be getting a phone call to ask why he had made the query. Cursing because he had made work for himself, he picked up the phone and dialled the number given for DCI Boyle.

'Ah, Simon. Good of you to spare the time.' The Prime Minister stood in the small anteroom to the left of the hall in 10 Downing Street looking at himself in a gilt mirror as a valet brushed white specks of dandruff off the collar of his dark grey suit.

'I trust you are enjoying your job at the Northern Ireland Office. Being a Parliamentary Private Secretary is the first rung on the ladder, my boy, and well deserved.'

Baines-Hickey smiled modestly and wondered why he had been summoned at such short notice to see the Prime Minister. He fingered his blue and silver Special Forces tie and composed his features in a blend of earnest endeavour and enthusiasm.

'There's a bit of a flap on. I'll tell you as we go.' He took Baines-Hickey by the elbow and steered him towards the door.

Baines-Hickey, who had spoken no more than three consecutive sentences to the Premier in his life, was flattered by the attention. Was there a siege situation? A hijack he wanted Baines-Hickey's advice on? All sorts of wonderful opportunities for glory swept through his racing mind.

'Go where, sir?'

Baines-Hickey saw the Premier's Jaguar and the escort car with armed detectives ready to leave.

'I've a lunch in the City. We can talk as we drive. Ready? Good.'

Baines-Hickey settled in the leather back seat of the Jaguar feeling proud and important.

'The Northern Ireland Office offers a rare chance, you know,' said the Prime Minister regarding Baines-Hickey with a keen glance. 'Too many politicians regard it as Boot Hill, but it's the place to make a reputation.'

Baines-Hickey thought of all the Secretaries of State and their Ministers who, if they hadn't wrecked their careers, had certainly blighted them in the Northern Ireland job and said nothing.

'Now, Simon, between you and me, the shit's about to hit the fan.' The Premier leaned towards him to emphasize their shared complicity. 'And as you know the buck stops here.'

Baines-Hickey took in the mixed metaphor as the car swept through the tall security gates at the end of Downing Street and turned left into Whitehall. The Prime Minister acknowledged the waves from the handful of tourists on the corner with a professional smile and an economic twitch of his arm.

'I've had the Cabinet Secretary on. Apparently the Joint Intelligence Committee are getting wound up about what they perceive to be a very real threat to the ceasefire in Northern Ireland. This information only came in yesterday afternoon so JIC have pulled out all the stops – it shows they consider it to be an emergency.'

The car slowed as the traffic built up at the end of Northumberland Avenue and immediately two police motorcycle outriders swept past to clear a path on the other side of the road. They swung on to the Embankment straight through a red light as other policemen held up traffic. Baines-Hickey was enjoying the ride.

'It's hard to believe, but it seems that there's a former SAS man on the loose looking for the killer of his brother – the last British soldier to be shot in Ireland. A lot of this is highly confidential, but I don't need to tell *you* . . .' The Prime Minister made a gracious gesture towards Baines-Hickey.

'Seems there's a chap called Fife with quite a reputation. Maybe you served together, hmmm?'

'Yes, Prime Minister. He was in my squadron in the Falklands. In fact, I was his troop commander.'

'Of course, when you won your MC.' The Prime Minister prided himself on his memory and liked to surprise colleagues with nuggets of information about themselves which made it appear that he knew them rather better than he did. 'Well, it seems he's in Northern Ireland and he's out to get their top gun. Between you and me, Simon, if it was any other time I'd say good luck and good hunting, but the imperative now is peace and we must do everything in our power to bring the two sides to the table in an atmosphere of mutual trust and goodwill. If the gunman was killed by regular forces then that would be acceptable under the rule of law, but if he falls to a renegade SAS man, a maverick with a grudge, then that is gun law.'

Baines-Hickey nodded eagerly. He knew how much the Premier had staked his personal and political reputation on the peace talks. He was more involved than a politician should be, said the pundits. If this splashed, he'd have an awful lot of trouble climbing out of the water before the sharks got to him.

'Of course, Prime Minister.'

'So it is vital, absolutely vital, that we head off this vigilante. Unfortunately the RUC seems to have lost him. We can assume this Fife is using his special skills to stay ahead of the game.' He put his hand on Baines-Hickey's knee and gave an encouraging squeeze. 'That's why it's a perfect operation for you to cut your teeth on. You have unique qualities to bring to the problem.'

'Any idea of the identity of the killer, sir?'

The Jaguar sped past the Inns of Court and turned up the slip road into Blackfriars Bridge Road. Ahead Baines-Hickey could see City of London police officers with red and white chequered bands on their sleeves waiting at Ludgate Circus to halt the traffic for them to turn right up Ludgate Hill.

'Security people say it's too dangerous to carry on down the underpass. Think it's baloney myself.' He gave a self-deprecating shrug. 'Ah, yes, well ... There's a chap in Special Branch who has this theory that he could be ... um ... another ex-SAS man. Get everywhere, don't they? Totally unsubstantiated as of this moment. Joint Operations Centre is meeting at two o'clock – 1400 hours I believe they call it. They know you've been empowered to attend. You served on that after the Falklands, didn't you?'

'Ah ... no, sir. I was in Special Forces Group HQ at the Duke of York Barracks in Chelsea. JOC is in the Ministry of Defence.'

'Humph. All these different security bodies. Gets confusing.' The Premier's memory had failed him and he was miffed to appear fallible in front of a minion.

'I haven't had the opportunity to inform your Secretary of State. As you know he's away today, but I'll clear it with him this evening. You have carte blanche on this. Use anyone you like. Obviously the Director Special Forces will be involved because he knows the man. Five and Six will weigh in with whatever they've got and you'd better speak to the SB officer who believes he knows the identity of the sniper. Whatever appointments you've got in the next few days, cancel them.'

The Jaguar glided to a halt outside the Guildhall.

'I don't need to tell you, Simon. This has top priority. If our ex-SAS hoodlum kills their sniper and it gets known, the talks will be off and we'll have handed the IRA their biggest propaganda coup since . . .'

The car door was opened by a liveried footman as the Prime Minister switched on his professional smile.

'. . . I don't know when,' he ended lamely.

'I'll do my very best, sir.' Baines-Hickey was about to pledge his loyalty and his life, if necessary, but the Prime Minister was already climbing out of the Jaguar, hand outstretched.

'Lord Mayor. How good to see you . . .'

The dignitaries moved away leaving Baines-Hickey stranded in the back of the car. When the party had disappeared inside the Guildhall he got out and crossed the road, where he hailed a taxi to the Ministry of Defence.

Sean O'Hanlon exploded out of his chair and thumped his fist on the beer-stained table, making the glasses jump.

'There's no fucking way we're going to give up our weapons. No way at all. You can tell the high fucking command that. If you want my fucking gun you'll have to take it off me.'

'No one's asking you to hand in your weapons,' repeated Patrick John Collins, but O'Hanlon wasn't listening.

'And it'll be a brave fucking man who tries to do that. It'll be the last fucking thing he does.' O'Hanlon's loose eye darted around inside its socket like a mad goldfish inside its bowl. Spittle bubbled and frothed on the corners of his mouth.

Two hard-faced men either side of him growled their assent. Five others around Collins narrowed their eyes. One spark would ignite the high octane atmosphere and there would be an almighty brawl.

'You are a soldier in Oglaigh na hEireann.' Collins chose the Gaelic deliberately, knowing O'Hanlon spoke not a word of the language. 'You have been given an order by your superior officers. If you disobey that order, you are liable to be court martialled.'

'Yeh, and what? Shot?' spat O'Hanlon. 'So this is what this fucking ceasefire is all about. We don't kill bastard Brits any more. We shoot each other instead. In 1916 the boys were ready to die and willing to die cheerfully and proudly preserving Ireland's honour. Now it's all gobshite. We're more worried about upsetting fucking England.'

Collins poked around in the overflowing ashtray until he found room to stub out his roll-up. He was surprised at O'Hanlon's use of Padraig Pearse's words, even if they were misquoted, so he said as patiently as he could, 'We

341

have to present a united front. No one wants you to give up your arms, but there must be no incidents. We must be able to deliver what we promise.'

'Aye, and I suppose the Crown will keep their promises,' snarled O'Hanlon with heavy sarcasm.

Collins decided on a show of reasonableness. 'What's the first thing on the agenda when three IRA men enter the room? The split. It's an old joke, Sean, but a true one. The factionalism has to end.'

'There's nothing to say INLA cannot carry on the fight, though, is there?' asked O'Hanlon, slyly.

'You're not going to fight by using INLA proxies,' warned Collins. '*Odi profanum vulgus et arceo.*'

'Why don't you speak fucking English if you're going to betray us . . .'

'Watch your fucking tongue.'

Frannie McFadden, his red face blotched and purple with fury, kicked over his chair and lumbered across the floor, his banana-like fingers on the end of short tree trunks reaching for O'Hanlon's throat. O'Hanlon stepped back, his right hand snatching under his coat for either gun or knife.

'Leave it. Leave it. Frannie, sit down. Please. Everyone sit down. Have you all taken leave of your senses?' For once Collins raised his voice and a silence fell over the room as McFadden and O'Hanlon eyeballed each other. They sat down glowering and breathing heavily.

The silence was broken by a timid knock on the door. Wee Dermot oozed into the back room.

'Will any of youse gentlemen be wanting a drink?'

'We'll tell you when we want a drink,' snapped Collins. 'And don't be coming in here until we say.'

Wee Dermot felt the electricity in the atmosphere and became scared.

'I didn't mean no harm. The guvnor thought . . .' He looked as if he was about to burst into tears. His legs wobbled under him. McFadden grabbed him by the collar and propelled him out of the door, slamming it after him.

'What's wrong with you, Patrick John? The barman was only offering a drink. He's one of us.'

'No one's one of us until he's dead,' replied Collins crisply.

'Not even the big man. Your secret weapon,' taunted O'Hanlon.

'Leave it,' warned Collins as others looked up in interest.

'Is he willing to lay down that big rifle of his?'

There was a triumphant smirk on O'Hanlon's face and just for once Collins was swept with an overwhelming urge to sink his fist into the gloating loudmouth.

'You don't know what you're on about,' he said shortly.

But O'Hanlon was not going to give up. 'He'll not want to see all his good work go to waste on the foul word of an English politician.'

'He'll obey orders.'

'Yeh, but whose orders? It's a bit of a waste, don't you think, Patrick John, to have a one man army and not use him. Others might see it differently to you, don't you think?'

Just then Collins could have killed Sean O'Hanlon. Instead he looked sadly over his glasses at his tormentor and silently vowed to have him killed when the ceasefire broke down – if O'Hanlon didn't kill him first.

It was a warm night and men still prowled in twos and threes along the main roads even though the pubs had emptied almost an hour before. Wee Dermot scurried along in his brisk, short-legged gait, his gaze fixed on the pavement a few yards ahead. His lips moved as he talked to himself.

'Look how close he's walking to that wall,' observed Boyle conversationally to his sergeant sitting diagonally ahead of him in the driving seat of the car. 'He's the sort that invites mugging. A professional victim.'

Boyle was in a good mood. It had been a remarkably

good day and it was about to get better. Dermot turned the corner into a narrow street of small redbrick houses opening directly on to the pavement. The car followed him. Ashanti Terrace had been built to house workers at the dark, looming mass of the mill at the end of the street. The mill was now derelict and used by the close observation platoon of the resident battalion.

Wee Dermot lived in a back room of a house halfway down the street and now he was almost home he quickened his pace as though seeking sanctuary. He was trotting under the one light in the whole street which worked when the car glided alongside him. The rear passenger door was flung open blocking his path. Sweat erupted under Dermot's armpits. He couldn't see who was in the car, but whoever it was meant trouble. He clenched his key in his pocket and gathered himself to make a break for his front door. Another car parked directly outside his home flashed its headlights. It told him he was trapped.

He stifled a sob, sniffed and slid into the car feeling he was climbing into his coffin.

'Wee Dermot. How are you?'

Something deep inside Dermot snapped and he flew at the big detective, pummelling his broad arms and shoulders with his fists.

'Bastard. Bastard. Bastard.'

'What the fuck!' Boyle gathered Dermot's two thin wrists in one of his hands. 'What do you think you're doing? Quit it.'

Dermot collapsed, limp and shaking.

'Leave me alone, can't you. Leave me alone,' he snivelled.

'Where've you been tonight?' demanded Boyle, ignoring Dermot's tears.

'Minding my own business.'

'Haven't been working, have you? In a pub in Short Strand by chance?'

Oh Mary mother of Jesus, how did he know that?

'Serving in a private room, maybe, were you?'

'No. No, I wasn't. Leave me alone.'

'Who was there, Dermot?'

Wee Dermot swallowed and ran his tongue over his lips.

'No one.'

'You served no one.'

'I didn't serve anyone. They didn't want anything.'

'Who didn't?'

'I don't know.'

'You didn't recognize any of the faces?'

'No.'

'Are you sure, Dermot?'

Dermot dared himself to look up. He felt exposed and vulnerable sitting in the detective's car so close to his home. But he didn't want them to drive him away. They might never bring him back.

'Yes.'

'Yes you knew someone, or yes you're sure?'

Dermot said nothing.

'You're lying to me, aren't you?'

Dermot could smell his own fear.

'Do you want some money, Dermot?'

'No, I don't want any money.'

'Like a holiday, would you, somewhere away from here?'

Two men walked past the car parked under the street light and stared in unconcealed curiosity. Dermot sank into the seat.

'I've left you alone,' said Boyle in almost friendly manner. 'I left you alone until I thought you could help me so I could help you, but you say I was wrong. You say you can't help at all. There's no way you may have made a mistake, is there?'

It occurred to Dermot that Boyle was taunting him somehow, that he wasn't actually after information.

'Well, is there?' Boyle barked and instantly Dermot forgot his fancy.

'No. No. I swear.'

Boyle sighed in defeat. 'All right. Maybe you could do with a rest. Times are changing. Maybe the block will come off a passport. Maybe.'

Dermot's face lifted. If he could get out of Ireland. America. London, Kilburn. Somewhere new.

'Keep your nose clean and your ears open and I'll think about it.' Boyle tapped his sergeant on the shoulder and he started the car.

Dermot took his cue and slipped out. His legs were trembling, but he covered the pavement to his front door in double time. He fumbled, finally managed to insert his key in the lock and disappeared from view.

The two men who had stared into the car watched his progress from the shadows. Boyle gave one of his sour smiles.

Dermot, Dermot. You've outlived your usefulness. Soon you will have outlived your life.

Chapter Thirty-three

The hollow crack of a dried twig startled Fife. He remained motionless but instantly alert and tingling in anticipation. A rustle in the darkness. Someone or something was moving slowly and carefully along the other side of the hedgerow. Fife pressed into the wall of the ditch, his head on one side and his mouth open. He made out one black form then another. Fife sunk lower, trying not to look directly at the strange figures drawing closer. He believed that you could feel eyes upon you in the darkness. He knew he could. The beings were level now, advancing in large, weird masses with no beginning or end. Looking up he picked out the barrel of a weapon against the night sky. Gotcha. Two men covered in netting to soften their outlines. Now he knew what to look for, he could make out their bergens and a radio pack.

An undercover team moving into position.

They were running late, thought Fife. From the fading stars he judged there was only an hour or so to dawn. He put his night vision goggles, a souvenir from the Regiment, to his eyes and swept back the way they had come. When he was sure there was no back-up team he moved aside a clump of cow parsley and stood up. The figures halted at the corner of the field near the young oak and sank from view.

Fife slipped back into his ditch, drew the scrim netting over himself and turned the goggles towards the darkened bungalow a quarter of a mile away. He wasn't happy about the company. He preferred to be the only watcher on the hill. As he waited for dawn, he considered the implications. The men would be under the orders of the regional Tasking and Co-ordination Group at Gough Barracks, Armagh. Why had they targeted the bungalow? Were they a surveillance team or part of a fighting patrol setting up an elaborate ambush? What intelligence were they acting on? Had they followed him to the area? Was the man of the house expected?

The girls were up and about by nine o'clock, tacking up the pony and then taking it in turns to ride around the rear field. Mary brought them out glasses of an orange drink at ten and thirty minutes later began hanging more washing on the line. The girls' clothing this time. The lane was quiet, he noted. Just a few farm pickups, the milk tanker and an occasional tractor.

At 11 AM a Lynx helicopter scudded over the hill at zero feet, its rotors sending out a downdraught that flattened the vegetation around Fife's hide. It swung over the bungalow, sending the washing billowing and frightening the pony, and then sped off south towards the border. A breakdown in communications. You insert the watchers then freeze the target area. You didn't buzz it from the air.

The presence of the observation post nagged at Fife. If O'Keefe turned up it would be hard for him to act without being seen. Untrue. It would be impossible for him to act. They'd clock him and call in the cavalry.

He was taking a sip of water through a straw from a racing bottle covered in a grey sock when a pale blue car slowly manoeuvred up the potholed drive. A red-cheeked, middle-aged woman climbed out carrying a shopping bag. Half an hour later she left, Mary escorting her to the car. It was really hot now, the sun beating down from a hazy, cloudless sky. The warm grass smelled sweet and insects buzzed and moths fluttered over the white fronds.

The Lynx returned at midday, skimming over the top of the ridge so it was on Fife before he heard it. He cowered in the ditch and wondered if it was looking for him. If so, the left hand really didn't know what the right hand was doing. He could imagine the fury of the two guys in the OP.

This lack of liaison mined covert operations. They should get on the net and pull that chopper off. The Lynx gave the bungalow the once-over and then contour chased the lane off to the north towards Belleek.

Bloody pointless to stay now. No one was going to turn up with that chopper split-arsing around the place. May as well put a uniformed copper on the front gate. Snatches of young voices drifted on the breeze. Rolling on his side, he made out a party of twenty or so teenagers with three adults a couple of fields away. They carried brightly coloured haversacks and they were coming in his direction. This was the last bloody straw. The hillside was turning out to be busier than Sauchiehall Street on Saturday night.

Pull out. Pull out now. And if he was going, so were the bloody opposition.

Fife took a damp face cloth and sponge from a plastic bag and scrubbed his face clean of the dirt he'd smeared on instead of cam cream because it was easier to get off. He inspected himself in a tiny mirror cupped in the palm of his hand before replacing his camouflage shirt with a nondescript blue one. He wasn't worried about his camouflage trousers. Everyone from building labourers to ramblers wore them. He packed his bergen, draped binoculars around his neck and put on his glasses to complete the image of a hiker or bird-watcher.

'Hello. Lovely day.' Fife met the group at the edge of his field.

An earnest, bespectacled young man waved back. 'Glorious. A joy to be alive.'

The youngsters did not think so. They were pale, surly and bored, scuffing their feet through the grass and slashing at the blackthorn with sticks. Slum kids. He should know; he'd been one.

The Lynx reappeared and three of the boys instantly put up their fingers in V-signs.

'Fucking Brits. Hope you crash. Bastards.'

The earnest man squirmed in embarrassment. 'They're

from West Belfast. This is a holiday club for the disadvantaged. Only their second day. I'm afraid they haven't got used to the countryside yet. Sorry.'

He waved a limp hand in farewell and hurried off to get ahead of his straggling band.

'What you doing, mister?' demanded a boy with freckles and a running nose. If he'd been bigger, Fife felt the kid would have challenged him to a fight.

'Minding my own business.'

'Sod you, then.'

'You three. Here.' Fife's word of command jerked them out of their sullen hostility. 'Is it right you don't like the Brits?'

The boys jeered and one spat on the ground.

'So if I told you there were two soldiers hidden on a stake-out, what would you do?'

'Piss on them,' replied Freckles.

'Yeh, piss on them,' echoed his mates.

Fife made a play of looking around to ensure they were not overheard. 'You'd be doing the Boys a favour if you would.'

Suddenly he had their attention. 'You right, mister?'

'See this hedge. Follow it to the left.' The boys spun around. 'Don't stare. See that small oak in the corner. About ten yards this side there're two soldiers with guns. They're well hidden, but they're there. Do you reckon you can find them?'

The boys' mouths dropped open.

'This is straight up,' insisted Fife. 'Take your mates and make a lot of noise so they know you're coming. You don't want to get shot.'

'I'm not scared,' boasted Freckles.

'You won't help the Boys by being dead,' snapped Fife. 'Now go and ask those Brit soldiers what the hell they're doing. Really go to town.'

Three fields away, Fife looked back. The teenagers were standing around the hedge shouting, taunting and pointing.

A black car was slowly negotiating the potholes up to the bungalow. He watched through his binoculars as a large, tall man uncurled from the front passenger seat. Definitely time to go.

Collins and Jenny Dove stood three feet apart looking through the metal-framed windows at the small vegetable garden with its rows of runner beans climbing up trellises of hewn branches. In the field beyond the low concrete wall, a herd of Friesians chewed placidly. The weather forecast said rain, but they seemed not to have heard it.

'Fide, sed cui vide.'

'I'm sorry, Patrick John, you have the advantage of me.' There was no apology in Jenny's well-modulated voice.

'Just a line from Horace. So you'll play the honest broker, then?'

'I didn't say that.' Jenny tossed back her tumbling hair. 'You know my loyalties will lie with my partner, but I'll not mislead you.'

Collins looked at the woman before him and thought she had changed somehow. Her outward impression of serenity had collapsed in on herself and he was more aware of her sharp white canines.

Jenny handed him a cellophane packet containing two sets of photographs taken in a booth in Enniskillen the previous day.

'How long before the passports will be ready?'

'A week, maybe longer. The money will be on hand once we have the passports.'

Jenny snorted. 'I'd hurry it up if I were you. He's getting restless doing nothing.'

O'Keefe was certainly getting restless but not for any reason she'd tell Collins. He was restless to give up and get out. But she wouldn't say that.

A cow rubbed against the pillar at the end of the wall, a look of pure joy on her gentle face. Collins always liked this safe house, fifteen miles to the south of Belfast, with its air of rural simplicity and peace. Again he felt that weariness creep over him. He was tired, tired to his marrow. The tonics from the doctor didn't seem to be doing any good. He'd see what the tests would show – although he already had a chilling idea.

In the past few days Yeats's Irish Airman had been constantly running through his mind. Fighting those he did not hate, guarding those he did not love. He balanced all, brought all to mind. *The years to come seemed waste of breath, A waste of breath the years behind, In balance with this life, this death.*

Snap out of it. One last mile. Just one last mile.

'I'd like to see Paddy. These things are best discussed face to face.'

'I don't think that would be a very good idea at the moment. Let well alone.'

Collins ruminated. The silence deepened like a slow, heavy fall of snowflakes building on itself until the landscape was transformed.

'Answer me, Jenny. Is the man thinking of throwing in his lot with the hardliners?'

The stark directness of the question took her by surprise. Most unlike the urbane obliqueness of Old Holborn's normal interrogative technique.

'Not yet.'

It was the only answer which sprung to mind.

'Not yet,' repeated Collins. 'Has he thought about doing so?'

'I think he's thought about a lot of things,' answered Jenny slowly.

'Will he heed the ceasefire? No more Duncans. Will he stop killing?'

Collins was ardent in his need for reassurance, his eyes burning brightly behind his spectacles. Jenny sensed the pendulum swing towards her.

'Help him, help us go far far away. As soon as possible.'

'You mean you wouldn't trust him if he stayed here?'

Maybe to humour the old careworn man Jenny quoted Padraig Pearse's words from his prison cell before his execution.

'We are ready to die and shall die cheerfully and proudly. Personally I do not hope or even desire to live. You must not grieve for this.' She smiled and looked serious at the same time. 'I know I couldn't control him.'

As Collins nodded she fancied he became enveloped in a cloud of sadness.

Driving away she congratulated herself on not telling a single lie. Clever girl.

'So you see, Secretary of State, it is imperative for me to be in Belfast to oversee the operation.'

His political master slowly raised his large head to glower at his Parliamentary Private Secretary standing before him.

'And just what do you think you can contribute?'

The Secretary of State for Northern Ireland did not bother to conceal his anger. He'd learned of Baines-Hickey's new responsibility only that morning and then through the Permanent Secretary at the Cabinet Office. The PM hadn't had the courtesy – or the guts – to tell him personally that he had put his subordinate in charge of an operation that was his by right.

'Well, the PM did say to pull out all the stops and do whatever I felt was necessary. I can't really get on top of the operation from here.'

Baines-Hickey felt like the jam between two heavyweight slices of bread. The PM had put him in a difficult position, but it wasn't of his making and the Secretary of State should understand that. Stuff him. With the Premier behind him, what could he do to him?

The Minister supported his heavy chins on his thumbs and continued to glare at his PPS. God! How he despised this cocky upstart posturing across his desk. He hadn't even bothered to put on a jacket when he was summoned. Poncing around in red braces. Such overweening confidence. He'd been aware his speech at the weekend calling for Britain to stand aside from Europe would anger the PM, but he hadn't expected anything so underhand and despicable as this. Typical of the bloody man. Petty and vindictive. One to store in the memory bank for the future.

'The security forces over there have their own ways of doing things. Don't you think you might get in the way?'

'That wasn't the way it was put at JOC.'

This was news to the Secretary of State. He couldn't restrain himself. 'What JOC?'

Now he'd made it appear as if he was really being kept in the dark.

'Full meeting yesterday afternoon, sir. When you were in Scotland. Five, Six, FCO, Home Office, RUC and NI DSF from Belfast came over specially and of course the military and SAS Group. Quite a turnout, really.' Baines-Hickey failed to keep the smugness out of his voice.

'And did you get anywhere?' asked the Secretary of State in a silky voice.

'We agreed to co-ordinate all intelligence efforts through Five's DCI at Stormont, with the day-to-day running up to the RUC.'

'So, the NIO's not directly involved.' The Minister was quick to distance his department from the possibility of failure.

'Er . . . no, sir.'

'So you're on what might be seen as secondment, then?'

Baines-Hickey did not like the way this interview was heading.

'I suppose so. The PM didn't spell it out . . .'

'No, dear boy. He seldom does.'

Mary O'Keefe did not offer Boyle a cup of tea. She received him coldly if correctly and showed him into the living room with the french windows. She was sensibly dressed in trousers and a long-sleeved cotton shirt and she wore no make-up. Boyle noted she'd recently had her hair done and there wasn't a photograph of Paddy O'Keefe to be seen.

Boyle exuded an air of authority, but in her unspoken way Mary's compact dignity challenged that authority in a manner which indicated she accepted neither the power he represented nor his personal manifestation of that power.

'It's a lovely part of the world,' he began.

Mary nodded solemnly.

'Bit out of the way, though. I'd have thought the girls would have preferred to be in a town.'

'They're fine.' She took his reference to her daughters to mean that this big policeman was saying he knew all about her and her family. 'Well, Mr . . . Boyle?' She made a play of searching for his name.

'It's regarding your husband . . .'

Mary looked at him blankly while someone released a swarm of butterflies inside her stomach.

'My husband is dead,' she said with a finality she did not feel.

'Yes, the explosion . . .' Boyle let the words slip into the silence that grew between them.

Mary began twisting her wedding ring on her finger.

'I knew Paddy, Mrs O'Keefe.' Boyle wondered how much O'Keefe had told his wife about his efforts to recruit him as an informer. 'I was talking to him about a job the very day your son Liam was . . . um . . . hurt. A few years ago now.'

'Yes, time flies.' Mary's mouth was set severely, but her heart was beating so violently that she was sure the detective must be able to see its rise and fall.

'I won't ask you when you last saw your husband.'

'No,' retorted Mary briskly. 'That would be an impertinence.'

Boyle didn't flinch. He admired the way Mary was conducting herself. He respected the formidable working-class

Irishwoman of whatever religion: the matriarch who kept home and family together in times of feast and famine. The men might be weak and feckless, but the women were capable and daunting. His mother was just such a one.

'It is my duty to inform you, Mrs O'Keefe, that we believe that someone is about to make an attempt on your husband's life.'

'My husband is dead, and anyway why should you care?'

'Mummy, mummy.' Boo burst into the room waving a painting book.

'Not now, pet, mummy's busy.'

'Hello,' smiled Boyle.

'Don't talk to her,' snarled Mary. Her lips turned white with fear and her eyes glared deep into him, defying him to say another word.

'Mrs O'Keefe,' continued Boyle when Boo had left the room. 'Perhaps we know more about your husband's activities than you do.'

Not likely, he thought, but he'd give her a window of opportunity if she wished to climb through it. Mary said nothing.

'Do you see Patrick John Collins often?'

'Why?'

'He was helpful to you when you were in Belfast.'

'That was in Belfast, but what has this to do with someone trying to kill my husband?'

Mary wondered if she'd slipped up in her choice of words – she was in an impossible position. She was desperate to find out more about the threat to Paddy, but in maintaining he was dead she couldn't display any curiosity. What if it was a trap?

'We have reason to believe that a former colleague of your husband will try to kill him,' continued Boyle ponderously. 'We believe they served together.'

'The British Army is a big place.'

'In the same regiment.'

'There are three parachute regiments.' Mary recalled the endless hours Paddy and Fife had spun stories of their time in Para Reg together.

'In the Regiment. In 22 SAS.' Mary frowned her disbelief. 'A Scottish soldier called Fife. Duggie Fife.'

'Jimmy Sands,' gasped Mary. She snapped shut her gaping mouth before she could say anything more.

She glowered at Boyle who, under his lugubrious mask, was pleased at the reaction. Mary recovered from the initial shock.

'Never. Never in a thousand years. You're making it up.' Her eyes hardened. So it was a trap after all. 'Get out. Get out of my house with your lies.'

She rose and pointed at the door, but Boyle did not move.

'Let me explain. The last British soldier, killed at the border checkpoint near Middletown, was a private William Agnew of the Royal Highland Fusiliers . . .'

Mary suddenly divined what he was about to say. She turned linen white.

'Billy! Young Billy! But he was Billy Fife.'

'No,' corrected Boyle. 'Billy was adopted. He enlisted under his real name.'

'Oh, Billy.' Mary pressed her fist to her mouth and sank her teeth into her index finger until Boyle thought she would draw blood. She would not, could not accept the awfulness of what this policeman was saying.

She took her hand away, a semicircle of bloodless indentations crowning her first knuckle.

'You're lying.' Hysteria rose inside her and her voice was again that of the Falls, guttural and grating. 'Don't fucking lie to me. Get out of my house, copper. Get out of my fucking house, now.'

Boyle let her resentment and pain break over him.

'I'm sorry. It's the truth.'

Mary put her fingertips to her forehead, her thumbs on her cheekbones and tried to focus on a stable point of reference in her whirling kaleidoscope of thoughts and emotions. The phone calls from Fife had become irregular and infrequent, especially after he'd left the army. But . . . but . . . she closed her eyes. Billy had joined the Paras, yes, she remembered that. He'd hurt himself. She'd sent him a get well card to some military hospital in London. That's right. Then what? He'd learned to walk again. Yes. He'd left the Paras but he was army mad. He was going to join a Scottish regiment.

Oh Mary Mother of Jesus and all the saints, forgive us.

She heard Boyle talking on in that deep, monotonous voice, but she could not make out what he was saying. She merely shook her head helplessly. If Fife approached her, she was to call him straight away. Boyle offered her his card which she accepted. Did she want a panic button? A what? No.

When he had left she poured herself a large gin and tonic. A little later she phoned the classified ads department of the *Belfast Telegraph*. The advert would run for three days. If Paddy did not respond, she would place another one.

A little later still she thought that her phone must be tapped. Too late, too late.

'This is it?' Baines-Hickey's voice rose in insolent disbelief. 'This is the incident room?'

He looked contemptuously around the dusty room with its massive iron radiator and old-fashioned coat stand behind the door. A blackboard stood in a corner. Baines-Hickey's leather soles squeaked on the linoleum as he crossed to the grimy window and looked down on to the tarmac of a deserted car park. He hadn't known what to expect, but certainly not this forgotten room at the end of the long gloomy corridor.

'There's been no incident yet,' rumbled the heavy Special Branch detective. 'And we are not fully up and running.'

'You can't run a major manhunt from here,' snapped the politician in disapproval, putting down his locked leather attaché case. 'You do know the Prime Minister has a personal interest in this, don't you? Eh? I'm disappointed, frankly disappointed, and I shall tell the PM so.'

Boyle's jaw muscle twitched. He and Major Taylor had been under orders not to attract attention while setting up a comprehensive operation. He angrily regarded the politician's aristocratic features. You may be well-bred, sunshine, but you'll not bully me on my own patch.

He walked to the door and opened it, indicating with his free hand that Baines-Hickey should leave. 'I'll conduct you to a direct line.'

'What for?'

'You said you wished to phone Downing Street.'

Baines-Hickey gave the detective a haughty scowl, his head drawn back so he looked along the pronounced arch of his nose. Boyle in turn returned an unblinking stare from under bushy eyebrows and again indicated the door.

'Later. Later. We've things to do. Bring me up to date on Fife.'

'Fife was last seen at 8.15 the night before last in Belfast,' said Boyle. 'He didn't return to his lodgings that night. They are still under surveillance. We are systematically checking all the hotels, guest houses and B and Bs in Belfast and the towns near Mrs O'Keefe's home. We'll widen the search throughout the Province if we draw a blank. Metropolitan Police Special Branch are keeping observation on his girlfriend's flat in south-east London. Her phones at home and at work are being tapped. There's no indication that Fife has left Northern Ireland, but we are covering all eventualities. He's just gone off radar.'

Boyle crossed to the large-scale map of the Province. 'The target's home phone is being monitored. He might make contact with O'Keefe's wife. I saw her this morning. She seemed shocked by the news of Billy Agnew and Fife's involvement.'

'Was she play-acting?' asked Baines-Hickey.

'No. I don't think so.'

'Will she help us?'

'No.' Irish women did not turn against their men. Boyle continued the briefing. 'Fife didn't have a car when he arrived, so we're checking to see if he's hired one.'

'And where is O'Keefe?'

'We don't know, sir.' Fucking stupid question.

'Why not?'

'If we knew where he was, sir, we would arrest him on suspicion of the murder of a dozen or so police and army officers.' Boyle spoke with the exaggerated simplicity with which one would address a child.

'Oh, I don't think the PM would want him arrested just now.'

'That's all right then, sir. We don't know where he is,' said Boyle sweetly. 'We've circulated Fife's picture to the RUC. We haven't explained why, but we warned to approach with extreme caution, preferably seek back-up.'

'What about the army?'

'Many soldiers, especially in Special Forces, will have served with Fife.' Major Taylor took up the briefing. 'They'll want to know what this is all about. It'll inevitably get to the press and we're instructed that a press blackout is essential. We judged the potential for embarrassment outweighed the usefulness of involving the armed forces directly at this time. All we've really lost are the mobile patrols and they're not geared to look for an individual. We are employing all intelligence-gathering agencies including 14 Int, but they are trained not to talk.'

'I expect Fife is living rough,' observed Baines-Hickey. 'Using his training. Doing a rogue male. You should look around O'Keefe's home to see if he's lying up there.'

'The local battalion's COP is sweeping the area as we speak, then we'll freeze it and insert a team from the Det.'

'Good.' Baines-Hickey was pleased he'd come up with a valid idea.

Boyle didn't believe Fife was out in the cuds. He and

Taylor had discussed it at length that morning. Boyle reasoned that Fife would not find his quarry by lurking under a hedge. He had to track him down. He only wished he knew what leads Fife had.

'Do you want us to ask the Garda for co-operation in case he's holed up south of the border?'

'Um.' Baines-Hickey looked helpless. 'What do you think?'

'IRA men hide out in the Republic all the time,' growled Boyle. 'We can't take the Garda fully into our confidence, but if we spin them a cock and bull story and the truth gets out they won't be best pleased and they have a way of letting their irritation be felt in Whitehall – but I'm sure you can handle that.'

Baines-Hickey looked at him with loathing. 'What about known associates?'

'Apart from O'Keefe's wife, the people who know Fife best are members of the Northern Ireland troop of 22. They've been ordered, under threat of RTU, to report any contact from him.'

'What are the chances of finding Fife?' Baines-Hickey looked up from his note-taking.

'We'll find him,' Boyle assured him. 'We always find them. But in this case we have very little to go on and it might take some time.'

'Time.' Baines-Hickey jerked out of his languid pose. 'Time is the very thing we don't have. It would be a disaster if he strikes before we find him.'

'You must appreciate our difficulties, sir. We are trying to find someone to prevent him committing a crime against a second person. But we don't have a clue of the victim's location. There are too many variables. It's a bit like blind man's buff across six counties with everyone blindfolded.'

Baines-Hickey felt a prickle of apprehension. In the RAF Puma on the way over he had pictured a quick success and then back to the congratulations and the glory. The prospect of a long-drawn-out manhunt stretching over weeks opened out before him like a bleak moor. What would he do? Fester in Belfast or return to London to be sneered at by his Secretary of State? And then there was the Prime Minister, desperate to make these talks a success. On his back. All the time. He could see the operation turning into a bloody nightmare.

'You must admit it's a little rum that we should be busting a gut to protect the IRA's top gunman when we should be busting a gut to catch him,' continued Boyle.

Baines-Hickey was thinking at a tangent.

'I assume the IRA could find Fife,' he said slowly. A knowing, supercilious look crept across his face. 'I think we should ask for their co-operation in this matter.'

'What!'

Boyle's glare of outrage and fury made the politician more determined. These parochial policemen ran on rails. It needed a fresh mind.

'Yes. Ask the IRA. You do have unofficial channels, I presume.'

'Yes, sir.' Boyle had turned a deep mahogany and he was having difficulty keeping his thoughts to himself.

'Set up a meeting. Completely and utterly off the record, of course.' Baines-Hickey closed his notebook with a flourish. 'Nothing is set in concrete, inspector. You have to be flexible – in your thinking as well as your dealings with the other side.'

Boyle didn't know which he objected to more, being demoted or being lectured at by a pompous prick. On the whole he thought it was the latter.

'Phuket looks lovely, doesn't it? Or we could go up country to Chiang Rai or Chiang Mai. It's supposed to be beautiful there.' Jenny sat at the farmhouse kitchen table, a pile of holiday brochures in front of her. 'I suppose you'll want to go to one of those sex shows in Bangkok. I've heard some very weird stories about those girls. Razor blades, flags of all nations, even bursting balloons. Perhaps I'll learn a few tricks.'

She prattled on, enthusiastically planning their holiday. After leaving Collins she had called at travel agents and bookshops, gathering everything she could find on Thailand. She had also visited an old flame. It had been pleasant and convenient to spend an hour in his bed, but it had made her forget to buy the fourth security camera. She told O'Keefe that they still didn't have them in stock.

'How long did Old Holborn say till the passports will be ready?'

'About a week, he hopes.'

'I would have liked to have spoken to him face to face.'

'He says it's too dangerous, Paddy.'

She watched him out of the corner of her eye for any sign of suspicion, but he settled over the Lonely Planet guidebook. He seemed to be enjoying the prospect of getting away.

Indeed, O'Keefe was delighted at the chance to get out of Northern Ireland. He would never come back. Start again. Mary and the kids would come out to Thailand. Then he would move on. He thought about them vanishing together, but feared their disappearance would only put the police on his trail. And there was Liam. He couldn't go to Thailand, but he certainly wasn't going to be left behind when they emigrated. Mary would return to sell the house and get everything in order. She had distant cousins in Perth; she'd put out the word she was taking the family to Australia to live.

Jenny watched Paddy begin to make notes and after a while snuggled up to him.

'Where're we going then?'

'Around.'

'The seven Ps,' she said gaily. 'Proper planning prevents piss poor performance.'

'That's only six.'

'Pollocks.'

She threw her arms around his neck and touched his cheek with her lips, feeling the rough dark growth of bristles although he'd shaved that morning. She sensed him stiffen. She rested her fingers lightly on his thigh and let her hand stray towards his groin as her hair brushed his neck. Paddy jerked his head back in irritation and removed her hand gently but firmly.

Bastard. He was rebuffing her in the same way as she had rebuffed amorous, heavy-handed schoolboys when she had been a schoolgirl. Before she went to university and wondered why she had troubled to rebuff anyone at all.

He looked into her burning green eyes and shook his head. She wanted to grab his black curls and pull them out in handfuls. Instead she rose and stood behind him, placed her hands on his broad, muscular shoulders and began kneading them.

'You can have lots of this in Bangkok. If you like we can have a threesome or foursome. Whatever you fancy. Something you haven't done before.'

O'Keefe was reading about the bridge over the River Khwae at Kanchanaburi. He'd love to see Death Railway, but he wasn't so sure Katie and Boo would. They'd be happier on a beach.

'When can we book flights?'

'When we know what names we'll be travelling under.'

'What about visas?'

'Easy peasy.'

She dug her thumbs into the base of his neck, working away at the knots that clustered there like ganglions. He didn't stop her; instead he rolled his head in appreciation.

'Do you think we could have some target practice before we go?' There was a moment's silence and Jenny hurried on. 'Not necessarily with the Robar, but with the AK or even the Browning. Just to keep our hands in.'

'No need.' O'Keefe dismissed her idea without looking up. He couldn't see her passing spasm of angry disappointment and she kept on working away at his neck and shoulders.

'Wonder how they feel about nudity on the beaches in Thailand. It's so sensuous to swim naked.'

O'Keefe didn't answer and Jenny's sharpened intuition told her she was being excluded from his anticipation of the holiday. No way was she being left behind. She'd control the airline tickets and passports. She'd stick with him like superglue. No one dumped Jenny Dove. No one.

Chapter Thirty-four

'Thank you for agreeing to see us.' Baines-Hickey managed to make it sound as if it were he who was bestowing the favour. 'You understand this meeting is under Chatham House Rules. Off the record.'

'Yes, I did know what you meant.'

'Good.' Baines-Hickey was unabashed.

Collins switched his gaze to Boyle standing four-square behind the slimmer politician. 'Is this room clean?'

'It was swept before we entered. I haven't bugged it. It's not in our interest.' Boyle's deepset eyes challenged Collins to doubt his word. He pulled back the curtain and looked obliquely at the still, grey waters of Strangford Lough. Boyle was not prepared to jeopardize one of SB's safe houses; Collins was not willing to enter a police station or a military base; so borrowing the office of the catering manager, known to Boyle, in this quiet two-star hotel near Newtownards had been a typical compromise.

'We don't trust each other, do we?' stated Collins, cigarette paper dangling from his lips as he prepared a roll-up.

Baines-Hickey was confused by Collins's scholarly appearance. He had been expecting a tattooed demagogue and was nonplussed by the tall, painfully thin schoolmaster with the silver hair, shapeless sports jacket and shiny grey trousers. Boyle too was using the opportunity to study the opposition close up, but he saw beneath the horn-rimmed spectacles to the grey tinge of Collins's skin and the angry cough that broke out of him.

He hoped the politician would not cock things up and leave him to clear up the mess. The Prime Minister had phoned just as they were setting out to demand a progress report – Boyle didn't know whether he was expecting miracles, or whether he was deliberately giving Baines-Hickey a hard time. Either way it rattled the politician just when he needed a cool head.

Baines-Hickey cleared his throat. He sat in the manager's chair, putting himself in the position of power. Collins, across the desk from him, appeared the supplicant.

'We're concerned that a former member of Her Majesty's armed forces is preparing to break the ceasefire by committing an illegal act.'

Collins rasped the wheel of his old petrol lighter and peered through the smoke that rose in front of his face.

'Then how can I help you?' He implied the problem was of their making. Nothing to do with him.

Baines-Hickey hesitated. 'He's seeking to avenge the death of his brother who was killed by the IRA.'

'Mr Baines-Hickey,' replied Collins with a show of forbearance. 'If the IRA reacted every time a dead soldier's relative threatened revenge, they'd not sleep in their beds at night.'

'It's not quite that simple, Mr Collins,' said the politician tetchily.

'It seldom is,' murmured Collins.

There grew a silence as Collins inspected the end of his cigarette and Baines-Hickey nervously cleared his throat again. In the growing atmosphere, Collins compared the two men representing the Crown. The politician was a sleek racehorse, fine-boned, highly bred, liable to kick out in any direction, and not to be relied upon. The policeman was a lumpen workhorse, long-backed and large-hoofed. He knew which he'd trust if he had to – but then, he wasn't about to trust either.

'We expect your help.' Baines-Hickey finally jabbed a manicured index finger in Collins's direction. 'It's in your interest as much as ours to maintain the ceasefire. Probably more so.'

'Do you think so now?' mused Collins quietly. 'I don't think you're in a position to expect anything.'

'Don't tell me you're one of those who wants to see the peace talks fail.' Baines-Hickey threw himself back in the chair. 'It's impossible to deal with you people. No two sing the same song.'

'Belua multorum capitum?' he mused. 'No, I don't think we are. Do you know Horace, Mr Baines-Hickey?' Collins took off his glasses and held them so he peered through the lens at the politician in a calculated gesture of disdain.

Enough, thought Boyle, impatiently shifting from foot to foot like an unsteady wardrobe. He's playing with this bloody politician, but I'm the one who'll get the fallout. He decided to intervene.

'The man seeking revenge is a former sergeant in the SAS.' Boyle knew the IRA's fear of the Regiment. 'His name is Duggie Fife and he has a reputation, even inside Special Forces, for being ruthless and indefatigable. He is seeking the man who killed Private Billy Agnew. We believe he knows the identity of the killer. There is a real possibility that he will find the gunman and kill him. We feel that act might jeopardize the peace talks.'

Boyle spoke succinctly and harshly and the words cost him a lot in pride.

Collins seemed to understand, for he pinched the end of his nose and regarded Boyle with sympathetic eyes. He was calculating furiously.

'Can you help?' insisted Baines-Hickey.

Wrong question again, thought Boyle. It should be: Will you help?

'Possibly, possibly.'

'Good. Excellent.' Baines-Hickey was prepared to feast on any crumb of comfort.

'There may be a quid pro quo.'

'Fine, fine.' The politician rose out of his chair. 'Must be getting back. I'll let you two sort out the details, that sort of thing. Take the back-up car,' he instructed Boyle. 'Mr

Collins. Hopefully this will be the first of many other joint operations.' He held out his hand.

There was silence in the room after Baines-Hickey had left. Then Boyle exhaled noisily. As though he could now relax, Collins began to cough in short hacking gulps for breath. He pushed a handkerchief to his mouth and bent his arms into his narrow chest.

'You should give up the cancer sticks,' advised Boyle.

'You must be taking this threat seriously for your political master to come from London.'

'I'm taking it as seriously as any other job. Fife is a Glasgow Catholic. I reckon he'll stay on your turf where he'll feel more at home. Here's his picture. There's a description on the back. O'Keefe knows what he looks like. They were mates once.'

'O'Keefe?'

'Just a name.'

The two men regarded each other with a flicker of mutual respect before they resumed the blankness of antipathy.

'Do you want any help?' asked Boyle.

'And how do you think you can help me? I thought you were the ones asking for aid.'

Boyle shrugged. 'You might be able to give this task more of your undivided attention if we removed distractions like Sean O'Hanlon.'

'You think so?'

'That wandering eye of his is going to go to war by itself one day and it might go to war on you. We wouldn't want anything to happen to you – at the moment.'

'I thank you for your concern, but I don't think I know what you're talking about.'

'So be it, but he doesn't like being sworn at, even in Latin. Watch your back.'

'Me?' exclaimed Collins, stubbing out the cigarette. 'I'm just a Sinn Fein councillor and don't you forget it.'

Collins stopped on the outskirts of Dundonald and made a

call from a phone box in a layby on the A20. By the time he arrived at the Community Aid Centre a score of teenage messengers had gathered. An earnest young electronics graduate of Liverpool University carrying a small metal case assured him that the building was free from listening devices, but reminded him to stay away from the windows, draw the curtains and to switch on the noisy and vibrating fan if he intended a delicate conversation. It was a well-worn litany, but one which Collins himself had instigated and he was pleased that the expert was going by the book.

Under the guise of distributing Sinn Fein literature, Collins put out the word to the company intelligence officers in every Catholic area of Belfast. To the remaining slums of the Lower Falls and to the newer slums of Andytown and Divis; to the Murph, The Markets and Short Strand and New Lodge; up to Ardoyne and The Bone and to the heartlands of Turf Lodge, Dermot Hill, Westrock and Whiterock, Beechmount and Clonard.

He covered every street and block of flats, private houses as well as guest houses, boarding houses and small commercial hotels. He added his authority, that week's code word and a Double A priority. When the man was found, on no account was he to be approached. He was to be put under surveillance only, and Collins repeated *only*, if it was possible without arousing the slightest suspicion. He wanted reports by nine the next morning at the latest.

To an outsider it was an impossible task. For anyone enmeshed in the tribal lands of Belfast it was straightforward. In the closed communities, everyone knew everyone; strangers stood out. If Fife was there, someone would know.

Collins closed the door to his office, made sure the tobacco tin and papers were at hand and swung his feet up on to the desk. He lit the first roll-up and stared through the curling smoke at the whitewashed ceiling. A three roll-up problem.

What was Boyle trying to tell him? Did Special Branch suspect that O'Hanlon was plotting to kill him? Their intelligence was invariably sound and now it was in their interest to keep him alive. Collins remembered that O'Hanlon's eye had been like a marble rolling around in a jam jar at the last meeting. He was glad Frannie McFadden had been at his side.

'He doesn't like being sworn at in Latin.' Collins furrowed his brow trying to remember his exact words. He used his Latin tags like sharp dartlets, sometimes for his own amusement, sometimes to rile others; sometimes, indeed, he didn't know he was doing it. No doubt a psychologist would say he was subconsciously trying to compensate for not using his learning.

What had he said? O'Hanlon had spoken about using INLA to carry on the fight in their name. And he had become cross. He'd quoted Horace. *Odi profanum vulgus et arceo.* I loathe and shun the profane rabble. Who else in the room would understand that? The smoke drifted to the ceiling in blue-grey wisps. It wouldn't matter who would understand if it was being taped. Wee Dermot had been there. He'd come in uninvited and unannounced. He'd long had doubts about wee Dermot. There was already a report that Dermot had got into a car with two men outside his home after the meeting last night.

Was he being debriefed? It was a careless place to do it, if he was. But to be sloppy is human. Not everyone regarded truth as the layers of an onion to be stripped away one at a time as he did. Dermot would have to be interrogated with all the necessary consequences. Not O'Hanlon. He would enjoy torture for torture's sake. He'd send Frannie McFadden. He'd send him with the authority to do whatever was needed.

And then there was the mention of O'Keefe. Did Boyle really know his identity or was he just fishing? It didn't really matter but . . .

Golden Virginia found him deep in thought, still staring

sightlessly at the ceiling. No one else dared to disturb him, but his sister had no such fears. In repose, she noticed his eyes burned unnaturally fiercely.

'Mary's been on the phone.'

Collins seemed to come back from somewhere a very long way away.

'Mary. From a call box. She had a visit from a detective named Boyle who told her Paddy was still alive and some-one called Fife was trying to kill him.'

'I met Boyle this morning. He didn't mention he'd seen Mary.'

'I can't see how anyone could ever find Paddy.' Virginia automatically began tidying up the office.

'The Crown are taking this man Fife very seriously,' replied Collins. 'O'Keefe is the centre of a lot of grief and uncertainty at the moment. O'Hanlon hinted a couple of days ago that O'Keefe might throw in his lot with the hardliners and then there was something Jenny said which disturbed me. She and O'Hanlon both quoted the same passage from Pearse. In O'Hanlon's case he mis-quoted it, but it makes you wonder if they've been talk-ing.'

'I've never trusted that woman,' sniffed Virginia, her long formal face becoming prim.

'I have the feeling that she is not being totally straight with us,' agreed her brother.

Virginia paused as she emptied the full ashtray into the wastepaper bin. There was a mound of lighter grey ash among the cigarette butts. Kneeling behind her brother, she poked around until she picked out the charred corner of a small photograph showing a red curtain.

'Why don't you go and see him?' She kept her voice steady as she examined the remnant.

'Jenny didn't think it was a good idea . . .' Old Holborn seemed to drift back into his own thoughts.

'The sooner they are both out of the way the better,' asserted Virginia.

'I don't know that short-term answers are any answers at all,' said Collins in a dreamy fashion.

'What do you mean?' She put the corner of the photograph in her jacket pocket and moved around in front of her brother.

Collins continued to gaze at the ceiling. It seemed he was thinking aloud. 'What do you think would happen if Fife took out the pair of them?'

'It would blow a hole in the peace talks,' replied Virginia promptly.

'Exactly. That's the point. His act would blow a hole in the talks, but they would still remain. And if the Crown were the transgressors think how many more concessions that would bring us. State-sponsored terrorism would not go down well in Washington. It could work to our advantage.'

'Surely not, Patrick John.'

'But what would happen if O'Keefe and Jenny Dove return in a month or whenever and start picking and choosing their own targets? The Brits wouldn't stand for it and we would have shown that we were incapable of keeping our house in order. We'd appear to be the ones breaking the ceasefire. We'd lose public and international sympathy.'

Suddenly Virginia recognized the charred remains.

'But you're the one who preaches there's always a tomorrow; never close the door finally because no one knows what tomorrow brings.'

'*Carpe diem.* Seize the day,' intoned Collins. He coughed and swung around to face his sister. 'Do you know the full line from Horace? *Carpe diem, quam minimum credula postera.* Seize the present day, trust the least possible to the future.'

'I took the liberty of getting you one in. Where's our master now?'

'He's spent the past hour trying to get the SIS involved.

Quite what he thinks they can do, God only knows. Cheers.' Boyle took a large gulp of his Guinness and idly looked around the ramshackle hut which passed for 14 Int's bar and mess.

'Everyone's going to earn their bread in the next few days,' said Major Taylor. 'The increase in radio traffic alone will scare the Russians into believing we're about to go nuclear.'

'The Northern Ireland Office will go nuclear when they see the overtime bills.' Boyle took another long pull. 'We've been put on a war footing. All Special Support Units are on alert. E3 and E4 are buzzing. Collators are being kept on through the night. 4A and 4B have never been so loved and cherished. We're in the attic of Collins's neighbours and also across the street.'

'Collins is putting out the word far and wide. While I remember, there's going to be some action concerning Ashanti Terrace or someone who lives in Ashanti Terrace . . .' A shadow passed over Boyle's face and continued on going. '. . . Big Ears came up against some interference in the shape of a petrol tanker.' Major Taylor laughed. 'I mean. They can pick up the beat of a butterfly's wings at half a mile, bounce it off a satellite somewhere out in space and then tell you the butterfly's wingspan. These parabolic devices can do everything apart from give their operators a blow job and then a bloody petrol tanker parks in the line of sight.'

Boyle pulled a wry face. 'In my experience, you gear up in one direction, commit God knows what resources, manpower and technology and then the village bobby has a chat to the local postmistress and you discover chummy is staying with the vicar.'

'Say we caught O'Keefe,' said Taylor thoughtfully. 'Would we be able to prove he murdered those men?'

'No,' replied Boyle, slowly. 'Let's say we ignore supergrass evidence, which is discredited anyway. If he admitted the shootings then we're home and dry, but he'd never do that.

If we found him with the sniper rifle and ammunition he could say he was carrying it from one location to another and that he'd never seen it before. We could do him for illegal possession and possibly as an accessory after the fact, but not even a Special Court could go further. He'd get ten years. If we found him without the rifle, then we'd have nothing. Some awkward questions as to why he's alive when he's supposed to be dead, but not much else.'

'Does Fife know that?'

'I shouldn't think so. All he wants to do is find O'Keefe and kill him.'

Virginia Collins did what she always did in times of trouble; she made herself a pot of tea. She didn't agree with her brother and the tea made her calm and resolute. She was a strong woman who acted on her beliefs, so she fetched her writing case and with a determined look began writing a short but important letter. It was seldom she crossed her brother, but this time he was wrong. She had just time to catch the last post.

It was almost 9 PM and PC Paul Robinson was hungry. He'd called at dozens of small hotels and boarding houses in St James and now he was working his way along the Donegal Road. He was four hours into overtime. St Mary's Road was next and he had just one address there, a Mrs McNally who infrequently took in paying guests. He decided to take a meal break before going on with the list towards Milltown Cemetery. With overtime like this he'd have enough to buy that sailing dinghy. He turned the police car and headed back to the police station.

Fifteen minutes later two young men knocked politely on the door of a semi-detached villa in St Mary's Road. Mrs McNally knew one of the boys. Yes, she said, she had one guest. A Scotsman. Fair-haired, early thirties. Arrived yesterday. The men thanked her and asked her not to reveal the man's presence to the police if they came calling. It's no big deal, they explained. It's better they didn't know you had anyone here. Think of the tax people. Of course, said Mrs McNally.

When PC Robinson returned forty minutes later, Mrs McNally told him in a friendly fashion that she had no one staying there. In fact she didn't take paying guests any more.

Wee Dermot was picked up by Frannie McFadden and two other men as he approached the pub in Short Strand. He was hooded and taken to a house in New Lodge just off the Antrim Road. They didn't need to beat the truth out of him. By the time Dermot was hurled on the floor of the cellar he was a limp, blubbering mess. He confessed to being an informer immediately. McFadden insisted that Dermot had told Boyle about the plan to assassinate him. Dermot did not deny the accusation. He agreed he had listened at meetings above the bakery and when McFadden put it to him that he had spied on the row with O'Hanlon, he was so overcome with mortal dread that he could not speak.

Dermot's incoherence and choking sobs wrecked McFadden's efforts to tape his confession. It became a farce as McFadden was forced to give a running interpretation of Dermot's grunts and nods as he lost the power of speech and continence.

'Did you tell DCI Boyle of the Special Branch of the plan to kill him?'

Incomprehensible gurgles. McFadden's voice. 'The accused is nodding his head.'

'Where did you meet him?'

'Mother of God, mercy.'

Another man's voice. 'The dirty bastard's pissed himself.'

'Where did you meet him? Was it in a car?' A pause. 'The accused is again nodding his head.'

'How often did you meet him. Once a week, twice a week? Hold his head up.'

376

'No, no. Please, no.'

'You were seen talking to a man in a car outside your home at approximately 12.15 AM after the council meeting. Were you being debriefed by Special Branch?' The sound of Dermot howling in anguish and self-pity. 'You don't deny you told Boyle what was said? The accused is nodding. Jesus. He's shat himself now.'

The nearness of death emanated from the tape in coldly shivering waves.

More whining mumbling and sobs. 'Absolution, contrition. How the fuck would I know? He says he wants to make confession. You are making confession. I shall hear your confession. Bless me father for I have sinned . . .'

The tape recorder did not pick up McFadden's mockery; pressing his thumb on Dermot's damp forehead, his eyes, his bound hands and his trembling lips as he coarsely imitated the actions of a priest.

It did register the explosion. The tape recorder was held too close to the gun and the sound of the shot came deafening and distorted. The bullet entered the top of Dermot's skull, passed through the cerebral hemisphere, down through the corpus callosum and the thalamus before lodging finally against the left side of the jaw.

It was four days before his landlady reported him missing. Boyle was surprised she had acted so quickly and surmised aloud that she must be very keen to relet Dermot's room.

Usually an informer's body was put on public display but Dermot's body was never found – in deference to the peace movement.

Chapter Thirty-five

Collins was already up and sitting at the kitchen table filling the ashtray with the leftovers of his breakfast when the knock came at the side door. He had not shaved and the white bristles made him look older and closer to death. His open shirt exposed the sunken V beneath his neck and he coughed a lot. Although he was very tired he could not sleep. He'd woken in a pool of sweat before dawn and had risen to drink tea, smoke and think.

He thanked the messenger, reassured him that it was not too early, listened to the address and dismissed him with dignity. As Virginia got up to make toast and more tea, busying herself around the kitchen in her old pink nylon housecoat, he went to shave. Just after seven-thirty he left the house, out into a drab, gusty September day – one of the first days of autumn. He was quiet and thoughtful.

'Take care. All the best,' Virginia called after him. Then she sat down and she too wondered what the day would bring.

Outside the bedroom door he hesitated while he adjusted the two mugs of tea, then turned the handle, found it unlocked and walked in. He had taken one pace when an arm encircled his neck and something cold and hard was pressed against his skin. It was done so swiftly and delicately that he did not spill the tea.

'I didn't hear you knock.'

'Around here, Mr Fife, all doors are open to me.'

'It's one way to get yourself killed.'

'You're too well-trained to make that error, I trust. My name is Patrick John Collins. Will you have the one with the shamrock or the black cat? There's no sugar in either.'

'I've heard of you.' Fife took the black cat mug with his left hand.

'I've heard of you, too. You can put that down. I'm alone and I never carry a gun.'

'If you don't mind . . .' Fife ran his hands over Collins in a brisk but efficient search which Old Holborn viewed with amused detachment.

The room was small with a single bed, a wash basin, a table and a representation of the Virgin hanging above the bed. The window looked directly at the brickwork of the house next door. A helicopter could be heard in the distance.

Fife was shorter than he'd expected. He was already dressed in jeans and shirt and at first glance looked like any other sandy-haired Jock. But then Collins caught the vivid anger of the cold blue eyes, always trying to probe deeper than they could, and sensed more than saw the contained power and energy in the wiry frame. A dangerous combination of frustration and strength.

'A lot of people are looking for you, Mr Fife.'

'I hope you haven't brought them here to see me then, Mr Collins.'

'I have tried not to.' Collins had spotted the strange van as he'd walked to his car. He knew every car in his street and their number plates. He'd used the growing rush hour traffic to double back twice and had cut through the garages of a council estate. He was confident he had shaken off any tail before he left his car three hundred yards away, approaching the house along the alley at the end of the back garden. He'd been aware of a helicopter to the south and another away to the west, but they were too distant to worry him.

'What d'ye want?' Fife put the combat knife down the back of his jeans.

'I think it's more of what you want. I understand you are searching.'

'We're all searching for something.'

Collins sat down at the small square table and took a sip of tea. He appeared to summon reserves of strength to continue; in contrast Fife stood near the door vibrating with nervous energy.

'Are you a philosopher, Mr Fife?'

'No. A reader.'

Collins nodded slowly as if that explained a mystery. 'So you've not come to seek for truth?'

'Isn't truth the first casualty of war?'

'One of your great leaders said truth was protected by a bodyguard of lies.'

'Churchill was not one of my leaders. He was English. I haven't time for games, Mr Collins. Tell me what you want or leave.'

Collins did not appear to be put out by Fife's abruptness. He took another sip of tea.

'Have you ever visited the shores of Upper Lough Erne in the county of Fermanagh, not far from the border? It's especially attractive south of Lisnaskea.'

The thwup thwup thwup of rotor blades swept closer. Both men looked up instinctively.

'You get used to it,' said Collins. He pulled out a cheap notebook and a soft pencil from his battered sports jacket and wrote an address. He folded the paper in half and, with his elbow resting on the yellow plastic laminated surface of the table, held it out between thumb and forefinger.

'It's a farmhouse standing alone. I would advise caution.'

Fife took the paper and glanced at the address. He frowned, peering at Collins as though seeking an answer to the puzzle.

'Why are you doing this?'

'It's not a trap, if that's what you're thinking,' replied Collins with a resigned smile. 'Let's say history, Mr Fife. Ireland's history has been entwined with blood sacrifice and more will be spilled yet before we are free.'

'Ireland will not find Christ's peace until she has taken Christ's sword, ye mean.'

Bloody Padraig Pearse again. 'You SAS men are a strange breed,' conceded Collins, standing up to leave.

'As I said, I'm a reader.' Fife was quietly proud he was able to demonstrate his learning.

By the door, Collins pointed to the medallion around Fife's neck. 'I wish you a safe journey. May Saint Christopher protect you.'

'It's not Saint Christopher, it's Saint Michael, patron saint of parachutists.' Fife clenched his fist around the saint. 'I gave him to someone once and God's warrior failed him. Now he's mine again until I lay him to rest.'

'We all have to hold on to something, Mr Fife.' Collins dabbed at his mouth with his white handkerchief as he opened the door.

'I don't believe I'll be seeing you again, Mr Collins.'

'No, Mr Fife, I don't believe you will.'

In the Wessex helicopter flying an exact pattern around the guest house, the sound technician grimaced and pressed his left hand to his earphone while finely adjusting a slide tuner.

'That's it, he's gone,' he announced over his throat mike.

'Well?'

'Some, not all. A general location. I think he wrote down an address.'

'Was it chummy?'

'Dunno. Scots accent. I'll clear up the tape back in Aldergrove. We had interference on the 14 band and a treble resonance echo, down to the proximity of the house next door . . .'

'But a Scots accent?'

'Yeh, no doubt.'

The Wessex swung away from the area, beating a path back to the sound labs in Aldergrove as the co-pilot pressed the button on the top of the control yoke.

'Mike delta. This is Army five seven.'

'Army five seven go.'

'Mike delta. Confirm tango at location.'

'Army five seven, roger.'

On the streets below, half a dozen Land-Rovers, four Saracens and two armoured Ford Sierras began moving into position.

Fife memorized the address, shredded the paper and put the pieces in the pocket of his green fleece jacket with the large blue collar. On the landing he smelled bacon frying and heard the radio in the kitchen.

'I've got to go out early, hen.'

Mrs McNally, plump and caring, looked from Fife to the bacon in the pan.

'You cannot waste this. It's too cold a morning to be going out with nothing inside you. It'll only take a minute.'

But Fife did not have a minute. If Collins could find him, others could. Time to go time.

'I'll take a bacon sarnie with me, if that's all right, Mrs McNally. I'll eat it as I go.'

He'd gone fifty yards down the curling, leafy hill when he heard the unmistakable sound of a Saracen grinding in low gear. Through a gap in the houses on the lower side, he caught sight of a long radio aerial. Two steel grey Land-Rovers turned the corner and halted in a V formation. Policemen in green flak jackets, carrying M1 carbines, climbed out. An APC stopped ten yards behind the police picket. The Divisional Mobile Support Unit to cordon off the area with the resident battalion's QRF as back-up.

A few policemen were taking stock of him and he took a bite of his sandwich. A man walking is less suspicious than a man running. A man walking towards you is less suspicious than a man walking away. A man walking slowly is less suspicious than a man walking quickly. A man walking and eating is not really worth bothering about. That's what they'd taught him on the intelligence course in Ashford. Fife thought he could improve it.

He picked a young copper with red cheeks at the end of the line and stared at him to generate eye contact. It worked. When he saw the policeman give him the once-over, Fife pulled the large jacket collar up to his left cheek and moved his lips. Then he took a hefty snatch at the sarnie.

Clocked him. Clocked him in the act. PC Peters was delighted. Peters was young enough to be fluffy about the Det's undercover operators. When he'd first seen the man slouching down the road, he was going to stop him and demand ID. Then he saw the man pull up his collar. A natural act in the drab morning, but his lips moved. There must be a mic hidden in the collar. He was talking to the net on his hidden comms. God, those guys were cool. Now he took in the man, he perceived a vaguely military look. He was delighted with his own sharpness.

The man was up to him now. Three paces away, their eyes met again. The man dropped his eyes to his hand. Peters followed the glance and was rewarded with a flash of an ID card. He looked up again and caught the slightest of winks as the man walked past still chewing on his sandwich.

Peters felt ten feet tall.

The troops, seeing the man walk through the police cordon, ignored him. As Fife turned the corner, two Sierras drew up outside Mrs McNally's house. A red and white city bus was pulling up at the stop on the main road and Fife ran for it. Slumping in an upstairs seat, he prayed the car he had tucked away still had its wheels. He was going to need them to get to his heavy weapon dump.

The mush of communication equipment, the hum of computers and the smell of warm dust and paper filled the shabby room. Signals sergeants with earphones and pencil microphones sat at radio tables connected to the helicopter,

RUC and army nets. Different coloured phones linked directly to Downing Street, the Cabinet Office Briefing Room, SB HQ Knock and the brigades littered the long metal desk. Large-scale maps covered the walls.

'Two voices. Male. One Irish,' reported the signaller. 'One with a Scottish accent . . . He's talking about Upper Lough Erne. Fermanagh. Lisnaskea . . . You'll get used to it.'

'Get used to what?' snapped Baines-Hickey, drumming his fingers with impatience.

'A farmhouse . . . Atmospherics are very bad, sir. It's breaking up.' The signaller felt obliged to apologize on behalf of the heli team.

'That has to be Fife,' concluded Boyle.

'What the hell is Collins doing?' demanded the politician, the only man in the room not in uniform.

'He's pointing Fife at O'Keefe.' Boyle and Taylor frowned at each other.

'He's double-crossed us.' Baines-Hickey was furious. 'Arrest him.'

'He used us,' corrected Boyle. 'We used him, but he just did it that much better. Assuming, of course, that he's given the correct address.'

'Can we assume that, Chief Inspector?'

'There've been rumours that O'Keefe was unhappy with the ceasefire, sir. We've heard he might throw in his lot with INLA. Maybe this is Collins's way of cleaning the slate. Disposing of an embarrassment, if you like.'

'I don't like and he won't get away with it. He must learn he can't do this sort of thing.' Baines-Hickey's mouth became petulant. 'Fucking Irish. You can't trust any of them.'

Boyle crossed to a large map of the province and pulled a face as he looked at the confused, sprawling mass of Lough Erne with its hydra of watery fingers, inlets, islands and rivers. They needed a specific address.

'What are they saying now?'

'They're not talking. Now the Irishman says it's not a

trap. They're talking about blood sacrifice. It's coming over twos, sir. Lots of interference.'

'Blood sacrifice,' snorted Baines-Hickey. 'What the fuck are they on about?'

'He's leaving, sir.'

'All units in position. Confirmed.'

'Why didn't the RUC find this house?' demanded Baines-Hickey, irritably. 'Collins had no problems finding it, did he?'

'You're witnessing some of the problems we face every day,' maintained Boyle stoutly. 'Their intelligence is bound to be better than ours in their heartlands. They know the people; they *are* the people.'

'Just as well we turned to them then, isn't it?' said Baines-Hickey smugly.

'Army five seven's pulling out,' reported the sergeant. 'Ground units going in now.'

There was enough muscle in those two Sierras to overpower a bull elephant. Just collar Fife and the legal fiction of finding a charge would come second. If he assaulted a police officer all the better.

'Army five seven's ETA at Aldergrove is eight-ten, sir. They'll clear up the tape and squelch it from there.'

'Urgent message from the ground unit, sir.'

Baines-Hickey, Boyle and Taylor all looked expectantly towards the signaller.

'Negative on tango.'

'What do you mean, negative?' Baines-Hickey leapt towards the sergeant as if to strike him. The sergeant touched his earphone.

'Tango left the house before the officers arrived.'

'Get a description of what he was wearing from the landlady and circulate it to the back-up,' barked Boyle. 'Instruct all ground units to let no one, repeat no one, through. Copy that to the army QRF.'

'Get a chopper back overhead,' ordered Taylor. 'Status Red. Half a mile radius cordon. Flood the area.'

'Bollocks, bollocks, bollocks.' Baines-Hickey was white with rage. 'I'll have someone's guts for garters. What a fucking fiasco. The IRA lead you to the man we are desperate, the PM is desperate, to capture and what do you do? You let him slip through your fingers. What a fucking display of rank amateurism. Why did Fife leave immediately after Collins? Did Collins warn him?'

'Don't know, sir,' replied Taylor. 'Probably his training. He knew he'd been compromised.'

'How did he get through the cordon? I want a bloody inquiry into this gross incompetence. We've got to start all over now.'

'No we haven't, sir,' pointed out Taylor. 'We have a general location for O'Keefe. Our best chance now is to find O'Keefe and then apprehend Fife in the neighbourhood before he can close with him.'

'Why not catch him now? For Christ's sake, he can't have gone far.' Baines-Hickey wiped a smear of spittle away from the corner of his mouth.

'If we don't get him in the next ten minutes he'll lose himself in the city. We'll stand a better chance in the countryside where he'll be more exposed.'

'Downing Street. For you, sir.'

Jesus Christ. Now of all times. The PM must be bloody psychic. The politician reluctantly took the phone and straightened up until he was standing to attention.

'Good morning, Prime Minister.' He turned his back to exclude the others from his conversation. 'Quite well, thank you, sir. The situation has moved forward. I now have a general location for the sniper and I believe that Fife will head in that direction . . . If I might venture an opinion, sir. I believe the best opportunity of apprehending Fife will be to trap him in that area before he's had a chance to close with the gunman . . . Thank you, sir, I employed rather unconventional methods and they paid off . . .'

Boyle avoided Taylor's eye and instead made a show of scrutinizing the wall map.

'It's actually around Upper Lough Erne. Difficult country, sir. Not as you think of a lake with recognized shoreline. No, sir, this information has come to light within the last fifteen minutes . . . Excellent idea, sir. We'll concentrate there. Of course, we may be able to pick him up en route . . . Yes, sir, I'll keep you informed. And I have your authority for that? . . . Thank you, sir.'

He hadn't mentioned that Fife had slipped through the net, noted Boyle. Not out of loyalty, he guessed, but so he wouldn't be associated with failure. Baines-Hickey turned round, his face flushed with success.

'The PM has suggested we use the boat troop of which-ever squadron is on the special projects team. Major Taylor, will you task it through DSF Belfast?'

He registered Taylor's bemusement.

'The PM enjoys regular trips to Hereford. He especially enjoys being the hostage in the killing house when the assaulters use real ammunition. That's not well known, you realize,' he added quickly as though he had dropped a state secret.

'I'll speak to Brigadier Doughty, sir,' decided Taylor. 'The Northern Ireland troop will have to be deployed. With them and G Squadron boat troop we should be able to intercept Fife. Of course, it would help if we knew exactly where he was going.'

'Army five seven's landed, sir,' reported the signals sergeant. 'They're cleaning up the tape, but they say there's a silence when it seems the Irishman is writing something. It could be the address.'

Boyle was already on a secure line to Enniskillen RUC headquarters. 'Get the bobbies out and about around Upper Lough Erne. Get them into the shops and bars. We're look-ing for reports of a stranger buying supplies more than once or stocking up. O'Keefe's not in hiding, he's lying low, so he may have gone to the local for a jar or two. We'll get his picture and description and Fife's sent down the line to you, but get your men out on the streets now.'

Boyle and Taylor examined the road map. 'If Fife heads directly to Upper Lough Erne, he'll take the motorway to Dungannon and then drop down the A4,' said Boyle. 'We'll insert vehicle checkpoints on the motorway and outside Ballygawley. He could drive down to Armagh, then take the A28 to Aughnacloy so we'll place VCPs on the A3 and again between Augher and Aughnacloy. Of course, the countryside is covered by a spider's web of lanes. If he wants to take the time and go across country we don't have a hope in hell of catching him.'

'Why not saturate the area south of Lisnaskea?' demanded Baines-Hickey.

Boyle shook his head. 'If we flood the area with police and troops, not only would we frighten off Fife but we run the risk of driving away O'Keefe in search of somewhere quieter. Lose O'Keefe and we lose the magnet which draws Fife.'

Major Taylor addressed the sergeant standing next to him. 'The Royal Anglian Regiment is based just ten miles from Lisnaskea at Enniskillen. We'll use their close observation platoon to set up OPs on high ground around the approaches from the east and north. Posts on the B36 at Rosslea, the A34 south of Lisnaskea and again outside Newtownbutler.'

'It would help if we knew what he was driving,' complained Baines-Hickey.

'No response from the hire companies so far,' retorted Boyle. 'But Fife has got ten grand. He could have bought himself a secondhand car. We'll try Belfast garages. Nothing too grand. Back street and cash.'

Chapter Thirty-six

O'Keefe flicked the remote control button of the cameras now concealed in the grey roof tiles and scanned the empty fields on three sides. He was restless to get out of the farmhouse. He'd released his pent-up energies by running for six miles and swimming in the Lough yesterday, but he was keen to see the newspaper. If he drove into Newtownbutler he could buy a *Belfast Telegraph*. If there was no communication from Mary today, he'd place an advert to alert her he was about to make contact. They weren't far apart as the chopper flies – around forty miles, he guessed – but most of it lay over the great bulge of County Monaghan in the Republic. That's where they'd meet. Option number three of the five prearranged at different directions and distances from Mary's home, depending on where he was hiding.

He knocked formally on Jenny's bedroom door and caught a flicker of hope in her eye as she sat up, sleepily exposing her breasts.

'I fancy getting out for a bit so I'll go to the shops. Is there anything we need?'

Jenny flopped back on the pillow, languidly rubbing her breasts.

'I don't think so. I filled the freezer and we're all right for vegetables for a few days. Just bread, milk and a good morning fuck.'

O'Keefe grinned and gently closed the door. Jenny wondered if cracks were beginning to appear in Paddy's indifference to her. She closed her eyes and, smiling to herself, continued stroking her nipples with her left hand until they grew hard and erect. She slid her right hand down over her

389

belly and her trimmed pubic hair. She opened herself and arched her back in feline pleasure.

O'Keefe parked his car twenty yards away from the small general store in the single long street with its numerous bars, offering live music. All closed now at 8.30 in the morning. Maybe one night he'd come in for a drink. He warmed to the idea. May as well enjoy his last week here before beginning his new life. Paddy O'Keefe of old. Hell raiser and firebrand.

He waited until he saw the store was busy and then quickly picked up a loaf, a carton of milk and a *Bel Tel*. The woman at the till was chatting away to regulars so he handed over his money and left with a friendly smile.

He drove to the outskirts of the town before stopping and opening the newspaper, leafing through until he came to the classified ads page. His eyes ran down to section 12-3. Prayer to the Holy Spirit . . . Grateful Thanks . . . A Bible Fact . . . Find that Special Person . . . Gay? . . . Miss you. Only 9 days. M.

Yes. O'Keefe clenched his fist and punched the air, a broad grin on his face. At last. Mary would be expecting his call at 9.30 AM or 9.30 PM for the next three days. He'd phone her at 9.30 AM. He could wait until then. Former SAS men were good at waiting – at least for under an hour.

G Squadron's boat troop were mooching around the Blue Team basha, drinking tea and browsing through the newspapers they'd brought in. As usual they'd finished the sandwiches and crisps that were supposed to be lunch. It was raining heavily in Hereford and they were considering how to fill the day.

The word that they were going over the water in one hour was welcomed with a buzz of excitement. The hangar came alive as the black counter-terrorist gear was stored and the Gemini inflatable boats brought out together with their dry bags divers' suits. Ops bags were filled with G3s,

390

Heckler & Koch 9mm MP5s, Brownings and M203s. Land-Rovers filled up at ammo bunker and the Chinook came in low and hard on to the helipad.

In the thirty minutes before they took off, the Squadron OC tried for more information on the job. An exercise in containment, possibly a seek and destroy. Even an OP React ambush. It was difficult to say at that moment. The situation was still unfolding. Not knowing the specific task, the boat troop threw in everything from flash bangs to 66mm rockets.

ETA Aldergrove 1100 hours.

'Now are you sure you've got everything? Sandwiches, chocolate bar, lemonade, money?'

'Yes, mum. Stop fussing.'

'A fine thing when your nine-year-old daughter tells you to stop fussing,' exclaimed Mary in mock exasperation. If only the girls knew what an effort she was making on their behalf. She was so tense she could be sick. 'And make sure Boo doesn't go near the water. I don't want her falling in.'

'No, mum.' Katie pulled a face of long suffering. 'I'll go and see what she's doing.'

Katie assumed an air of world-weariness befitting her third annual Sunday school picnic. It was a shame it wasn't a nicer day, but they'd eat their sandwiches in the huts in the Slieve Gullion forest park and play rounders. She wondered if Ryan Kilcrane would be there. She liked him even if he could be childish at times.

She found Boo trying to cram Flopsy, her favourite stuffed rabbit, into her small rucksack and bullied her little sister into leaving it behind.

'Hurry up,' Mary called. 'The bus will be here soon and it won't wait.'

It would wait, Katie knew, but her mum was uptight this morning. She'd been ill at ease since that big man had called yesterday morning. Katie had caught her crying softly to herself last night. When she'd asked what was wrong, she'd been rewarded with a smothering hug.

Katie adjusted the rucksack on Boo's back, took her hand and led her into the living room. Mary instinctively pulled up one of Boo's ankle socks and brushed a wayward strand of yellow hair from her eyes.

'There it is, there it is,' cried Boo excitedly.

Along the lane they could see the top of the minibus slowly snaking towards them. Waving, they skipped down the drive to the gate. Mary saw them climb on board, then she made herself a cup of tea and settled down to wait for the phone to ring.

'Do you want to hear the good news or the bad?' Boyle asked Taylor, quietly so Baines-Hickey would not hear.

'Let's have the good first.'

'The good news is we've found the garage which sold Fife the car. A Toyota Corolla.'

'Great.'

'The bad news is we don't have a registration number. The garage owner is sure his partner sold a car to a man who matches Fife's description on Sunday, but he hasn't done the paperwork. If it was cash he wouldn't want it to go through the books. The bloke's off this morning playing golf. He doesn't know where. We're on the way to his home now.'

'At least we can add a Toyota Corolla to the picture. Every detail helps,' said Taylor. 'There can't be that many of them in the Province.'

'Three thousand one hundred and nine,' replied Boyle sourly.

Baines-Hickey strode across the operations room to join them. 'The boat troop and the Northern Ireland troop are deploying directly to Enniskillen. It would make sense for us to go there as well – nearer the action.'

'What are comms like there?' Taylor asked the signals sergeant.

'Every bit as good as here, sir. There's a built-in facility for secure satellite comms at Grosvenor Barracks, or if you wanted we could patch you through from here. It takes less than forty minutes to get there by chopper, sir. I did it last week.'

The sergeant seemed keen for them to go.

'Right, we'll move to Enniskillen,' decided Baines-Hickey. 'Set up an FOB there. No reports from the VCPs?'

'No, sir, but we now know Fife is driving a black Toyota Corolla. No registration yet.'

'Put the word out, then,' barked Baines-Hickey, scurrying away to pick up a phone. 'Put the word out.'

'Arsehole,' murmured Boyle without moving his lips. 'What's an FOB?'

'Forward operations base,' grinned Taylor, who enjoyed Boyle's dour professionalism in contrast to Baines-Hickey's hysterical outpourings of frustration and blame. 'Why aren't the VCPs picking up Fife?'

'Maybe he's using the lanes, in which case we don't stand a chance until he gets nearer. He'll know O'Keefe is armed so I expect he'll be carrying something himself. That'll make it easier for us. We can legitimately charge him with illegal possession of firearms.'

'Chopper on stand-by, sir, whenever you want to go,' announced the sergeant.

Baines-Hickey flicked a hand in acknowledgement as he rejoined the other two. 'Why don't we ask Collins for the address?'

'He wouldn't give it us,' said Boyle firmly.

'He led us to Fife,' argued Baines-Hickey.

'Not deliberately – and then he pointed Fife at O'Keefe. He'd mock you if you asked him.'

Baines-Hickey didn't like the idea of being laughed at.

'Mrs O'Keefe has had an incoming phone call, sir. A wrong number.'

'Play it,' ordered Boyle.

Chapter Thirty-seven

Matthew, Mark, Luke and John and Graham. The five meeting places. Mary sat in the corner of the sofa looking from the small carriage clock on the mantelpiece to the green phone next to her and recalled the code Paddy had taught her.

She'd giggled when they had settled on Graham for the fifth.

Time.

Even though Mary was expecting the call, she leapt when the phone rang. She let it ring twice then, trembling, picked up the receiver.

'Hello,' she said softly. It was all she could do to stop herself blurting out a warning.

'Is Luke there?' Paddy's voice. Bless him.

'Who?' she heard herself say in a neutral tone.

'Three two one two?'

'Three two one two,' she repeated. 'No.'

The phone went dead and Mary replaced the handset, damp from perspiration. She sighed deeply, wrapped her left hand around her right fist and squeezed to try to regain control. Luke. Rafinny Lake, 12.20 PM. The last two digits of the phone number gave her the time on the twenty-four-hour clock. Then add twenty minutes so the meet was never on the hour or the half hour.

She mentally pictured Rafinny Lake. Almost half a mile long and a quarter of a mile broad, tucked away in pretty, hilly country about eight miles south-west of Monaghan. A few scattered farms and lonely lanes. Sightseers at summer weekends; deserted the rest of the time.

There was a problem, she realized. If her phone was

tapped then her home would be watched. They would follow her. And she would lead them to Paddy.

'Good morning, Mrs Finnegan.' The shop-door bell jangled behind the policeman.

'Constable Thorogood. A very good morning to you. And how may I be helping you?'

'Have you had any strangers coming in to buy provisions recently? He'd be a man in his thirties, big built like, dark hair. Not from around Newtownbutler.'

The policeman nodded to the old man poking around in the piles of vegetables at the rear of the store while Mrs Finnegan pursed her lips and pulled at the single white hair on her chin.

'A man came in this morning and bought a newspaper and one or two things. I didn't take much notice of him, to tell you the truth, but I don't think I'd seen him before. And what'd you be wanting with him?'

'The bigwigs in Belfast are after finding him. I'll take twenty Embassy while I remember. Was he driving or on foot?'

'I don't rightly know. As I said, I wasn't taking that much notice.' Mrs Finnegan reached behind her for the cigarettes. 'No, the only regular stranger, if you like, is an Englishwoman. She's been coming in all this week. Always buys a paper and she bought a load of potatoes, vegetables and meat on Monday.'

'How old is she?'

'Early twenties, I'd say. Good-looking. Funny coloured hair, sort of yellow, reddish orange. Don't know how you'd describe it. Real, though. Beautiful fingernails painted bronze. Very well spoken.'

'On holiday, is she?'

'She didn't say. Pleasant enough but not chatty. She drives a big foreign car and we don't see many of those in Newtownbutler. I see it parked outside. With all the food she's bought she must have company. Is this any good to you?'

'I don't rightly know, Mrs Finnegan, but I'll report it. That way no one can say Percy Thorogood is not doing his job. Do you know we have to fax these reports to Enniskillen? That's technology for you. Good-day now.'

When PC Thorogood had left, old Josh Rafferty who had been slowly selecting potatoes from the sack, brought them to be weighed.

'She's staying at the old Cavanagh's place.'

'And how do you know that, now?'

'I saw her turning up the track in that posh car of hers.'

'Why didn't you tell Mr Thorogood, Josh?'

The old man rubbed the back of his hand on his silver bristles. 'He didn't ask me.'

E & E. Escape and Evasion. Fife had escaped the trap set in Belfast. Now he must evade the police until he got to his target. They knew his mission and they were looking for him. Looking hard.

He was relieved to find the car still had its four wheels and his spare bag containing a change of clothing untouched in the boot. Out of the city Fife changed his jeans and fleece for cords, a country shirt, beige v-neck sweater and a Barbour with a small enamel Union Jack on the lapel. He put on a cloth cap and a pair of glasses.

He'd altered his age, his class and his religion.

Fife crossed the bridge into Dundalk, the first town in the Republic, and bought a spade in a hardware store before heading west on the N53. Five miles out of the town he turned south towards Maghereagh Cross. A mile later he turned into a track leading to a wood which sprawled down one side of the ridge overlooking the distant sea.

Fife stood with his back to a sign proclaiming *Bridle Path* and took a compass bearing on 290 degrees. He nodded, satisfied the bearing agreed with his memory. He paced out 130 metres and came on a beech tree with the initials TV still deeply scored into its bark. The letters meant nothing.

They were the easiest to slash. Twenty paces to the left, among the rotting damp leafmould, under the sprawling roots of a copper beech, he found the fox hole.

Ten minutes later he was carrying a heavy duty plastic sack back to the car. He'd known one day the Seven Ps would pay off. He drove further up the track until the trees gave out and he found himself on a deserted hilltop where the wind blew long waves in the grey-green grass. Alone in the world Jimmy Sands unpeeled the plastic to reveal a hessian sack full of objects wrapped in oiled paper. He set about examining his own personal private arms dump.

'What d'you mean, you won't tell me?'

'It's nothing to do with you,' replied O'Keefe, tolerantly.

'But you just can't go off and leave me,' insisted Jenny. 'Where're you going?'

'I'll be back this afternoon.'

'No.' Jenny didn't like the idea of O'Keefe going off and not telling her where. 'You must tell me.'

O'Keefe tapped the side of his nose.

At the back of her mind, she had the niggling suspicion that he had been waiting for something. Twice she had caught him looking at the classified adverts page of the *Belfast Telegraph* he insisted she bought daily. She had a funny feeling about today. An uncomfortable feeling she was unable to define. Maybe he was going to see his wife. Jenny felt pangs of jealousy and the stirrings of hatred.

Then she turned cold as a worse possibility dawned on her.

What if he was secretly meeting Collins? What if they'd been communicating behind her back through the bloody newspaper? Christ. She'd been so clever playing one off against the other. If they met . . .

She wound herself up like a top until her fears and suspicions spun and wobbled out of control. She knew a

397

lot. She knew too much. They would kill her just as they'd killed others.

'Are you going to see Collins?'

O'Keefe was surprised at the question but he didn't miss a beat. 'Might be, might not.'

'Why won't you tell me?' Jenny stamped her foot.

'Need to know,' teased O'Keefe. 'And you don't need to know.'

Jenny snapped.

'You're not going by yourself.' She sprang to the door and locked it. 'I won't let you. You must take me.'

Tears of anger and frustration welled in her wide, staring eyes.

'Don't be silly,' said Paddy gently.

'For the last time, tell me where you're fucking going,' screamed Jenny, her face red with fury. God, how she hated being thwarted.

'It's no concern of yours.'

'If you go now I swear I won't be here when you come back.'

'Key.' O'Keefe held out his hand. 'Or I'll get out of a window.'

'Bastard.' She hurled the heavy key in his face.

O'Keefe closed the door behind him. He heard the crash as Jenny hurled a mug at the wall. Temper.

Jenny, tears streaking her darkened face, snatched up a plate and flung it at the door. She was behaving like a spoilt brat, she knew. So fucking what! She heard O'Keefe start his car and dashed another mug against the wall.

The phone rang in the flat in Lewisham and in the basement of the large office block off Millbank the spools of the tape recorder began soundlessly to revolve. Two minutes earlier the machine had been triggered into action when the caller, speaking to the Accident and Emergency Department of Greenwich Hospital, spoke the name Lizzie Gough. The caller, male with a Scots accent, sounded disappointed when he learned that Sister Gough was on nights.

The call came from the Irish Republic. A telephone box in Dundalk.

The technician listened as the phone in the flat rang twice and the answerphone cut in.

'I'm sorry I can't take your call at the moment. Please leave a message after the tone.'

'Lizzie? Are you there, Lizzie? It's me.' A pause. 'The hospital said you were on nights so I thought I'd try you at home. Maybe you're asleep. I'll try you later. Take care, hen.'

The same Dundalk number. The technician ran back the spools and prepared to relay the tape to Northern Ireland.

Mary didn't spot anyone as she drove over the cattle grid and into the lane. That didn't mean they weren't there. At the ramshackle farm she stopped to let Yvonne's eldest son Danny lead a docile-looking bull into a paddock.

She found Yvonne in the old dark kitchen, up to her elbows in flour.

'Hello, my dear. Girls gone off with the Sunday school, have they?'

Mary nodded and wondered how she was going to phrase her plea. She didn't have a plan. Just a big request and however she put it, she knew it was going to sound strange. Yvonne bustled around adding currants to a large mixing bowl and stirring steadily. She chattered on as Mary sipped the ubiquitous cup of tea and listened to the grandfather clock ticking loudly away in the hall. She did not have much time.

'Yvonne?'

'Yes.' Yvonne continued rolling pastry on a large slate.

'I've a favour to ask. Um . . . It's going to sound silly, as if I'm imagining things but it is important, honest.'

The imploring note in Mary's voice made Yvonne turn and wipe her white, floury hands on her apron.

'Well, what can I do to help?'

Now Mary had Yvonne's attention, she didn't know where to begin.

'Um. It's . . . um . . . I've . . . You see . . .' She looked hopelessly into Yvonne's honest apple-red face.

'Is it about Paddy?' asked Yvonne gently. Mary's eyes snapped as wide as saucers. 'Don't you worry. No one will say a word.'

Mary opened and closed her mouth like a goldfish in a bowl. 'How do you . . . how did you . . . ?'

'Farmers,' shrugged Yvonne. 'Out at all times in all weathers. Perhaps see things they weren't meant to. But we don't know and we don't want to. Now, how can we help?'

Mary burst into tears of relief.

'There, there, there,' comforted Yvonne. 'It's all right.'

'Someone's going to kill him. I have to warn him, but they're watching, I know they are.'

'So you've got to get away from here without being followed. You don't want to lead anyone to Paddy.'

Mary nodded gratefully.

'Well that shouldn't be a problem. Take the Metro. Now, finish your tea.' Yvonne, elbows pumping, bustled out of the kitchen, calling for her youngest son Ted. She returned minutes later to lead Mary through the scullery to the old milking parlour and into the adjoining small barn where Danny had backed in the pickup truck.

'Ted's taken the Metro down to Five Mile Cross. Get down behind the seat of the pickup and Danny'll drive you to meet him. You take the Metro and Danny will smuggle Ted back here. Anyone watching will see your car parked and believe you're still with me.'

Yvonne looked pleased with herself and Mary could not help giving her a big squeeze and a kiss on the cheek.

'Away with you. Best of luck. You deserve it.'

Frank and Winifred Johnson cruised slowly through the car park looking for a space. Friday was always busy in Newry and today they were later than usual starting their weekly shopping. The man who had promised to come to fix the washing machine first thing hadn't arrived until eleven. The morning had been lost and Winifred was cross. They had to go to the chemists to get Frank's new prescription for his emphysema. Then they'd see what was cheap on the vegetable stalls and go to the supermarket before dropping their neighbour's green and blue jacket, now lying on the back seat, to the cleaners. Finally they would finish off with a couple of glasses of stout and something to eat in the pub which did special meals for pensioners. Winifred didn't think they had time to do everything before their meal. It meant changing her routine and at her age she didn't like that.

'There. There.' She jabbed a finger to where a woman was backing out. Frank got a bumper in ahead of a rival car and Winifred felt the balm of victory partly compensated for the morning's frustrations. Frank manoeuvred backwards and forwards until the black car was plumb with the white lines. He locked his door and walked around to check Winifred had locked the passenger door. They'd bought the car second hand in Belfast only the week before and Frank didn't want it stolen.

Jenny was still fuming as she switched on the security cameras. She thought about going into Newtownbutler but rejected the idea. No decent shops, just a load of understocked butchers, empty bars, ironmongers and greengrocers selling potatoes and cabbages. A rolling picture of empty fields emerged on the screen, the view from her window looking west. She pressed the remote control button and the hill at the back appeared; another press and the track to the lane and the water beyond came up. Having only three cameras, O'Keefe had decided to leave the eastern approach unwatched, arguing that the long stretch of fields offered so little cover that no one would approach from that direction.

Jenny stared hard at the screen. Something had turned up the track towards the house. It flashed through her mind that O'Keefe had left her alone because he knew someone was coming. He'd plotted with Collins after all. This was her executioner.

She made out a van lurching up the track. The guns. Get the guns. Jenny leapt up the stairs three at a time, panting in fear. In Paddy's bedroom she dived into the wardrobe and pulled out the AK47, its front sight snagging on the canvas bag. She heard the van approach as she fumbled for a magazine, swearing in frustration at her clumsiness. Hell, shit and damnation.

Jenny peered around the edge of the curtain. A red van was drawing to a halt outside the front door. She finally clipped in the long banana magazine and flicked off the safety catch. A man slowly rose from the driver's door. A man in a blue sleeveless jerkin.

You stupid cow. She closed her eyes as a tidal wave of relief broke over her. A postman.

When the nausea subsided she went to pick up the envelope off the dusty hall floor. She expected it to be a circular or addressed to a previous occupant, but it was addressed Mr Liam Katie, The Cavanagh Farm.

Jenny recognized the names of Paddy's children. Nice lilac-coloured linen envelope. A woman's hand in blue ballpoint. She held the letter in her hands for a long time trying to fathom its meaning before putting it on the mantelpiece. She would go for a walk up the hill; get some fresh air and try to blow away the dark cobwebs of paranoia and suspicion clouding her mind.

'What the hell is he doing south of the border?'

The news that Fife had made a phone call from Dundalk in the Irish Republic was waiting at the Forward Operations Base at Grosvenor Barracks in Enniskillen. It put Baines-Hickey in an even worse mood.

'What's Fife doing there?' he demanded of Boyle.

The broad-shouldered detective hunched behind a trestle table covered in a blanket and let his head sink so far forward on to his chest that his body sagged in his dark suit.

'He might be seeing contacts, enlisting help. We haven't come across anything to suggest that he's not working alone, but we can't rule it out. Then again, Collins could have sold us a dummy. If he suspected for one minute that we were eavesdropping, he could have written down a completely different address from the one he mentioned.'

Baines-Hickey shuddered. 'Let's ignore that possibility for the moment.'

The heavy thump of a Chinook's rotors swamped the room and they waited until the helicopter landed.

'The boat troop from Hereford,' announced Taylor.

'He could be collecting his weapons,' guessed Boyle. 'It makes sense to hide them there.'

'Alert the Garda.'

And a fat lot of good that'll do, thought Boyle. The Garda had recently stumbled across a Special Branch operation targeting known terrorists who lived in Monaghan but killed north of the border. They hadn't been pleased to find the RUC trespassing on their patch. Now they were sulking. Boyle didn't think the local Garda would be putting in much overtime to find Fife.

'Any news of the car salesman?'

Boyle shook his head. 'He's not where he told his wife he'd be.'

They paused while a second large helicopter landed outside.

'Puma,' declared Taylor without looking. 'Brigadier Doughty and the Northern Ireland troop. Quite a party.'

'Mr Boyle, sir. Telephone.'

Boyle picked up the indicated receiver. 'What. When? Anyone see the driver? How long's it been there? Deploy the local SSU to stake it out covertly. Liaise with 3 Brigade. Call me soonest anything happens.'

He came off the phone looking tired.

'A black Toyota Corolla has been found in the market car park in Newry. Belfast plates with a jacket like the one Fife was wearing on the back seat. It's only fifteen miles from Dundalk, where Fife made the phone call. The registered owner claims he sold it ten days ago to a secondhand car dealer in Belfast. He's hazy about which one. We're helping him remember.'

Baines-Hickey scowled at the map. 'But that means Fife has driven north again – back into the Province. Is he going back to Belfast?'

'He may have swapped cars,' suggested Boyle. 'He's a wodge of money to play with. He might have bought another car and dumped the first. We'll check all garages, secondhand car salesmen and hire companies around Newry.'

'Hell,' swore Baines-Hickey. 'If Fife is heading here from Newry or Dundalk, he'll come south of the screen.'

'If he's coming here at all,' said Taylor.

'We're going backwards,' summed up Boyle. 'We don't know where Fife is, what he's driving or really where he's going. We only know what he's going to do when he gets there.'

The three men fell silent.

The clouds were parting and the butchers' aprons of blue sky were reflected on the rippled waters. A plover sent up its melancholy call to be answered by another from the reeds at the far side, the falling cadence of hollow notes drenching the lonely upland lake in sadness. O'Keefe climbed the hillside above the waters and looked around. There was not a soul nor a dwelling to be seen. After a few minutes of solitude, he made out a small pale blue car slowly coming up the lane from the south. It stopped near the stile. A woman climbed out and looked uncertainly around.

He bounded down the hillside. Mary climbed the stile, waved and ran towards him over the springy turf. They halted five paces from each other, both breathless and high in colour. Paddy caressed her face with his eyes, seeing her as he had done the first day in that bar in Glasgow and later lying in the heather. Warm, challenging, pugnacious, sardonic. His Mary.

He held out both his hands. She hesitated; she grasped them and she was in his arms. She wept with her head on his shoulder and he stroked her hair.

Then Mary held him away from her and she too saw him as she had done all those years ago. The sparkle was back in his eyes and it seemed that a weight had been lifted from his shoulders. They held each other silently, both feeling as though something had passed. Something was over.

'Oh, Paddy, Paddy.'

She wanted to go away with him then and there; to protect him from the world and all its evil.

'And I thought you didn't want to see me,' confessed Paddy.

'Don't be silly. I always want to see you.' She took his hand and together they walked around the lakeside looking for all the world like young lovers. In reply to his questions she told him the girls were on a Sunday school picnic, Liam was unchanged and she had borrowed the car from Yvonne. There was so much to tell him. She savoured the moment of togetherness, then, slowly and painfully, she recounted Boyle's visit. Yes, he recalled Boyle.

'He said he offered you a job the day Liam was injured.'

Yes, he had. It was all a long time ago but Paddy remembered.

'It could have been so different.' Mary spoke his thoughts.

'Come on, hen. What's done is done. We can't relive the past.'

'He knows you're alive.'

'Oh!'

'There's worse, Paddy.'

Mary began sobbing and they stopped while Paddy held her close again, wondering what she was about to say.

405

Then she told him about Billy and Paddy felt his guts twist and wrench. He'd never guessed. Never associated the name he'd heard on TV with young Billy.

Jesus. The happiness and joy emptied out of him. He'd brought him that bayonet back from the Falklands, had seen him grow up, had taken him into Stirling Lines, watched him play with Liam and sit at their dinner table listening to stories with rapt attention. He'd received Billy's hero worship. Jesus Christ. He hadn't pulled the trigger. Jenny had. Bastard Jenny.

He tried to tell himself it was his fault. He should never have given way to her wheedling and cajoling, but he wasn't that big a man. So he allowed it was Jenny's fault – although he couldn't tell Mary. Not now. Maybe in the weeks and months ahead.

Mary watched the emotions sweep his face like a rain squall damping and then extinguishing the light in his eyes. And there was still worse to come.

'Boyle said Duggie Fife is in Ireland. He's going to kill you. Oh Paddy, what's going to happen to us?'

She was crying openly and Paddy was helpless. He hated seeing Mary cry. Competent, level-headed Mary who would confront the world for her family's sake. Mary didn't cry; she got on with life. Feeling worthless, he looked at the shadows of clouds scudding over the forlorn green hills.

'I didn't kill Billy, I swear.'

'Who did?'

'Don't ask.'

'You and Jimmy Sands were best friends. But now he's going to kill you. Boyle said he would never stop until he found you,' sobbed Mary.

Jimmy Sands, the Lean Mean Killing Machine. Need an impossible job done, give it to Fife. He'd get it done whatever the cost. Ruthless, unstoppable and professional. He knew better than anyone.

O'Keefe wasn't frightened, just saddened. He'd fight his

best mate if he had to for the sake of Mary and the children.

Briefly he told Mary of his plans to leave Ireland for ever. Never to return. But first the holiday with Mary and the girls. He wanted to take them to Pi Pi Island where there were bungalows right on the beach and clear waters where he could teach the girls to snorkel and to dive. Thinking of his family increased his longing to be with them.

'Join me in Thailand and we'll plan our future.'

'But we've just had a holiday and the girls are back at school.' Mary couldn't help her motherly commonsense asserting itself. She burst out laughing through her tears. 'Oh Paddy, of course we'll come.'

He laughed too. Same old down-to-earth Mary. 'I'll get life sorted out in Australia and then you, Liam and the girls come over and we'll start afresh.'

'I think Old Holborn owes you that,' agreed Mary.

'If I don't hear in a couple of days, I'll go and see Collins personally. It's a risk, but he'll speed up things.'

A dark cloud passed in front of the sun and Mary shivered. 'I have to go. The children will be back from their picnic soon.'

'Don't worry. Everything will come out all right, you'll see.'

Helping her over the stile, he swung her in his arms and kissed her. Mary began to cry again, warm salt tears trickling down her cheeks. For an eternity they held each other.

'I love you.'

She held him hard, unwilling to release him.

'It's a long time since you said that.'

'It doesn't mean I haven't been thinking it.'

'Take care, my love.'

He stood granite still and watched as she drove slowly and reluctantly away; her small pale hand waving out of the window until the car disappeared from view and O'Keefe was completely alone.

*   *   *

407

As Frank and Winifred Johnson turned into the cobbled alley, Winifred spotted two men in black overalls climbing a fire escape on to the roof of a bank overlooking Newry market square. They carried rifles over their shoulders. A uniformed policeman, watching his colleagues disappear, hesitated as the old couple approached.

'I wouldn't go into the square for a while if I was you,' he advised quietly. 'There may be a bit of trouble.'

'But our car's there,' complained Winifred.

'Shouldn't be too long,' assured the policeman. 'We're not stopping people going to the square, but you don't want to be around if there's any bother, do you?'

'We could go to the supermarket first,' suggested Frank.

'But we've got to carry all these vegetables. And there's the dry cleaning.' Winifred was becoming increasingly annoyed that the morning's rhythm was being disrupted.

'I'll manage,' said Frank. 'Don't you worry. Thank you, officer.'

From the top of the slope behind the farmhouse Jenny saw a group of men launching two boats in the far distance. She sensed they were soldiers. She didn't feel they had anything to do with her and she promptly forgot about them. Her nerves were still jangling from the post office van but, now that her antennae were twitching, she was beginning to suspect that the letter and Paddy's unexplained disappearance were connected. The more she thought about it, the more convinced she became.

Back in the kitchen, Jenny picked up the blue envelope off the mantelpiece and turned it over in her hands. Definitely a woman's writing. Posted in Belfast the previous evening. She knew she was making trouble for herself, but she couldn't help it. Her burning curiosity outweighed the fear of the consequences. Jenny had to know what was in the letter. She considered trying to steam it open or scroll up the paper tightly and pull it out as they did in spy books. Fuck it! Jenny picked up a sharp knife from the kitchen drawer, inserted the blade and in one brutal upward movement, slit the envelope.

She held her breath. She listened to the sound of silence and withdrew the single sheet of lilac paper.

'This is to tell you that the last man you killed was the brother of your former colleague Duggie Fife. He is in Ireland seeking revenge. He will try to kill you. He knows where you are. Do not bank on going to Thailand. Trust no one. Leave the farmhouse as soon as you get this letter. You are in immediate peril.'

Jenny twice read the terse sentences. It was unsigned. O'Keefe often talked about his old mate Fife, or Jimmy Sands as he called him. The hardest man he knew. You'd have to kill him to beat him.

Christ. Paddy didn't kill that stupid squaddie. I did. What if Paddy told his mate who really pulled the trigger. Then this hard man would kill her – and Paddy would let him.

You are in immediate peril.

Fear settled over Jenny like freezing fog, penetrating and chilling her to immobility. How did Fife know where to find them? Something was going on she didn't know about. Something which terrified her.

Do not bank on going to Thailand.

Had Collins been stringing her along while planning their execution?

She switched on the security cameras and flicked from view to view. Clear. Get out. Escape now. But what if Fife was lying in wait for her outside? Maybe he was already in the house; perhaps he'd entered while she was out walking. He was silently creeping down the stairs now, knife in hand.

Stop it. Jenny made her somersaulting nerves stand still. Get a grip.

Suppressing an urge to scream, she put the letter back in the envelope and buried it deep inside her handbag. Breathing quickly and shallowly, she forced herself to climb the stairs to the empty rooms above. She folded her clothes neatly, remembering her toiletries in the bathroom and even her tee-shirts in the airing cupboard. In the kitchen she washed and dried the few dishes and picked up the broken crockery. Within five minutes she had removed all trace of her presence.

No one will ever know I was here. I told O'Keefe I'd be gone by the time he returned. He didn't believe me. He's going to have a surprise.

Jenny decided to take the Robar. It was as much hers as his. She'd find a use for it in the Ireland of tomorrow. It was her trophy. Her blood trophy. She'd leave him the AK.

Going out of the side door, she felt a chill despite the sunshine. A coal lorry was making heavy work negotiating the lane two hundred yards away and a small stream of cars followed it. She couldn't attach the Robar under the car by herself so she put it in the hollowed-out back seat which was used to conceal their other weapons and the ammunition. She drove away looking neither to left or right and certainly not behind. Jenny Dove was going back to Dublin and Trinity and academe. She didn't know that the bolt of the sniper rifle was still taped to the inside of the wardrobe. Without it the Robar was just a chunk of metal.

Major Taylor repositioned the screen of troops north of the B36 leading from Rosslea to Lough Erne in case Fife came from Newry. The land was hilly and forested, made for infiltration and penetration. G Squadron boat troop covered the eastern edge of the lough and in between he spread a line of HMSU units across roads from Clones. The Northern Ireland troop and their helicopters waited in support in Enniskillen.

The waiting, Taylor knew, was the hardest part.

Not far now. Time to turn off and find somewhere to zero the M16. He had already stripped the weapon, ensuring the working parts moved smoothly, and loaded three magazines. Fife wasn't expecting a firefight, but P is for Plenty and old habits die hard. He was calm and focused as he always was on a job, ridding himself of emotions and fears until he became a machine – the Lean Mean Killing Machine.

He'd preferred Jimmy Sands as a nickname, but there was really only one man who had the right to call him that – the man he was on his way to kill.

Jesus Christ. Right on the blind bend. A herd of bloody cows across the road. He hit the brakes and screeched to a stop. Another ten yards and they'd have been hamburgers on the hoof. The cows ignored his dramatic halt and continued plodding towards him, their heavy udders swaying in time to a bovine rhythm. The tide of white and black swirled and eddied around Fife as he sat helplessly in his car. One cow tried to squeeze through between the car and the verge. He heard a shrill whistle and a mongrel dog dashed up barking so the cow backed away and rejoined the herd. Another paused alongside and regarded Fife curiously through the window with big brown eyes. A teenage boy with a ragged coat held together by baler twine ran up behind her, hollering in an unknown tongue, and beat her viciously with a stick. The cow didn't seem to feel the blows but rolled her wondrous eyes and lurched on, pushing back his wing mirror.

Mary O'Keefe inched forward behind the herd and admired the way the two dogs worked to keep them together. This was Ireland for you. A herd of cows blocking a trunk road. She felt sorry for the driver of the black car on the other side of the road as the herd brushed past, bending back its wing mirror.

She was struggling to come to terms with the wonderful idea of their new life together. And trying not to count her chickens. The idea of the Far East was entrancing, but she wouldn't say anything to the girls yet. She'd wanted this so much for so many years. She wouldn't feel homesick this time. No, not the tiniest bit. She closed her eyes and prayed to Mary mother of God to keep Paddy safe until they could all be together. Don't let Paddy and Fife meet.

Let no harm befall Fife, but above all protect my Paddy.

The last cow swayed past the black car and the driver accelerated away with the impatience of someone in a hurry.

Chapter Thirty-eight

Boyle scanned the reports coming in from local police stations. There was no sign of the missing car salesman in Belfast, nor had anyone approached the black Toyota parked in Newry. Boyle suspected it was a deliberate plant, but checks on garages around the town had drawn blanks. He was having doubts if they were even in the right area. Baines-Hickey was like a cat on hot bricks; one moment revelling in command and the hot line to Downing Street, the next panicking because they were no further forward.

Concentrate on the reports. No sighting of a dark, curly-haired stranger in the shops or bars for the last fortnight. There were strangers enough, the tourist season was still limping to a close, but no one fitted the bill. Two men matching the description in Enniskillen had turned out to be English fishermen, another man was found to have a wife and four children in a holiday cottage; there were families on late holidays, a pharmaceutical rep who had stayed over one night in Newtownbutler when his car broke down, an attractive young Englishwoman with striking red hair, a couple of cyclists who appeared in the reports more than once, a Scotsman from Stranraer on his way to visit relatives . . .

He suddenly halted and went back. The Englishwoman had been seen around Newtownbutler since the weekend buying supplies for more than one person. Early twenties, well-spoken, drove an unidentified large foreign car. Her hair, described as reddish, was a distinguishing feature. Boyle remembered the whisper after the prison officer had been shot. The woman seen going into the flat from where the shot was fired. Red hair and English accent. And then the watchers had seen a woman talking to Collins . . . attractive, auburn-haired. Red, flame, copper, auburn. All the same if you weren't a hair stylist.

'Get me PC Thorogood.'

'Sorry, sir, PC Thorogood has gone to collect a prisoner in Omagh.'

'Then raise him.'

'Sorry, sir. There's no radio in the van.'

Boyle lifted his eyes to Heaven in exasperation. 'What time's he due in Omagh?'

'Wait one, sir.' There was a pause. 'In about half an hour, we think, sir.'

'Leave a message with Omagh control for Thorogood to call me the moment he arrives. Do you know a Mrs Finnegan who runs a shop in Newtownbutler?'

'Yes, sir. She runs a small general stores and news-agents. There's always a rabbit's hutch and metal buckets outside.'

Boyle considered. About twenty miles. It was the only lead he had and better than sitting here. He'd go to Newtownbutler.

Winifred Johnson shaded her eyes from the sun which had appeared while they were in the supermarket and scanned the rooftops for the black-clad policemen with their rifles. Not one to be seen. Everyone in the square seemed to be going about their business normally.

'We can't hang around Newry all day,' she complained. 'We still haven't been to the dry cleaners and I've things to do at home.'

'The policeman said we should be careful.'

'Well, I can't see anything wrong. Come on.'

Winifred bustled ahead of her laden husband over the pelican crossing to the parked cars. They took no notice of the street cleaner with his broom and dustcart, nor of the couple peering under the bonnet of their car. There were a number of drivers looking for a parking space, but that was normal on a Friday afternoon. All the phone boxes were occupied and two men in tracksuits, carrying sports bags stood aside for them to pass.

As Frank raised the hatchback of the black Toyota, he suddenly became aware of a policeman in a flak jacket alongside him.

'Excuse me, sir. Is this your car?'

'Of course it is,' Winifred answered sharply. 'Who else's car do you think it is?'

Frank became conscious that they were at the centre of a ring of a dozen or so fit-looking men, including the road sweeper, the phone queue and the ones in tracksuits.

'May I ask you when you bought the car, sir?' The policeman still addressed his questions to Frank. This time Winifred let him answer.

'In Belfast about a week ago.' A terrible thought occurred to him. 'It's not stolen, is it?'

'No, nothing like that, sir,' reassured the policeman. 'May I see your documents?'

As Frank pulled out his wallet and searched for his driving licence and insurance details, Winifred with her sharp eyes saw one of the sportsmen talking into a small radio hidden inside his tracksuit top. He seemed disappointed.

Fife climbed the hill until he could see where the Republic's T45 became the A34 as it crossed the border near Clones on its way north to Newtownbutler and Enniskillen. Two Gardai went through the motions of examining a driver's documents at the raised green and white barrier and waved him on in ten seconds flat. Fife wasn't satisfied. He tacked on upwards until, through his binoculars, he could see the British checkpoint a quarter of a mile away on the reverse slope.

A bloody battle group. Two long Land-Rovers, one bristling with aerials, a Saracen APC and two armoured Sierras. Four civilian cars and a bus queued at the barrier watched by squaddies carrying SA80s. Two soldiers lay behind a GPMG on the high ground looking over the checkpoint. All vehicle registration numbers and personal identities were being radioed back to Lisburn for verification.

Okay, he wouldn't go through the front door. He'd sneak in around the back. Fife marched briskly down the hill, got into his car and headed back to Clones. There was something he had to do first.

'What the fuck d'you mean, wrong car! Then you've put the Royal Anglians in the wrong place. If Fife was never in Newry then he won't be coming through Rosslea. They're defending against thin air.' Baines-Hickey was quick to blame Major Taylor.

'The Prime Minister, sir.'

Jesus. The bastard must have a sixth sense. Baines-Hickey racked his brains for some good news.

'Good afternoon, sir.' He tugged at the creases in the back of his pinstripe suit jacket and turned away from the others.

'I apologize for disturbing you,' said the Premier silkily. 'But I was wondering if there were any developments before I set off for Chequers?'

Baines-Hickey decided to gamble. 'We now know the make of Fife's car, sir. It's just a question of time.'

'Good, good.' The Prime Minister sounded genuinely pleased. 'You're at Enniskillen, I'm told.'

'Yes, sir. I like to be right on top of the job. The boat troop are deployed on the lough and RUC Support Units are on the ground along the border. I'm keeping the Northern Ireland troop as an airmobile reserve, sir.'

'Splendid. You sound in control of the situation.'

'We're doing our best, sir.' Emboldened by the Premier's compliments, he pressed on. 'As we don't know what situation we will actually be presented with, I'd like to run through some actions on with you, if I may, sir?'

'Actions on?' The Prime Minister sounded puzzled and

irritated. Baines-Hickey remembered too late that while the PM liked to throw in the occasional military term, he was basically an amateur who hated being exposed as such.

'Well, for example, sir,' he stuttered. 'Actions on finding Fife are straightforward. We will take him into custody. But actions on him resisting arrest? Minimum force, I assume, sir?'

'Oh, actions *on*. Bad line, Baines-Hickey. Do something about your comms. Deal with Fife with whatever force is needed. Just don't leave a mess for someone else to have to tidy up behind you.'

'Yes, sir. Actions on finding O'Keefe before Fife, sir?'

'He's supposed to be dead. I'm sure he's broken some law. Use whatever force is needed. Just don't leave a mess.'

'Actions on Fife penetrating the cordon . . .'

'Unthinkable,' barked the PM.

'Special forces have to think the unthinkable,' replied Baines-Hickey with oleaginous charm. Behind him, Brigadier Doughty raised his eyes to heaven.

'Yes, yes of course.' The Premier was becoming bored with the litany. 'Match the force to meet the threat. I'll leave it up to you. After all, I put you there to take these decisions.'

'Yes, sir.' Baines-Hickey didn't know whether to take it as a compliment or a dressing-down.

'Do you think you'll still be there next week? Your Secretary of State is fretting about your absence. If this drags on, I'll have to accede to his demand for another PPS.'

Baines-Hickey jerked as if he had been smacked on the nose.

'I hope to have everything sewn up by then, sir,' he said fervently.'I intend to be present personally at the conclusion of the operation.'

'Rather like Churchill at the siege of Sydney Street,' mused the PM.

'Not really, sir,' blushed Baines-Hickey.

'No, perhaps not. Must go. Keep me informed. I'll not speak to the Secretary of State until Sunday.'

The line went dead and Baines-Hickey sat down heavily.

'Lizzie. Lizzie are you there? Lizzie, it's me. Answer the phone. The story of my life. No one's there when I need them. Lizzie, hen, I didn't mean it that way. I'm not easy I know, but I love you. I just wanted to talk to you. You'll not want. Take care of yourself now, you hear, take care.'

The tape was played at Enniskillen within two minutes of being recorded at the Millbank basement.

'It sounds as though Fife is trying to say goodbye,' reflected Major Taylor.

'He is,' affirmed Doughty.

'The call was made from Clones, sir. Just over the border,' announced a signals sergeant.

'Jesus.' Baines-Hickey erupted. 'He's almost here. We need the Anglian Regiment on the ground – now. '

'If we chopper them down to the border, it'll scare away Fife and O'Keefe,' observed Doughty.

'Drive them down, then. Put them in private cars, buses, lorries. Do what you fucking well like, but get them to the right place. We have to intercept Fife.'

Baines-Hickey was losing his cool, Doughty saw. Cracking up under pressure. Just as well he'd left the army. He was more fitted as a politician.

'Inform all ground and water call signs of Fife's current location,' instructed Doughty crisply. 'Northern Ireland troop to go to instant alert. Exfil the Anglians' COP towards Magheraveely. Deploy immediately once forward elements reach the FRV.'

A boding air of gloom descended over the now quiet operations room. Pressing on everyone was the weight of feeling that something terrible was about to happen.

* * *

A slight, fair-haired man, leaving the telephone box, held the door open for Jenny Dove. She smiled her thanks and opened her purse to look for change. She needed to tell friends in Trinity College she was returning to make sure she had a bed for the night. She had almost finished dialling the number when a police car skidded to a halt and two large, red-faced Gardai snatched open the door.

She went cold at the thought of the Robar and the ammunition hidden in her BMW.

Jenny and the Gardai stared at each other.

'Sorry to trouble you, miss,' said the sergeant. 'Did you see a man in the phone box before you?'

Jenny swallowed, relief breaking over her like a comforting warm shower.

'There was a chap,' she replied in her most English accent. 'He drove off as I arrived. That way.' She pointed vaguely up the street.

'Did you see what he was driving, ma'am?'

'A black car. Japanese. Sorry, I didn't really notice.'

'No problem, ma'am. We're sorry to have disturbed you.' They were in a hurry to get on their way.

Jenny had to wait for her hand to stop shaking before she began to dial the number again.

The first thing O'Keefe noticed was the BMW missing from the stables. The kitchen door was unlocked and as soon as he entered the house he knew something was different. He stood stock still and eased the automatic out of his waistband. An alien silence permeated the unfriendly farmhouse. O'Keefe inched the door closed and let his eyes traverse the room. Jenny's coat had gone from behind the door and she had tidied up the crockery she had hurled in her tantrum. Strange. Jenny wasn't the neatest of women.

O'Keefe slipped off the safety catch and with his left hand cupped around his right, padded soundlessly into the hall. He hadn't believed she would carry out her threat. He moved from room to cold hushed room. Jenny had gone, but that didn't mean he was alone. He climbed the stairs with one hand grasping the banister and the other holding the pistol out in front of him. The sides of the stairs were less likely to creak than the centre and if he fired with two hands he could be thrown off balance. At the top, O'Keefe hurled himself around the corner, Browning level with his eyes.

He didn't feel foolish when no one was there – just relieved. You only felt foolish when you felt the smack of metal tearing into your flesh. Too late to run then. No one runs faster than Mr Browning.

O'Keefe cleared his bedroom and swung into Jenny's room. Empty. He took in the made bed and absence of her clothes lying over the back of the chair. When he was satisfied he was alone in the house, he went from window to window, standing back in the shadows, and peered out over the surrounding fields. Something on the lough was disturbing the gulls, but he couldn't make out what.

He looked again in Jenny's room. It was as though she had never been there. That wasn't like Jenny. She was the sort to deliberately leave a mess for him to clear up.

The Robar. He strode back into his bedroom and looked in the wardrobe. Its metal case had gone. He slid his hand inside the wardrobe and tugged at the taped envelope. Jenny didn't know it, but she'd done him a favour. He'd been wondering what to do about the big gun. Later he'd throw the bolt in the lough. There was no reason to keep the AK immobilized now. He inserted the firing pin and considered his plans.

So Jenny had gone for good. That changed things. He didn't know what damage she would do, if any, but he couldn't stay here.

And then there was Jimmy Sands. He could find him only if someone betrayed him. Collins reckoned there were more traitors than martyrs in Ireland. True enough.

He decided to lie up here tonight and set off for Belfast before dawn tomorrow. Then keep moving around until he went abroad. Mary should be home soon. His thoughts kept straying to her and the children. It'll be good to see them grow up again. Jesus, he'd missed so much. Don't dwell on the past. *Carpe diem.* Seize the day, as Patrick John used to say.

Ronnie Franks was grinning like the cat who had the cream and stole the saucer as well as he strode confidently to his white Jaguar car. He'd be back at the garage in ten minutes spinning his partner Tom a yarn about his round of golf. Tom always asked about his game. How many he went round in, how many birdies. Stupid git. There was only one birdie. Tom's missus Wendy.

Ronnie's golf clubs were strictly for show. He'd even convinced his wife that his games on Mondays and Fridays were good exercise. They were, but not in the way she thought.

Ronnie felt life was good and getting better. Wendy knew the score. She wanted exactly what he did. A bit of sex and fun on the side with no strings attached. Two of a kind, they were. Not like their boring bloody partners.

He opened the car door and jumped like a frightened jack rabbit as a heavy hand fell on his shoulder.

'Mr Ronald Terence Franks?'

He spun round in horror at the uniformed policeman. Another officer watched him from the wheel of an unmarked car across the road.

'Yes.' Jesus. It couldn't be a crime to nob someone's missus.

The policeman regarded Franks with interest. A typically smooth car dealer but obviously terrified. Why? The officer told himself not to be deflected from the top priority inquiry.

'We believe you can help us, sir. You sold a black Toyota Corolla car to a man last Sunday . . .'

'Y-e-es . . .' Franks confirmed unwillingly.

'Do you know the registration number? It is important.'

Franks exhaled like a pricked balloon.

'Yes. It's in my briefcase. Here. Why? Nothing wrong with the car, is there?'

He scrabbled to spin the numbers on the lock and pulled out the sales documents.

'Nothing for you to worry about, sir.'

'I was going to register the change of ownership this afternoon, honestly. Here.'

Franks held out the sales receipt with the registration number. The policeman snatched it out of his hand and marched across to his colleague, already holding the radio transmitter.

After a while he returned. 'We thought you were playing golf, sir.'

'Oh, um. Who told you that?'

'Your wife and your business partner, sir?' The officer was frowning. Something was going on. Something more than avoiding tax and VAT on the sale. They'd have a closer look at Mr Franks when this one was over.

'I changed my plans. How did you find me?' Franks asked hesitantly.

'Every policeman in Belfast is looking for you, sir. We just happened to spot your car.'

Franks screwed himself up to ask the vital question. 'Does my wife know I wasn't playing golf?'

'I don't know, sir. You'll have to ask her.' That wiped the smile off the smoothy's face.

Fife turned north at Belturbet and followed the minor road until he found himself on an isthmus between the River Erne on his left and one of the innumerable lakes on his right. The road petered out into a track ending in a pine wood with scattered picnic areas and spaces cleared for parking. He drove to the furthest, darkest spot and smelled the sweet resin as he changed out of his Barbour and cords into camouflage trousers and smock. On his belt he wore his water bottle, three magazines, hunting knife and Browning automatic. In a day pack he put para cord, adhesive tape, biscuits, chocolate bars, scrim netting, plastic bags and a few special odds and ends. He carried his M16.

Northern Ireland was just across the narrow stretch of shallow water in front of him. His journey's end was less than two miles away, directly ahead as the avenging crow flies. But he wasn't a crow and SAS men never take the obvious route. He began tabbing back through the wood the way he had come.

'Political expediency allows no conscience,' Collins managed between rasping coughs.

'But you have a conscience,' chided Virginia.

'*Post equitem sedet atra cura,*' intoned Collins, picking at a unravelling strand of wool in his cardigan.

'Which means?'

'Behind the horseman sits black care.'

'Pah. I don't believe you turned that killer loose on Paddy.'

'It had to be done, Virginia.'

Collins was racked with another coughing fit and Virginia forgot her anger in her concern for her brother's health. It had deteriorated since he'd returned home that morning. Had he lost a small part of his will to live, she wondered or was she being too fanciful.

'You must go and see the doctor about that cough. You've had it some time and it's not getting any better. You're losing weight and you're working too hard. Perhaps we should take a holiday. Have a rest.'

'I'll have a rest soon enough,' gasped Collins. He mopped the sweat off his gaunt face with a large white handkerchief. 'But we can't stop now.'

'Go and see Dr Hatton. This cough linctus isn't working. He'll give you something.'

He'd been to the doctor but he couldn't tell his sister. The results of the tests would be back tomorrow morning. He reckoned he knew anyway, but he wanted it medically confirmed before he burdened Virginia. On balance, he thought he would be unable to bear the pain or rather he would choose not to suffer the pain. He'd have a quick end. He had already chosen his epitaph. A quotation from his beloved Horace.

Exegi momumentum aere perennius.

I have reared a monument more lasting than brass.

Collins hoped it would appeal to the Movement's professed love of learning, otherwise he would end up with some patriotic claptrap.

He had decided to groom McFadden as his successor as head of Special Operations. He hadn't seen McFadden as his cupbearer, but really there was no one else. McFadden had handled the Wee Dermot affair well: decisively and discreetly although his interrogation technique was still lacking. It was a shame he had assumed Dermot was the only traitor. McFadden had made him take the blame for all the leaks. Collins, personally, didn't think it was that simple.

Virginia was the obvious one to take over but the hard men would never accept her. What did they know! She had more steel in her backbone than the rest put together.

Collins went into a spasm, his thin body contorted by the tight, searing bands crushing his chest. Virginia handed him a glass of water and he gulped it gratefully.

'I had to do it, Virginia. For the good of all.'

She shook her head gently in disagreement. This illness was affecting his judgement. She wouldn't tell him about the letter she'd written. She just hoped it would arrive in time. Paddy would know what to do. He'd guess it was from her and make contact. She'd keep him safe until her brother saw reason. She'd send that Jenny back to Dublin and then Paddy and Mary and the weans could leave Ireland. Paddy would be available for the troubles of the future and out of harm's way at the same time.

Virginia told herself that was how Patrick John could have played it – if he hadn't been so ill.

Chapter Thirty-nine

'Hallelujah and about bloody time. Where was he?' demanded Baines-Hickey impatiently.

'Don't know, sir, but the Toyota's registration number is being circulated to the RUC and the Garda,' replied Major Taylor.

'I trust the Garda are co-operating?'

'We've briefed Dublin, sir. They've told the local units to pull their fingers out.'

'Huh! Let's just hope they're in time. Nothing from DCI Boyle?'

'No, sir.'

Bob Doughty traced a route on the wall map with his pencil.

'I've been trying to put myself in Fife's shoes,' he said slowly. 'He was last heard of just over the border in Clones. He knows we're after him so it makes sense to stay in the south. That way, he would catch us off balance by crossing the border where we least expect it.'

'So?' Baines-Hickey implied he didn't have time for baseless speculation.

'So I'd place a bet that rather than cut directly from Clones to Upper Lough Erne, he'll follow the border to the town of Belturbet,' continued Doughty. 'From there it's only six miles to Newtownbutler. That way he'll come from the south-west while we're guarding from the east. He'll outflank the screen totally. I'm going to move the boat troop to the southern end of the lough.'

'Is that wise?' queried Baines-Hickey.

'Sir. The Garda have found the car.'

'Where?'

'Near Killylea Lake, sir.'

'Where the hell's that?' Baines-Hickey's voice rose to a screech.

Doughty jabbed his pencil at the map. 'Three miles north of Belturbet in a straight line with Newtownbutler.'

'Well, we know he's here,' summed up Taylor. 'But where the hell's he going?'

Maeve and Connor had enjoyed many hours hidden in the cleft on the top of the grassy hillock that summer. They'd left school but there was no work, so they had spent their time in their secret love nest. The depression was just five feet deep, but until you climbed the eighty feet to the summit of the steep knoll you would never know it was there. From the top you could see over the sparkling tongues of water as far as Newtownbutler in the north and Belturbet in the south. But Maeve and Connor didn't go there to look at the scenery. On fine days they took flagons of cider, stripped off and spent hours naked, making love.

They were naked now, sheltered in the dip from the breeze which propelled flat-bottomed clouds across the blue sky.

'Hang on a minute. Let's have a fag.'

Connor slowly rose to his feet and walked to his jacket. He idly peered over the grassy rim and froze. Beneath him a man was stealthily making his way along the low hedge. In ten paces he would have to either turn towards the lake or climb the hillock. He was carrying a gun. Maeve came up and began rubbing her breasts against Connor's back and her belly against his buttocks in slow circular movements. Connor signalled for her to stop.

There was something menacing about the man which inspired fear. He wore camouflage clothes and carried a small rucksack on his back. Connor recognized the M16, but didn't think he was army or IRA. Living on the border he was used to unexplained men, but there was a sense of purpose and stillness about this one which wasn't natural. The man halted as if he sensed he was being watched and turned his head slowly from side to side. Connor ducked out of sight.

'What is it?'

'There's a bloke down there with a gun,' he whispered.

'Maybe he'll like a threesome,' joked Maeve. Before he could stop her, she peered over the edge.

Directly below her, coming up the slope, the man dropped flat, his rifle snapping up to his shoulder aiming at her head. Maeve gave a shrill scream of terror and fled for her clothes.

'Mother of Jesus!'

Scrabbling, she desperately pulled on her jeans, hopping on one foot at a time and stuffing her knickers in her pocket. Connor raced to keep up with her. In her haste, she got her arm trapped in the sleeve of her shirt. Frantically she pulled it off, snatched up her bra and slipped on her sandals.

Connor dared himself to look over the rim one final time. Fucking hell. The man was just thirty yards away. He stared straight at the teenager, a cold look on his hard face. Connor fumbled with the zip of his jeans, bundled up his clothes and grabbed Maeve's hand. They scrambled over the far edge and pelted topless down the slope as fast as they could. Only when they reached the edge of the wood did they stop, breathless and frightened.

'He would have killed us,' gasped Maeve.

They looked back up to the top of the hillock, but there was no sign of the man who had dispossessed them. Maeve did up her bra and knew she'd never go back up there again. Summer was over.

The two teenagers running half naked down the steep hillside were witnessed by Corporal Jason Williams through his powerful binoculars from his observation post on high ground a mile away. Lucky bastards. He wished he was romping naked through the countryside with his bird. He kept the glasses on the area for a while in the hope of seeing

428

them at it, but they didn't reappear. He lingered over the idea of screwing naked in the breeze, then wrenched his attention back to the boring job in hand. He continued to scan a 180-degree arc across the lake and promised himself an al fresco fuck as soon as he got back over the water.

Fife could see the farmhouse from the top of the hillock – a grey square set against a green hill in the distance. He was too far away to make out any details. The flash of the sun on glass betrayed someone with binoculars half a mile away on high ground to his right. An observation post. Near the lough he sank on to the soft turf and crawled 200 yards across the exposed promontory, snaking between the small rocky outcrops until he reached the rushes on the foreshore.

He couldn't see any sentinels in observation posts, but that didn't mean they weren't there. He was searching for a lying-up point. They were harder to find than rocking-horse shit. He'd planned to use the fingers of the lough as cover for his approach, but the terrain was working against him.

The westerly wind brought the quiet purr of the Yamaha engine before the Gemini inflatable turned the headland. There was only one place to hide. Fife lowered himself into the clear water, gasping as the coldness took his breath away. From behind a clump of rushes he watched as the patrol glided past 100 yards away. Six men in greens carrying G3s and MP5s. Nice reception party.

Fife took stock. If he started across the lough and the Gemini caught him in the open then he was a sitting duck. Nowhere to run. Nowhere to hide. He'd stand out like a bulldog's bollocks.

He shivered as the cold water lapped around his chin, only his weapons and his pack dry in the black bin liner which floated in the rushes. He stayed submerged for another thirty minutes, trying to discern a patrol pattern as the Gemini unhurriedly vanished and reappeared from behind various islands and spits. There wasn't one. They certainly weren't protecting the bank leading to the grey square house. They were holding the southern perimeter of the lake to prevent infiltration. The very route he'd chosen.

When the inflatable disappeared behind a headland to his left, Fife pulled himself out of the water and leopard-crawled on his elbows and knees to a stand of pine trees at the base of the narrow peninsula. He scooped a shallow hole in the soft earth, smeared mud on his face and rolled in pine needles so they stuck to his soaking wet clothes.

The Gemini inched around from the east, making headway on its own throttle. Too late, Fife could see the trail of water where he'd crawled across the grass. Like a snail trail glistening in the sun. Leading straight to him. Hell!

The cox in the Gemini cut the engine and headed for a tiny shingle beach. Two men leapt on to the peninsula and the boat backed off and purred away. The men, one diagonally behind the other, pulled their rifles into their shoulders, sights raised and began to make their way across to the trees. They weren't playing games. There was a round up the spout and a finger ready to squeeze the trigger.

Fife saw a shadow moving towards him over the lough. It was going to be touch and go. Just in time, a cloud drifted slowly in front of the sun, blotting out the bright sparkling reflections across the grass.

From his shallow scrape, Fife watched the men make their sweep while out of the corner of his eye he clocked the circling Gemini.

He could drop the men with two three-round bursts.

Or he could call their names and welcome them as the old friends they were.

He did neither.

When they had boarded the Gemini and moved on to the next peninsula, Fife pulled his map out of its waterproof case and reconsidered his plan of action. He wasn't coming this far to give up. Jimmy Sands never gave up.

*   *   *

430

Mary had been home less than five minutes when the sound of a horn told her the girls were back. Boo was full of the picnic, but first she wanted to know why Aunt Yvonne's car was in the drive instead of theirs. Mary sidestepped her questions and asked about their day.

'Look what we've got,' chirped Boo, holding out the soggy brown bag her sandwiches had been wrapped in. 'Blackberries. I picked them specially for you.'

'And I've got some for Liam,' announced Katie.

'Thank you.' They were good girls.

'Katie held hands with a boy,' piped up Boo.

'Tell-tale.' Katie gave her little sister a hefty shove.

'Well you did,' insisted Boo indignantly, putting out her tongue.

Katie blushed and began plaiting her hair to hide her embarrassment.

'It was Ryan Kilcrane. He's Katie's boyfriend,' proclaimed Boo, savouring the moment of power over her big sister.

'Beast.'

Soon, too soon, Katie would grow up. Mary smiled sadly. They were adults for a long time, let Katie remain innocent for as long as possible. As innocent as Liam would always be.

'Shall we have Liam to stay this weekend?' As usual Mary felt guilty when the girls enjoyed themselves and Liam was excluded.

'Oh yes please, mum. I can give him the blackberries.'

'And I'll tell him about your boyfriend.'

And I can have my whole family together – always.

Boyle recognized Mrs Finnegan's shop by the rabbit's hutch and the metal pails. She was at the till talking to three women, none of whom seemed in a hurry to pay and leave. Boyle showed her his warrant card and asked for a word in private.

'You were telling PC Thorogood about an Englishwoman

431

who shops here,' Boyle began when they were standing alone in one corner.

'And what of it?' Mrs Finnegan scowled suspiciously through her thick glasses and tugged at her solitary chin hair. Talking to Percy Thorogood was one thing. She'd known him since he was a boy. Being interviewed by this walking wardrobe with his rough Belfast accent was different. Whatever he wanted, it was nothing to do with her or hers.

'Has she been in today?'

'No.' Mrs Finnegan folded her arms defensively.

'When was she last in?'

'Yesterday. She bought butter and a newspaper.'

Boyle set about getting a description of the foreign car and the woman herself. Like drawing rotting teeth. By now Mrs Finnegan thoroughly disapproved of this strange woman who was causing so much bother, so the outsider ceased to be pleasant and attractive and became full of airs and graces with red hair and a mouth that was far too wide.

'Any idea of her name?'

Mrs Finnegan indicated her lack of interest by adjusting her glasses.

'And you don't know what she's doing here?'

'She's on holiday,' replied Mrs Finnegan firmly.

'You told PC Thorogood you didn't know why she was here.' Boyle was not going to be caught out in the shop-keeper's imagination.

'She's on holiday,' she repeated firmly.

'And how do you know that?' asked Boyle, gently. He had a feeling he was close to something. This difficult woman held a key. He had to persuade her to use it.

'I know,' insisted Mrs Finnegan with defiant pride.

'Something she said?' hazarded Boyle. 'Something you saw? Something you remember?'

'I know where she's staying.' She almost chanted the words in her triumph. That showed this bloated detective. Boyle went absolutely still.

'And where's that?' he asked in a tone which would have lulled a baby to sleep.

'Old Josh Rafferty saw her drive there in her car. Almost took the bottom off, he said.'

'And where might that have been?' Boyle dropped into the speech of the countryside while resisting an intense desire to take this stupid woman by the throat and beat her head against the wall.

'The old Cavanagh place.'

Boyle kept the gleam of victory out of his eyes. Mrs Finnegan jerked her thumb at the doorway. 'Speak of the devil. Josh'll tell you. He's got more time to be nattering than I have.'

An old man wearing a purple pullover with holes in the elbows and a collarless shirt shuffled through the door. He raised his flat cap to the women still clustered around the till.

'Josh. Come and talk to this policeman,' ordered Mrs Finnegan. 'He wants to ask you about the woman you saw drive into the old Cavanagh place. I'm busy.'

'Why? What's she done?'

'Nothing. When did you see her?'

Josh rubbed his white bristles in thought. 'I've got a couple of pigs near the lough so I cycle past the Cavanagh place every day. About five days ago I did see her, and again yesterday. Didn't know there was anyone there until I saw her turn in.'

The detective slouched to avoid towering over Josh. 'And where's the Cavanagh place?'

'Near Galloon bridge, up from Derrydoon – maybe a couple of miles from here. Stands by itself. It's a decent enough farmhouse, but no one's lived there for four years or more. Not since the old woman passed away. The sons had already left for London.' His eyes clouded over as though he was remembering his own misfortunes. 'They try to let it as a holiday place, but it's never really taken off. Nice spot, but the house is not friendly, if you understand.'

'Have you seen anyone else there recently?'

'I saw a man in the fields near the house. I don't know what he was doing. He was looking at something near a hedge. I didn't take much notice.'

'Could you see what he looked like?'

Josh hesitated. 'I was cycling past, but I thought he had dark hair. Quite burly.'

'Why didn't you tell PC Thorogood this?'

The old man squinted slyly up at Boyle.

'He didn't ask me,' he said for the second time that day. 'Is there a reward?'

'Alpha kilo to all units. Alpha kilo to all units. Return to Newtownbutler. Repeat return to base. All signs acknowledge.'

Lying almost under the police car in a culvert, Fife picked up the message as clearly as if he'd been in the driver's seat.

'November three, roger. Returning to base.'

Special Forces were freezing the area and they didn't want wallflowers at their party.

Fife thought there was just one copper in the police car. It didn't matter if there were two, but then he'd probably have to hurt someone and he had no quarrel with country bobbies. The unmarked maroon patrol car was a sitter. Plonked on the narrow bridge linking an island to the mainland, its occupant had a clear view for miles. It could also be seen for miles.

Fife snaked alongside the driver's door and reached for the handle, waiting until he heard the key turn in the ignition. It was a fair bet the RUC man was right-handed and that hand was now holding the car key, well away from his Ruger pistol. As soon as the starter motor engaged, Fife flung open the door and jabbed the Browning into the policeman's ribs under his armpit.

The copper was alone. Fife was glad he was not wearing a flak jacket. He didn't want him to have delusions of safety.

Fife had decided on his pistol instead of the M16. The assault rifle was more intimidating, but the pistol was easier to use in a confined space if he'd been faced with two men.

The RUC man froze in terror. Fife could understand. The speed and the implicit violence in the attack were intended to petrify. One moment the copper had been secure in his nice new police car, on his way back to base and a cup of tea, and the next, a soaking wet, wide-eyed, mud-smeared madman covered in pine needles was bending your ribs with a Browning.

'Easy now and you'll not get hurt.'

The policeman gulped.

'Put your hands on top of the steering wheel where I can see them.'

Fife, his automatic in his left hand, grabbed the keys.

'Now open the driver's side rear door.'

The policeman leaned back and did as he was told. He was fresh-faced, in his mid-twenties, and wore a wedding ring. Fife hoped he wouldn't try to be a local hero.

'You haven't a chance.' The RUC man was recovering his spirit. 'You pull that trigger and everyone will come running.'

'Not everyone, sunshine.' Fife threw his pack and his M16 on to the back seat. 'You won't be running any-where.'

He flipped up the leather band restraining the Ruger pistol in the policeman's holster and pulled out the weapon. The radio was strangely quiet. Fife guessed that the important transmissions were on a separate secure net.

'Sorry about your nice clean police car. Here're the keys. Now drive, nice and slowly.'

Fife lifted the police hat on the passenger seat to make sure nothing was hidden beneath. There might be other weapons in the safe, but they didn't interest Fife. The copper couldn't get to them before he could take care of him. He crouched on the floor and screwed the M16 into the man's ear. The policeman let in the clutch and pulled away.

'Left,' commanded Fife. He had memorized his route. 'At the top of the hill turn right.'

Halfway up the single-track road they met an ancient Morris 1000 driven by an elderly woman. Both cars halted, the woman peering uncertainly through the windscreen.

'What would you normally do?'

'I'd reverse and let her through.'

'Then fucking well do it.'

The policeman backed until there was room for both cars. As she drew level, the woman wound down the window.

'No tricks. You don't want me to kill the old woman now, do you?'

'There's a lot of police cars around. Is there anything happening?' Fife heard the woman's quavering voice and jabbed the rifle barrel hard into the back of the driver's seat.

'Just an exercise, Mrs Fallows. Nothing for you to worry about.'

'That's all right then. Thank you, officer.'

When the lake was out of sight, Fife sat upright in the back so it appeared as if he was a passenger. A British squaddie in full kit in the back of an RUC car. These things happened. As they passed a lane he caught sight of two Land-Rovers, their long aerials bending in the breeze.

'Slow down but don't stop.' He slumped in the corner of the seat so the driver couldn't see his eyes in the mirror. They were passing the square house two hundred yards or so away up a track on their left. A geometric block, rendered in grey, slate roof, outbuildings on one side. One roof tile was askew. He noted another tile was out of line on the side roof. Security cameras.

'What did they tell you about me?' Always glean what information you can.

'Nothing. Only a description. Not to approach you. To call in.'

'I've no quarrel with ye. Do you know why I'm here?'

'No, they didn't tell us.'

436

That was probably true. A little too sensitive for the ears of a hick bobby.

'Is all this activity for me?'

'I wouldn't know.'

Yes you would, thought Fife, but he let it pass.

'Do you mind if I smoke?'

'Go ahead,' replied Fife, his mind on the grey house and its approaches. The copper reached forwards in a natural movement.

'No,' screamed Fife so fiercely that the copper swerved across the road. 'Keep your fucking hands on the wheel.'

He realized at the last second that the car smelled of plastic, polish and aftershave. There was no odour of stale tobacco. He screwed the muzzle into the vertebrae on the base of the policeman's neck and then moved it down three inches.

'Paraplegic or tetraplegic. You choose.'

The RUC man stiffened, his frightened eyes pleading with Fife's ice-cold ones in the driving mirror.

'No. No. Please don't. There's a panic button under the dash.'

'Turn left. Nice try,' said Fife conversationally. He took the gun away and looked out of the window. He had seen three sides of the grey house. As much as time allowed. Time. The one possession he did not have and could not acquire. The clock was running.

They drove through an old farm on both sides of the road. As they passed, a black and white sheepdog bounded on to the stone wall barking furiously. Finally they halted in a sunken lane under a tree. As soon as the copper's feet touched the grass, Fife knew he was keying himself up to have a go. When the attack came, it was slow, clumsy and predictable. The lad was tall and well built and he lunged forward, arms outspread as though making a rugby tackle. Fife leaped back so his attacker's momentum was spent in thin air. When he was extended and off balance, Fife pushed down his head with his left hand

and clubbed him behind the ear with the butt of the Browning.

He arranged the unconscious policeman on his side in the car's boot so he wouldn't choke on his own vomit and secured him with his own handcuffs. He'd have a headache and a fright when he woke in the darkness, but otherwise he'd be all right. Fife quickly chopped branches and ferns to cover the maroon car from the air. It wasn't perfect, but it would buy a little more precious time. He stuffed the Ruger down the front of his waistband and, tossing the car keys over the hedge, set off across country towards the stark grey house.

'I don't want to hear any more about the rule of law. We are the law. We make the rules.' Baines-Hickey now wore a parachute smock over his suit, giving himself a quasi-military appearance. 'Thanks to Boyle we know where O'Keefe is holed up, so we expect Fife there. We'll pick him off and get two for the price of one.'

'We don't know that Fife has committed an illegal act yet,' cautioned Doughty.

'Pah! If he reaches O'Keefe, he'll try to kill him.' Baines-Hickey was prepared to ride rough-shod over civil niceties. 'That's an illegal act.'

'A shoot-out with Fife will alert O'Keefe. That could result in a drawn-out siege,' said Major Taylor.

'No.' The vehemence of the politician's reaction surprised the two officers. 'The Prime Minister was most insistent that we leave no mess. We can't have journalists asking questions and TV cameras camped out here for weeks. It would be a public relations nightmare. This has to be ended clinically once and for all. How far away is this Cavanagh farmhouse?'

'Just the other side of Newtownbutler. About twenty miles. Less than ten minutes in a chopper.'

'What arms capability does the Regiment possess in Ulster?'

'The boat troop brought everything but the kitchen sink. The resident troop can call on weapons depending on task,' replied Doughty.

'Mortars. Anti-tank missiles?'

Doughty didn't like the way the conversation was going. Special Forces succeeded because they had clear mission objectives and precise sets of orders. Baines-Hickey was behaving like a loose cannon and the operation was running out of control.

'Each squadron has its own 40mm, 60mm and 81mm mortars. Anti-tank capability comes in the Milan and the LAW 90. Maybe since your time, the LAW is the new anti-tank rocket. Range about 400 metres. Pretty lethal. The boat troop wouldn't have brought those, but we can call on them here.'

'Get them off the Royal Anglian Regiment,' snapped Baines-Hickey. He was called to a phone at the far end of the operations room as Doughty gave the necessary orders.

'I don't know what his thinking is on this one, but I've a feeling I'm not going to like it,' confided Major Taylor.

'We do our political masters' bidding and hold our noses,' rejoined Doughty, in what Taylor took as part rebuff and part agreement.

Baines-Hickey returned, a sly look suffusing his aristocratic face.

'What if the farmhouse was being used to store explosives and the storekeeper blew himself up playing with his toys? An own goal.' Baines-Hickey warmed to his idea. 'The Provos would know it was fiction, but if they made a fuss we'd see to it that Collins would have some explaining to do. One up for us. Eh, Brigadier?'

Doughty winced.

'Sir!' A signaller sergeant tried to attract their attention. 'One of the RUC cars in the area has failed to return to base and it's not answering its call sign.'

'I knew we should have sterilized the area sooner,' carped Baines-Hickey.

'We'll have to put a chopper up to look for it,' said Taylor.

'That will jeopardize the operation,' complained the politician.

'The RUC will go potty if we do nothing to find their missing copper,' pointed out Taylor.

'Could Fife have kidnapped him?'

'The copper could have stumbled across him and then . . . who knows? We are all aware of Fife's capacity for ruthlessness,' replied Taylor.

'That's made up my mind,' proclaimed Baines-Hickey. 'We can't have Fife stalking the country kidnapping or killing police officers. He'll have to be taken out.'

He saw the objections forming on the lips of the two army officers and held up his hand to forestall them.

'I am authorized by the Prime Minister to take any action I deem suitable. We have an RUC man missing, believed dead. We shall meet fire with fire. Get your men in position, Brigadier, and make sure they are suitably armed.' Baines-Hickey straightened as if he was on parade. 'I shall lead them.'

'They were both honourable men once.' Doughty did not need to name the men. Nor did he trouble to hide his contempt for the politician.

Baines-Hickey ignored him. 'We'll make this an SAS only party. Let's get the Northern Ireland troop off their backsides, into the air and surround that fucking farmhouse. The boat troop can stop fannying around on the lough and get there as well.'

'How will you explain Fife's body?' demanded Taylor. Soldiers abided by the rules of war. Baines-Hickey played by the rules of the Westminster jungle. And they had no rules at all.

'What body?' sneered Baines-Hickey. 'Remember, gentlemen. Who dares wins.'

*   *   *

440

O'Keefe caught the sound of a helicopter to the north-west as he was stripping and cleaning the AK47 on the kitchen table. He felt happy with a weapon in his hands and it gave him something to do. A change from dreaming over the pile of holiday brochures. The AK was a good reliable weapon, except the thirty-round magazine was too cumbersome. The safety catch was the opposite to Western weapons, reflecting Eastern bloc tactical thinking. One click down for automatic, two for single shot. When in doubt, hose it down.

He glanced up at the monitor in the corner and again wished he had cameras on all four sides. O'Keefe pressed the remote control switch and a picture of different fields filled the screen. He pressed again and found himself looking at a perfect picture of a cloud. O'Keefe swore. The camera was pointing at the sky. He pulled through the AK, cleaning the barrel of oil and replaced it in the wardrobe. In the dusty attic he tightened the loose butterfly screw holding the camera and targeted the lens at the fields leading to the lough.

In the distance a Puma helicopter was sinking behind a hill towards Newtownbutler. Pumas were troop-carrying choppers. His senses tingled. There were choppers flying today which hadn't been there yesterday. You didn't begin an army exercise late on a Friday afternoon.

In the narrow road a maroon car slowed down opposite the farmhouse. O'Keefe fancied there had been an increase in traffic today. Again he felt a prickle of anticipation and again he thought of Jenny's disappearance. The more he thought about it, the less likely it became. She might throw a wobbly, but she wouldn't have upped and left in a fit of pique just as they were about to spend a month together in the Far East.

What did she know that he didn't? Had Jenny been abducted? Got out of the way so someone could have a clear run at him. The more he thought about it, the more it made sense. He'd move out at nightfall. O'Keefe retrieved the AK. He had the feeling he was going to need it.

Fife crept towards the farmhouse using every blade of grass, every six-inch dip and depression. He didn't know why one side lacked a security camera, but its absence made that the obvious approach. Maybe too obvious. Maybe he was being channelled into the killing zone. Crawling through the long grass, his outstretched hand brushed a taut line a foot off the ground. A basic trip wire. Cautiously Fife followed the line up to an old gate post.

Think thin. That's what they taught you if you were parachuting near power lines. Think thin. Lying on his back Fife squirmed under the alarm wire using his buttocks, elbows and shoulders to ease himself sideways. With his head bent into his shoulder he crabbed inch by inch, delicately picking the line off his chest so the tension did not alter. Once he was clear, he carefully pulled through his pack and his M16. A Puma helicopter lifted off from behind a hill and he wondered at its presence before returning to the task in hand.

He was going to have to make a break for the drystone wall which led to the derelict outbuildings and remains of the pigsty. The short grass in the gateway offered no cover. Better to run for it. He stared intently at the grey house for ten minutes without detecting movement. He didn't know if his quarry was at home. He was about to find out.

Fife gathered himself and exploded upwards and forwards in a lurching, wide-legged sprint. As he did so, he suddenly saw the patches of yellowing grass leading to the gateway.

Traps. Primitive but effective. Fife desperately extended his stride to miss the withered vegetation. Only one way to do it. He squelched heavily through the crust of a cow pat and leaped again to reach the next pile of cow dung. Islands of safety. He jumped from cowpat to cowpat, sending up sprays of manure until he reached the shelter of the stone wall. There he knelt stock still for five minutes M16 to his shoulder.

When he was satisfied he hadn't been seen, he laid down his weapon and reached in his pack. Kit for task, it was called in the Regiment. He wasn't in the Regiment now but he reckoned he had enough kit for the task.

'Contact. Contact.'

The two camouflaged men on the hillside above the farm dropped flat as they saw the figure beneath them lumber in an ungainly dash to the cover of the stone wall. They were too far away to be sure of a hit. Nor had their comrades reached their final assault position. All they could do was report the target had arrived.

The Knock Knock charge blew off the lock, sending the side door banging against the whitewashed passage wall. Before the echo of the explosion died away, O'Keefe was crouched at the end of the passageway, the AK to his shoulder, safety catch down just one notch to automatic. The splintered door hung on one hinge.

Through the gaping doorway he saw the corner of the outbuildings and the fields beyond falling diagonally down to the lake. A chill ran through his bones. Give me a target. Give me someone to fire at and I'll fire. But I must have something to shoot at.

At the top of the stairs Fife looked along the barrel at O'Keefe's broad back.

'Ye didn't think I would forget you, did ye, Bobby Sands?'

O'Keefe did not move. He was watching men in green camouflage smocks running behind a hedge a quarter of a mile away. One was carrying a general purpose machine gun.

'I thought you might drop in, but I didn't know you were bringing the Regiment.'

Something about the finality of O'Keefe's tone told Fife he wasn't bluffing. Fife glanced out of the landing window and saw figures scurrying for cover. They were carrying something heavy.

What the fuck were the Regiment doing here? Fife stepped closer to the window. A volley of shots jack hammered against the thick brickwork.

Jesus. They weren't messing about. With a sinking heart Fife realized he had led them to this isolated farmhouse. They'd used him and now they were going to have to kill him.

I've been set up. The bastards used me to get to Paddy. Shit, shit and holy shit.

'I'm not going to surrender. You can tell them that.'

The window exploded in a thousand shards of glass.

'They don't want you to surrender, Bobby Sands. There's no surrender. For you or me. We're an embarrassment to them.'

O'Keefe ran up the stairs into the front bedroom commanding the view on two sides. The enmity between the two men disappeared. Time and anger fell away and they found themselves performing the same drills as they did all those times all those years ago.

Fife darted after O'Keefe and smashed out one window with his rifle butt. O'Keefe did the same with the other. They were rewarded by a hailstorm of gunfire.

'Lousy fucking shots. Couldn't hit the side of a barn.'

'What happened to the fucking yellow card? I know my rights, you bastards,' shouted Fife.

O'Keefe crouching at the window saw a tall figure rise up beyond the lane and point to the right with his outstretched arm.

'Baines-Hickey, M-fucking-C.'

O'Keefe leaned out for a snap shot as Baines-Hickey again popped up behind the hedge, waving his arms to urge someone forward. The front and rear sights lined up on the sleek face, his finger tensed on the trigger. Hell. Hell. A small girl in a cornflower blue dress was cycling desperately along the lane, fair hair streaming behind her.

444

About Katie's age. That useless cunt. He hadn't even sealed the area and now this poor terrified girl was pedalling into the firing line.

O'Keefe hesitated.

The bullet caught him in the chest, smashing his ribs and catapulting him backwards. He came to rest sitting against the bottom of the bed, his rifle resting on his thighs, with a look of surprise on his dark Irish face. He made an effort to smile, showing his large white teeth, but then he coughed and spewed up blood.

Fife snapped off two rapid bursts and knelt beside O'Keefe. He pulled a field dressing from his pack, cut and ripped away O'Keefe's shirt and inspected the wound. Not much to look at. A clean entry wound, leaking blood. No exit wound. The bullet was still in there. From the rasping of O'Keefe's breath and the blood trickling down the corner of his mouth, he guessed it had pierced a lung. He pressed the pad on to the wound and secured it with tape.

O'Keefe who had drifted off with faraway eyes, returned to squint at Fife.

'Fuck this,' he gasped, and through the pain Fife saw laughter in O'Keefe's eyes. 'Let's show these bastards how men fight.'

He dragged himself back to his firing position and Fife returned to his window. He fired a neat three-shot group and had the satisfaction of seeing a man disappear backwards into a ditch.

O'Keefe fired two rounds, but the recoil jarred and juddered through him and he felt his mouth fill with blood.

'Listen. You must know. It wasn't me who fired that shot. I swear.' He crawled to the other side of the window and fired from his left shoulder, clenching his teeth with the agony of each shot.

'I'm glad.' Fife didn't turn around. He was firing individual rounds now, picking a target for each. Cool and deadly. The Lean Mean Killing Machine.

The stench of cordite, lead and gun smoke filled the room.

445

A ragtime of shots smashed into the ceiling, bringing down flakes of whitewash and plaster on to their heads.

'It was my fault.' O'Keefe coughed, spraying blood on his sleeve. 'I'm just a stupid, pig-ignorant mick.'

'I don't reckon they'll put us on the clock tower in Hereford, do you, Bobby Sands?'

'I'm sorry about your Billy. He was a grand boy.' The words emerged with difficulty. He turned to look towards Fife. 'And the name's Jimmy. Jimmy Sands.'

Through the blue curling smoke, Fife met the creased blue eyes.

'Ay.' He too smiled. 'Jimmy Sands.'

O'Keefe looked again out of the window. This thing was flying towards him, getting bigger and bigger, coming straight at him. What the fuck.

'Jimmy Sands.'

The high explosive anti-tank rocket arched through the window and the room exploded in a sheet of flame.

Epilogue

The two men were buried on the same day. In Belfast, Paddy O'Keefe was buried among the decaying black and grey headstones in Milltown cemetery. The Movement wanted him interred in the Republican plot surrounded by metal railings, close to the cemetery's perimeter, next to the industrial refuse depot. They wanted speeches and threats and a green, white and gold tricolour over the coffin. Mary denied them. She had lost Paddy to them in life. He would be hers in death. There was just Mary and the girls, Patrick John Collins and Virginia. Old Holborn looked pale and faded. There were a few of Mary's relations, but no one from Paddy's side. DCI Boyle watched from a respectful distance. He wore a black tie. An army surveillance helicopter hovered in the distance.

In Dalbeth cemetery on a day as grey as the Clyde itself, Shug Fife stood alone with wee Kate at the edge of the deep, ugly grave. They'd stood in this grim place three weeks before, but then they were accompanied by a burial party of fine Scottish soldiers and a lamenting piper. Neither spoke, but they clung to each other's arms for comfort. They were old and tired and shrunken. The fire had gone out of Shug's eyes, leaving the ashes of hopeless age. They watched their son being buried in the dank earth and turned to go home to an empty house.

Six weeks later Simon Baines-Hickey was made a junior minister at the Ministry of Defence. A discreet MBE followed in the New Year's Honours.

The body of Jenny Dove was found in the River Liffey in Dublin the following week. The inquest returned an open verdict. Trinity College mourned the death of a brilliant Irish scholar.

Patrick John Collins stayed alive until the day after Jenny Dove's body was found. Sinn Fein ignored his chosen epitaph. Instead they imposed Padraig Pearse's hackneyed lines: *Life springs from the dead and from the patriot dead spring living nations.*

Mary, Katie and Boo did go to Australia, although Mary did not take much interest in life. She had lost her husband once; losing him for the second time broke her. Changed and lost, she let Katie run the house. They left Liam behind.

Even though Boyle continued to record a series of notable successes against the IRA, he remained a chief inspector.

And the ceasefire . . . was for another day.

Glossary

APC	Armoured Personnel Carrier
ASU	Active Service Unit
Basha	Camp, barracks, shelter
Beat the clock	To die in action (and have your name put on the Memorial Clock in Stirling Lines)
Bergen	British Army rucksack
Black Mafia	Royal Green Jackets
Cam cream	Camouflage cream
CLF	Commander Land Forces
COP	Close Observation Platoon
Crucible	Intelligence computer in Northern Ireland
CRW	Counter Revolutionary Warfare
CTR	Close Target Reconnaissance
DCI	Director and Coordinator of Intelligence
Det, The	Army's élite undercover surveillance squad, also known as 14 Int.
Dicker	Lookout
DMSU	Divisional Mobile Support Unit; SAS-trained heavily armed RUC units used mainly in towns
DSF	Director Special Forces
DZ	Drop Zone
E4A	RUC Special Branch surveillance department
E4B	RUC Special Branch electronic listening and intelligence gathering department
Egg banjos	Fried egg sandwiches
ERV	Emergency Rendezvous

ETA	Estimated Time of Arrival
Exfil	To exfiltrate, pull out
Five	MI5, the Security Service
FOB	Forward Operational Base
FRV	Final Rendezvous
Garda	Southern Irish police force
GPMG	General Purpose Machine Gun
Group	Special Forces Group Headquarters at Duke of York Barracks, Chelsea
Hexy	Hexamine block of solid fuel
HMSU	RUC Headquarters Mobile Support Unit; rural equivalent of DMSU
INLA	Irish National Liberation Army: Republican paramilitaries
JIC	Joint Intelligence Committee, working to the Cabinet Office
JOC	Joint Operations Centre in the Ministry of Defence; the clearing house for joint operations in major crises
Kevlar	Body armour
LUP	Lying Up Point
NIO	Northern Ireland Office
NVG	Night Vision Goggles
OP	Observation Post
PE	Plastic Explosive
PIRA	Provisional Irish Republican Army: Republican paramilitaries
QRF	Quick Reaction Force
Regiment, The	22 SAS
RUC	Royal Ulster Constabulary
Rupert	Officer
SB	Special Branch
Schermully	Parachute Flare
Six	MI6: Secret Intelligence Service
Slime	Intelligence Corps: from the green colour of their berets
SMIU	Special Military Intelligence Unit

SOCO	Scenes of Crime Officer
SSU	Special Support Unit, trained by SAS to be RUC Special Branch's reserve
Stick	A working group, usually of four infantrymen
Stickies	Official IRA
TACBE	Tactical beacon radio
TCG	Tasking and Coordination Group
TCGLO	Tasking and Group Liaison Office
UDR	Ulster Defence Regiment
UFF	Ulster Freedom Fighters: Loyalist paramilitaries
UVF	Ulster Volunteer Force: Loyalist paramilitaries
VCP	Vehicle Checkpoint

Provo

Gordon Stevens

Two women. One war. No rules.

Catcher is the codename of Cathy Nolan, working under-cover for MI5 in Northern Ireland, fighting against not only a major IRA threat, but also the internal politics of her own side.

Sleeper is the perfect assassin, put in place years ago, unknown even to the top-ranking members of the Provisionals' Army Council.

PinMan is the target of this, the ultimate coup. Now there is no way of stopping the mission.

Provo is the novel that redefines the modern thriller. From Whitehall to Belfast, Hereford to South Armagh, it is an adrenaline-pumping, white-knuckle ride behind the head-lines to a land of danger and betrayal.

'Hugely enjoyable and gripping tale . . . with a refreshingly non-partisan approach'   *Time Out*

ISBN 0 00 647632 5

Kara's Game

Gordon Stevens

'A blockbuster . . . a lesson in political reality'
Guardian

Once, behind the lines in Bosnia, she saved the lives of two SAS soldiers. And they made Kara a promise. 'We will never forget. Anything you want, you have. Anything you need, you get.'

Now the tables are turned. Kara's in the West – Paris, Amsterdam, London. And she's dangerous. Now the powers-that-be call her a terrorist.

Now the SAS have been sent to kill her.

So what about their promise?

'A cracking thriller with all the pace and tension and authenticity of *The Day of the Jackal*'   *Publishing News*

'Luminescent . . . Anger and compassion shine through the characters'   *Daily Telegraph*

ISBN 0 00 649781 0

King's Shilling

Mike Lunnon-Wood

King's Shilling is an explosive novel of action and character, pitching the men and women of a British warship into a nail-biting race against time to evacuate civilians from the bloody cauldron of an African civil war.

With the country suddenly plunged into political chaos, and insurgents only a few miles from the capital, the Western powers need to get their people out of Liberia. HMS *Beaufort* is diverted to make the pick-up.

It soon becomes clear that even in the age of smart weaponry and sophisticated geopolitical planning, the modern naval commander must still rely on courage, ingenuity and guts to survive.

King's Shilling is a superb portrait of the modern navy, and thrillingly describes how a brilliantly drawn cast of characters reacts to a life-or-death situation.

ISBN 0 00 651162 7

Angel Seven

Mike Lunnon-Wood

Angel Seven is a high-tech, high-drama, high-emotion ride to the brink of the end of the world in an aircraft built at the edge of today's technology.

Global nuclear disarmament. So many people have dreamed of it, so many more have dismissed it as an impossible dream. One such is Peter Carson, a former RAF pilot, whiling away his premature retirement in the Caribbean.

As a new Middle East crisis threatens to plunge the world into conflagration, Carson is approached by a clandestine organization with an apparently preposterous idea: they want him to fly an aircraft they have developed that is faster and more lethally effective than any the world has seen and they want him to use it as the spearhead of their plan to create world peace.

Carson is an unlikely knight in shining armour, and the team that wants him is pitted against unimaginably powerful forces. Can they succeed?

A superbly orchestrated narrative of worldwide action and suspense, *Angel Seven* is a thriller of the future that could be happening now.

ISBN 0 00 649979 1